WINDLASS IN MY BELT

First impression 2002
Waterways World Ltd
The Well House
High Street
Burton-on-Trent DE14 1JQ
Tel: 01283 742950

Paperback ISBN 1 870002 96 2

A CIP catalogue entry for this book is available from the British Library

Originated by M-J-P, Doveridge, Derbyshire
Printed in the United Kingdom by Page Brothers, Norwich

John Thorpe

WINDLASS IN MY BELT

A Canal Adolescence

Waterways World
Burton-on-Trent

To Alec and Lil
who gave me so much friendship

CONTENTS

Preface

This book fulfils a long-felt desire to set down my experiences as a boy growing into manhood on and around the Midland canal system. It is over forty years ago and a busy professional life has come and gone, but those early years and the values they imbued in me have remained steadfast in my heart.

As a youth I was obsessed by the cut and by the life of the narrowboats and the families who worked them. All its varied moods were witnessed as I strove to play my part in keeping the boats forever moving. Soaked by the rain and burnt brown by the sun, raising blisters with a shovel or enjoying the ease of the tiller around a long winding pound. The contrasts were there and so were the people I was fortunate enough to work with. Truly the salt of the earth, they gave me so much kindness and generously forgave my mistakes. I thank them all from the bottom of my heart.

The cut has brought me so much that is precious. Along its banks I met my wife whose love and encouragement has never wavered, enjoyed the company of some wonderful and irreplaceable friends and experienced many magical and never to be forgotten moments. If this book can give pleasure and interest by way of return then it will all have been worthwhile.

*****

Chapter 1

Early Days

In the autumn of 1954 I was eleven. Having successfully cleared the hurdle of the eleven-plus examination I nervously began attending the local grammar school in my home town of Northampton. In those far-off days the roads were much less busy than is now the case and, self-consciously wearing my new blazer and cap, I was allowed to begin cycling to and from school. The journey was just over three miles each way and each morning would usually take me about twenty minutes to complete. However, a bicycle gives flexibility and I did not always take the most direct route home. Even then I possessed a certain wandering spirit and an inquisitiveness which took me down paths and alleys into the more obscure parts of the town. There was no particular hurry as both my parents worked and never arrived home until about six o'clock in the evening. Very usefully from my point of view there was no-one at all to wonder about my whereabouts between four o'clock and just before six o'clock!

As an only child of working parents mine was a fairly solitary childhood. Knowing nothing else I was quite happy with this and had my own interests centred on books, cycling and wandering in the leafy countryside to the west of the town. In the course of these explorations I had discovered the towpath of the Northampton Arm of the Grand Union Canal and followed it up to Gayton where it joined the main north-south route of the same waterway. Using an ancient ex-W.D. linen-backed Ordnance Survey map given to me by my grandfather I had also noted the long canal tunnel joining the villages of Blisworth and Stoke Bruerne. This seemed very worthy of investigation and several days had been spent during the previous summer holidays exploring this area and looking with interest into both ends of the dark dripping cavern. I had also noticed the long canal craft passing by, carrying coal southwards and returning empty or with their cargoes mysteriously hidden under large tarpaulins. These boats seemed to be crewed by families who acknowledged my shy smile with a grave "How-do" as they passed by. The little cabins interested me greatly with their gaily painted sides and smoking brass-rimmed chimneys. Presumably, I thought, these people lived aboard permanently. Once, returning along the narrow lane between Gayton Arm End and Rothersthorpe, I encountered a barrel-topped horse-drawn wagon drawn

1

up on the wide grassy verge, the family busily sorting themselves out and getting a fire going having evidently just stopped for the night. There was a striking resemblance to the canal people in the dark weathered faces of the gypsies and the bright and immaculate paintwork of the wagon. Cycling very slowly past I met their eyes and, after venturing a shy "How-do", was gratified by the smile and the quiet response.

Not long after beginning at the grammar school an event occurred which was to change the course of my entire life. That much can be indisputably stated with the benefit of hindsight although at the time I had no inkling of what was in store. It was a particularly warm autumn afternoon as I left school and cycled along with only a small amount of homework in my satchel. There was plenty of time before I needed to actually go home. I considered detouring down to have a look at the lock on the river Nene in Becket's Park, it was always interesting and I might be lucky enough to see a boat. Alternatively there existed the possibility of cutting across the path behind the gas works which led under the bridges where the rail tracks left Castle Station to cross the unnavigable part of the Nene at West Bridge. Standing under these cavernous bridges with steam locomotives rumbling overhead was always good fun. Both could have been fitted in on my way home to the St James' area of the town where I lived but, with the fickleness of youth, I chose neither. Instead, quite unknowingly, I made the fateful decision to go home straight through the town-centre calling in at Billingham's on my way. Billingham's was a small second-hand bookshop situated in the narrow thoroughfare of St Giles Street, just opposite the bottom of the Co-op Arcade where I was in the habit of having my hair cut. I was reasonably in funds as both my grandparents had been pleased by my passing for grammar school and had responded positively to the suggestion of a ten-shilling note each to buy books.

Billingham's was run by a pleasant middle-aged lady and had a good range of stock which was also relatively inexpensive. It seemed likely that I would get something of interest as the door bell tinkled to announce my entrance into the shop. I was at an in-between stage on books being past Blyton and then Ransome, my early favourites, but not quite sure what to go on to next. I investigated the small Transport section to see if there were any interesting train books and there, tucked away on the end, was the slim volume that would irrevocably change my life. It was the dust-cover that took my eye, a panel of brightly coloured roses, the same roses that I had seen on the canal craft out at Blisworth. I took the book out and glanced at the title, *Narrow Boat* by L.T.C. Rolt. There was a canal map at the front and a sequence of black and white etchings of canal scenes depicting the author's journey on a boat called *Cressy*. This looked interesting and at 6s 6d was well within my current range. Making my purchase I stowed the book carefully in my satchel and pedalled home forthwith, having an eye on homework first and then to begin my new acquisition later that evening.

EARLY DAYS

Initially the remainder of the afternoon and evening followed a pattern similar to many in my childhood. Dinner would be followed by a cup of tea, sipped whilst listening to 'The Archers', and I would then get down to my homework at a small table tucked into the corner of my bedroom. We had no television until much later and distractions were few. Having stowed the completed homework back in my satchel ready for the morning I sat down on the bed and picked up *Narrow Boat*. It was the map which first took my attention. I had never really given much thought as to where the canals went and was intrigued by the sheer scale of the network. Looking at it I realised how my local waterways linked into the overall pattern and ran my finger along the line of the Grand Union as it made its way down towards London or up to Braunston where there was a choice of directions. As I read that evening I lost track of time. I was hooked. This was fascinating stuff. Here was a previously unknown world and much of it was right on my own doorstep. Even Banbury was only twenty miles away although, if truth be told, I had never been there. Buses, boots, and bicycles took us everywhere in those days and my horizons, in common with those of my friends, were fairly limited when judged against the experiences of today's children. I had just seen old Mr Tooley off to catch his bus back to Banbury, after accompanying *Cressy* for the first few miles up to Cropredy, when my mother opened the bedroom door with a cup of Ovaltine in her hand.

"New book?" she queried, seeing me hunched over with *Narrow Boat* on my knees.

I showed her my latest acquisition and told her of the origins of the superb dust-jacket. She knew nothing of canals and I think probably considered it an odd, if essentially harmless, purchase.

That week-end I read the book right through and then re-read it the following week. I absorbed it factually but, more crucially, I imbibed the philosophy of life which underlay the story of the journey. Everything was suddenly different and life took on a deeper meaning. All my spare time was now spent exploring the local canals in the company of my faithful cycle. I savoured the dripping silence of Watford Locks on the Leicester Section, no motorway in those days but apparently no waterborne traffic either. Although just once, early in the following Spring, I was lucky enough to see a British Waterways pair south-bound with stone chippings descending the flight. The Leicester Canal was quite weedy with just a narrow channel through in some places and exuded the air of a lost and forgotten waterway. Cycling down to Norton Junction and the top of Buckby Locks was like entering another world. Beyond the swingbridge at the entrance to the Leicester the canal was wide and deep and still commercially busy. I considered myself somewhat hard done by if I did not see at least one pair of boats as I made my way down the flight to Whilton Bridge before pedalling off up the long hill which gave on to the ridge leading back through Little Brington and Nobottle to home. It was a little unfortunate to have become so enthused just as winter closed in and the dark evenings restricted my explorations to week-ends only. I was expected home by dusk at the latest and, even with a sandwich for lunch, could not expect to get much beyond the line of the waterway from Blisworth to Buckby Locks. Throughout that winter I made many runs out to this long pound and became very familiar with the beauty of the quiet Northamptonshire lanes that led to it. Arm End, Banbury Lane, Bugbrooke, Heyford, Stowe Hill, Weedon, through Brockhall to the spinnies below Whilton Locks, these were my access points and the towpath between them the object of my explorations. It was not easy at times and that first winter I battled with mud, long clinging wet grass, and large holes where the flush from the empty pairs had washed out whole sections of the towpath. The boats of the Samuel Barlow Coal Company Ltd were my favourites and I always felt a shiver of joy when I saw the white-painted fore-ends, decorated with a knot of roses, coming towards me before passing to reveal the beautifully painted green cabin sides, the mop and cans resting just in front of the brass-rimmed and decorated chimneys. That winter I also saw for the first time a new company on the waterways as the distinctive roundel of the Willow Wren Canal Carrying Company, proudly carried on the motor-boat *Warbler*, passed me along the Weedon Embankment.

Naturally I wanted more, but it had to be worked at. An exploration of the Public Library revealed *Idle Women* by Susan Woolfitt and *Maidens Trip* by Emma Smith. Both were hardback editions and were tucked away on a bottom shelf in the Transport Section. There was also a copy of *Narrow Boat*! But nothing else was available and a scouring of the Index confirmed this. Both the wartime memoirs were eagerly devoured and kept out on extended loan. I especially liked the detail given by Susan Woolfitt on the many different trips she undertook, my favourite part being the descriptions of the long run up the Leicester Section to Langley Mill for coal. Emma Smith's story also appealed greatly and her feel for the essence of the canal mirrored much of what I was inwardly experiencing. At the very back of *Narrow Boat* mention had been made of the fledgling Inland Waterways Association and an address at 11, Gower Street was given. A hopeful letter resulted in a friendly response from Robert Aickman no less and my subscription to the IWA was paid for by my great-aunt's Christmas present that year! Aickman made no allusion to his falling-out with Rolt, of which I was then completely unaware, and would remain so for quite a little while yet. Those slim little IWA bulletins with their central pages of black and white photographs only fanned my enthusiasm and I began to live and breathe waterways. My parents were not oblivious to my new-found interest and certainly did not discourage it. Pictures of canals cut from magazines such as 'John Bull' found their way into my bedroom and were either pinned onto a makeshift notice-board or put into the three old photograph frames which I had acquired from my grandparents' spare room. Pride of place was given to a colour magazine photo of a pair of loaded Barlows ascending the Marsworth flight on the Grand Union with their washing flapping in the breeze on the butty.

That Christmas I received a most unexpected present. I had, after reading *Narrow Boat*, been searching hopefully for a 'Bradshaw' which I knew would give me all the distance tables and factual information on each of the canals and rivers in England. None of the second-hand bookshops in Northampton had even heard of it and held out scant hope of locating a copy. At the Public Library I drew a similar blank and I suppose at some point I must have mentioned my fruitless quest to my parents. That morning a large package was awaiting me. That it was a book was beyond doubt and it was also clearly a weighty tome! A pale-blue dust jacket enclosed *Inland Waterways of Great Britain and Northern Ireland* compiled by Lewis A Edwards; it contained a foreword by Robert Aickman and had a publication date of 1950. Every waterway was listed giving mileages and details of locks, tunnels, bridges and other general information. It was not the much sought after Bradshaw, but it was the next best thing. My 'Edwards' became a prized and much thumbed possession from which I derived many hours of pleasure and considerably enlarged my knowledge of the fine detail of the system.

Spring came and with it a welcome resumption of my explorations. My interest had not waned in any way during the dark months of winter, instead it had increased to become a veritable passion. If my family had been waiting for the craze to pass they were to be disappointed. Other than school work, which had to be done, I thought about little else. My cycle and I became familiar with every bump of the towpath on the Northampton Arm, a favourite venture being to cycle down to Duston Mill on the western branch of the stripling river Nene, cross the field beyond and thereby gain access to the towpath by the old hump-backed bridge. This same path, if continued upon just a little further beyond the bridge, merged with the access road leading to the Blackwood Hodge plant which manufactured large yellow earth-moving equipment, fascinating vehicles with tyres bigger than myself! However I rarely ventured beyond the bridge, instead I would pedal off along the green squelchy towpath threading its way between tall rushes and the unkempt hedge to the solitary lock at Duston. Here the branch railway line to Blisworth ran right alongside and every couple of hours the two coaches and tank-engine of the 'Blizzy Flyer', as it was affectionately known locally, would pass by on their push and pull journey to link with the main London Midland & Scotland Railway line at Blisworth station. The canal then drifted away from the railway as it curved round the base of Hunsbury Hill, surmounted by the old iron-age fort of Danes Camp, before coming to another hump-backed bridge carrying the lane to Rothersthorpe, with the next lock immediately adjacent. Great banks of reeds and bulrushes grew far out into the waterway giving only a very narrow channel for the occasional pair taking wheat to Wellingborough, a few miles downstream on the Nene. Beyond this next lock railway and canal came together once more for the gentle ascent out of the valley and up to Blisworth. The railway climbed steadily up a long gradient and the canal did likewise by means of a flight of thirteen locks complete with two tall drawbridges and two lock cottages. The first of these cottages stood tucked back and neglected about two thirds of the way down the flight and has long since been demolished, the second and much smarter one still stands in whitewashed splendour by the top lock.

That summer of 1955 I came to know the lock-keeper, a man called Meadows, later to be killed in a traffic accident in Blisworth village. I had seen him about from time to time but we had never really spoken. I was a rather shy youth and he had always seemed rather gloomy and surly as we had passed each other on the flight. That he was nothing of the kind I was soon to discover. One day I was sitting on the balance beam of the top lock eating a sandwich and drinking milkless tea from my flask when he came out of his cottage and accosted me grumpily.

"You b'aint sposed to ride bikes up erem," he proclaimed.

Through the IWA bulletins I had foreseen this problem and prudently armed myself with a pass which for 4/- a year allowed the bearer to cycle anywhere on the towpaths. Never before had I been required to produce it but now with a relieved flourish I did so.

"I ain't never heard of these," he rejoined, looking at it doubtfully.

"It's valid," I said helpfully, smiling as I did so.

He looked at the pink form and then back at me. I wondered if he could actually read it but this was something I never did find out. His gaze drifted over me taking in my blue denim shirt and the old patched grey trousers I wore for this sort of day; on my feet were thin canvas 'baseball' boots which were quite fashionable at the time. He, as always, was dressed in a white collarless shirt, old waistcoat, thick serge trousers tied with twine below the knee and strong black boots. White stubble sprouted on his chin but his faded blue eyes were not unkind.

"What are you doing then anyhow?"

My shyness quickly dissipated and became replaced by an unusual degree of animation as I spoke of my interest in canals. Perhaps he didn't want to blunt my enthusiasm or the warm sunshine had induced a measure of benevolence, whatever it was he sat down on the beam beside me and reminisced about the Arm and his job as lock-keeper. The ice was broken and from then on I had a friend. I never pushed myself on him but would always stop and chat, if he showed signs of being willing to do so, as we met along the arm. Although he lived at the top lock his patch extended the full length of the arm from the maintenance yard at Gayton Arm End to the entrance lock into the river Nene five miles away. I knew from previous observation that he had a habit of helping the crews of the wheat boats which by then were the only regular commercial traffic on the arm.

The butty would normally be bow-hauled down the thirteen locks, an arduous undertaking, and two-handed crews especially must have been very glad of his help in taking the motor through ahead, filling the locks behind him as he did so.

A couple of weeks later at about midday I arrived at the bridge below the second lock of the flight having pedalled out by road via Kislingbury and Rothersthorpe villages. As I puffed up the last slope towards the bridge I could distinctly hear the unmistakeable rhythmic beat of a diesel engine and the rattle of paddles. Peering over the parapet I saw Meadows working a loaded boat through the lock with a butty being bow-hauled into the top lock above. Wheeling my cycle through the little access gate I made my way to the lockside. Eagerness was no doubt written all over my young face.

"Shall I open the bottom gates for you?" I said, rather too quickly.

He looked at me gloomily as was his way and then gave me a rare slow smile.

"You can help me down if you've a mind," he rejoined. "Gimme yer bike."

I had longed for this moment and the sight of my bike propped against his on the motor's back-end was confirmation of my first step into real boating. Of course I was brimful of theory and had watched lots of boats pass through locks, but that afternoon would be a case of theory into practice and I had to learn quickly so as not to disgrace myself. Meadows was getting on in years while I, on the other hand, was full of youthful zeal and I like to think I became of increasing use to him. The locks were empty and had to be filled whilst the motor was in the lock above. Meadows would not entrust me with a windlass on this first afternoon as, doubtless, he did not want to risk his job for any mangled fingers I might incur. Instead he would leave the motor just ticking over in gear to keep her nudging up to the bottom gates and, having drawn the bottom paddles, would then amble down to the next lock and draw the two ground paddles there. I watched the motor descend in the lock and, upon his return, was shown by Meadows how to take off the catch with a twist of the spindle and then let the paddles drop. My job was to open the two bottom gates and drop the paddles and I seemed to be expected to step across the yawning gap between the gate I had just opened and the other still closed gate in order to do so. This was initially nerve-wracking but if boatmen could do it then so could I! He, in the meantime, drew a top paddle in order to flush the motor out of the lock before rejoining the boat at the tail of the lock. I then proceeded to shut the bottom gates with a most satisfying crash leaving the lock to refill for the following butty. It was then a case of moving fairly smartly as I was expected to reach the next lock in order to open the top gate before the motor arrived.

The intervening pounds are short on the arm and I frequently found myself having to run hard to reach the next lock with Meadows making no concessions by slowing down in any way. I was having the time of my young life that afternoon and even got a ride on the boat down the last slightly longer pound as a fisherman had offered to open the final top gate. Sitting on the cabin top opposite the can and mop, afloat for the first time and with the diesel exhaust blowing in my face, I was in a seventh heaven! It was over all too soon as we walked back to meet the oncoming butty. The crew were a young husband and wife who acknowledged me with an acceptance which made my heart glow. I was all for accompanying the pair down into the town but Meadows suggested I come back with him for a cup of tea, an unprecedented offer which I could not possibly turn down. That day was an important one in cementing my love for the canals or the cut as I now always called them. For the first time I had helped meaningfully at the locks and had, albeit only very briefly, been afloat on a working boat. I arrived home sweaty from pedalling and with hands dirty from the gates and paddle spindles. I was so proud of that dirt that I didn't really want to wash it off!

Throughout the long summer term of 1955 things continued in much the same fashion. The Arm and I saw a great deal of each other but, as chance would have it, there was not another opportunity to assist Meadows on the flight. The wheat traffic was unpredictably spasmodic and very dependent on the arrival of shipments from North America. Meadows told me that it was brought up the river in dumb barges pulled by tugs to Brentford where the wheat was transhipped into narrowboats for the journey to Whitworth's Mill, twelve locks down the Nene at Wellingborough. The traffic tended therefore to occur in flushes with several pairs making the trip and then a lull leaving the arm to doze in the summer sunshine. The river Nene itself was more difficult to explore as, once out of the town, there was no real towpath as such and it was largely a case of walking with the bicycle rather than riding it. Nevertheless I penetrated downstream past Rush Mills, the first lock encountered beyond the town lock in Becket's Park, to Abington Lock where a particularly noxious tannery made its presence very much felt. At Weston Mill was a further lock and an old-established boat club whose little huts, built on a spit of land between the lock cut and the mill channel, were supported on brick pillars to combat the regular winter floods. At Weston Mill the towpath changed sides at the tail of the lock-cut and a bridge had been built to facilitate the passage of the boat horses, unfortunately this had been eroded over the years by floodwater and had recently collapsed. I found it necessary to detour up the bumpy narrow access lane before passing through a gate and continuing across the flat rather featureless fields to the next lock at Clifford Hill where a gelatine factory overlooked the wide reed-fringed pool above the weir.

Clifford Hill, after which the lock was named, was a singularly curious feature. It stuck up beyond the little factory very much in the manner of a small tumulus. My parents could throw no light on its origins, but for me it constituted an excellent vantage point. Climbing up through the assorted trees and bushes I emerged onto a flat grassy platform from where it was possible to see right back up the valley towards the town as well as downstream to the locks at Billing and Cogenhoe. I remember standing up there one day and noticing a pair of wheat boats leaving Weston Mill lock – needless to say I was down the hill in very good time to help shut a gate! The next lock along at Billing formed the outer limit of my explorations in those days as from there a narrow lane gave swift pedalling back to the town. The Nene valley seemed flat and rather uninspiring and was never a favourite of mine, although my passion drove me to explore it. My strong preference was for the world of the canals on the west side of the town, here I felt increasingly at home and it was in this direction that my wheels usually took me as the long summer term drew to an end.

The other great adventure of that summer came about in August. I had read about the canalside village of Braunston in some detail but had yet to visit it. Calculations on my old map showed it to be about fifteen miles from home, this meant a thirty mile round trip which at that time seemed to me a rather daunting distance to cycle. It so happened that my parents decided to spend their two weeks annual holiday at home that year dealing with some much needed paintwork on the bungalow. Whether or not my father saw his chance to escape I cannot say, but he suggested that we cycle together to Braunston the very next day as the weather seemed set fair. He had recently become more interested in my canal doings and I was overjoyed at the suggestion. The morning dawned fair with very little wind and, with sandwiches and old Tizer bottles filled with water in our saddlebags, we set off in high spirits westward. Our journey took us up over Berrywood Hill and along the old Roman Road, sweeping across the crest of the ridge and past the lonely tower and steeple which was all that was left of the church at Little Brington, before rushing down the long slope of Whilton Hill and coming to a halt on the hump-back bridge overlooking the second lock up of the Buckby flight. This was a familiar enough route for me by this time but beyond the railway arch facing us was new and unexplored territory. This was what we had come for and, eating our apples and drinking some water, we scanned the old faithful linen map for the direction. A short stretch of the very busy A5, or Watling Street trunk road, was followed by idyllic lanes leading down and over the summit level of the canal, through the village of Welton, and along an undulating road to the long main street of Braunston itself. In the summer of 1955 Braunston was an unknown and undiscovered place, a far cry from today when it has featured in books, magazines, and even films and is one of the busiest and best-known canal centres in the country. At that time I had seen no photographs of the village and knew of it chiefly from the chapter in *Narrow Boat*. My expectations were probably of a classic canal scene bustling with boats and activity, but that seemed very definitely not to be the case on this particular afternoon.

WINDLASS IN MY BELT

We cycled slowly through the long main street, knowing that the canal ran below us, and then turned down to the modern concrete bridge carrying the A45 over the waterway. Nothing moved. The waterway lay slumbering in the August sunshine and all was still. We had a look at the junction with its superb cast-iron bridges and the little triangular island created by the two narrow channels giving access to the route for Birmingham or Oxford. The long straight stretched away towards Wolfhamcote Church but, with the exception of a pair of mallard ducks steering purposefully through the junction and heading off northbound towards Hillmorton, there was no traffic to be seen. All was peace! But peace was not what I wanted; I wanted boats! We retraced towards Barlow's Yard. Here surely would be the clamour of a busy boatyard with a number of boats under repair and overhaul. A familiar white fore-end stuck out to greet us from under the curved cast-iron bridge giving access to the arm just beyond the old toll house, this looked more promising!

We wheeled our bikes up onto the bridge for our first view of the boatyard, to be greeted by virtual silence. A pair of empty boats, which I recognised, were tied at what was clearly an oiling point just inside the arm but no-one seemed to be aboard. Behind them, alongside the dock, was a butty under repair but not at that exact moment! A couple of other derelicts were moored at the very end of the arm and a faint hammering could be heard emanating from one of the group of sheds which comprised the dock. Busy, it most certainly was not. With the benefit of hindsight I can see what had happened. The collieries which provided Barlows with their trade were taking their two weeks annual holiday and, doubtless, the yard was doing much the same. Most of their pairs were idle, or becoming so as they returned to the coalfields, and we had caught what I later knew as a busy and interesting yard at one of its slackest moments. It was all rather disappointing but I determined to get the most out of the day and, after consulting the map closely, I persuaded my father that we should see the flight of six locks and then follow the horse path across the top of the tunnel to rejoin our route home. Like many plans it sounded fine in theory, but proved to be much harder in practice.

All went well as we cycled up the flight hoping for, but not seeing, some traffic. Our problems started beyond the top lock as we entered the cutting leading up to the tree shrouded and silent tunnel entrance. It was mid-August and warm but the towpath suddenly became very muddy and squidgy. Water was seeping out of the sides of the cutting and oozing onto the soggy towpath. It was too far to go back and we were becoming uncomfortably aware of passing time and the distance still to be covered. Nothing ventured, nothing gained. We squelched through, acquiring wet feet on an otherwise beautiful summer's day, and peered into the dark portal of the tunnel. A few drips were all that could be heard and no headlight was visible in the blackness. It had really been astonishing, not a single boat all day. The horse path more than made up for the struggles with the mud. Unlike Blisworth, where the bulk of the horse path is actually a road, this was a green path wandering through the fields between its own hedges amid a glorious silence broken only by the humming of bees and the occasional murmur of a distant tractor. The only disadvantage was that clearly no horses now passed this way. The grass was long and tussocky with an occasional spiky thistle rearing up. Cycling was impossible and we walked in the sunshine, sitting down halfway across for a drink of warm water and a tea-time jam sandwich. It was drowsily warm and the green countryside was very beautiful as we idled contentedly, I pictured in my mind's eye what the scene must have been like fifty years earlier when boat crews regularly walked horses across here whilst their boats were towed through the stygian depths beneath us by the steam tug. How many generations of boots must have passed this way but now, with the advent of the diesel engine, all was still and forgotten, a lost path meandering through the silent fields. Eventually we roused ourselves and pressed forward, crossing the Daventry to Kilsby road, and coming to the south end of the tunnel where two rather dilapidated cottages overlooked the canal in its leafy cutting. A tall bridge gave us access to the road and, passing once more through Welton, we pedalled steadily home without further incident. It had been very bad luck to have seen no boats on the move but, lying drowsily in bed that night, I felt contented with the memories of another fascinating day.

The bonds tying me to the waterways were getting stronger and stronger. I might arrive home tired, often sweaty, sometimes wet, frequently muddy and windswept, but I loved it all and was not to be deterred. News of my interest in the canals had by now spread around family and friends and that Christmas my small stock of books was very considerably enhanced by Rolt's *Inland Waterways of England*, Hadfield's *British Canals*, and de Maré's *The Canals of England*. All three books were eagerly received and then read and pored over with great interest, considerably adding to my growing knowledge of the system. What I lacked was another enthusiast to strike sparks off, but where to find such a person? In those days canal enthusiasts were very few and far between particularly in the small provincial town world I inhabited, I talked to Meadows as often as I could and he would tell me tales of a pre-war world of Joshers (Fellows Morton & Clayton boats) and the big Grand Union Canal Carrying Co expansion of the thirties. All this was fascinating to hear about and I learned a good deal, but otherwise the towpaths I wandered seemed to be deserted of any other kindred soul with whom I could communicate. This was soon to change, but in these early days I was very much alone with my all-consuming interest. My parents obviously noticed the solitary nature of my spare-time activities and began to take more of an interest themselves for which I was grateful and it was this that led me to venture, in the Spring of 1956, an idea that had been simmering in my mind for the last year or so.

As a family we might not be able to buy a boat as Rolt had done but it might be possible to hire one from the small, but very slowly increasing, number of companies offering this service. On a warm April day both my parents had accompanied me up the Arm on their bicycles for an afternoon's excursion and about half-way up the Rothersthorpe flight we encountered a small motor cruiser locking down to the Nene. Greetings were exchanged and I busied myself helping with the opening and closing of the gates. My mother seemed quite taken with the little cruiser, it was a sunny day after a long winter and the canal seemed very much a place of peace and quiet attraction on that afternoon of early springtime. I was quick to point out that such boats could be hired by the week but unfortunately not from Northampton or the surrounding area. Despite their interest my parents' knowledge of the waterways system was minimal, mostly confined to a glance at the Stanfords map hanging on my bedroom wall. If we were to do such a thing then where did I suggest?

Today we are spoilt for choice and the waterways are positively bristling with marinas and hire boat companies, but this was most definitely not the case back in the mid-1950s when such bases were only infrequently encountered. In a slim volume entitled *Know Your Waterways* by Robert Aickman I espied an advertisement for Canal Pleasurecraft (Stourport) Ltd. I had never even set foot in Worcestershire, let alone been anywhere near Stourport, but I knew my canal history and this looked to be an interesting start-point. It seemed feasible to me, and this was confirmed in the thin brochure we subsequently received, to go from there to Market Drayton and back in the week available to us. In the Staffs & Worcs this would give a taste of one of the early canals forming part of Brindley's 'Cross' and then on to Telford's much later Birmingham & Liverpool Junction Canal now forming the main line of the Shropshire Union system. The two waterways would, I hoped, form a complete contrast in engineering techniques and ambience. My parents were persuaded. I would be properly afloat at last!

It was decided that we should go in September when hire-rates were cheaper and thus, with me rejoicing in an extra week off school, we travelled cross-country by rail to pick-up a centre-cockpit cabin cruiser called *Bredon Hill*. It is difficult to remember nowadays, when travel is so much more widespread from an early age, what a relatively narrow existence I had hitherto led. Born during the war in 1943, with my father away on service, I had had a week on the Norfolk coast in 1952 and occasionally been to London by train. Otherwise I had hardly ever left my home area, my explorations being confined to the distance I could pedal in a day. The journey to Stourport was a memorable adventure in itself. After changing stations from New Street to Snow Hill in Birmingham we made one further change and finished the journey in what appeared to be a bus on flanged wheels. It was, in fact, a Great Western Railway diesel-powered railcar which took us the last few miles along a single-track line to Stourport. Our progression was decidely rattly and noisy and it was my first experience, apart from the Underground in London, of anything other than steam power on the railways. We found *Bredon Hill* lying in a large and mostly deserted basin from which two sets of entrance locks, one broad and one narrow, led down to the grey and distinctly uninviting waters of the river Severn.

"Glad we're not going down there," my father commented, as he surveyed the scene.

"Canals are much better," I affirmed cheerfully. "Rivers are always a bit bleak."

In terms of the Thames, which I had then never seen, this was blatantly untrue but, in terms of the Severn on that September day and coupled with my experiences of the Nene immediately below Northampton, it was a justifiable opinion to hold.

Of the small hire fleet available, ours was the only boat going out that week. My excitement was almost uncontainable as we were shown how to steer across the basin and given instruction at the first lock. At last we were off, with me at the wooden spoked wheel, steering steadily and with great concentration out of the town and into open country. It was a dull rather cloudy afternoon as, after a couple of uneventful miles, we reached our first lock at Falling Sands. The bottom gates were resting slightly ajar, an indication that the lock was empty and ready for us. Meadows would have eased right down before using the strong fore-end of the narrow boat to push open the gates and then steer in. *Bredon Hill*, on the other hand, was a small lightly-built cruiser and not at all fitted to ramming open lockgates, however gently the approach was made. We pulled in below the lock and I investigated the narrow dripping chamber overlooked by a rather neglected lock-cottage. There was one significant difference between this lock and those on the Arm, here the top gate boasted a pair of gate paddles in addition to the conventional ground paddles on either side. This was a great improvement in my eyes. Not only did the lock fill more quickly, but I also had more paddles to wind up and the roar of the water surging into the chamber to appreciate. All very satisfying! Everything went smoothly at Falling Sands and *Bredon Hill* was soon safely through, with the top gates shut behind us and all paddles dropped. Our instructions from the hire company on this business of gate closing and paddles were different from those given today; there was then very little commercial traffic left on the Staffs & Worcs and we were asked to shut top gates to reduce the leakage of water. Conversely, when locking downhill on our return, the bottom gates could be left open. Once on the Shropshire Union, on the other hand, we were told not to bother with the business of the top gates as the traffic was more regular. That afternoon we worked up through Kidderminster, where the wooden balance beams of the bottom gates had to be cranked in order to avoid fouling the adjacent bridge, and tied for the night below Debdale Lock. We had met no other boats since leaving Stourport but the canal was very picturesque with a succession of locks and tight bridge holes giving never a dull moment. I was enchanted by the sheer narrowness of it all and the low angles of the lock steps and bridge arches, a complete contrast to the much more open Grand Union in Northamptonshire.

Bredon Hill proved to be a most comfortable boat. She was about 30ft in length and possessed two cabins separated from each other by the centre cockpit. The back-cabin, with two berths, was rather smaller than the fore-cabin, where I slept, which also contained a small sink, a four-ring cooker powered from a calor bottle, and a fold-down table. The petrol engine was under the floor of the centre cockpit with a trapdoor giving easy access for oil checks and so on. Again, by some of today's standards, she would appear rather basic and most definitely a 'noddy-boat'. This, however, was a term which I had not encountered at that time, I thought she was just great and spent time that first evening mopping her off and making sure she was tied just so with her fenders preventing any unnecessary rubbing of her paintwork.

The next day dawned clear and sunny with no sign of any of the predicted autumn mist along the waterway. Bacon and egg was the order of the day before we once again set off with our first full day's boating ahead of us. Cookley Tunnel was of immediate interest. I had often peered into both ends of the long Blisworth Tunnel and had also looked into Braunston and Crick Tunnels, but I had never been inside a canal tunnel before. Cookley was cut out of the red rock which is prevalent in the Kinver area and was only sixty-five yards long complete with towpath. In all honesty it was not really much more than a long bridge, but it was classified as a tunnel in 'Edwards' and I steered carefully through taking great pains not to touch at any point. A few more locks brought us to Stewponey where a couple of T & S Element's 'joey' boats were moored. They were empty and looked as if they had been there for some time, as did the old LMS railway boat tied adjacent to the turn into the Stourbridge Canal. We had a sandwich at Stewponey and I took the chance to walk up the opening four locks of the Stourbridge. All the locks were empty and the chamber walls were quite dry, an indication that no boats had passed this way recently. The paddle spindles, shiny from constant use on the Grand Union, also appeared rusty and little used with the pound above the locks narrow and somewhat weedy. It would have been very interesting to go up there, I thought, traverse the Netherton Tunnel and drop down the Wolverhampton 21 to Autherley. But, if we had done this, there would be no time for the 'Shroppie' so stick to the plan!

The afternoon was spent working steadily and enjoyably northwards and, after successfully negotiating our first staircase locks at Botterham followed by the exquisitely named Bumblehole Bridge and Lock, we reached one of the undoubted high points of the trip, the unique staircase of three locks at Bratch. Bratch, like much of the present waterways system, is now cleaned up, tidied-up and is justifiably the object of considerable interest. Its future is assured, but it has lost some of the other-world charm that we found that afternoon. It was quite late when we arrived at the bottom of the three, there was no-one about and grass, weeds and crumbling stone were much in evidence on either side, but this was a fascinating place for a young enthusiast. I had read about the Bratch and looked with great interest at the three separate locks with their tiny intervening pounds. The steps at the sides of the flight were worn into deep curves by the boots of the boat crews, but the once very heavy coal traffic had now almost entirely departed and, amazingly by today's standards, we had not met another boat on the move all day. We tied above Bratch that night which gave me time, after more diligent mopping-off and cleaning of *Bredon Hill*, to have another thorough exploration of this most unusual flight.

Part of the charm of travelling by water is the planning and anticipation of the day ahead, the next day was no exception to this as we would reach Autherley Junction and change onto the Shropshire Union Canal, or 'Shroppie', as I was already knowledgeably calling it. I knew from Rolt that the Staffs & Worcs was colloquially known as the Stour Cut, somehow though this never slipped off my tongue with the same ease as 'Shroppie'. The last few miles from Bratch to the summit lock at Compton were memorable for the state of the canal. The water had grown increasingly brown as we had worked up towards the summit and small flecks of white foam were now becoming quite large lumps which floated along like miniature icebergs. At the locks the churning and rushing of the water caused even more froth which near the summit reached well up the boat sides and spilled out across the locksides to be blown about and snagged in the towpath hedge.

"It's the sewerage!" we were gloomily informed by the lock-keeper at Compton.

"It's Wolverhampton!"

Shortly after leaving Compton the source of the problem was finally seen in the form of a steady gush from an outflow into the canal accompanied by veritable Everests of foam, all of which, pulled by the downhill locks and their overflows, headed towards Stourport. Beyond this the water remained distinctly uninviting, but this could now simply be put down to the proximity of much heavy industry at nearby Wolverhampton. Passing the bridge, its arch picked out in whitewash, which led into the bottom lock of the Birmingham Canal Navigations. at Aldridge we swung left into the Shroppie at Autherley or 'Cut End' as the boatmen called it.

Thus far we had seemed to be navigating deserted waters but here, at last, there were signs of life. We exclaimed at the width of the Shroppie, stretching away long and straight to a distant bridge, and came to a halt in the stop-lock where we were hailed with extreme friendliness by Sam Lomas, the toll clerk, emerging from his office on the lockside. Sam was a shortish man with a receding forehead and was surprisingly attired in a suit, white shirt, tie, and grey pullover. Suits in my limited experience were a rarity on the cut and this seemed to indicate that Sam was a figure of some importance in the Shroppie world we were about to enter.

"Hallo my dooks!" he greeted us with a beaming grin. "Are you enjoying you'm holidays on our old cut then?"

My mother and Sam seemed to take to each other immediately and the kettle was soon hissing away for tea and, I hoped, a digestive biscuit. Sam said he would just fetch his cup and re-emerged from the toll office bearing an enormous white cup and saucer that looked as if it would take an entire potful of tea! He assured us the commercial traffic on the Shroppie was still holding up and that he remained quite busy in his little office. He also talked of the very heavy traffic there had been in coal to Stourport Power Station handled almost entirely by 'joey' boats and horses. This I would have loved to have seen but it had ceased in 1949 and the unloading gantries had been destroyed. The northern section of the Staffs & Worcs, he said, had carried very little traffic for many years unless there was a stoppage on the Shroppie main line in which case all the traffic went via the Trent & Mersey, but the shallow pounds and general neglect of the waterway made this an unpopular option among the boat crews. Sam was pessimistic about the future for trade on the Staffs & Worcs, conversely he was very optimistic about its potential for pleasure cruising given that the canal was so very pretty and would surely attract holidaymakers. I am sure, however, that even Sam would have been astonished at the degree of change on the Staffs & Worcs and everywhere else over the intervening forty years.

Also tied at Cut End was *Mistress Mine* which I had read about in IWA bulletins. Her skipper was Pat Saunders and the boat had recently won the cup for longest distance travelled to a rally. I suppose I had expected *Mistress Mine* to be a smart large and gleaming fifty-foot boat but found, on the contrary, a boat smaller than *Bredon Hill* and looking extremely functional. Her captain responded to my shy enthusiasm for him and his craft with great friendliness, taking me aboard *Mistress Mine*, and showing me photographs of her in places all over the system. I would have greatly enjoyed spending longer in his company but our tea-break had already extended to an hour and a half and we needed to get going. I had my 'Edwards' on the cabin-top and Sam, having spotted it, insisted on signing the inside of the front cover adding the official British Waterways stamp for added effect. Pat Saunders, who had come down for a can of water, was also roped in by Sam for pen work and his signature was added; the date stamp reads 27th September 1956.

After the pleasant but solitary journey up from Stourport I remember this meeting with great affection and recognise now how kindly both Sam and Pat responded to my intensely youthful enthusiasm. To add to the excitement a pair of boats were approaching from the north, hurriedly we vacated the lock and set off up the broad reaches of the Shroppie. The oncoming pair were Thomas Clayton (Oldbury) Ltd tar boats sliding deeply laden through the water with the tanks in their holds covered by planking. The cabin-sides were red but still with brass-rimmed chimneys, painted cans, and spirally decorated mop handles, just as on the Grand Union. I had heard of, but never seen, Clayton boats before and was pleased to add another pair and a new company into my 'spotters' notebook. With only the one lock at Wheaton Aston in the twenty-five miles to Tyrley Locks near Market Drayton we needed to put some miles in today and accordingly ate our sandwich lunch on the move. The Shroppie, wide but very shallow-edged, was a completely different proposition to the Staffs & Worcs with very long straights, many cuttings and embankments, and even another small tunnel at Cowley to add to the interest. Although only 81 yards long it was again listed officially in 'Edwards' as a tunnel – now I had passed through two canal tunnels! The Shroppie had a strange elusive charm all of its own, but I must confess I rather missed the tree-shrouded secretiveness of Brindley's canal.

We were not alone that day either. I recall we passed a converted pontoon as used for bridge-building in the war and powered by an outboard motor which looked none too healthy as it passed us, amid clouds of blue smoke, just short of Wheaton Aston. Sam had told us we would likely meet *Mendip*, skippered by Charlie Atkins, on the run from Knighton to Cadbury's at Bourneville with chocolate crumb and this we duly did on the long level beyond that solitary lock. We nodded gravely and exchanged the customary "How-do" with the steerer. In the lovely reaches beyond Norbury a small convoy of traffic was encountered led by two single motors, what I now know to be Josher 'pups', closely followed by a pair of British Waterways craft. The boats were deeply laden and had to stay centre-channel, but they slowed for us and we followed Sam's advice to stay close to them, squeezing past without any problems. *Bredon Hill* had a shallow draught and went quite fast on a waterway as accommodating as the Shroppie. We just kept going that day, changing steerers from time to time and having tea whilst still on the move. The long pound seemed to go on and on and it was deep twilight as we came through the spectacularly tall bridges of the 'rocket' cutting to tie at the top of Tyrley with darkness closing in. Hardly time to mop off that evening but I did, of course, sploshing about happily in the dark before finally going below for a well-earned dinner after a really memorable day.

Time, which crawled by at school, was passing with horrifying rapidity. It was already Tuesday, the mid-point of the trip, and I felt like we had hardly started! Slipping easily down the lovely little flight of five locks at Tyrley we came to our destination at the little town of Market Drayton. Here was a chance for necessary shopping and also sadly where we had to turn round ready for the return journey. My parents walked up into the town for provisions but I elected to remain and 'look after the boat', savouring the sensation of being alone and in charge and even indulging myself in a fantasy of continuing on and on around the system without the inconvenience of having to attend school. Sweet dreams! My reveries were interrupted by the steady diesel beat of an oncoming boat and I was rewarded by the sight of another single motor passing by, presumably returning empty to the north-west for orders. I proudly exchanged a "Hey-up, mate!" with the young steerer and wished I could do that!

The plan for the day was to return to Norbury in time for a walk down the disused arm which headed off towards Shrewsbury. As we entered the cutting it began to rain heavily for the first time that week. I was undeterred and, wearing my blue gaberdine school mack, stood stoically but happily in the completely exposed centre-cockpit getting steadily wetter and wetter. My parents remained below, doubtless buoyed by my assurances of being fine, and in any case the trip was my idea! As I said at the time we couldn't stop anyway or we might not get back in time, so on we went! The rain perversely intensified, if that were possible, and by the time we did finally reach Norbury it had set in for the evening. This was very disappointing but even I, after a complete head to toe change, had to concede that a walk down the arm was inadvisable as the rain drummed relentlessly on the cabin roof and my wet clothes caused all the windows to steam up. It was all most unfortunate. There would not really be time the next morning and so the chance was missed and, to this day, I have never returned to Norbury for that walk. Such is life. On the Wednesday, after a prompt start, we reached Cut End in early afternoon encountering the same pair of Claytons at Wheaton Aston returning empty to Ellesmere Port. By contrast to yesterday the day was proving mild and sunny and there was a little time in hand!

I had read of the 'narrows' on the Staffs & Worcs north of Autherley and the round house at Gailey Lock at the end of the summit. It was only a small detour, I reasoned, and with unique features of interest! No more locks involved! My parents were persuaded, helped by Sam's assurances that the plan was perfectly feasible, and *Bredon Hill* headed north that afternoon. This was all a bonus as I had not really expected to be able to fit in this extra pound, despite it being privately in the back of my mind! It also made up for the disappointment at Norbury the previous evening. The 'narrows' proved to be as interesting as they sounded and for several hundred yards the boat had to be steered very precisely with the rough-hewn banks alarmingly close on both sides. The contrast to the earlier part of the day on the wide breezy levels of the Shroppie was like chalk and cheese. Canal boating, like most pleasurable activities, should not ideally be hurried but we had only limited time and, despite this being a supposedly 'short' detour, it was still eight miles from Autherley to Gailey and then naturally the same distance back. A sixteen mile pound no less. Time was pressing and *Bredon Hill* was turned smartly round with just enough leeway to see the round house and observe the very busy A5 trunk road below the bottom gates of Gailey Lock, the same road that we had cycled briefly upon on our trip to Braunston. Back we went towards Cut End and I glanced with interest at the junction with the Hatherton Branch and the neglected looking locks beyond. It looked as if no traffic came down there either. This would also have made for an interesting walk but, alas, time was running out and it was once more almost dark as we tied adjacent to Autherley that night. My parents confessed that, much to their own surprise, they were actually enjoying the trip and relishing the change of pace and the different angles on town and country which boating gave. This was excellent news as, unbeknown to them, I was already mentally plotting another trip for the following Spring!

We awoke the next morning to the steady, but seemingly persistent, noise of rain on the cabin-top. We had two days to get back and would have to move eventually but there was no desperate rush to be gone. A leisurely breakfast was followed by reversing *Bredon Hill* into the stop lock to top off the water tanks. This was not strictly necessary as we had ample water to get us back to Stourport but I wanted to do it and it also gave us the chance of a last chat to Sam before departure. He was as cheerful as ever and gave us the weather forecast which promised rain clearing from the west. We were fairly west already so it looked quite promising. By dithering about we avoided a soaking as the rain had petered out by mid-morning and, with a last farewell to the beaming Sam, who I can see now standing waving to us in the doorway of his little office, we set off back towards Stourport.

At Compton the foam seemed worse, perhaps it was the rain. It reached up to the cabin windows as we entered the lock, the action of the paddles exacerbating an already frothy situation! As we sank down in the chamber it fell from the lockside on top of the boat in great lumps of soft bubbles. The froth followed us down that day towards Bratch, gradually dispersing as the outflow was left further and further behind. We had improved considerably as a team in boating through the locks with my mother steering and my father and myself active with gates and paddles. There were a lot of little tricks of the trade that I did not know of at that stage, but I can honestly say that we were becoming quite proficient that afternoon as we dropped steadily down, lock after lock, to tie finally at Kinver which would give us a comfortable last day regardless of the weather. Once again we were very much alone and had encountered no moving craft south of the junction with the Wolverhampton Locks. In later years I became aware that an item of interest, totally unlinked to waterways, had slipped through our hands the next morning. None of us knew of the existence of the nearby cave dwellings built into the distinctive soft red rock of the the area. I now know that there are a number of these cave houses and I believe that they were still lived in at the time of our visit. With hindsight, it is annoying that our lack of knowledge cost us the chance to see this unique but vanishing way of life.

WINDLASS IN MY BELT

There was absolutely no hurry at all on this last day and the weather was pleasantly autumnal as we retraced through Cookley Tunnel to reach Kidderminster at mid-day. With time in hand I wandered up to the railway station there, finding myself rewarded by the spectacle of several unfamiliar GWR locomotives passing through including one of the well-known 'Castle' class engines. It struck me then how the regional nature of things changed in such short distances. We were not that far from Northampton as the crow flies but the environment was so different. Here on the Stour Cut the long distance family boats of the Grand Union system were unknown and the railway reflected its golden past with an ambience somehow lofty and superior when compared with the more mundane workaday world of the old LMS back home. The boat had to be back by ten the following morning and, trying to cram in everything of interest, I suggested that we work through the last couple of locks and spend our final night adjacent to Pratts Wharf Lock which apparently led through to the river Stour. It was sad to be finishing so soon but this should at least make for an interesting last evening. The arm to the river Stour was situated a short distance below Falling Sands Lock and went off at a right angle from the main canal with an immediate entrance lock. Any optimistic thoughts of navigation were quickly dispelled at the lock, which was derelict. The paddles were securely tied up with barbed wire and the gates rendered unusable by heavy chains fastened with rusty padlocks while rushes and weeds sprouted profusely. Below this sad relic of a busier past a very narrow and extremely weedy waterway wandered through the fields. Sitting on the bottom gate on that quiet autumn evening it was difficult to imagine the clip-clop of the approaching horse and the rattle of those rusting paddles as a heavily laden narrowboat passed through. Dusk came on and a ghostly white barn owl passed through the nearby trees with a soft hoot, water trickled gently through the old and unwanted lock. In that still moment of twilight I felt very strongly the spirit and charm of the canals and was at one with myself.

The return to reality was not easy. During the next few weeks, as autumn gave way to winter and the dark evenings drew on, my thoughts often drifted back to those few short glorious days exploring the intricacies of the near deserted Stour Cut, the lonely windswept pounds of the Shroppie, the high embankments giving way to deep fern shrouded cuttings and the passage of deeply-laden craft. Dreary days of French and Algebra were mitigated by my private dreams. The romance of the cut had entered into my soul and it would not easily be dislodged. A little of the mysterious charm of the canals had communicated itself to my parents who had also enjoyed their week and seemed not averse to trying another trip. That winter I immersed myself in the cut, re-reading my books, poring over the distance charts in my 'Edwards', cycling around in Northamptonshire at week-ends and talking to Meadows when our paths crossed. There was only one chance of actual boating for me that winter when, on a gloomy and misty Saturday in late January, I helped Meadows bring an empty motor up the Rothersthorpe flight.

He knew of my trip and this time I was entrusted with a windlass, spending a happy afternoon dealing with gates and paddles whilst he steered. I learned uphill techniques that day as he taught me the routine. Upon his signal I drew half to two-thirds of a paddle to stop the boat as it approached the sill at the head of the lock, he meanwhile had left the boat as it entered the lock and, walking up the steps provided for the purpose, shut the bottom gates with a resounding bang. I then drew the rest of the paddle before crossing over to draw the other side, thence remaining on the outside of the lock watching the swirling waters settle as the levels equalised. Meadows had the boat in gear and, as it began to nudge the top gate open, I quickly dropped the outside paddle and stepped smartly on to the already opening gate, crossing over to drop the other paddle with a satisfying clatter. The motor chugged steadily forward and, when she was about half-way out of the lock, Meadows would draw about four inches of bottom paddle before briskly regaining his steering position as the boat drew clear. My task was to shut the top gate behind the receding motor, allowing the lock to empty in time for the approaching bow-hauler to be able to open the bottom gates to admit the following butty. I then followed Meadows up the pound to the next lock where we repeated our routine.

Pounds are short on the arm. Mostly by dint of running I would be there in time to open the bottom gates, if not, Meadows would nudge them open with the motor. What was really important was that I was there ready to draw upon his signal as the motor entered the lock. I always was! At the top lock Meadows disappeared into his house and had not re-emerged when the lock was filled. Noting that the boat was not in gear I dropped both paddles and, having opened the top gate, ambled back down the lockside where, having looked with interest through the engine-hole doors, I stood gazing down the flight to where the boatman was just emerging from the bridge-hole below the second lock with the long towline stretched across his shoulders. Meadows emerged into his porch and grinned at me.

"Well, go on then! Take her out!"

I knew what to do from watching and needed no second bidding! Standing on the footboard I turned the large wheel on the right-hand side to engage forward gear, following this with a gentle twirl on the speedwheel to move us forward. Meadows was strolling along the side of the lock, apparently casually, but actually watching me closely.

"Steady," he intoned, as I came abreast of the gate.

I throttled back and then took her out of gear allowing her to drift forward.

"Hold her back!" he commanded, as the counter cleared the gate and he pulled on the beam to close it behind me. I thought I had stopped her rather well and, without any further prompting, tied her to the adjacent stump to prevent her drifting back into the gate.

"Good lad!", remarked my friend, as he wandered down to draw the bottom paddles.

High praise indeed. I grew an inch on the spot!

Cycling home through the soggy lanes with my little lamp playing a thin beam of light on the familiar road ahead I felt truly exhilarated. However briefly, I had steered a narrowboat for the first time! I had noted her name, of course, and in years to come the sight of *Dorado*, GU No 36, would always remind me of that memorable winter's afternoon. Narrowboats were the real thing, I reasoned. *Bredon Hill* was good fun, but a narrowboat was better. Upon reaching home that evening I was full of my adventure, proudly displaying the patches of paddle-grease on my hands before reluctantly going to wash. My parents seemed quite amenable to another canal trip in the Spring as again the cost would be lower than in Summer. Once more it was left to me to come up with the suggestion for a hire company and an interesting route. What I really desperately wanted was a narrowboat As January gave way to February and with each passing day the evenings began to lengthen out I determined to find one.

*****

Chapter 2

Canada Goose

There was no time to be lost if a booking was to be made for the coming Spring and this time I did not have to look very far afield. Set beside the Grand Union Canal at Leighton Buzzard was the base of The Wyvern Shipping Company Ltd. This small company had been set up to take part in commercial carrying in the very early 1950s and had even acquired the well-known motor *Heatherbell* as part of their small fleet. Carrying had not been a great success but the company, instead of selling out as John Knill had done, switched the focus of their activities and moved into the hire boat business and some accompanying boat yard work. I had, on a number of occasions, seen their blue painted craft in Northamptonshire and had noted that one of their boats was indeed a narrowboat with the name of *Canada Goose*. Upon acquiring the Wyvern brochure it was immediately obvious that the most suitable craft for three people was a boat called *Princess* which I had also seen along the Blisworth pound. She was tiller-steered, which I was keen on, but against that she was only about thirty-five or forty feet in length. *Canada Goose*, on the other hand, was a six-berth converted narrowboat and really far too big for our needs. Oddly the price differential for hire was not that great and I managed to persuade my parents of the desirability of *Canada Goose* and the validity of experiencing travel by narrowboat, just like Rolt and *Cressy*. In the face of my immense enthusiasm about the whole idea they had very sensibly opted for the line of least resistance! *Canada Goose* was booked for a week in early May and route planning began at once.

Southwards towards London was one possibility; a heavily locked route with interesting highlights such as Tring Summit, the paper mills which received the bulk of the southbound coal, and the large ex-GUCCo, now British Waterways, carrying base at Bulls Bridge which I had read about in *Maidens Trip* and *Idle Women*. I considered the northbound alternative and, upon referring to the Wyvern Shipping Company's brochure, was informed that those of an energetic disposition could reach Banbury and back in a week. That settled it! We were very definitely of an energetic disposition, there was absolutely no doubt about it! The challenge had been laid down, northbound it would be with the diverse experiences of the Grand Union and Oxford canals giving yet another contrast in engineering techniques and ambience. What we did not then know was just how much the voyage on *Canada Goose* was to change the whole future course of our family life.

Winter, after a dismally cold and grey March, finally gave way to Spring and I spent several days of the Easter holidays wandering the towpath between the Arm End and the dark northern portal of Blisworth Tunnel. Leaning round I would peer into the gloomy depths and see the gleam of headlights, the echoing reverberation of the engines, and presently the emergence of a north-bound pair, sometimes loaded but often empty. Unfortunately for me none of them had wheat for Wellingborough, trade on the arm was in one of its slack spells and I was unable to get in any lock practice at all. Nevertheless I revelled in my time at Blisworth Tunnel End secure in the knowledge that, in a matter of only a few weeks, I too would be passing through its dark and mysterious interior. At long last May arrived and so did the eagerly awaited Saturday! The train trip was considerably shorter this time and afforded two good views of the cut, firstly as it wound its way through Wolverton and again just before we dived through a short tunnel to arrive at Leighton Buzzard station. Our second adventure was underway with the considerable added bonus of yet another week off school!

A short walk up a narrow lane brought us to the base of the Wyvern Shipping Co Ltd lying on the straight tree-lined stretch of waterway between Leighton Bridge and the town's solitary lock. *Canada Goose* was alongside looking enormous by comparison with *Bredon Hill*. Narrowboat steering was going to have to be learnt quickly! It was once again theory into practice with a vengeance! *Canada Goose* still had her boatman's cabin, albeit partially stripped out, and a conventional engine-hole. From here the cabin-work stretched forward to culminate in a spacious well deck, separated from the fore-end by a cratch tastefully decorated with a panel of diamonds and a bunch of roses on either side. A short plank led from the cratch across the well deck to the cabin roof and canvas could be rolled down to enclose this area if the weather was inclement. Rather unusually the headlight was not to be found in the conventional position on the foredeck just in front of the cratch, instead it was mounted on the cabin roof directly above the double doors giving access to the main cabin. A galley was situated halfway along, again with double doors opening out for ventilation in fine weather, with the three little double sleeping cabins further aft. It was certainly true to say that we had plenty of room! My parents, although happy with the luxurious cabin space, seemed rather uneasy as to what we had taken on and were clearly apprehensive about manoeuvring this long craft along the narrow waterway. I, just past my fourteenth birthday, had no doubts at all. With all the confidence and innocence of youth I was simply raring to go!

We were escorted the short distance along to Leighton Lock and then waved off around the Jackdaw pound. A reading of the books on wartime boating had alerted me to the fact that this pound had a bad reputation for awkward bends and clinging mud. Gripping the tiller I was ready to give of my best! Experience is all with narrowboats, I was very much the raw tyro and on this trip had no one to teach me. The theory of it all had been diligently read up, I knew all about keeping straight, going round the outside of bends, slowing down when passing, and giving way to loaded boats. But it was the practice of it that had to be learned and inevitably it would be learned the hard way, especially with an itinerary as ambitious as ours. Looking back on it one can only smile at some of the errors, but I lacked then the expertise I would later acquire and had to learn quickly as problems presented themselves. Once round the first gentle turn out of Leighton Lock we forged along in style, happily passing The Globe inn and getting the feel of her as much as possible. Tiller steering was more responsive than wheel steering, I decided, and felt quite pleased with progress along that first straight stretch. Indeed I began to wonder what all the fuss was about over the Jackdaw pound. I was soon to learn! Beyond this straight stretch the canal curves in a U-shape round the side of a hill and the first real bend taught me my first hard lesson. I came into the bend too fast, not realising how far round it went, and then added to the problem by turning too early. Instead of going steadily round the outside I found myself cutting the corner. Realisation of my predicament came too late and the length of the boat made the necessary adjustment a very difficult one. It was beyond me, and *Canada Goose* came to a halt, stuck unceremoniously across the very first bend. It was not a good start and my confidence had taken a knock which was no bad thing. When travelling on an unknown waterway with a narrowboat a little caution and prudence from the steerer can prevent a number of problems. As is so often the case in life I had learned my lesson the hard way, but at least I had learned it.

Luckily we were not seriously aground and, by shafting the fore-end across the cut and holding it there, we were able, with a combination of engine and shaft, to force the back-end free and find ourselves afloat once more. One of the great advantages to be had when steering a narrowboat is an intimate knowledge of the waterway. The working boat people had this, of course, knowing every bend, bridge hole and lock, and all the quirks and foibles attached to each. It is a knowledge that can only come from experience, without it navigating a narrowboat along a strange waterway most definitely requires a sensible degree of caution if major problems are to be avoided. Stowing the long shaft back on the top of the cabin and re-coiling the ropes we set off once more. Not surprisingly we had never run aground with *Bredon Hill* and were all somewhat chastened by such an early mishap, especially myself who was steering. I resumed at the tiller with my father, perched on the narrow gunwale next to me, offering moral support, whilst my mother, a boat's length away in the well deck, scanned the route ahead. It was a nervous time. The boat felt heavy and unfamiliar and the intricate details of the route ahead were unknown.

Very steadily we edged cautiously round the next turn and then slid smoothly through a bridge hole to be confronted by a pair of loaded Barlows bearing down on us. I eased off and moved over to the right but not too far as I knew their deep draught would suck the water out from under us. They also eased well down in the customary manner and we passed with two or three feet between us exchanging the usual "How do's" with the steerers. This successful manoeuvre served to lift morale considerably and, feeling rather more confident, we pressed on carefully and were pleased to reach the top of the three locks at Soulbury without any further misadventures.

We had developed the custom during our previous trip of my mother steering through the locks leaving my father and I free to deal with the gates and paddles. Nothing daunted she saw no reason to change this routine just because of the difference in size of boat and we organised ourselves accordingly. The three locks are straight and very close together which afforded her a relatively easy initiation that afternoon. Meeting the Barlow pair had left us with 'a good road', all three locks full with gates open and paddles still up as was the custom on the Grand Union. Locks were invariably just left as they were after use with no dropping of paddles and shutting gates every time; all that was still a long way in the future. Our instructions from the Wyvern Shipping Co on lockage followed this pattern of working, the only departure from it being the custom for boats to close the top gate of the summit locks at Claydon and Marston Doles on the Oxford. *Canada Goose* dropped slowly down the Soulbury Three that afternoon emerging to follow a winding course through the water meadows to the next solitary lock at Talbots which was also ready for us.

By now the shadows were lengthening and evening was well advanced. The original aim had been to tie for the night by the single lock at Fenny Stratford, but everything had taken a good deal longer than I had thought. What with the time lost extricating ourselves from the mud and our subsequent more cautious approach around the pounds, this target began to look rather doubtful. It probably would have been sensible to have stopped below Talbots on that first evening but, with half an eye already on Banbury, we decided to push on in an attempt to to reach Fenny if at all possible, the alternative being to tie up 'when it got dark'. The pound along towards Fenny is not a difficult one to steer but the fading light began to play on my nerves and still there was no sign of the lock. To have attempted to continue in the dark on a strange waterway really would have been to court disaster and so, having just cleared a particularly gloomy bridge hole, we elected to tie up. This proved to be another mistake. Tying up in the middle of nowhere with a narrowboat is not to be recommended and *Canada Goose* was secured, none too comfortably, about two feet out from a grassy and somewhat broken bank. The first day had gone quite well, it was decided, as we ate dinner in the spacious cabin that evening. We had got stuck once, but had got off again and learned something along

CANADA GOOSE

the way. Our routine in the locks had gone smoothly and we must be very close to Fenny, our planned destination. My parents felt with some justification that life was less stressful on *Bredon Hill* but, on the positive side, they certainly luxuriated in the extra space and superior comfort of *Canada Goose*.

Next morning we were stuck again! We had been woken by the passing of a southbound pair who, as it was only a little after six o'clock, we assumed must have started from Fenny Stratford. Although they thoughtfully slowed right down to just a tickover the suction of their wash nevertheless lifted *Canada Goose* slightly, before dumping her firmly down again a little nearer the towpath. She was undoubtedly stuck and listing at a slight angle. It was not a good start. My father and I decided to get her off and then have breakfast at Fenny Lock. At least the same method worked again. With the fore-end already shafted out I pushed hard with the other shaft against a dolly on the counter. Very grudgingly *Canada Goose* moved, slowly at first but then with gathering momentum, floating out into the channel and leaving me stranded on the towpath. My father had steered only very briefly the day before and was far from confident but there was no question of trying to get back in again to pick me up. Gingerly he set off, with me walking alongside, rounding a slight bend before sighting the A5 road bridge which preceded the curve that took us round into Fenny Lock. Here we found a comfortable deep-water mooring complete with rings, a tap, and the shop and all just half a mile from where we had spent the night on a shallow rocky mooring. The day was still damp and misty but a hearty breakfast of bacon and egg, safe in the knowledge that *Canada Goose* was tied securely to rings in deep water, worked wonders for the all-important inner man. Another lesson learned. We resolved that in future we would tie up only at recognised stopping places where *Canada Goose* could be drawn comfortably and safely into the bank.

With breakfast over and washed up we set off on our journey around the long pound towards Cosgrove Lock in bright spring sunshine with any residual early morning mist clearing rapidly. It developed into a glorious morning and, after successfully negotiating an extremely awkward S-bend with a bridge hole straddling the middle of it just beyond Fenny Lock, I felt my confidence growing as we headed north. The pound ran through remote and open countryside and several herons kept us company that morning. They would fly ahead of the boat for a while alighting on the bank from time to time until, having presumably reached the limit of their territory, they would wheel away and fly back towards their starting point. A number of hares were also spotted sitting motionless in the fields with ears erect before scampering for cover as *Canada Goose* approached. There were quite a few big bends around the pound but I was getting the hang of it now, slowing down in time as well as assiduously sticking to the deep water channel running round the outside of each corner. Everyone took turns steering that morning and enjoyment flooded back after the slightly faltering start of the day before, the sun was shining and life was good! We snagged slightly on the bottom at an awkward turn under a railway bridge just before the 'Black Horse' near Linford, but the boat dragged herself clear amid clouds of mud and bubbles churned up from the silt on the inside of the turn. It was the same mistake of cutting the corner again, but I was definitely getting better!

Winding under the dark low railway bridges at Wolverton we emerged to run alongside the extensive carriage works which were then in full operation, both for repair and restoration as well as the construction of new rolling stock. Glancing back over the bubbling wash I noticed the blue and yellow fore-end of a British Waterways motor emerging from the railway bridges; we were being quite rapidly overhauled by a fast-moving pair travelling back empty to the coalfields. To be overtaken was another first and as we were on a straight stretch I slowed immediately, even taking *Canada Goose* briefly out of gear to enable them to catch up. Which side were you overtaken on? I waved back to the oncoming steerer and indicated to my right being instantly rewarded with an encouraging thumbs-up. Edging over to the left *Canada Goose* drifted forward on tick-over as the high fore-end of the motor drew abreast, they had also eased off and the rushing wave, which had previously accompanied the motor's stern the full width of the cut, died away as the pair coasted past. The crew were a young couple I had seen before on the arm and they remembered me!

"Hey-up, young John! You're getting on a bit! Where you'm going then?"

"Banbury!" I shouted with a smile.

"You be careful," he responded, "Shallow down there!"

The butty came alongside and his wife, who was rather more demure but with a lovely smile, confined herself to the matter in hand.

"Whay-up, young John! You've loosed us by nicely!"

It was all slightly embarrassing. They knew my name from talking to Meadows and had actually remembered it whilst I, although I recognised them and their boats, did not know their names. This was something I must sort out with Meadows the next time I was up the arm, another little lesson learned.

They soon began to draw ahead, although remaining in sight, as we rounded yet another bend before passing through the bridge hole which gave access to the long straight leading up to Cosgrove Lock. A timber yard on the left was still served by water and I looked with interest at the pair of boats alongside being laboriously unloaded by hand, plank by plank. Then our whole attention was focussed on the point where the cut narrowed, halfway along an increasingly high embankment. It was here that the canal made the crossing of the river Great Ouse; it was my first aqueduct. An iron trough carries the cut high above the reedy and very shallow Ouse with a four inch rim on one side and the towpath, complete with protective iron railings, on the other. Bringing *Canada Goose* to a halt in the trough we all looked over the edge with interest as this was the same river that we knew from bus trips to Olney and Bedford. This really was the life! Warm sunshine, the rhythmic thump of the diesel, the pair ahead of us disappearing into the lock, and the interest of the aqueduct before us. What more could anyone want?

Stoke Bruerne was our intended destination that night and we were well up to time. Having dropped down to river level to see *Canada Goose* floating high above us we discovered and explored the little foot tunnels that ran under the aqueduct before tying above Cosgrove Lock for a sandwich lunch. Here the old Buckingham Arm ran off towards Old Stratford. Like the Wendover Arm and the small Welford Arm, off the Tring and Leicester summits respectively, it had steadily lost trade until in the 1930s despite the busy nature of the main-line, it had been allowed to fall derelict. Crossing the lock-gates at Cosgrove there was time for an exploration of the weeded and reedy first half-mile of the arm. Having not been able to walk down the Shrewsbury branch of the Shroppie the previous autumn it was, apart from the short River Stour Arm of the Staffs & Worcs, the first completely derelict canal I had seen. Reaching the first bridge I ran my fingers through the grooves worn in the bridge supports by the constant rubbing of many tow-ropes. All gone now. Tall banks of reeds blocked the channel and untrimmed branches bent low over the weedy waterway, even the towpath was unkempt and clearly very little used by walkers. A deep silence overhung the arm with just the occasional coot or mallard disturbing its still waters. It was all rather poignant and I was quite glad to make my way back to the main line where the canal was wide and clear, still very much a thriving commercial artery.

The pound up to Stoke proved to be much easier to steer than the preceding Fenny pound and we made steady progress that afternoon, passing through the ornately decorated stone bridge in Cosgrove village before once more moving out into open country. This was the valley of the small river Tove which made its winding way down through the pastures to reach a confluence with the Great Ouse; glancing up I recognised the sleepy Northamptonshire villages of Yardley Gobion and Grafton Regis overlooking us from the ridge. Across the other side of the valley rose the needle-like spire of Hanslope Church forming an ever-present landmark as we gently wound our way along to the bottom of the seven locks at Stoke Bruerne. We had passed three pairs of south-bound boats in the pound but we still had the empty pair ahead – as a consequence the first two locks were ready for us but the remaining five were not.

It had been a day of long pounds and we all welcomed the flight as a chance to be off and getting a little light exercise! The small brick pumping station at the bottom of the locks was working as, leaving the river Tove on our left, we eased gently under the white-painted wooden bridge and entered the lock. For Wellingborough-bound wheat boats the length from the top of Stoke to the top of Rothersthorpe constitutes a summit level and thus the Blisworth pound loses around 100,000 gallons of water for every pair that passes that way. Such losses need to be replaced, hence the pumping station which moved water from the Cosgrove pound, well fed from the river Tove, up to the Blisworth pound into which it bubbles forth from an outflow situated in front of the four tall cottages which front the canal side at Stoke Bruerne. Finding that the third lock, Bridge Lock, was against us my father opted to lock-walk, as against lock-wheel with a bicycle, ahead up the flight and prepare the locks for us. The locks were very fast filling being equipped not just with ground paddles but also with double gate-paddles, admitting water apace through two apertures in each gate. You had to be very careful, always drawing the ground paddles first and then waiting until the boat had risen sufficiently above the sill before drawing these highly efficient gate-paddles. If you drew too early the enormous rush of water would bounce up off the sill in a huge wave and flood the well deck and cabin of *Canada Goose*, a process not to be recommended! I thoroughly enjoyed working these big double locks and found the roar of the water churning through the gate-paddles and rapidly filling the lock most satisfying.

At the top lock, beyond the arches of the high double bridge, we were back in familiar territory. I had cycled out to Stoke Bruerne and explored its delightfully unspoilt canal side on a number of occasions and knew that the boatpeople's nurse, Sister Mary Ward, lived in the big old red brick house which lay adjacent to the top gates of the lock. Indeed, on two occasions whilst watching boats pass through the lock, I had seen her emerge in her blue uniform with white head-dress and chat to the crews. Needless to say, being rather shy and retiring, I had not managed to summon up the courage to speak to her! It was a surprise therefore to see my father, who was blessed with a similar temperament, sitting on the end of the top balance beam and apparently in animated conversation with Sister Mary. Glancing up the cut I noted that the empty pair preceding us had gone on and that not a single other boat was to be seen. Unless there was a late arrival it rather looked as if we would be all alone at Stoke Bruerne that night.

Rather shyly, after shutting the bottom gate behind *Canada Goose*, I made my way up the lockside to the outside top gate. Here I drew the ground paddle and then, as my father seemed deep in conversation, crossed over and drew the other one before finding myself being introduced to Sister Mary. She was a small lady dressed, as I had seen her before, in a nurse's blue uniform with a white head-dress fastened with pins around her greying curls and she smiled at me kindly as we shook hands. Up close, I noticed the deep laugh lines around her eyes and the engaging geniality of her smile.

"Hello, my dear," she said. "So you're John."

CANADA GOOSE

I liked her instantly and I'm quite sure that this had nothing to do with her almost legendary status. She was very open and genuine and you just warmed to her immediately. My father, having set the lock for us, had obviously been in the process of telling her all about my developing passion for canals and our trip to Braunston together. This had evidently met with her approval for we found ourselves invited in for a cup of tea just as soon as we had got *Canada Goose* tied up and snugged down for the night.

It was twilight as we stepped off the boat. We had tied just beyond the old warehouse which adjoined the four tall three-storied cottages which looked across to The Boat inn with its thatched roof and low windows. Reeds grew in the neck of the canal outside the inn and some old trestle tables seemed a permanent feature, whatever the season of the year. A narrow path led down the side of the cottages, reminding you that the canal was actually embanked at this point, and then came the long two-storied red brick house currently occupied by Sister Mary. There were two doors at the front and a light alongside the first of these seemed to indicate which should be knocked upon. Trim gardens fronted the house and foliage crept up the walls before spreading luxuriantly out over the porch to neatly encompass the main door upon which we now knocked. Warmth flooded out to greet us as Sister Mary hurried us inside and we found ourselves standing in what was evidently the boatman's surgery. Everything was painted white and was spotlessly clean. In the centre of the room a medical bed occupied pride of place and glass-fronted cupboards were filled with bottles, bandages, and other medical paraphernalia. A bay-fronted window with a low wooden seat afforded an excellent view of the lock and adjacent towpath. I knew that Sister Mary had been ministering to the boatpeople's needs for very many years, that through a mixture of kindness and selfless devotion she had acquired their complete trust and loyalty, and that she was paid only a small sum by the carrying companies for her efforts.

"This is where I look after my darlings!" she enthused cheerily. "I can deal with all the small matters, but anything major has to go to Northampton General."

As small matters apparently included assisting at births in the tiny boat cabins, it was clear that you had to be in dire straits to warrant a trip to the dreaded General Hospital in nearby Northampton!

"Come through," continued Sister. "Tea's all ready for us."

We passed across a narrow passageway into a comfortable sitting room amply furnished with settee and armchairs with several small tables scattered about. Two bookcases lined one wall and thick heavy curtains added to the atmosphere of old fashioned comfort. Photographs of family and friends, small ornaments and miscellaneous objects completed the friendly and welcoming effect. A tray of cups, plates and biscuits stood on a low table in front of a pleasant fire.

"Do sit down, dears," she said. "I'll just pop and fill the teapot."

She returned with a large brown teapot, not traditional Measham I noted, and settled us all down before talking about our trip and my interest, or some would say obsession, with the canals. She pulled out a pre-war Grand Union Canal Company handbook with many original photographs of the new wide locks between Napton and Knowle and of the spanking new boats built for the rapidly expanding carrying fleet. We talked of the boats and their crews who were her real interest. She was not in the least bit sentimental about them and recognised their hard and often rough lives for what they were. She told us of the pressures on the crews, of their problems with illiteracy, and their comparative lack of knowledge of the world outside the narrow strip of the canal. Pessimistic about the long-term future of carrying, which I had enthusiastically assumed would just go on for ever, she was concerned as to what would happen to the boatpeople if trade ceased. A life on a bleak council estate on the fringes of Coventry or Birmingham did not seem at all appropriate from her point of view. I think she rather hoped for a slow decline over a number of years, with many of the erstwhile crews switching to become lock-keepers, lengthsmen, or general waterway maintenance workers which would, at least, enable them to live by the cut and not in an alien world.

All too soon the tea was drunk and an hour had passed. My mother clearly felt that to stay longer would have been to impose although Sister Mary seemed very happy to go on talking. Reluctantly we gave our thanks and promised to call in on our return journey later in the week. A light rain had begun to fall and the boat lay shrouded in the gathering gloom, with the light outside the pub stretching a long finger across the wind-flecked ripples of the cut. We hurried along past the tall cottages from which emanated a faint glow through curtains drawn tight against the darkness. My attention was drawn by the cottage nearest to Sister Mary's house which stood dark and empty and looked to be in a rather dilapidated state. Clambering aboard we settled down in the snug cabin to a warm dinner followed by a quiet read. It had been a good day. Full of interest and with a steady improvement in my steering ability! I snuggled down that night with a feeling of warm satisfaction and the quiet anticipation of another good day's boating on the morrow.

Next morning dawned fresh and clear with only a light westerly wind to disturb the still waters. Cotton wool clouds scattered across a blue sky presaged a fine day. We did not linger over breakfast as I aimed to reach the bottom of Napton Locks that evening so as to keep us nicely on target for Banbury. For such a relatively inexperienced crew it was a long round trip to be contemplating, but I was steadfastly determined to achieve it and my enthusiasm led my parents to keep any doubts they may have had to themselves. No boats had arrived at Stoke during the night and my glance back, as I engaged gear and pulled away, revealed an empty waterway and a small queue of people waiting by the bridge for the Northampton bus. Somewhat naturally I was a mixture of excitement and apprehension that morning. The long Blisworth Tunnel was just around the corner and I was nervous about being able to match the level of skill needed to steer through in a professional manner. Meadows had told me in all seriousness that any unnecessary bumps or brushes either in locks, round the pounds, or in tunnels was regarded as poor boating. Naturally I was striving to achieve high standards in this matter and had already developed my own sense of professional pride with regard to steering and boathandling; bumping the tunnel wall was definitely to be avoided! My parents decided to sit in the well deck for the tunnel and leave all steering strictly to me, this also gave them the opportunity to retreat into the cabin if things became too wet outside!

I approached the dark mouth of the tunnel very slowly indeed. Reasoning that my eyes would need to get used to the dark, it seemed to me that to creep in on tickover and then slowly speed up was the most sensible option. *Canada Goose* eased into the darkness and the headlight began to pick out a yellowish halo along the brick lined roof and sides. I knew that in order to remain straight it was necessary to keep the cratch centred in this halo of light and this I endeavoured to do, gingerly increasing speed as I adjusted to the darkness. No boats had passed through since yesterday which meant clear air in the tunnel and presently, very far away and indistinct, I began to make out the arc of daylight at the Blisworth end. *Canada Goose* ran steadily on, periodically passing under the deep air-shafts driven into the hillside, a glance upwards revealing a circle of light to remind you of the world above. Some of these shafts let in cascades of icy water which ran along the top of the cabin roof before engulfing the hapless steerer who could only move out of the way in a limited fashion or he would fall off! I remember that one particular shaft near the Blisworth end was especially wet and seemed to have almost a small stream running out of it! My absolute priority was not bumping the side and I stood stoically at the tiller as the water drenched me thus ensuring that *Canada Goose* stayed straight. I had done it! Concentrating to the end we emerged from the north portal, rather wet it must be said, but having passed through without a touch. Not even the faintest brush against the wall! I modestly accepted a cup of tea and my parents' congratulations before concentrating again as we passed through Candle Bridge. This bridge is so named because candles used to be sold there from a stall in the days of horses and the rigours of legging through. The stall is long gone and, passing the gaunt and empty brick warehouse overshadowing the bridge, we wound steadily along past Blisworth village to the Arm End.

This was now all very familiar territory and I found that steering really is easier when you know the waterway and can anticipate its bends and twists. I also found that the world viewed from the towpath, and that same world viewed from a boat only a few feet out, look quite different and it was always enjoyable watching the familiar prospect unfold ahead of us.

WINDLASS IN MY BELT

Up as far as High House Turn, a little way beyond Heyford, this is a straightforward pound to steer and once again we took turns at guiding her up the long straights interspersed with occasional gentle bends. Through Banbury Lane and Bugbrooke, and then, rounding High House, we passed under our old friend the A5 at Stowe Hill and soon found ourselves running out along the high embankment at Weedon. Here we met our first boats of the day, two pairs of south-bound British Waterways craft deep laden with coal for Dickinson's paper mills. Pausing briefly by Weedon Bridge for bread and memorable flapjacks we pressed on, rounding the enormous railway turn with strong concrete coping along the outside which I just avoided touching, before passing once more under the A5 to wind through the spinnies at Brockhall.

These spinnies are a good example of a beautiful view seen strictly from the canal. They consist of a narrow band of woodland on the outside and a tree-lined strip along the towpath side. Beyond these quite narrow strips a couple of fields lead back up to the railway and the busy A5 beyond, whilst from the towpath the view was across quiet water meadows to the beautiful hamlet of Brockhall and the long ridge where I regularly pedalled out to the forthcoming flight of seven locks at Buckby. Seen from either a boat or the towpath the spinnies on a sunny morning such as this were idyllic. Fresh green leaves shrouded the cut, birdsong abounded and could even be heard above the rhythmic beat of *Canada Goose*s' engine. Every now and then a beautifully proportioned hump back bridge carried a farm track across, all was peace and beauty. Years later I heard tell of an old boatman's saying, "Never tie up in the Spinnies", presumably through fear of the supernatural. I could see little sense in this and there was a particular length of concrete coping, about half-way through the spinnies, that I had earmarked on my earlier rambles as a good place to spend the night. Years later I was able to finally tie there only to find that the sylvan peace of the spinnies had been irrevocably destroyed by the building of the M1 through those once tranquil water meadows. Reluctantly emerging from the leafy beauty of the spinnies and passing under a wooden accommodation bridge we saw the welcome sight of the bottom gates of the Buckby flight standing invitingly open for us.

The pairs we had met at Weedon had done us a good turn and it was another 'good road' as we began the process of locking up to the Braunston Summit. By this stage of our second trip we were getting quite adept at locking and no problems were encountered as we moved smoothly upwards to tie at the top lock for some well earned lunch. Although we had stopped at Weedon for bread we found that we needn't have done so as the little shop by the top lock, besides the usual stocks of tins, had good quality fresh-baked bread and an excellent choice of vegetables for sale. We took the opportunity to stock up here as we did not wish to lose time by climbing the hill into Braunston village and, judging by the map and my reading of *Narrow Boat*, we might well not find another convenient shop before Cropredy or Banbury. Everything was going swimmingly and we were well up to time as we set off once more, passing the swing-bridge guarding the entrance to the narrow weedy channel of the Leicester Cut as it set off on its lonely journey across the deserted wolds to Foxton, before moving on towards our second tunnel of the day at Braunston.

In the long straights of the summit we met no less than five pairs of boats including a pair of smartly painted Barlows followed closely by an equally shining pair of Willow Wrens. Brasses gleamed and cabin chimneys smoked bravely in the Spring air. Even the sometimes lugubrious and reserved boat people seemed to feel the glories of the day and warm greetings and smiles were exchanged as we edged carefully past.

"How am yuh!" exclaimed the first steerer.

"All of Buckby ready," I rejoined with a smile. I was getting more confident these days!

"Nice for me," he grinned, waving back at the next pair who would have to lockwheel behind him.

"Five pair behind us," said his wife, as the pristine butty swept past trailing that distinctive smell of East Midland coal smoke.

Easing down to tickover as we prepared to enter the tunnel I remembered her words. We had only passed four pairs behind the leading pair, therefore there must be another pair still in the tunnel as I did not doubt for a moment the veracity of her information. Smoke from the cabin fires was drifting out of the tunnel mouth as *Canada Goose* crept cautiously in. This was much worse than Blisworth had been in the freshness of early morning. The smoke was being sucked slowly out of the tunnel, apparently in my direction, with the halo of light upon which I was lining up the cratch only just visible through the haze. Somewhere ahead I knew there was a 'dog-leg' kink in the otherwise straight tunnel where the diggers, proceeding from both ends, had failed to meet quite straight and the tunnel had had to be adjusted accordingly. That was one problem, but there was also the problem of the other pair whose headlight I certainly could not see in the stygian smoke-filled darkness. To hit a working boat would be catastrophic and put a very severe dent in my efforts to build up a professional pride in boating. I was lucky, I hit the 'dog-leg' instead! We crept through the first part of the tunnel but, lacking any previous experience here, I did not know the exact location of the 'dog-leg' which occurs about one-third of the distance in from the Buckby end. In my defence, the smoke was particularly bad and my eyes were smarting and watering as I strained ahead, only for *Canada Goose* to bump gently against the tunnel sides as my straight course encountered the unseen 'dog-leg'. We only touched once as I adjusted the steering to compensate for the rebound, edging cautiously round the curving bricks of the kink and abruptly emerging from virtually all the smoke which was still being sucked out behind me. Losing the smoke seemed to make the tunnel lighter than would normally have been the perception. The halo of our headlight now arched brightly ahead illuminating the nicely central position of *Canada Goose*s' cratch and also, to my intense relief, the bright headlights of the final pair. I would not be disgraced now. All I had to do was ease right down and edge past, hugging the right-hand wall as I did so, and being careful not to swing out into the path of the oncoming butty. Everything went well amid the echoing reverberations of the diesels as the low fore-ends of the British Waterways pair crept past.

"How do!" from the steerer.

"How do!" I rejoined. "Very smoky back there!"

"Ooh Ah!" came the reply.

I repeated this to his wife who was steering engulfed in smoke from her cabin chimney.

"Bit more to come then," she smiled, indicating her brass rimmed chimney. "You got all the locks ready for you."

They moved away and presently the glow of her cabin light was swallowed up as she swung through the 'dog-leg' and disappeared into the smoke still filling the end of the tunnel. After all this excitement the remainder of the tunnel proved to be a straightforward matter and very soon we were back in daylight and easing through the wooded cutting leading along to the top lock.

My father came back and we looked at the very muddy towpath and reminisced about our bike trip over the top of the tunnel nearly two years before. I had learned a lot since then, I mused to myself, as mother took over the tiller to put *Canada Goose* neatly into the first of the six Braunston locks. We were locking downhill again now but our teamwork was getting even smoother and we made short work of the flight, passing the 'Admiral Nelson' to arrive by the boatyard, dry dock, and oiling point situated around the bottom lock. The Willow Wren Canal Carrying Company had made their base below the lock and occupied the yard opposite the small shed and oiling point used by British Waterways. Much was expected of this new carrying company and it was interesting to see several boats alongside in the process of renovation and also the pair featured in photographs of the IWA Banbury Rally of 1955. *Redshank* and *Greenshank* were tied close by the bottom lock and loaded with coal. This particular pair looked very smart with white strings stretched tightly across their cratches and a lovely white swan's neck, a classic example of purely ornamental ropework, adorning *Greenshank*'s rudder post. Nobody looked out to acknowledge our passing and so, having gazed under the arch of the iron bridge into Barlow's yard, we turned left at the junction and headed out along the long wide straight down which I had looked longingly two summers before. Once again we were back on strange waters.

The pound down to Napton is undoubtedly one of the prettiest in the Midlands. Gently rolling hills enfolded the waterway as it wound back and forth through the Warwickshire fields, rabbits ran in and out of the hedges and a black crow passed purposefully overhead. We had had a good day coming up from Stoke Bruerne and I may well have been getting over-confident as *Canada Goose* came up to the flat concrete road bridge at Shuckburgh. It was an awkward turn into the bridge but, being a relatively new and rebuilt one, it had greater width than the traditional hump-back variety and I felt justified in only a small reduction in speed. A mistake. I did not know the canal and found myself thumping under the road bridge with a great bank of tall reeds on my right and unforgiving concrete coping seemingly dead ahead. As I later learned, the correct way at Shuckburgh is slow through the bridge hole, edge round slightly, and then tiller hard over and turn on the power so that the boat swings fast without achieving too much forward motion. I was going too fast and wasted more precious seconds by panicking and wondering what to do. The bend was so sharp that the canal disappeared from view behind the reed beds on my right, it was like steering into a large pool. Too late I eased down and desperately swung the tiller over. *Canada Goose* lost way and began slowly to turn, but it was nowhere near enough. The back-end caught on the mud on the inside of the turn and all steerage was lost. Helplessly I watched the fore-end swing across to hit the concrete with a resounding thud and leave us skewed awkwardly across the cut. Pride comes before a fall, as the saying goes, and it was all my own doing. Through a combination of speed and over-confidence we were well and truly stemmed. It took quite a bit of sorting out as the afternoon began to drift towards evening. The back-end would not respond to shafting off and also resisted a combination of putting the engine ahead, then back, and then ahead again. No go. Still we were stuck. At least the fore-end remained in deep water resting against the coping on the outside of the bend. My father, seeing I was upset, pointed out the chips and paintmarks along the concrete coping where others had failed to get round. It was some consolation but my pride had taken quite a knock. In the end we had to get a line off across the cut and, with both of us pulling and mother giving some assistance with the engine, finally succeeded in dragging her off the bottom. Thereafter a bit of shafting and reversing saw us round the turn and get underway again, leaving a cloudy muddy mess in the water to mark my failure.

I would certainly remember Shuckburgh Turn as, somewhat chastened, we proceeded on to the junction for Birmingham or Oxford at Napton. Under a 'new' 1930s bridge passed the Birmingham route which took nearly all of the traffic, but our way was south onto the narrower and then little used Oxford Canal. The difference was immediately apparent as the banks closed in on us and the long lengths of continuous concrete coping, which were a feature of the Grand Union, disappeared. It felt just like being back on the Staffs & Worcs as we passed through our first low narrow bridge hole, easing down as the wash swirled along the banks and sucked against the bricks in the restricted opening. We had lost time at Shuckburgh and the shadows were gathering as we rounded Napton Hill. There was no question of tying up along here with shallow rocky edges predominating everywhere and so it was with a sense of some relief that we rounded the final bend to glimpse the balance beams of Napton bottom lock through the steadily enveloping darkness. No other boats were at the bottom lock and so we thankfully tied in the narrow length between bridge and lock. We had just made it! It had been another magnificent day and, other than the mistake at Shuckburgh from which a lesson could be learned, everything had gone really well. The die was now cast. We were in the Oxford and tomorrow we would need to tie at Banbury. That night I read my Rolt for renewed inspiration and fell asleep in a state of high excitement as I contemplated the next stage of our journey.

I was shaken from my reveries by my father's hand on my shoulder. A glance out of the window revealed it to be very early with a slow dawn breaking against the bulk of Napton Hill.

"It won't pump up!" he exclaimed, his voice had a slight edge of panic to it.

"What won't?" I responded, rubbing the sleep from my eyes and trying for some degree of alertness at such an early hour.

"The damn header tank!"

Canada Goose was fitted with the usual triangular diesel tanks in the corners on either side of the engine-hole. Diesel from these tanks was pumped manually into a header tank to supply the engine and we had been instructed to keep this topped up, always being sure to pump up a supply at the start of each day. My father had traditionally been an early bird and, knowing that a prompt start would be a prudent move given our aim of reaching Banbury that night, he had gone along to the engine-hole to ensure that everything was ready. No diesel in the header tank meant no engine, hence the note of alarm. Climbing into my clothes I followed him along the dewy bank before clambering down into the engine-hole and glaring at the red pump handle.

"See." He demonstrated by waggling the handle back and forth to no apparent effect.

Memory came to the rescue as I recalled an incident in the maintenance yard at the Arm End the previous summer. Hot from cycling I had been replenishing my Tizer bottle at the water tap just as some diesel cans were being filled from the nearby tank. Then there had been some very fast initial waggling of the handle followed by a steady back and forth pumping action.

"Let's have a go!" I said determinedly.

Seizing the handle I pumped vigorously from side to side and felt it 'catch' as the diesel began to come up and I was able to settle to a steadier pace. It was alright, disaster had been averted!

I grinned at my father who was well-known in the family as a 'worrier'.

"All OK!"

CANADA GOOSE

The clattering and banging had woken my mother and we decided to go up the locks on a cup of tea and have breakfast at the top, prior to setting out on the long and tortuous summit level. The Napton locks were light and easy to work and, except for the absence of top gate paddles, it was very akin to our autumn journey through the Tyrley locks. The first six locks were close together and empty which made it even simpler. A longer pound took us to the seventh lock, standing alone among the fields with a curious short side arm going off to the left above it. I had seen this on my old O.S. 1in map and there seemed little purpose in its narrow but clear channel. My attention was deflected from consideration of this little arm by a sight I had hardly dared to hope for. Coming round the slight bend ahead was a mule led by an old man wearing black boots, dark clothes, and a battered old hat. From the mule a towline stretched back to the mast of an empty narrowboat steered by an equally ancient lady wearing an old blue coat and black hat. It could only be the *Friendship*, Joseph Skinner, the last of the Oxford 'Number-Ones' and mentioned in *Narrow Boat*. It was the end of an era that we caught that morning, a sight that would very shortly vanish from the canal scene for ever. There were no cheering crowds, no exaggerated cult status, no talk about legendary characters, just us and the Skinners meeting in the early morning on the Napton flight. *Canada Goose* was down to tickover and the camera was out as we drifted past, this time on the left as we afforded them the towpath side. All the locks would be ready for them and we had even left the top gates open as was the custom in those days. I drank it all in. No cratch up, feedbox by the mast, top planks laid along the beams, the red cabin side and the lettering 'Jos Skinner'. A beautiful Tooley castle illuminated the cabin side and the chimney smoke mingled with the fresh green leaves along the towpath hedge.

"Morning!" greeted Joe as he guided his mule along the wet grassy path. "You left them locks ready then?"

"Morning! All ready!" we shouted back.

"Gates open too!" I added enthusiastically.

"Morning!" smiled Rose as we came abreast. "You've got a lovely day for it."

It would have been nice to say more, to have met them in a lock or even tied next to them, but it was not to be. The boats met, we smiled and greeted each other, passed by and went on. That was the way of the cut. I kept her on tickover and looked back at a bygone age as *Friendship* floated serenely down the pound behind the steady tug of the mule, who I later discovered was called Dolly. Presently we rounded the bend and she was gone, her passing etched indelibly into my youthful memory.

Working through the final two locks of the flight we reached the summit at Marston Doles and tied for a well earned breakfast. I discovered the small stable where the Skinners had obviously had their mule the night before, a neat pile of still warm ashes on the towpath marked where they had tied. We had been very lucky indeed to meet the *Friendship*. She was then trading between the Warwickshire coalfield and Banbury and, with us only being on the Oxford for two days, the odds were against us seeing her as we had. The long summit level, known as 'Eleven-mile pound', lay ahead of us and I viewed the prospect with a mixture of excitement and apprehension. This pound was noted for its solitude and beauty but it was also known for some fearsomely big bends, most notably the infamous Cabbage Turn. It was bound to be narrower and shallower than the Grand Union and the worry was in getting badly stuck and losing a lot of time. On the other hand, the sun was up again and it was another glorious spring day. We had been very lucky with the rain so far and the summit was looking its best as we set off from Marston Doles to commence our circuitous wandering along Brindley's old canal. One curious feature of the Oxford I noticed, as the first uneventful hour of the summit passed by, was the state of the towpath hedge. It was very tall and had clearly not been properly cut and laid for many years. The passage of Joe Skinner's mule had kept the hedge back for the first six to eight feet of its height but then the remainder of it arched over forming a shady bower in which to walk. Not knowing the summit I went very steadily indeed at every twist and corner and presently reached what I assumed must be Cabbage Turn. Glancing into a field on the approach I found myself looking straight across it to the top of a hump-backed bridge, a clear indication that the cut must very soon be about to make an enormous U-turn. Easing right down I crept into what looked like a dead end pool. A massive bank of rushes lay on the inside of the bend and the canal appeared to simply stop in the field. At that time no-one had taught me about big turns and the art of 'winding it on' at the critical moment. I preferred to try and creep round the outside thus avoiding getting stuck on the inevitable mud thrown up on the inside of the turn. Cabbage Turn was far too big for this method and about half-way round I realised that we would not make it, holding back hard as the fore-end touched. My new approach, albeit an undignified and incorrect technique, at least had the merit of keeping us safely in deep water. With a bit of shafting off and some forward and backward movement we succeeded in getting ourselves safely round with little time lost. Another huge turn followed at Griffins Bridge, Wormleighton, where we came up alongside one wall of a farmhouse, rounded the turn with an awkward bridge hole in the middle of it, and then made our way along with a view of the opposite wall. I confess to a single very gentle bump in the bridge hole, otherwise we made our way round these enormous turns safely if a little slowly.

Once beyond the George & Dragon inn, which constitutes the only recognised stopping place along the summit, we knew we had seen the last of the really awkward turns and shortly afterwards entered a long narrow cutting known as 'Tunnel Straight'. It had indeed been a former tunnel but, with only a shallow roof above, had been opened out in the last century thus speeding up traffic by obviating both a bottleneck and the rigours of legging through. It came as a welcome relief to be steering down this long narrow straight with the worries of the summit's 'big turns' behind me, how simple the Shroppie would seem compared to all this tortuous winding about! After passing a little humped bridge lifting the towpath over the narrow outflow from the summit reservoirs we slipped, with a sense of triumph, through a final bridge hole to see the white-tipped balance beam of Claydon Top Lock ahead of us. The summit had been rounded in four and three-quarter hours, a little pushing and shoving had been needed at Cabbage Turn and the time was a bit slow, but we had done it. As the top lock filled I allowed myself a private moment of quiet pleasure at the achievement. This really was the life! Last week and next week would be spent in school doing French verbs and algebra, but this week I was on the Oxford summit with the sun shining down, what more could anyone want!

We had met no boats round 'Eleven-mile pound' and rather expected Claydon Locks to be ready for us after our meeting with *Friendship*, instead all the locks were empty with bottom gates standing open and paddles still up. Wondering who was ahead of us I took a break away from *Canada Goose* by wandering down the flight and filling the locks in readiness. The pretty little flight of five at Claydon was followed by three more locks, Elkington's, Varney's, and Broadmoor, before another longish straight brought us to the beautiful canal-side setting at Cropredy where we met a small cruiser just emerging from the lock. It was mid-afternoon and we paused there for a pot of tea and a very welcome digestive biscuit. This gave just enough time for me to again follow in Rolt's footsteps, over the bridge and up to 'The Red Lion', situated in the lee of the impressive church. Coal was still piled on the wharf below the lock where the canal picks its way through between buildings and trees, but we had no way of knowing whether it had been brought by water or road. Should be water, I reasoned, but one never knew these days and the southern Oxford seemed to be carrying very little traffic. We pressed on down the gently winding pounds, through the soft water meadows of the Cherwell to Salmon's Lock and the final infamous pound into Banbury. I had read about this pound and its attendant perils and, very wary of its mud and accumulated rubbish, elected to travel at little more than tickover for the final couple of miles. None of us wanted to get badly stuck now as the first hint of twilight began to creep across the cut. The outskirts of Banbury were a sorry sight after the almost unbroken rural scene stretching right back to Leighton Buzzard. Railways closed in and a busy main road, crowded with fast moving traffic, ran alongside after the first drawbridge of the Banbury pound. Previous drawbridges had either been secured in the 'up' position or had been removed altogether, but here they were 'down' which was an added complication. At the first one, on a slight bend and adjacent to a garage, I very slowly and carefully laid the fore-end against the brickwork, holding back firmly so as not to hit the bridge itself whilst allowing my father the chance to leap ashore and raise it. The beams on the Oxford drawbridges were different from the tall structures on the Northampton Arm which could be held up by hooking a length of chain around a conveniently placed six-inch nail. Here they could not be secured in the 'up' position, instead one had to sit on the end of the beam whilst the boat passed through before getting up and allowing the bridge to fall with a resounding crash. My father opted to accompany us along the towpath as we crept on, with ominous muddy bubbles appearing on both sides, and soon had more work as a second drawbridge loomed ahead.

We had done well today and, although time was marching on, it was still quite light as we saw the Factory Street drawbridge ahead and tied securely for the night to shining mooring rings just opposite Tooley's yard. A very old and decrepit butty and a rather nice conversion were tied at Tooley's, but the yard had evidently finished work for the day as all was silent and deserted. There was just enough time to rush up Factory Street into the Square and buy the last apple tart left in the baker's for supper before darkness stole across the silent cut. It had been a long day but we had done it! We had reached Banbury! My mother's wry comment was that "we wouldn't have much time to look around it" as the return journey also had to be completed in three days, but I was simply pleased to have joined the ranks of 'boaters of an energetic disposition!'

As a misty morning dawned it was a case of up early for me and off into the town. We were desperately low on bread and I had been detailed to buy enough to last us back to the top of Buckby. Walking back down Factory Street I was surprised by the regular rhythmic thump of a narrowboat and upon reaching the drawbridge saw a pair of empty Thomas Clayton 'gas-boats' locking through. Forgetting breakfast for a moment I walked down to the lock where a large lady in a floral pinny had just drawn the ground paddles with considerable aplomb. She was very friendly and informative and I learned in short order that they were the Beechey family who, having just emptied at the Midland Tar Distillery below the lock, were now on their way back to Leamington Gasworks for another load. They, Joe Skinner, and the very occasional pair with coal to Oxford were now the only regular traffic left on this once busy waterway. She was quick to ascertain our plans for the day as they intended to remain in Banbury for a couple more hours due to the need for shopping. Realising that we would be going up to Claydon ahead of them she asked me if we would close the top gate and paddles and maybe draw a bottom paddle, if that wasn't too much trouble? It wasn't! Despite the extra work I readily assented to this request, anything to help a working pair! It was a measure of the lack of traffic on the Oxford at that time that such a plan, involving drawing off all the locks to the top of Claydon, should be a perfectly acceptable and feasible thing to suggest.

Whilst mother went shopping *Canada Goose* was slipped through the drawbridge and winded in the old basin just above the lock. As soon as she returned we were off, squeezing past the Claytons, and beginning the return journey. The Banbury run was really almost too far in a week. It gave plenty of boating but there was no time to spare for exploring Banbury and the villages along the way, many of which had much of interest to offer the more relaxed traveller. Going back should be easier than the outward jouney in that we had experienced the cut once and at least had some idea of the hazards in store. Quite rightly I was warned not to get over-confident, my parents being well aware of the difficulties of shifting a narrowboat badly 'stemmed-up' by an over exuberant steerer! The weather still held and we were blessed with yet another day of Spring sunshine as we locked steadily back up to Claydon that morning. Starting the locks for the Beecheys was not a problem, the technique being the same as I had worked with Meadows up the Northampton Arm. We had the advantage of being three-handed which made it even easier, mother steering her out as I drew about half a paddle and my father pulled the gate to. As far up as Broadmoor she held back in the head of each lock enabling us to clamber aboard, but for the three below Claydon and for Claydon itself, we were happy enough to walk the short pounds and enjoy the clear blue sky and invigorating air of Springtime. No other boats were met coming down which relieved me of one nagging doubt as to the wisdom of Mrs Beechey's suggestion, you certainly couldn't contemplate an idea like that in the crowded scene of today!

At the top of Claydon, having made good time with no hitches, we decided to tie up for lunch. This luxury had not been possible the day before but we were now getting more proficient with *Canada Goose* and just that little bit quicker as each day passed. Presently we heard the distinctive 'bomp,bomp,bomp' of the Clayton's motor as it approached the lock. Not wanting to miss anything we wandered back to assist as the young son, whose name I believe was Ronnie, brought the motor through, being closely followed by his parents easily bow-hauling up the empty butty. Clayton 'gas-boats' were never seen on the southern Grand Union and I enjoyed the experience of the flat boarded holds and the single wooden stand-cum-cratch, so different from the British Waterways fleet I was used to. The Beecheys were aiming for the top of Itchington Locks that night and doubtless would make considerably better time round the summit than us! We watched them move away, exchanging final waves as they disappeared through the nearby bridge hole. Time for us to follow as we shut the top gate, untied our lines, and started up.

The Claytons soon disappeared and were out of sight as we entered Tunnel Straight, but we were content with our progress. A little wind had got up and there were some high streaks of white cloud which might be ominous for tomorrow, but for today the sun still shone down as we wound our way round what was surely one of the most solitary and beautiful pounds on the system. We were taken completely by surprise at Griffin's Bridge by a fifty-foot conversion just coming through, used to having the cut all to ourselves I had to hold back sharply in order to allow them to clear the bridge hole and then pass us in what was a very narrow and awkward place. We edged through ourselves and this time cleared the bridge without a touch. Definitely getting better! At Cabbage Turn it was still a case of resorting to the long shaft, accompanied by a certain amount of backward and forward movement, in order to remain on the outside and get round safely. The technique needed for such an enormous turn was still to be taught me but the day would come when I would swing confidently round Cabbage Turn, although I never did so without fond memories of this early trip and *Canada Goose*. The bottom of Napton was reached comfortably enough that evening, despite the entire flight being against us due to the 'gas boats', and we even debated whether to go on as there was still about three-quarters of an hour of daylight left. But where to tie? After the experience of the first evening near Fenny we knew the folly of trying to get *Canada Goose* in just anywhere as we had with *Bredon Hill*. It was tempting to do a little more, but wisely we agreed that discretion definitely was the better part of valour and so settled comfortably into the length below the bottom lock.

During the night the wind got up and the boat nudged uneasily at her moorings. Clouds swept in and during the early hours an unwelcome pattering began on the cabin roof, swiftly becoming a steady drumming as the rain intensified. Dawn arrived grey and wet with rain falling from a leaden sky. It looked very unpromising, but we were a long way from Leighton Buzzard and had no time in hand. There was no choice but to get going and reach Stoke Bruerne that night, even if it rained all day! And that, apart from the occasional short cessation, which never looked likely to last, is precisely what happened. Luckily it was a day primarily of long pounds, divided by two flights of locks, and a welcome respite in the tunnels. I was to do most of the steering and soon became almost too wet to care about the rain. It was still much better than being at school and we made good progress along the wide deep pounds of the Grand Union, meeting pairs of loaded and empty boats from time to time, and exchanging the customary greetings with the equally bedraggled steerers. Braunston Tunnel offered a dry spell and, with no smoke problems this time, the 'dog-leg' was easy to see as we approached and came through without a touch of any sort. That afternoon the rain sheeted down in torrents as we made our way down the long pound towards Blisworth. It was running out of my hair and down my neck, my mack was letting in wet across the shoulders, but despite it all I remained perfectly content as we reached the very welcome shelter of the tunnel.

Lights were visible ahead and I slowed right down as I accustomed myself to the darkness and gauged the distance to the oncoming boats. However they didn't seem to be getting any nearer and, after fumbling along for a few minutes, I realised that what I was seeing was the cabin light of a receding butty and assorted headlamp haloes beyond this. A loaded pair was ahead of us and we were catching up. This was another new situation. I had no wish to come up close behind them, indeed I rather suspected that to do so in the tunnel would very likely contravene the unwritten laws of boating behaviour. *Canada Goose* was eased down to a very steady pace and contentedly followed in their wake, secure in the knowledge that we would be tying up above Stoke Locks in any case. After a rather prolonged journey underground and still taking great care not to 'get a touch' we emerged to find that it had actually stopped raining at last. An early dusk was setting in and the dark lowering clouds scudded along on a stiff breeze causing the trees overhanging the cutting to sway and groan with each fresh gust. The pair ahead of us had also called it a day and were tied in the first length outside the old Mill. We dropped in just behind and a very old lady with only a few blackened teeth stuck her head out of the hatch as I shared the mooring ring with them.

"Bit wet, boy!" she stated, her grin revealing still further the woeful lack of dentistry.

"Soaked!" I grinned back.

"Drowned rat you are, boy!"

With that our neighbour for the night disappeared below, leaving me to thankfully accept a towel and a complete change. It had been quite a day, but we consoled ourselves with the thought that it couldn't possibly be as bad tomorrow! Or could it?

It couldn't! I awoke to a suspiciously bright light and, peering through the curtains, was rewarded with sunshine and a promising blue sky flecked with large white clouds. Our neighbours, far from waking us up at at six o'clock, seemed to be in no rush to be gone and it was after eight o'clock, just as we were eating breakfast, that their engine finally thumped into life and they moved down to the lock. We also were in no particular hurry having confidence in our ability to reach the Stoke Hammond Three that night, leaving ourselves just the Jackdaw pound for Saturday morning. There was a shop just down the road from the bridge and mother and I walked down to pick up some bread and cheese for lunch, leaving my father with the drying-up and his shave. On our return we were hailed by the beaming Sister Mary who greeted us like her long lost family.

"Hallo, my darlings! Back again then. Did you get awfully wet yesterday?"

Acknowledging that today was much nicer we stood by her porch, discussing the weather with the intensity that only the English seem to manage. A door opened on the second cottage along and a short dapper man wearing strong boots and a black cap came past, the windlass tucked over his shoulder leaving a tell-tale bulge inside the jacket.

"Morning," he grunted to the three of us, as he crossed over the top gates and headed for a little whitewashed hut abutting onto the side of The Boat.

"Good morning, Mr James," rejoined Sister Mary heartily.

"He's the lock-keeper," she informed us in a lowered tone. "Sometimes a little grumpy in the morning, poor dear!"

I looked at the four tall cottages built of soft local stone, outside two of them black railings guarded steep steps leading to basements below canal level.

"Do they belong to British Waterways?" I asked. If the lock-keeper lived there this seemed a reasonable assumption to make.

"Oh no, dear," replied Sister. "They're mine, except for Mr James' who bought it from me. They all belonged to my father, you know."

We ascertained from Sister that the end cottage nearest her house was empty and had been for some time, then came Mr and Mrs James and their daughter, Christine. Next along, with a front door sporting a traditional boat castle and with miniature painted cans in the window, came Ricky and Olive. Olive was Sister Mary's daughter and the family apparently came down from London most week-ends, finally in the far-end cottage next to the Mill lived a very old gentleman called 'Gibbie' whom Sister Mary 'kept an eye on'. Once Sister Mary's father had owned most of the canalside at Stoke Bruerne, but we gathered that she was hoping to sell some of the property in order to gather much-needed funds to support her work among the boat people.

"You can't give them away!" she continued. "That end cottage has been empty for two years now, nobody wants it. You don't want a cottage do you, dears?"

I looked at my mother. She hadn't lived with a canal barmy son for the last two or three years without knowing what I was thinking! The position was superb. Right on the canalside, just up from the lock, and facing across the broad waters to the elegantly thatched 'Boat' inn. The lock-keeper on one side and Sister Mary on the other, what more could you possibly want? We shuffled together along the towpath and looked at the empty cottage more closely. A battered high brick step led up to a bright green front door with a brass knob, sadly in need of a clean. Sash windows were partially shrouded by an old climbing rose which also made its way across the top of the door and, Sister Mary assured us, gave beautiful deep red roses all summer. Similar sash windows opened out of bedrooms on the first and second floors and a steeply cobbled pathway, running between the cottages and Sister Mary's house, gave access to a cellar and wash-house at the rear of the property. It all looked rather sad and neglected but what a fabulous place to live! I couldn't resist asking the obvious question.

"How much would it cost?"

Sister Mary looked archly at me. She had already realised the degree of my canal mania and also knew that we lived in Northampton, a mere seven miles away. She transferred her gaze to my mother who was smiling at my enthusiasm.

"I would need to have about £150 for the cottages. That's each, of course."

My account with the Northampton Town and County Building Society had been opened for me in the summer of 1953 when my maternal great-grandad had very thoughtfully left me £20 in his will. Since then I had managed, by dint of saving some birthday money and a proportion of my florin a week pocket money, to add £5-14s-7d to the original deposit. The whole account was earmarked to buy myself a 'Bradshaw', if and when I was ever fortunate enough to come across one in the second-hand bookshops of Northampton. Of my parents' finances I had little idea. They both worked in offices and we lived in a small bungalow, built when 'licences' had become available after the war. Buses and bicycles took us everywhere locally and, in common with most people, there was absolutely no thought of owning a car. If we had the cottage for week-ends and holidays then we would have to come over on the bus or cycle. Used as I was to pedalling that seemed a minor consideration, but £150 represented a fortune and that was just to buy it. It had to be furnished, however simply, and paint and screws didn't grow on trees. No! I told myself sternly that the whole idea was just a fantasy. A week on a boat for a holiday was one thing, but a canalside cottage was very much another.

What I had not allowed for, or indeed even really considered, was my parents' spirit of adventure. This spirit was largely hidden from me by the humdrum nature of our daily lives, the sheer unremitting effort involved in making a living and holding everything together. But from time to time it did evince itself and my parents would happily divert down the road of a less conventional lifestyle. They had, if I had thought about it more clearly, already shown this propensity in a number of family forays, not least the recent trip on *Bredon Hill* and the present one on *Canada Goose*.

"Would you like to see inside?" continued Sister Mary after a slight pause.

My mother looked at her watch. We had to be moving shortly or we would be caught by darkness at the other end. I had already regretfully given up the wild idea. Things like buying a cottage happened to other people who lived in a different world to us.

"We don't really have time now," she replied. "But I would like to see it and I'm sure John and Jack would. Could we come over the week-end after next?"

We took Sister Mary's phone number, Roade 395, and left it there. We would ring if there were problems but otherwise would come over to see the cottage a week on Saturday.

I walked back to *Canada Goose* with my mind whirling at this totally unexpected turn of events. We'd only gone to get bread and cheese and now this!

"What are ..." I began finally.

"Say no more now," smiled my mother. "Remember I've got to talk to your father first. Come on, we'd better get untied and get going!"

It was the last full day's boating and I was resolved to enjoy it but, as we worked down Stoke Locks and wended our way along the Cosgrove pound that morning, I was already indulging in a fantasy of owning that cottage and enjoying week-ends and holidays spent right beside the cut in the midst of a genuine bona-fide canal community. Mind you, I still didn't see how it could even be considered. My mother was a practical woman and I couldn't really imagine either of my parents buying themselves a small country cottage, even if their only son was canal mad! We were after all just ordinary folk. Cash had not been very short in the family, but conversely neither had it been particularly plentiful and running two houses seemed a complete non-starter. It was nonsense! Of course it was! But if it was nonsense, then why on earth had my mother made an arrangement to view the cottage the following week? It was all getting beyond me and I finally decided, as *Canada Goose* passed over the Wolverton Aqueduct, that I would simply have to await developments and try hard not to get my hopes up too much.

Going back invariably seems shorter than setting out and so it was that day. Yesterday's rain had all cleared away, as is often the case at that time of year, and the Fenny pound was never more glorious than in the warm Spring sunshine. Once clear of the rail works at Wolverton the long pound wound its way southwards through lonely countryside, the herons once again flapping lazily along ahead of the boat before turning back at the end of their territory. A pair of Barlows returning empty were encountered near Linford Bridge and they were followed by a pair of loaded Willow Wrens, beautifully sheeted-up in fresh green cloths and riding very low in the water, just short of Fenny Bridge. Fenny was succeeded by Talbots and finally the three locks at Stoke Hammond were slowly ascended. It was nearly over and I felt rather mournful. No sooner did I get my foot in the canal world than it was yanked out again! It was not that I was ungrateful, far from it. I had relished the trip, but I wanted more. Much more. What I really wanted, I thought to myself, as I drew my ground paddle at the top lock, was a deeper more permanent involvement with the cut and its people. I didn't quite know how this could be achieved but I was determined to do my best to make it happen. Nothing ventured, nothing gained!

Rather to our surprise we found our companions from the previous night tied above the three locks and felt rather pleased that our day's journey had been the same as a pair of working boats. Mind you, it was a deeply loaded pair and the couple on board seemed unbelievably ancient to be still boating. Once again we found ourselves sharing a mooring ring and the old lady, who was sitting in the butty hatches peeling potatoes in her handbowl, smiled her near toothless grin.

"Dry today, boy!"

"Much better," I agreed, tying *Canada Goose* in snugly behind them.

"Short day for us," she added, thus emptying cold water on any ideas I might have had of keeping up with working boats. "We're getting a bit slow nowadays, can't jump about like you can, boy!"

Being unsure how to respond to this I changed the subject and asked her where they were going.

"Croxley," she affirmed. "Then back empty, they reckon we'm too old for Brummagem now. I tells 'em we ain't but they don't listen. Reckon they wants us orf, but we're stopping on so long as we can draw paddles!"

I wondered how old they were but it seemed tactless to ask, instead I complimented her on her butty's white strings and the little white 'bumper' or fender to prevent touching in the locks.

"Scrubs it every day," she said proudly, before slinging her peelings in the cut and disappearing down into the cabin.

They were gone very early the next morning, the steady beat of their engine receding round the Jackdaw pound in the cold light of dawn. We had breakfast and then followed on, going very steadily round the pound so as not to risk getting stuck on that last morning. Inevitably I was a little sad as we passed through Leighton Lock and drew alongside the hire wharf, but it had been another great week with so much to savour and store up in the memory. Little had been said about going over to look at the cottage at Stoke Bruerne and I knew better than to pester! But we were apparently still going and this thought swirled round in my mind as the local train made short work of the journey back to Northampton.

*****

Chapter 3

Stoke Bruerne

The following week passed painfully slowly. Back at school I spent my time feverishly trying to copy up the notes from my stolen week, not to mention completing all the work from the current one. We would not begin the GCE courses until the following September, but this was an old-fashioned Grammar School with an ethos of discipline and hard work and keeping up with everything when half your mind was still on the cut was not easy. At last the week was over and we were standing patiently in the Derngate Bus Station waiting to board the green United Counties double-decker bus which made hourly journeys to Stony Stratford and would drop us off at Stoke Bruerne along the way.

"We're only going to look," my parents had stated emphatically on several occasions during the previous week.

"But what if we like it!" I had said.

"We'll see," had been the only response. With that I had to be satisfied as the bus turned off the main road and ran down the hill into Stoke Bruerne before dropping us off by the familiar bridge where just a week before we had been with *Canada Goose*. It somehow seemed much longer than that.

A pair of empty British Waterways boats were just leaving the lock and we paused to watch the steerer expertly holding back as he came abreast of the butty's cratch and picked up a cross-strap. Heaving the butty over behind the motor he neatly dropped the eye of the strap over the dolly on the motor's counter. The second strap was hooked deftly on and, with only the slightest of jerks, the butty began to move out of the lock. Sister Mary was leaning out of her surgery window exchanging greetings with the crew and waving them off before emerging onto the towpath with a beaming smile.

"Hallo, my darlings!"

"Good morning, Sister!" I felt suddenly rather shy, silly really as she could not have been kinder. The problems of adolescence!   A pot of tea was insisted upon and, although I was positively itching to see the cottage, I sat demurely enough in Sister Mary's sitting room whilst she enquired about the remainder of our trip and how was I enjoying being back at school. Time passed, and eventually a large brass key was produced and we found ourselves standing expectantly in front of 4, Canal Side.

STOKE BRUERNE

The front door opened directly onto a squarish room with a broken-tiled floor. A somewhat rusty range stood on the left and facing us were two doors with latches which gave access to the stairs and a kitchen area so small that only one person at a time could fit into it. The whole cottage smelt musty and rather damp and a sadly forlorn air of abandonment hung about it. The last tenants had been a family called Dyke who had rented the cottage from Sister Mary before being offered a council house at the top of the village. Since their departure over two years previously it had stood empty for lack of tenant or purchaser. Unhelpfully the cottage had a 'closing order' on it; essentially this meant that certain work had to be carried out before the local council would pass it as being fit for human habitation. Sister was rather vague about the specific details, but assured us that she had the list of requirements 'somewhere in the house' if we were still interested. My heart sank at this news; 'essential repairs' to my mind made it even less likely that whatever interest my parents had would be sustained.

Lifting the latch on the door at the back of the room we found ourselves climbing up a curving wooden spiral staircase to the first floor. Here a thin wooden partition divided the available space giving about two-thirds of the floor area to a front bedroom facing out onto the canal and the remaining third to a 'bathroom' which was, in reality, empty except for a pedestal sink. The bathroom project had clearly got no further than the arrival of the sink as neither water nor drainage was yet laid on to this floor. A back window gave a view over a neglected looking yard with a rusting tin-roofed open-fronted barn opposite providing parking space for a couple of cars. Immediately below the cottages was a small block of brick-built toilet cubicles, one for each cottage, in which resided the Elsan bucket. Mains sewerage had not reached the village at that time, the buckets being emptied on a weekly basis by the Council's sanitation truck.

To the left a weedy and nettle-strewn area about ten yards wide led from the yard between stone walls right through to Chapel Lane, about seventy-five to eighty yards away. It transpired that this had been the ropewalk where, many years before, Sister Mary's father, Mr Amos, had manufactured lines of various length and diameter for sale, predominantly to the boat crews but also to the local farmers. With his death, and the near extinction of the working horse, the ropewalk had fallen into utter disrepair and, as I would later find, it was now so neglected as to make it nearly impossible in summer to force a passage from one end to the other. Beside the ropewalk a blue gate gave entry to a large and very neglected orchard which also backed down towards Chapel Lane. All of this yard, together with the orchard and ropewalk, still belonged to Sister Mary and the little access lane, running along from the bridge and passing behind her house and garden, was legally a shared access for her and the residents of the four cottages. It also afforded access on to land behind the empty Mill, this was owned by British Waterways who used only the ground floor for the storage of stop-planks and other material. The Mill, Sister assured us brightly, was hardly ever used and BW made virtually no use of the vehicular access to its rear, a decrepit gate leading from the yard and the completely rusty padlock affixed to it seemed to confirm this. The whole area behind the cottages was in a sorry state of benign neglect, exuding an air of melancholy charm as it slumbered in the sunshine.

An identical latched door gave on to a further spiral staircase which led up to a large top-floor bedroom whose low sash window offered a superb view of the canal. A watcher here could see right across the bridge to the second lock and the curve of the waterway beyond. Directly opposite lay 'The Boat' and, clearly visible over its low thatched roof, the village street winding up the hill to the church. By dint of craning one's neck the line of the canal could also be followed upstream until it curved away towards the cutting leading to the tunnel mouth. This room was the largest of all occupying the full length and width of the house, damp stains marked the old fashioned wallpaper on the outside wall and the ceiling bowed ominously. Leaving the view with reluctance we clattered back down the wooden stairs and emerged once more into the sunshine before turning down the narrow cobbled path between Sister Mary's house and the cottage.

This was known as the 'jetway', so named because of the propensity of water to rush down it from the towpath under conditions of heavy rain. The jetway admitted us to the rear of the cottage and to the dilapidated yard which we had first glimpsed from the upstairs windows. The canal was embanked as it approached the top lock and this had allowed a fourth room to be included in the form of a cellar, accessible only from below. Originally this had served as the wash-house and a broken and rusting washtub, heated by an adjacent coal-fire, stood forlornly in one corner covered in layers of dust and festooned with spiders webs. The chimney from this washing range ran right up the outside of the house and it seemed highly likely that damp getting into this long disused shaft was responsible for the stains visible in the top bedroom. The cellar had a very dusty earth floor with black cobwebs draped along the walls and ceiling and looked as if it hadn't been swept out for a century. Two of the cottages only were favoured with a railed-off flight of steps giving additional entry from the front, an odd arrangement and Sister Mary seemed unable to throw any light on the exclusion of the other two. Outside the cellar door a large concrete slab covered the top of a well, long since out of use, which had once been the sole water supply for the inhabitants. Nettles sprouted round this slab and the crumbling surround of bricks and stones looked suspiciously loose, I made a mental note never to stand on the well-cover. Just in case!

We wandered back up the jetway to where the waters of the canal glinted in the pleasant Spring sunshine, a bee sniffed around the fat red buds on the old rose tree growing up the door and an early butterfly drifted lazily past on the gentle breeze. My parents wanted to see the 'closing order' list and disappeared back into Sister's house leaving me alone in the silent cottage. Not an inspiring sight at first glance, it remained a sad prospect as I considered the possibilities. Badly broken tiles in the living room, range probably only partly usable, one cold-water tap in the miniscule kitchen was the only water supply in the house and the cracked brown sink it fed into the only washing place. The thick plaster on the walls was badly cracked and 'gave' to the touch and the base of the front door was rotten. The only positive thing was that the electrics seemed fairly recent and in good order. Upstairs was not quite so bad. Indeed the middle floor could almost be described as sound although the damp stains and bulging ceiling on the top floor hinted strongly at possible roof problems. Ambling around the three floors I imagined it somehow restored and furnished, imagined waking up in the morning and glancing out at the canal, imagined becoming a small part of the tight-knit canal community. Imagined...... What was the point, I reminded myself strongly. This cottage needed far too much time and effort for my working parents to cope with. It was all very well imagining, but what I could not imagine was them taking it on. It was simply not a feasible proposition.

I was just fourteen and my parents were still only in their early thirties having married younger than originally intended due to the war and my father's call-up. In common with most people of their generation early married life had been a struggle to make ends meet in the aftermath of the war and the lean years of austerity which had followed. We had lived in rented rooms, then a council house, and finally had moved to our present small bungalow in Duston on the western fringe of the town. Both parents worked and I had remained an only child, my interest in canals gradually drawing them into the far less frenzied world of the peaceful waterways and unspoilt countryside to the west of the town. My father's family hailed originally from Ecton and Great Billing, villages to the east of the town, and my great-grandfather had started life as a ploughboy. During the severe agricultural depression following the Great War, in which both my grandfathers had fought and been wounded, he had found work in the shoe factories of Northampton. At the time of our visit to Stoke Bruerne my great-grandfather was in his eighties and I had often heard him talk wistfully of his beloved wife, Polly. She was a shepherd's daughter from Shutlanger, the next village on from Stoke Bruerne, and he had walked eight miles each way at week-ends to court her in those far-off late Victorian days.

Unknown to me my father had long nurtured within himself a romantic notion of returning to the apparent simplicity of his family's roots and life in the quiet Northamptonshire countryside. Both their livelihoods and my schooling were firmly centred on the town, nevertheless he had clung on with secret tenacity to this dream of a quiet rural idyll. My mother, an energetic and practical woman, had few illusions about the true nature of country life. However she did suffer from a low boredom threshold and the somewhat mundane existence of suburb and office sorely taxed her spirit. She also had a deep rather possessive love for me and had strongly supported my unconventional interest in canals against some of those in the family who had clearly felt that I could be making better use of my time than consorting with 'bargees' up the arm. All these strands now came together in place and time and a decision was made that would dramatically change all our lives. For my father, Stoke Bruerne offered a distant link with his grandmother, whose family were well-known in the village, and he would be able to fulfil part of his dream by spending week-ends and holidays in the country. For my mother, it offered an outlet for her energies and the chance to become part of a very different community from that of our suburban street. For me, it was all an unreal dream as I saw myself being brought ever closer to the mysterious heart of my beloved canals. I was only too willing to plough what little money I possessed into the cottage, even at the expense of a possible 'Bradshaw'. What I did not know was that my mother had been left £1000 in the same will that had benefited me, that this money still remained intact and was earmarked for nothing in particular.

Sitting on the floor by the sash window at the top of the house I drank in the scene. Stoke Bruerne was far more beautiful in those days, being little known outside the immediate area, and almost completely unspoilt. Mr James, working quietly on the flower-beds of his prize-winning lock garden, was the only person in sight. A tractor and trailer briefly interrupted the tranquillity as they crawled slowly over the bridge and passed on up the hill. Even the locks were quiet and no pairs had passed through to disturb the still waters. I saw my father emerge from Sister Mary's and stand taking in the scene. He nodded to Mr James and they exchanged a few words before he came back into the cottage.

"John!" he called from below.

"I'm up here," I replied. "I'll come down."

"No. Stay there," came the response. "I'd like another look at it all."

His footsteps echoed up the wooden stairs and he joined me at the window. Together we looked out across the broad waters to where 'The Boat' was showing signs of life as lunch-time opening approached.

"Bit of a mess, isn't it?" I grinned, getting in first.

"It certainly is, but it's a lovely spot for all that."

I allowed my hopes, which I had kept most severely dampened down, to lift just a fraction.

"It's beautiful!" I agreed quickly. "Right by the cut, too. We'd get to know lots of people here. They'd all have to stop for the lock and it's a good overnight tying place!"

He glanced down once more at the peaceful scene below and then looked straight at me.

"If we bought it there'd be a lot of hard work. We'd have to do it together as a family."

"We could do it, we really could!" I said. "I'll help, of course I will."

He knew I was reliable about helping. I had done most of the gardening for two or three years now and invariably would set the table and make the fires up before they came home from work. There was a family tradition of working together and they both knew that I could be counted upon to pull my weight if needs be.

"In that case we thought we might buy it. We could come at week-ends and holidays and perhaps for part of the summer, just like Sister Mary's daughter does."

"Gosh!"

At that moment it really was all that I could manage to say!

Things moved remarkably quickly after that. A handshake with Sister had sealed the matter and, within a very few weeks, the legal formalities had been dealt with and the cottage was ours. Buying the cottage was one thing, dealing with all it's various problems was quite another. That Spring and Summer the scale of the undertaking soon became very apparent. Until the local council passed it as fit, that is to say took off the 'closing order', we could not live there on a permanent basis. Some of the work we could do ourselves, but some would have to be tendered out. My parents threw themselves into the task with a surprising degree of vigour and seemed to be thoroughly enjoying the challenge of it all. A considerable re-vamp was put in hand and each week-end found us busy with some task or other, pressing on with an eye on being able to live in the cottage, as opposed to camping in it, by that autumn. The downstairs living-room and tiny kitchen were in the worst state of all and, rather than tinker about with it, a complete re-fit was decided upon. The thick old plaster, bulging off the wall and badly cracked and fissured, was removed amidst clouds of dust, the broken tiles were chipped up from the floor, and the old range was deemed to be beyond repair and earmarked for replacement. A builder friend, who played football in the same team as my father, then took over and re-laid the floor with a smooth skim covering, the walls were re-plastered and a tile fireplace replaced the obsolete range. Similarly in the kitchen space a new deep sink superseded the old and badly-chipped original and an electric cooker was installed opposite. To meet the requirements of the 'closing order' a back door was fitted and a flight of wooden steps gave access to the rear courtyard. Hot water was a problem as there was no tank upstairs and the cost of fitting one, with all the attendant problems of plumbing, was high. My parents decided to defer this matter and continued with the time-honoured practice of boiling water as needed until a hot water system could be afforded. As is so often the way we found that, once we had settled into the cottage, we grew used to what we had and the planned system never did materialise.

On the second floor the plasterwork was surprisingly sound. The only real work needed was to connect up a cold water pipe to the sink in the bathroom with a kettleful of hot water being carried up from below as needed. The whole problem of the bath itself was linked to the arrival of a hot water system and was put into abeyance on the 'long list'. Further up, the damp in the top bedroom had to be addressed which led to more drastic measures. The ceiling was cracked and sagging and we decided to take it down, this was accomplished amidst further vast clouds of dust to reveal the actual tiles above. These were then 'torched' over the course of a week-end and the builder subsequently fitted a new plasterboard ceiling underneath. The chimney running up from the cellar was not needed so a protective cap was fitted in an attempt, which proved only partially successful, to eliminate the patches of damp on the outside wall. These seemed to occur only under certain conditions of wind and rain and eventually, like many dwellers in old cottages, we resigned ourselves to living with the occasional damp patch. With new wallpaper and coats of paint all round, the inside of the cottage neared completion as the long summer term drew to its conclusion.

Nearly all my summer holidays that year were spent wielding paint brushes and doing any other 'donkey work' in order to keep builder's costs to a minimum. It proved to be a warm and mainly dry summer and I was able to get on with re-painting the sash windows, giving the new wooden steps three coats of creosote, and considering the problem of the front door. The original plan had been to keep the solid old front door but a careful examination had shown it be badly rotted in its lower third with the cost of restoration outweighing the price of a new door. Mr James and Olive had obviously faced the same problem as their cottages both sported newish modern doors with glass panels which had the advantage of admitting extra light into the living room. We reluctantly decided to follow suit and the old door was replaced by a modern counterpart with two fluted windows in its upper half, another painting job for me during those long school-free weeks. Externally the cottage proved to be remarkably sound with only a little re-pointing under the front downstairs window being needed. The old broken brick front step was removed and new concrete steps laid with a low stone wall enclosing the tiny strip of garden. A similar stone wall flanking the jetway created another even smaller strip of enclosed garden.

By the first week-end of September all was ready. With considerable trepidation we awaited the visit of the council official from Towcester who would make the final decision regarding the lifting of the 'closing order'. He duly arrived on the Saturday morning in a dark suit and carrying an ominous looking file with the cottage's address inscribed upon it in large blue letters. We assembled with nervous smiles, ushering him deferentially inside only to have him decline the offer of a welcoming cup of tea. Perfunctory he most certainly was not! A very painstaking and meticulous examination of the cottage followed and much taking of notes and asking of questions was the order of the morning. We hung about in an agony of suspense until at long last he reappeared from his external inspection and announced that he would now take his cup of tea! Having ponderously downed one cup, he then made inroads on a second before brusquely informing us that we had met all the requirements laid down under the terms of the 'closing order' and that consequently the cottage was now fit for habitation. The fact that it had already been lived in for at least a century seemed a complete irrelevance! I had been told in no uncertain terms by my mother that under no circumstances was I to make comments of this nature to the official. He was to be humoured at all costs! With the business of the day amicably concluded we saw him politely to his car and waved him off across the bridge. We had done it! In great glee I led the charge back up the lockside to accept the congratulations of our neighbours, now at last we could move in properly.

The problem of furnishing the cottage was inadvertently solved for us by a sad event within the family. My maternal grandfather had died during the summer after a long and wearisome battle against the ravages of liver cancer. As a consequence of this my grandmother had decided to make the move from her large family house into a smaller bungalow more suited for her future needs. This change necessitated a very considerable reduction in furnishings, made greater by her wish to refit the bungalow with a certain amount of new furniture in order to "see me out". Gran had always been close to my mother and, having paid us several visits during the summer, was quite taken with the cottage. We found ourselves in the happy position of being offered first choice of the redundant furnishings. This, along with a couple of prudent visits to Ashby's auction rooms in Northampton, solved the matter of furnishings and by early October all was in place for our first week-end in comfort at the cottage. It was a celebration of the huge amount of work achieved that summer. As I sat on that first evening, watching the flames of the fire flickering in the gathering dusk, a deep contentment matched by a feeling of excitement stole over me and everything seemed to take its place in an harmonious whole.

It had not been all work for me that summer, of course. I mostly cycled back and forth to Stoke selecting a route that took me over Tunnel Hill to Blisworth, through the village to the yard of Blisworth Station and thence down the hill to the Arm End. Here I would invariably pause on the crown of the bridge, savouring the view across the waters of the junction and gazing along the straight to the distant roving bridge. From there, by way of two further bridges, the lane took me to the Rothersthorpe Locks. I had seen Meadows on several occasions during the summer and we remained friends, he being always interested in progress on the cottage. It turned out that he had not been to Stoke for a number of years and barely knew it, a measure of the insularity of lock-keepers lives in those quiet days. Occasionally, almost for old times sake, I would cycle down the arm to Duston Bridge and home up the long slope of Mill Lane. However the towpath was slower going and increasingly I found myself using the road, life was changing and time had become more precious. Gradually during the course of that busy summer we had begun to make friends and acquaintances at Stoke and, during the long summer holidays as I worked alone at the painting or other jobs, Sister Mary had taken me under her wing. Around mid-morning I frequently found myself being invited to share a coffee and biscuit in the small sitting room at the end of the house nearest the lock. Here a lovely bowed window overlooked Sister's sadly neglected garden and offered an excellent view of the lock itself. It became a similar tale in the afternoon when I would be hailed from my tasks for a cup of tea and frequently a generous slice of cake also!

I learned a good deal during those warm summer days chatting with Sister in the peace of her cosy little room. She was extremely unsentimental and realistic about the boatpeople to whom she had given such care and devotion, each family being treated individually with their foibles and idiosyncracies accepted and understood. Rarely critical directly, she nevertheless understood the often harsh nature of their working lives and the strict, almost Victorian, moral views that so many of them held. Sister gave them her unstinting support and always made herself available at whatever time their boats were passing. She knew that nearly all of them would make every effort to cope with their medical problems and families often travelled for several days to see Sister Mary rather than consult a local doctor This could have its drawbacks. On occasions problems had become much worse before Sister Mary could begin to deal with them. The boatpeople were undaunted by this, her devotion and their unswerving trust formed the bedrock of a unique relationship. From Sister Mary I learnt a good deal about the people of the boats who passed regularly up and down past the cottage during the course of the summer and being an accepted friend of Sister Mary counted very much in my favour as slowly they also began to accept me.

I had made an early point of getting off on the right foot with Mr Jack James, the lock-keeper, who lived next door to us. Sister Mary and he were pivotal figures along the canalside at Stoke. Always referred to by me as Mr James he initially seemed to be a gruff rather reserved man but, as trust became established, I discovered him to be exceptionally good-hearted and a veritable mine of information about the waterways. Once he realised the committed and passionate nature of my interest in canals he became much more friendly, giving me his blessing to help boats up and down the flight if I was so minded and even going so far as to personally introduce me to various two-handed pairs who, as he put it, "Could often do with a hand." I disciplined myself to work primarily on the cottage during those sunny weeks, but all work and no play could not be countenanced and I would sometimes break off for a bit of lock work. It was a measure of my acceptance when, as I was painting the undercoat on the front door, Mr James emerged from his cottage and, after a few complimentary remarks about my progress, produced a windlass from under his coat and held it out to me.

"Happen you'll need your own," he announced, with the very faintest of smiles playing around his mouth

I took it gratefully and found myself holding a brightly shining 'Willock', originating from Wheelock in Cheshire and reputedly the best windlass to have. A small pipe mark on the haft just below the square indicated its origins.

STOKE BRUERNE

"Gosh! A 'Willock'! Thanks very much!" I was completely taken aback by the gesture and felt myself shyly reddening.

"Can't help properly without one!" he continued. "You can keep it and make sure you use it nice and safe."

I took the point. My activities on the flight doubtless contravened all manner of rules and regulations and we both knew that by giving me a windlass and encouraging me to help the passing pairs he also was in breach of the rules. Like Meadows, he had acknowledged both my enthusiasm and my respect and admiration for the boatpeople and I shall always be grateful to them both and cherish their memory.

Armed with my windlass, which I carried tucked in my belt in the professional manner, I could be a lot more use to the often elderly two-handed crews whom Mr James particularly liked me to help. It was either a case of lock-wheeling the flight or, if the locks happened to be ready, of dealing with the butty's side of the lock. This gave the hard-pressed boatwoman a welcome break, the more so if the pair elected to go down 'breasted-up'. I became 'known' that summer, my quiet help always accepted by the crews with the usual gruff but friendly comments as we worked through the flight together. Slowly I was building up a knowledge of carrying practice, cargoes, destinations, tonnage carried, boating techniques, and most importantly of all, was gaining a steady insight into the nature and attitudes of the boatpeople and the problems and pleasures generated by their unique lifestyle. I added the 'Ovaltine' boats, which carried coal to the A. Wander factory at Kings Langley, to my list of companies seen and indeed helped them through the flight on several occasions; sadly the following year they were gone and the boats sold. The main carriers were the many pairs of the large British Waterways fleet made up predominantly of ex-GUCCCo boats augmented by a scattering of Joshers, ex-Fellows, Morton and Clayton boats. Also to be seen were the beautifully painted boats of the Samuel Barlow Coal Company Ltd known as 'the Limited' to distinguish them from the boats of S.E. Barlow of Tamworth. Both these companies were coal carriers, whose pairs normally returned empty, but they remained two completely separate companies until 'Essy', as he was affectionately known, sold out to 'the Limited' in February of 1957. The third carrier on the Grand Union at that time was the newly formed Willow Wren Canal Carrying Company Ltd whose smart green-painted boats carried all manner of cargoes and, with a steadily expanding fleet, inspired fresh hope for the future.

Throughout the winter of 1957 most weekends were spent at Stoke Bruerne and, although the daylight hours were short, I was able to begin my explorations of the surrounding area. Below the locks all was pastoral tranquillity but not especially interesting. The river Tove crossed the canal at this point and a series of arched weirs carried the towpath above the waters which, in times of winter floods, ran through surprisingly strongly. Extra side-paddles were available for Mr James to use if the river threatened to overwhelm the towpath but, despite these added precautions, he assured me that such submergence did occur from time to time. Water meadows accompanied the canal as it wound in a great curve round to Grafton Bridge from where it was possible to cycle by road back to Bridge Lock, third up in the flight. Usually though I preferred to retrace along the towpath and thereby avoid the steep hill up into Grafton Regis and the rather unpleasant ride along the busy main Northampton to Stony Stratford road.

Much greater reward was to be found by exploring northwards from the cottage. The towpath up to the tunnel consisted of a narrow grassy thread running between long grass and bushes as it entered the tree-lined cutting leading to the dark portal and the faint musty smell of damp and dripping brickwork emanating from it. Just around the first gentle corner from the top lock was a raised piece of brick piling of exactly a boat's length and furnished with several mooring rings. The hedge was broken half-way along this length and a sharp eye could discern the narrow grassed-over rails of a short length of tramway running across the field and disappearing into a small disused stone quarry etched into the gently rising hillside. All was nettles and dereliction. In the mind's eye it was easy enough to picture the once busy scene as stone was cut from this small local quarry and hauled in little tubs along the short length of tramway to the waiting boats, neatly tucked alongside this purpose-built length. Such short-distance and local traffic had virtually disappeared from the rural canal scene by this time, yet here was another forgotten but poignant reminder of what once was.

Blisworth Tunnel has always been plagued by problems of water leaking in from underground springs and runnels and it is a notoriously 'wet' tunnel, especially when compared to the much dryer tunnel at Braunston only a few miles north. Considerable difficulties were encountered during the digging of the tunnel and it was not opened for traffic until 1805, being nearly five years in its completion. The canal owners, with the rest of the waterway completed, decided to construct a temporary tramway across the top of the tunnel in order to facilitate the transhipment of goods and get trade moving. There are very few traces of this enterprise to be found and the rails were soon removed and used as part of a temporary link down to Northampton whilst the arm was under construction. However a careful exploration along the top of the cutting beyond the quarry field revealed a distinct 'shelf' which was too pronounced to be natural. Initially everything was very overgrown and I had difficulty in squeezing through the bramble patches and nettles which crowded amongst the trees on the slope. The line was there, but it was hard to visualise. Suddenly I emerged into a grassy field and there it was, the course of the tramway clearly discernible as a flat 'shelf' running across the top of the cutting before disappearing once more into the trees to merge with the old horse-path climbing up from Tunnel End. There was really very little to see, indeed a casual walker could have been forgiven for not even noticing the difference in the lie of the land, but I found it all fascinating and another silent reminder of the canal's past.

At Tunnel End itself the two huts, formerly occupied by the gangs of professional leggers who had worked the boats through before the advent of the tunnel tug, stood mutely as further witness to changed working practice. We had been lucky enough to meet Joe Skinner still working on the Oxford but horse boating on the main line of the Grand Union was gone for ever, the days of legging through now just distant memories in old men's minds. The little used horse path over the top of the tunnel angled up the slope between the huts, deep banks of nettles and brambles rendered it just passable in high summer and merely a muddy thread of a path during the rest of the year. A stream trickled alongside in a brick-lined culvert before disappearing into its own small tunnel to emerge bubbling and swirling out into the waterway between the two huts. An unusual feature along the culvert was a rectangular cistern clearly designed to catch rubbish in order to prevent it clogging the underground section further on. When the stream was flowing well this would fill to a depth of anything up to two and a half feet and offered scope for a refreshing dip, so much so that my mother christened the spot 'Tramp's Bath'.

Pressing on up from here I soon discovered the railway which crossed the horse path on a narrow bridge. This lonely single track line was part of the cross-country network run under the aegis of the Stratford-upon-Avon & Midland Junction Railway, the S.M.J., or the 'slow, mouldy and jolting' as it was known locally. The main route ran from its own platform at Blisworth Station through to Towcester prior to wandering across the Midland shires, crossing the Oxford Canal in Tunnel Straight, and eventually terminating at Stratford-upon-Avon. It was now little-used although I could remember when my father took me to Towcester once by this route, changing from the jolting two coach 'Blizzy Flyer' to an equally slow and jolting three coaches pulled by an ancient locomotive and tender whose exact class and lineage I can no longer recall. It took a noticable amount of time longer than the bus but most certainly was, as my father said at the time, "much more fun!" If anything the line at Stoke Bruerne was even more remote. Leaving the S.M.J. at Towcester the single track meandered across country, over the main line of the L.M.S. at Roade, before going on to Olney in Bedfordshire. It rejoiced in the name of the East & West Junction Railway. Passenger traffic had long since ceased although the old Stoke Bruerne station was clearly visible below the bridge carrying the road from the village across the hill to Blisworth. Very few trains now passed this way but sometimes I would be lucky enough to spot a rattling line of mineral wagons being laboriously hauled up the long incline from Roade by an ancient wheezing locomotive whose belching clouds of steam mingled incongruously with the leafy hedgerows of the soft Northamptonshire countryside. Such was the S.M.J. I explored along the tracks as far as Towcester in the west and Roade to the east and

WINDLASS IN MY BELT

I still have the old pre-nationalisation loading tickets, headed 'East & West Junction and Stratford-upon-Avon, Towcester & Midland Junction Railways', which I found in a disused platelayer's cabin overlooking Easton Neston Park, the seat of the Hesketh family, near Towcester. The S.M.J., like so many small cross-country lines, was soon to close and is now just another memory in the folk-lore of the district.

Beyond the railway the horse-path continued upwards before joining the road which followed the line of the tunnel vents to the north portal. This was reached by diverting down another nettle-strewn and very short stretch of path leading off the road just prior to Blisworth village. This confluence with the road to Blisworth was often the limit of my explorations but, if feeling particularly energetic, I would take a green track leading off to the right which wound along to the woods on Stoke Plain where a good afternoon's exploring could be had. From there another wide green track led directly down under the S.M.J. and into the lower end of the village, just opposite Ursula White's shop, a very interesting and rewarding round walk.

By the Spring of 1958 we were settled in and an increasingly accepted part of the small Stoke Bruerne canal community which, although part of the wider village, owed its first allegiance to the cut. My parents had made good friends with the James family and with Olive and Ricky in the next cottage. They also enjoyed going together over to 'The Boat' of an evening to chat and play skittles under the eagle eye of the indomitable Emily Woodward who, although getting on in years, still ran the pub with the able assistance of her son Jack and Zoe, his wife. Old 'Gibbie', in the end cottage next to the Mill, we saw less of. He was a very old gentleman, one arm permanently held in a white sling which was changed regularly by Sister Mary. He was, nevertheless, very adept with his good arm and could often be seen tottering out to the edge of the cut with a bucket on the end of a rope. This he deftly lowered in to collect water, presumably for his toilet, as he was never seen 'round the back'.

During that Spring I took to helping Sister Mary in little ways as I was very conscious of her many kindnesses towards me and naturally wanted to give something in return. I began by tidying and weeding the gardens which ran along under her front windows, an activity which also pleased Mr James considerably as it enhanced his efforts to be 'champion lock'. Sister's gardens were not part of the area to be judged but they were very much part of the background and, from his point of view, every little bit helped. Heartened by this I moved on into the main garden which ran down besides the lock to the road-bridge. This was a considerably more formidable proposition, but a satisfying place to be working as it gave me a clear view of everything going on at the lock. Gardening was something I was used to, having done most of our home garden since I was about ten or eleven. Doggedly I progressed down Sister's patch creating several large piles of weeds and debris which, when thoroughly dried out, could be burnt on an evening when the wind was in a favourable direction to carry the smoke out across the nearly empty fields opposite. Most of the garden was put down to vegetables which grew very successfully in the dark soil and generated enough produce to be shared round along the canal side. Hints were dropped about the long neglected orchard as being a good place for vegetables, but at this I baulked. It was an enormous task which would have taken all my spare time and energy and left none for my first love, the cut.

All this time I had watched and helped with the steady stream of working boats passing to and fro along the waterway coming to know an increasing number of crews by name and others by sight. Pleasure boats were also to be seen in very slowly increasing numbers and the blue craft of the Wyvern Shipping Company, including our own *Canada Goose*, became a familiar sight on Sunday evenings before we returned to the town for our week's labours. Despite the enormous enjoyment which the cottage was giving to the entire family I was hankering to get afloat again. The big question was, how?

I was a youth with a rather romantic view of things, not greatly interested in the new world of rock music and teddy boys which was currently engulfing my generation, but much more into narrowboats with a separate soft spot for horse-drawn gipsy wagons which were then still quite a common sight in the Northamptonshire lanes. I began to style myself on the boatpeople and went about in old clothes, including a jacket that had seen much better days, and sporting a strong brass-buckled leather belt bought on Northampton Market through which my windlass could be securely held. It was all beginning to be very much of a double life. In the week I donned uniform and went to school to do GCE's like everyone else, but it always seemed so confining and I chafed inwardly at much of the pettiness of grammar school life. Week-ends and holidays were what I lived for. Then I could be free. My ideal was to be a boatman wandering the waterways on an immaculate single motor picking up loads all over the system and with the liberty to stop and start when I pleased. Boating was not actually like that but we must all be allowed our dreams. Reality was just around the corner.

One afternoon I was hoeing in Sister Mary's garden when I heard the familiar rhythmic beat of a south-bound pair coming through the cutting from the tunnel. I waited for the clatter of the lock-wheeler's bicycle, a 'bad road' would very often have people leaping off with the bike at the narrow place just beyond the old quarry. But, when no panting figure arrived and the engine beat eased off, I emerged from the garden and shut the bottom gates. A BW pair were breasting-up beyond the Mill and I recognised the old couple we had tied behind on *Canada Goose*. They were one of the pairs I helped regularly through the locks and, having ascertained by hand-signals that they weren't tying up, I fetched my windlass and filled the lock for them. Idling in mid-stream, with an ease born of a lifetime's experience, they waited for me to begin opening the gates before coming steadily in. Invariably they worked down the flight breasted-up which, when I was helping, gave the old lady a welcome chance to catch up on her cabin work.

"Hey-up, John," wheezed the steerer, waving a claw-like hand.

"Whay-up," I responded in kind as I took the butty's side of the lock. This would be better than hoeing!

That afternoon I happily lock-wheeled and also dealt with the butty's side, I could pedal back and forth fast in those days! It occurred to me, as I scurried about, that if two-handed crews welcomed help up and down the locks, then perhaps they would welcome similar help for the length of the school holidays! This particular pair were a very kind old couple and I was able to have a ride down to Grafton Bridge before cycling slowly back up to the top lock and my tea.

I turned the idea over in my head that evening. Could it be done? Who could I go with? I still felt almost too shy to ask anyone myself and also knew that my parents would have to approve this venture which would involve stepping into a world vastly different from the one I was used to. I slept on it and then broached the subject with my mother the next night after school.

"But who would you go with?"

I knew what she was getting at. I was an only child and inexperienced in the ways of the world. Clearly if I was going to be handed over to live and work on narrow boats for several weeks at a time, then it was going to have to be with someone she approved of and trusted. Both parents recognised my enthusiasm and were not at all opposed to the idea in principle, it was really a question of how it could be done.

"We could ask Sister Mary," I suggested.

The idea just came to me. It was blindingly obvious that this was the thing to do and I wondered why on earth I had not thought of it before. Sister Mary knew all the boatpeople and there was deep mutual trust between them. She would not put me into a situation in which I would be unhappy, similarly the boatpeople would take her word for it that they were getting an enthusiastic and hard-working lad! My mother trusted Sister Mary's judgement and would accept her point of view. It was quickly agreed that we would talk to Sister Mary the following week-end which meant the cut gave me yet another week of anxious anticipation! I was very excited and could already see myself steering an immaculate motor south to the Mills. It would happen but first I had a lot to learn about real professional boating. Mind you, I was very willing!

Sister Mary listened to my enthusiasm with her customary smile. She would give it some thought, she said, and with that I had to be content. The summer holidays were looming and I got increasingly nervous as a couple of weeks drifted by with no word. Would it happen or would it not? I disciplined myself to silence and went doggedly about my business as if nothing whatsover was being planned. Privately, in the seclusion of my bedroom, I spent much time looking at all my photos of narrow boats and re-reading relevant chapters in my books. The real world of the canals seemed to be so close now, surely something would turn up.

Something did! That next week-end I had no sooner put my bike away in the cellar and was walking up the jetway to join my parents, who had come over by bus, than Sister was greeting me with her news.

"I've got someone for you, John!" she beamed, as we stood together by her front door.

"Young Ronnie'll have an extra pair of hands!"

Ronnie, it turned out, was captain of the *Warbler*, the original motor boat in the Willow Wren fleet. He currently had a close girl friend called Phyllis, but the rigid lore of the cut meant that she shared a cabin with Young Lily, the daughter of Alec and Lily who ran the Willow Wren pair *Redshank* and *Greenshank*. All three boats worked together due to this arrangement and Ronnie was even hoping to take on a butty that summer whilst continuing to work as two pairs. Further enquiry revealed that Ronnie was Lily's son by a previous marriage and that therefore Young Lily, who shared the *Redshank* with Phyllis, was his half-sister and Alec his stepfather.

It all sounded a rather complicated arrangement but Sister Mary assured me that they were a lovely caring family and that Ronnie was happy for us to share *Warbler*s' cabin together. I knew the boats by sight, of course, and had got used to seeing *Warbler* paired with 'Wagtail'. This arrangement had recently broken up and *Warbler* was currently operating as a single motor, although in practice working with *Redshank* and *Greenshank* who were noted for being a very smart and beautifully turned-out pair. I had admired these boats as they passed through Stoke, but had never really had the chance to speak at any length to the crew. Be that as it may, they apparently knew all about me! News can travel with surprising speed on the cut and few secrets are possible. My presence on the Arm had been appreciatively noticed by boats I had helped, with Meadow's endorsement of me a further point in my favour. The habit of enthusiastically rushing out and filling the top lock at Stoke for approaching south-bound pairs had also not gone unnoticed, and neither had my quiet help with two-handed pairs through the flight. The fact that I appeared to be always courteous and considerate to the boatpeople and the tacit support of Mr James and Sister Mary had all worked to my advantage. In their slow considered fashion the canal folk had weighed up the young enthusiast and had accepted him. Not just a foot in the door now, I was in!

Sister informed me that the three boats were presently travelling back empty from Croxley Mills and were likely to tie at Cosgrove that same night where they had relatives living in the lock cottage. This meant that they would be through Stoke the next morning! I immediately proceeded to spend the entire evening and a good part of the night in a state of high anxiety, my father was not the only worrier in the family! My parents naturally wanted to meet the family just to satisfy themselves that all would be well and I had to meet them too, a sudden ordeal which brought all my wretched shyness to the fore. It was decided that nothing would do but that I should get up early and get down to the bottom lock to meet them. I would then have broken the ice and would be much more comfortable when everyone came together at the top lock. Cosgrove was about an hour and a half away from the bottom lock for empty boats and it seemed unlikely that they would be there much before half-past seven or so. But I was taking no chances on this one and had been awake since half-past four! I heard Mr James go out to take the lock off at about a quarter to six and, peering through my bedroom curtains, watched him pedal off to do the same at the bottom lock. No point now in lying abed! A very quick cup of tea and a slice of toast sufficed and I pedalled down the flight in a state of eager but nervous anticipation. I half-expected to meet the boats in the flight, but all was silent except for the exuberant outpouring of the birds as the emerging sun promised another fine day. Leaning on the wooden footbridge I looked down the long straight below the bottom lock. No sign. I debated cycling further and thought about getting on at either the first accomodation bridge or Grafton Bridge, but I didn't really know them. No, much better to meet properly at the lock as originally envisaged. Leaning my bike on the fence by the side-ponds I settled myself down on the bridge to await their arrival.

Time passes slowly when watching a kettle boil and it also passes slowly when waiting for a pair of boats. The lock was all ready and I mooched about as the sun rose higher and the early dew began to burn off. There was not a cloud in the sky and a magnificent summer's day was in prospect, but I remained fidgety and anxious. Perhaps they weren't coming! Perhaps they'd decided to have a day off! Perhaps they were...............! Faintly at first, but growing ever louder, I heard the familiar 'bomp-bomp-bomp' of a single Bolinder accompanied by the slightly different and more regular beat of a second diesel engine. A cratch appeared riding high out of the water as it came round the slight curve along the overflow arches, and behind this single motor was an empty pair. They were here! I stood on the footbridge watching as *Warbler* eased down by the river Tove, the steerer raised a hand and I waved back before moving to the bottom gate as she came in. Ronnie smiled up at me as he 'worked the rods' to bring *Warbler* to a standstill just short of the sill. I had seen him before but took in anew his strong overalled figure, his fair hair and the blue twinkling eyes, shirtsleeves rolled up above the elbows.

"Hello, young John," he greeted me, climbing up onto the lockside to shut his gate.

"Thought you'd be here!"

We walked up opposite sides of the lock and drew our respective ground paddles before Ronnie crossed over and shook hands firmly. I could feel myself going red. Awkward and suddenly shy I fumbled for words, but he seemed to have no such problems and thankfully came straight to the point.

"So! You want to come with me this summer then?"

"If you'll have me," I managed.

"What'd you wanna do that for?" he grinned. "Work, instead of a holiday."

"I like boating," I rejoined a little more confidently, as the ice began to break.

Ronnie drew the gate paddles and the water surged in with a satisfying roar. I was about to cross over and draw the other side when he intervened with a grin.

"Come on, leave that. Come and meet the old man!"

Redshank and *Greenshank* had breasted-up by this time and were in under the bridge, their fore-ends nudging against the bottom gates. Down the brick steps I went to meet the family that would come to have such an enormous influence on my life and whom I would later regard as almost second parents. Very very unusually, as I would later discover, all four of them stepped off *Redshank* via her centre-beam and greeted me on the towpath. Alec was a tallish thin man possessed of a vice-like hand-shake and dressed in old trousers and a rather worn jacket. He was deeply tanned and, upon returning his firm gaze, I became aware of an inner strength and kindness which I took to at once. Lil, as he introduced his wife, was a slight figure with a soft smile and faded blue eyes, from the corners of which cats-paws wrinkled in the sun. Young Lily and Phyllis seemed to be of a similar age to each other, beaming and joking with me and wondering why on earth I wanted to go boating! Fresh and clean in the morning sun their skirts and tops were overlain with traditional long-sleeved working pinafores to protect them from the grime naturally encountered in a day's work along the cut. Everyone seemed to know all about us as a family, they even remembered we had passed them in the 'Finney' pound whilst on *Canada Goose*. Our progress with the cottage over the course of that year had been watched and they knew all about my passion for the canals. Clearly the canal world had been observing and commenting upon us and the judgements seemed to be positive.

It was quickly agreed that I would help Ronnie up the flight with *Warbler* and that Phyllis and Young Lily would lock-wheel behind us. My bike was stowed in the empty hold below the back-beam and, almost before I knew what was happening, I was standing on the gunwale holding on to the cabin rail as *Warbler* thumped up the short pound to the second lock. By now I knew pretty well the order of things in the Stoke flight and we competently worked one side of the lock each as we progressed up that morning. Following the usual practice I walked up through the thick of the locks, with Phyllis and Young Lily arriving ready to draw off each lock as *Warbler* moved out. Another ride followed up the longer pound to the top two locks which Ronnie suggested I 'start' behind us to save the girls walking up the long pound. Suddenly we were at the top lock. *Warbler* lay above the gates as the surging waters lifted the pair and everyone was meeting everyone else under the beaming guidance of Sister Mary. One glance was enough for my mother to realise that these people would most certainly see that I came to no harm and with smiles all round the details were agreed upon. There were three weeks more of school and then I would be welcome aboard the first time they came through Stoke after the holidays had begun. They absolutely would not hear of any payment for my food, insistent that they would enjoy having me and that my labours would earn my 'eats'. With agreement reached everyone prepared to get going once more, my bicycle was still on board and I jumped at Ronnie's suggestion that I should have a ride through the tunnel with him. Off we went, with my parents doubtless realising that they wouldn't see me again till late afternoon!

This was the life! I positively tingled with excitement as *Warbler* forged past the old quarry landing and curved round towards the tunnel. The single Bolinder 'bomped' distinctively and the whole cabin shook under the strain. Talking had to be conducted in loud clear tones and sometimes after a day of this you could find yourself sounding unusually loud and hearty until adjusting back to the normal flat Midland intonation. I resisted suggestions to be in the cabin through the tunnel, instead I sat centrally on the back-end beam where there was no danger of being brushed off by the sidewall if we had to pass anyone! Unlike my own cautious approach on *Canada Goose* Ronnie just went straight on into the tunnel at full speed, steering *Warbler* with apparently effortless ease unerringly down the centre. As it was summer the tunnel was fairly dry and this time I managed to avoid the gush from the 'bad' vent by dropping down into the empty hold and simply stepping aside at the last moment, a practice which is not always so easy when you are steering. We were quickly through and swinging round the Blisworth cutting as *Redshank* emerged behind us with Young Lily at the tiller. It became a question of how far I allowed myself to go, each extra mile extending the distance to cycle back. Brasses were polished as we came through the railway bridges towards the Arm End and the boat made a brave show in the summer sunshine as I gave a final wipe to the cabin port-hole.

"What are you like at steering?" asked Ronnie, as we approached the blue brick bridge and outbuildings of the Arm End. I hadn't quite expected this but he knew about our *Canada Goose* trip, conversely I knew better than to claim narrow boat expertise that I did not possess.

I had not steered for some time but, when Ronnie stood aside and gestured me to occupy the footboard, I had no hesitation in clasping the smooth wooden grip of the long shining brass tiller bar. Looking forward I found that I had to steer by watching the top of the cratch and, looking down at the three rods and one speed wheel before me, also realised that I had no real knowledge of how the controls worked on a single Bolinder. I needn't have worried. Ronnie had no intention of even temporarily absenting himself that day, in this new world I was very much a learner, but loving every minute of it. He had picked a good place for me to start steering as, other than Banbury Lane Bridge, the long straights beyond the Arm End offered no real challenges to my limited ability. After a couple of bridge holes were successfully negotiated I began to relax a little and enjoy the experience, even finding time to glance casually back to *Redshank* coming steadily on about a hundred yards astern. Ronnie was a good teacher and I had the vital 'rods' sorted out for me as we approached the turn into the bridge hole at Banbury Lane. I was nervous here, not wanting in any way to disgrace myself on my first day.

"You take it," insisted Ronnie, standing close enough to take over if necessary.

"Not too fast ... oil rod out ... slowly ... speed wheel ... round the outside ... don't turn too early ... good ... good ... well done!"

Warbler swung round and was nicely centred for the bridge hole. As I turned the brass speed wheel and shoved in my oil rod I felt a great wash of happiness and confidence surge over me. Pride comes before a fall, so goes the old saying, but thankfully it was not the case today as I forged happily on. Very reluctantly I had decided that I would have to get off at Heyford Furnaces Bridge; there were still two essays to be written for homework and time was marching on. No other awkward turns confronted me as we thrashed along through Bugbrooke and then closed once more with the railway at Heyford.

It had been lovely steering again and it was very tempting to go further, but cycling back would take time. The morning had been a very emotional one and I was aware of my tiredness and the essays still to be written, a summer of boating lay ahead and it would be silly to overdo it! I leapt off with my bike at Heyford and, amid shouted goodbyes and thanks, watched *Warbler* move away before turning to say my goodbyes once more as the high bows of *Redshank* swept into the bridge hole. Alec passed through making jokes about my steering and followed by the smiling Lil on *Greenshank* who assured me he was only kidding! Standing on the bridge I watched them until they had moved out of sight beyond the towpath hedge with Lil and the girls giving a final wave as *Greenshank* disappeared. Climbing into the saddle I set off back along the familiar narrow lanes feeling about six feet off the ground! It had been a marvellous morning and I had been made so welcome. My hands were rather dirty from paddle-grease and Brasso and my eyes prickled with tiredness from lack of sleep, but I was sublimely happy with life and felt on top of the world. For the first time I had travelled on working boats instead of watching from the towpath. I had been an integral part of the scene and my feet fairly danced on the pedals as I recrossed Blisworth Hill and dropped down the horse-path back to the cottage. For me the freedom of the long summer holidays could not come quickly enough.

*****

Chapter 4

First Trip

Exams helped. I had them at the end of that Summer Term and they had
to be passed, which kept me busy with notes and revision for all but the
last week of term. Everything was ready at the cottage, my oldest clothes,
specially selected to be in the boatman 'style', were complemented by
strong boots from the market with a pair of canvas shoes for the cabin. A
narrow little blue flock mattress, which would roll up in the day, had been
acquired and would fit neatly either on *Warbler*'s floor or the side-bed
whichever was more convenient. The 'Edwards' and a blank notebook for
a diary completed the filling of my small bag. Space precluded taking too
much but everything was double-checked, I even packed a spare pair of
bootlaces just in case!

At last term was over and I rang the Willow Wren office to find out
where 'my' boats were. From this information I could work out
approximately when they would arrive at Stoke Bruerne. Stanley, the
clerk, told me they had gone to Cannock to load coal for Hayes Cocoa, a
very long trip indeed. The three boats had loaded that day, Friday, and
were headed south. I was not very knowledgeable about calculating the
speed and distances involved but, after consulting with Mr James who was
very knowledgeable indeed, we came to the conclusion that the boats
would most likely come through Stoke on Tuesday afternoon, if Alec was
following his usual practice of arranging things in order to tie at Cosgrove
overnight. Accordingly I was left at Stoke on the Monday morning with
admonishments to be careful and enjoy myself in that order! Having
ascertained from Mr James that the boats had not come through
Braunston, and therefore could not arrive that day, I spent most of the time
wandering up the horse path and along the track of the S.M.J. seeing
rabbits, a hare, lots of birds, but no trains and eventually found myself
ambling off to inspect the badger setts in Stoke Plain Woods. On Tuesday
morning Mr James told me that the boats had tied at the bottom of
Braunston the previous night, passing up the flight early that morning thus
confirming his forecast of Alec's intentions. In great excitement I had
everything ready by the front door and, at just after half past three, the
long awaited 'bomp-bomp' of *Warbler* could be heard and presently the
three boats swung into sight and the waiting was abruptly over.

FIRST TRIP

Suddenly everything seemed to happen very fast indeed. A north-bound pair of boats had left the flight ready and *Warbler* swept straight into the lock, with the pair breasting-up level with the old Mill.

"Ready?" grinned Ronnie, as *Warbler* shuddered under the strain of reverse gear and came to a standstill just short of the bottom gates. I needed no second bidding, heaving aboard my rolled-up mattress and blankets followed by the bag, all of which were immediately stowed at the far end of the cabin underneath the seat-board. Paddles were flying up, Sister Mary was waving good-bye, bottom gates were creaking open and paddles crashing down with a long rattle. I was off! The dream was becoming reality. Working down the familiar flight that afternoon I was under no illusions as to the magnitude of the undertaking. I was just fifteen and the world of the canals was much harder and rougher than the world of school. I knew that I would be expected to keep up and always work uncomplainingly hard if the genuine recognition and friendship of the boatpeople was to be won. There was an awful lot to learn but sheer enthusiasm bolstered my efforts, I was doggedly determined to enjoy the chance I had hankered after for so long. Having made all these promises to myself the first afternoon turned out to be a deceptively easy start, the rigours were still to come!

We left the bottom lock, watching Young Lily and Phyllis swing the gates to behind us, and set off at a steady beat down the pound. Ronnie steered and I could see nothing that needed doing with which I could occupy myself. All the outside brasses were already gleaming and had clearly been polished anew that day. Water cans were full, mop and short shaft neatly aligned along the cabin top. The counter also looked freshly scrubbed and the strips of ash along the edges shone white in the sunshine. Planks were laid in a neat line along the coal as far as the mast where a short top-plank connected with the cratch. The obligatory three white strings and the finishing strip of canvas across this also appeared fresh and clean. A bicycle and the long shaft lay in the coal and a line from the mast-head 'looby' was coiled neatly on the top-plank ready to hand. Naturally I was keen to prove my worth and had no desire to be an ornament!

"Anything wants doing?" I enquired casually.

"Can you light a primus?" rejoined Ronnie, as we eased down for the first bridge-hole. I had to admit I couldn't. I knew the theory from reading Arthur Ransome, but I had never actually done it.

"Cup of tea!" said Ronnie. "Hold this and I'll get it going."

With no more ado he dropped down into the cabin leaving me to step on to the footboard and clasp hold of the tiller bar. Immediately I discovered the very considerable difference between steering a loaded boat and an empty one. The strength required to move the tiller bar took me by surprise and I was soon wondering about my ability to get round even modest bends successfully, never mind the famous 'big turns' which were littered up and down the cut.

71

Here the cut was wide, but with muddy broken edges, and our wash flooded in and out of the holes sucking a little more silt out to clog up the waterway. Glancing down into the cabin I saw that Ronnie had the primus going and was pumping it up with steady even strokes before placing a rather dented old 'whistling' kettle on top. I concentrated very hard on keeping *Warbler* exactly in the channel and, as we approached Grafton Bridge, eased back the oil rod to reduce speed in the manner I had watched Ronnie do previously. We slid neatly through the bridge-hole and I pushed the oil rod back in, feeling rather pleased with myself at the first hurdle successfully negotiated. Presently Ronnie emerged from the cabin with two steaming mugs of tea, one in each hand. He looked round quizzically and then back at my reasonably straight wash.

"Alright?"

I nodded happily. Ronnie hoisted himself on to the cabin top, sipping tea and leaving me to steer down the long and, it must be said, easy reaches of the Cosgrove pound. We got to know each other a little more that afternoon and I told him all about *Bredon Hill* and the Stour Cut where, surprisingly, he had never been. Apparently Northern boats and London boats were two separate communities with few points of contact and only rarely did they stray on to one another's waterways. I also felt it prudent to point out that I was having my first steer of a loaded boat that afternoon as, much as I was enjoying it, I did not want to be left alone just yet for anything even faintly tricky.

"You're doing fine," was his comment, and with that I was content.

Although I had to learn fast that summer I can say, looking back on it after all these years, that I was patiently shown how to do things, expected to remember what I was taught, and learned a great deal by observation and copying. Ronnie did occasionally have a tendency to credit me with more knowledge and skill than I actually possessed, but I was never tested completely beyond my limits and took a pride in my increasing skill and professionalism as the days and weeks passed.

Ronnie took over again as we passed 'The Navigation' and confirmed that we would stop below Cosgrove Lock that night as was their custom. It was quite early to be finishing by boating standards, but the Beechey family living in the lock-cottage were close friends and Alec was in the habit of arranging his trips to include a night there. The three boats lay quietly in the evening sunlight, tied just below the lock on the long straight leading down to the aqueduct and the timber wharves beyond. I had been given a large bottom drawer under the bed-hole in which to stow my kit and, having squared this away, was suddenly shy of going back to *Greenshank* where the others had congregated. Instead I settled down to write up the first part of my diary, but I was not to be left in peace for long!

"What you'm doing?" enquired a gruff voice, the boat lurching slightly as Alec stepped aboard and grinned down at me. I would eventually, as our trust and friendship grew, come to regard him as almost a second father but, on that first evening, he was virtually a stranger and I reddened as I stammered out my reply.

"Couldn't keep up with you!" he bantered, as he sat down on the footboard and began eliciting details from me to fill out the picture he had obviously already been given by Sister Mary. This would be the first of many jests about my steering, but they were never malicious, serving only to draw me in to the family and encourage me in my efforts.

"Coming for a pint?"

This was so unexpected that I was momentarily taken completely aback. I was only just turned fifteen and although I knew pubs existed I was not in the habit of frequenting them!

"I'm not old enough," I countered. He must know that already, I thought.

"Don't matter!" came the reply. "You're with me, ain't yer?"

It was one of those moments again. I wanted to be a boatman. If boatmen went for a pint, then so would I!

Lil and the girls apparently intended to spend the evening in the little cottage and so, feeling rather self-conscious, I found myself descending into a very narrow foot-tunnel which led us under the cut and into the convivial bar of the 'Barley Mow', where the clatter of crashing wooden skittles mingled with the soft burr of South Northamptonshire. I was subsequently to spend many an evening in the pub with Alec and Ronnie but this, the first one, lingers in the memory. Surprised not to be summarily ejected because of my age, I found myself sitting at a round wooden-topped table with strong curving metal legs and a pint of Phipps' in front of me. This I proceeded to drink with the utmost nonchalance as if I had been doing it for years. Conversation swirled around me, baccy-tins lay open on the table, and thin pungent roll-ups filled the little bar with a blue haze and the distinctive reek of Old Holborn. It was all 'cut' talk and I mostly listened, absorbing the atmosphere and trying to piece together all the disjointed pieces of information which were coming my way. Soon I was pressed into making up a four at skittles and had to confess my ignorance. Skittles is a very local game and I have not seen it in a pub beyond a twenty-mile radius of Northampton. A large cushioned leather-topped table was set in a corner of the bar upon which nine wooden skittles, about six inches high, were set up on pre-determined spots in a diamond formation. Armed with three round wooden cheeses, each of which fit neatly into the palm of the hand, you take up position anywhere behind a line drawn on the floor of the bar. It is a simple game, the idea being to knock skittles down to achieve as high a score as possible. All nine skittles can be removed simultaneously by striking the leading skittle in such a way that it goes one way, the cheese goes the other, and a fortunate combination of rolling skittles bouncing off the side cushions will demolish all the rest. I also found that the cheese could be thrown right through the diamond without actually hitting anything! This is a feat that looks nigh on impossible at first glance, but I assure you it can be done! Theoretically a top score of 27 was possible although rarely achieved, but 'overs', that is to say scores beyond nine which entailed re-setting the diamond after the first or second cheeses had done their worst, were much more common. The game, I found, was not as simple as it appeared. A good eye and a steady throwing hand are needed in order not to hit the front edge of the table and bounce out by throwing too low, or to miss the diamond altogether by simply throwing too high. Being quite good at ball games and possessed of a reasonable eye I managed to acquit myself creditably as Alec's partner, even managing 'overs' on several occasions. Needless to say the next few years saw me become a competent pub-league standard skittle player although I must confess I never did score the hallowed '27', my personal best being a memorable '24' scored in the 'Admiral Nelson' at Braunston.

We left the 'Barley Mow' at closing time and not a moment before. I had not been expected to keep up round for round with the others for which I was grateful. To do so would have meant being carried back as Alec, in particular, was clearly very fond of his beer! I made sure I bought my round however, already perceiving that failure to pay one's share would go very much against the canal code. Four pints stood me in good stead that evening, a modest quantity by future standards but enough for now. We strolled casually back, chatting about getting an early start on the morrow, with an owl hooting in the trees along the old Buckingham Arm, the world of home and school seemed very distant and I felt a thrill of pleasure at my acceptance on the boats. Upon reaching the lock we joined the others in the Beechey's cottage for a cup of tea and a cheese sandwich and it was past midnight before I finally snuggled down on the side-bed, only to have to get up a couple of hours later in order to 'top the pound up'!

The next morning I was rudely awoken by Ronnie's response to a bang on the slide and a strident call of "Let's be having yer!". It was just six o'clock. I felt decidedly bleary, but my first full day's boating lay ahead and I was nothing if not determined to be a useful member of the crew! A three hour pound to 'Finney' and another hour beyond that to Talbot's Lock meant an easy start in many ways. Everything was done on the move as time was money. All our efforts were directed to 'getting the boats ahead', keeping them on the move, with all the various domestic routines and shopping being fitted in around this requirement. It was a pleasant sunny morning and the three boats worked together for the first part of the day, a long 'snubber' reached from *Warbler* back to *Redshank* with another similar length going back to *Greenshank*. This arrangement kept us close and enabled people to swop about on the steering whilst other jobs were attended to. The locks would come steadily after Talbots and these long pounds were the last opportunities to keep up with the tasks of cleaning, washing, ironing, making pies, splicing lines, before the rigours of the lock country ahead. Keen to be seen to be busy, I washed up our tea mugs and then was given a lesson in how to light a primus by Phyllis, who had come over from *Redshank* just by Linford. Like many things on the cut, technique was all important. I soon learned to watch for the precise moment, as the meths fades in the little cup, to pump up the primus and be rewarded by the roar as it bursts into life. Phyllis herself, I learned, was a comparative newcomer to the cut and was happy to share her expertise with me, proving to be a good friend in these early days. I was initiated into the cabin layout, everything had a place and everything in its place was an essential requirement if chaos and dirt were to be avoided. Keeping everything swept out and the cabin brasses polished now fell to me, as mate, and I'm sure Phyllis was very happy to get me into the weekly ritual of black-leading the range, not my favourite job, but someone had to do it and it was all part of the learning! Outside, the cabin sides and top would be mopped-off and, unless it was raining or really dismal, the outside brasses were polished and kept up to the mark, with shining brass rings on the chimney matched by the brass rings and curved hoop of the 'cutter' on the exhaust pipe. This emerged through the engine-hole roof, somewhat to the right of the steerer, and blew diesel fumes into his face all day long, particularly if the wind was in the wrong direction.

I did a little more steering that morning on the easier stretches before being sent forward to pump up the bike tyres, prior to jumping off at 'Finney' bridge and pedalling furiously along to get the little six-inch rise and fall lock ready as we began our climb up to Tring summit. Up as far as the Wyvern Shipping Company's base at Leighton was, whilst it could hardly be described as familiar, not unknown territory and it was on the bends of the Jackdaw pound that Ronnie taught me my first lessons on getting round the 'big turns'. I knew all about keeping on the outside but had previously been defeated by attempting to edge slowly round the really big turns, especially those on the Oxford summit. The trick was to ease off coming into the corner, how slowly depended upon the degree of turn, whilst just nudging the fore-end round in the right direction. Too far would mean cutting the corner and the boat would catch in the middle, not far enough and you would not get round being doomed to hit the coping or, even worse, plough into the soft shallow muddy edge of the field! It was all a matter of fine judgement and, at the critical moment, it was a case of speed wheel on, oil rod in, and tiller hard over. The sudden surge of power would turn the boat, almost in its own length, with a most impressive gush of spray as the wash deflected off the rudder. I survived supervised practice around the muddy turns of the Jackdaw but this would prove to be my last steering of the day as, once beyond Leighton, I was needed for lock-wheeling.

We had met several north-bound pairs that morning but, according to the ancient lock-keeper at Leighton, a pair of Croxley-bound British Waterways boats were not far ahead having spent the previous night at Black Horse Bridge safe in the knowledge that we were sure to stop at Cosgrove.

Consequently it was they who were benefiting from the locks left ready by the north-bound pairs whereas we had everything against us. Lock-wheeling was to become very much an integral part of my work over the next few weeks and, like most things on the cut, there are a few things to be watched for. Once again, timing is of the essence. You have to have the lock ready for the boats when they arrive, gates open, or one gate in our case, and paddles dropped. Failure to achieve this negates the whole point of lock-wheeling and the unfortunate involved comes in for much joshing about slowness on a bike and lazing about on the job generally. The other danger is pedalling too hard, inadvertently getting too far ahead of your boats in your zeal to have everything ready. Meeting a pair coming in the opposing direction, who then reach the lock you have just drawn off before your own boats get there, will result in a large dollop of venomous opprobrium being heaped on your head and, doubtless, directed at your boats also when they eventually meet. Bearing both these points very much in mind I pedalled off, windlass in belt, into the unknown beyond Leighton. Lock-wheeling on a fine day can be a very pleasant activity. It is necessary to watch the path ahead for any unexpected holes or erosion down which an unwary front-wheel could descend, but otherwise, if your timing is kept right, you have few worries. On a wet day it is not, by any stretch of the imagination, such a desirable occupation. Towpaths become a sea of puddles and soft clinging mud which makes the effort of pedalling so much greater, quickly resulting in sodden feet and filthy trouser legs which simply get worse as the hours pass on long climbs, such as those on either side of Tring summit.

Today, however, was warm and sunny and I felt pleased with myself as we passed up 'The Fields', as this part of the cut was known. Later I would learn that, on some of the longer intervening pounds, it was possible to get back on for a short rest, but I was happy enough that day pedalling up to the top of Maffers. Lock-wheeling is a solitary occupation. I saw Ronnie and Phyllis only briefly at each lock, and even more briefly as I waited to open and close the swing-bridge above the Nags Head Three, before pedalling energetically past *Warbler* to set the two below Maffers. Alec caught up to us in the Maffers flight to tell us that *Redshank* had developed some sort of shaft problem and that we would have to stop at the workshops on the summit to get it fixed. This inevitably took longer than anticipated and we finished up remaining at Bulbourne overnight which would, I was assured grimly, leave us a long days work to get down to Hayes Cocoa the next night.

The next day proved to be a very hard one indeed, making me realise in no uncertain manner what an easy life I had of it at school. Mind you, I never failed to prefer the harder life of the cut even on the really exacting days such as this one. I was inexperienced but immensely keen and, after a rapid sweep and tidy-out of the cabin as we crossed the short summit, I was once again lifting the bike off at Cowroast and girding up for what I knew would be a day of locks as we made the long descent to Cowley.

FIRST TRIP

Once again the locks were nearly all against us, a veritable 'bad road'. North-bound traffic seemed very light with only the Barlow pair of *Ian* and *Iona*, whom I met at Gas Two, offering any respite. They assured me that Berko would be against me as the Croxley pair were not far ahead. ... so keep pedalling! At Berko everyone was going to work as I cycled under the bridges to set the lock, it was all rather disconcerting as I seemed to have been up for hours!

I was under instructions to wait at Berko for breakfast where a very welcome bacon sandwich and mug of tea were downed as the lock emptied.

"Alright?" grinned Ronnie, taking the mug back from me as *Warbler* thumped out of the dripping lock chamber and Phyllis swung the bottom gate to in order to 'start' the lock for Alec.

"Mmmmm!" I replied through a mouthful of bread and bacon. "Fine!"

Fine I most certainly was. Indeed, I was in my element and enjoying every moment of it. Lock-wheeling that day gave me the time to have a good look round as the cut descended towards London and houses and railways began to close in. At Apsley I counted six pairs waiting to empty, with another four at Nash, and looked with interest for the first time at the huge John Dickinson's paper mills upon which so much of the canal's trade depended. I gave and received greetings from the waiting boats, feeling glad that we were bound for Hayes and not for the back of a queue at the Mills. On down past the Ovaltine factory at Kings Langley where a pair of Barlows were under the grab, emptying out the East Midland coal that would fire the boilers beneath that tall brick chimney. Then on into the long pedal through the pretty winding Cassiobury Parks before finally catching up with the pair ahead as they tied fifth in line at Croxley, the largest Mill of all. They grinned at me and I paused by them for a breather.

"Kept you busy, have we!" they joked. "You'll be alright now you'm past. Everything ready for yer!"

This seemed a pleasant prospect and I looked forward to a bit more steering practice that afternoon as I dawdled down to the lock, confident that all would indeed be ready.

I should have known better! Bottom paddles were being furiously drawn as I reached the lock and peered down on to a pair of British Waterways boats who had just finished emptying at Croxley and were now headed for Brentford. Any benefit we might have gained from north-bound pairs leaving locks ready for us would be cancelled out by this pair working just ahead of us. Being empty, they could be expected to draw slowly away from us, but not sufficiently to make any appreciable difference to my task for the rest of the day!

"Hallo boy!" they greeted me. "You're a long way from home!"

I knew the pair slightly, by virtue of a bit of assistance given on the Stoke flight, and grinned back as I explained my sudden appearance beside them at Croxley Lock.

"Oh, ah!" came the response. "Got you working then!"

They chugged off and, after checking for possible north-bound traffic, I filled the lock and waited for *Warbler*, feeling that Ronnie should be appraised of the new situation. At least he would know that I wasn't just drifting on ahead, merely dropping paddles on already full locks and generally messing about! Presently *Warbler*, with Phyllis steering, came slowly past the boats emptying at the Mill and eased into the lock. She smiled at me as, with much pushing and shoving of control rods, she valiantly engaged reverse gear bringing her to a halt just short of the bottom gates.

"Good road?" Phyllis enquired, as she shut her gate and watched me draw the bottom paddles. I explained and she nodded sympathetically as *Warbler* sank downwards.

"Ronnie's back with Mum having his tea," grinned Phyllis, pointing back up the cut.

"Who's lock-wheeling?" I responded, gazing expectantly in the same direction.

"Young Lily probably. We've been taking it in turns. Hour on, hour off."

I had not been included in the hour on, hour off, equation but I knew better than to comment on this. I was still very much wearing 'L' plates, still on trial, and I had to earn their respect by working uncomplainingly at any task set for me to do. I decided to be extra helpful and shut the bottom gate and drew a ground paddle as *Warbler* moved off. This started the lock for the following pair and, hopefully, got me in Young Lily's good books!

With the locks becoming more spread out, and with north-bound traffic conspicuous by its absence, I was able to do this several more times before Ronnie pedalled up to us at Ricky to change over again. I had eaten nothing since breakfast, although I had had a drink out of the tap by Nash Mills. But I could do it, I said to myself, as Ronnie swopped over with Phyllis.

"Hey!" he called. "Ain't you hungry?"

I conceded that I could do with a bite and was informed that I should have stopped and got on through the Parks! I mumbled something about locks and their state of readiness at which Ronnie smiled and nodded at Phyllis.

"She'll do a couple! You wait for Mum and have your tea. Then you can do the last few for them whilst Young Lily comes with us."

So the changeover was effected, smoothly and with no loss of momentum, 'getting 'em ahead' remained the priority. I was clearly expected, finding myself received with a beam by Alec as *Redshank* nosed into Batchworth Lock at Ricky.

"Tea-time!" he joked at me. "You've earned it. Yer done well today."

Nothing more was said about my efforts, but it was enough. I had been noticed and my sweat and toil had apparently been acceptable. I was tired, almost very tired, and was happy to get on *Greenshank* for a break, leaving

FIRST TRIP

Young Lily to pedal off in pursuit of *Warbler*. I had seen little of *Greenshanks*' cabin so far on the trip and looked around with interest as a very welcome plate of tinned stewed steak and 'taters' was taken out of the oven by Lil and put on the flap of the table cupboard for me. I sat myself down on the side bed with her discarded coat lying next to me and weighted down by a windlass gleaming from years of constant use. Dirty plates were piled into the handbowl which was on the floor under the gleaming black-leaded range with its twinkling brass fittings, and warmth from the oven washed over me as I tucked in. Drying towels were looped over the polished brass rods which led from the ticket-box drawer to the curtains shrouding the bed-end of the cabin. A fine display of ornamental lace-edged plates hung down the side of the table cupboard next to the range and further plates were intermingled with old family photographs arranged amongst the crocheted curtain top. A kettle hissed gently on the top of the range and the plates rattled in unison as *Greenshank* bumped slightly in leaving the lock.

Lil leaned into the door-holes as we cleared the dripping chamber, her weathered fine-boned face breaking into its characteristic almost shy smile.

"Thought we'd lost you, young John!" she joked. "Is it alright? I've been keeping it warm for nearly two hours!"

If you were being fussy then it was slightly dried around the edges, but I was famished and right now it looked absolutely five-star!

"Mmmm!" I responded, wiping a trickle of gravy off with a grimy hand. "Lovely!"

She resumed her position on the footboard to steer and I ate contentedly, occasionally glancing past her legs at the trees drifting past and the blue sky overhead. It was much quieter on the butty, the water gurgled and swirled past with the 'pop-pop' of *Redshank* a distant beat somewhere ahead. Lil suggested I make a pot of tea as I added my plate to the others in the handbowl. I was obviously supposed to know where everything was! Not that it took much finding in such a small space nor, with the kettle already simmering on the range, would I have to test my fledgling skills with a primus. A large brown teapot was to hand in the table cupboard and a flower-patterned tin just above proved to contain tea. How many spoonfuls? We had it weak at home, on the other hand my Grandad Thorpe had it nearly thick enough to stand a spoon up in! Lil was leaning in the door-holes humming softly to herself and steering effortlessly with one outflung hand. Must be an easy bit, I thought, and tapped her foot gently to enquire about spoonfuls. Two. Middling tea, neither weak nor strong, but in my view, just about right. Climbing out of the cabin with two mugs, leaving one waiting ready on the table to be passed to Alec at the next lock, I sat on the side of the butty hatches ready to move if the swing of the great wooden tiller necessitated it.

"Coming on," remarked Lil conversationally.

I had slightly lost touch with where we were and it was my first trip, but I agreed anyway. I commented favourably on the beautiful white-scrubbed swan's neck ornamental rope-work which adorned *Greenshank*'s rudder post or 'elum'. All this work and the making of the various fenders and tipcats was done by Alec and I was suitably impressed. I wouldn't have known where to start at that time and, once again, I realised that boating wasn't just steering along the pounds but a whole and all-encompassing way of life about which I had a lot to learn.

"Ronnie's teaching you steering then?"

I agreed with this and then had my quiet sit in the hatches abruptly ended in the best possible fashion!

"You hold this then while I wash up!" said Lil.

With no further ado she disappeared down into the cabin leaving me with the curved wooden tiller and a half-drunk mug of tea! I had never steered a butty before but was more than pleased to be trusted to do so. Stepping onto the footboard I clasped the tiller firmly, concentrating hard on the way ahead. After all, if I had a problem, Lil was right there to be asked. It was all part of the learning again and Lil knew I was good enough to steer along the wide straights which were much in evidence that evening. I strove to keep *Greenshank*'s mast in line with *Redshank*'s door-holes and the reclining figure of Alec, seemingly effortless at the tiller. All went well and I had emptied the passed-up handbowl of dirty water and re-filled the kettle from the can standing by the chimney on the cabin-top before the next lock hove into view. I knew the theory of strapping a butty into a lock, jumping off with a short strap as the boat enters, taking two or three turns round the stump or strapping post and easing the heavily laden butty to a standstill before it collides with the bottom gates. Surely, however, I was not expected to do this operation now? When, years later, I became a teacher myself I frequently espoused the theory of 'learning by doing' to the young children in my charge and it was this very same method that was now about to be applied to me!

"Lock's coming up!" I called into Lil, confident that she would emerge and take over.

"You know about the strap, don't you?" she responded, on her hands and knees sweeping up the cabin floor.

"I know how, but I've never actually done it," I confessed. Surely she would take over now!

"Go in on the right, keep her straight, and take it gently! You'll be alright!"

I hoped so! I very much hoped so! In we went, with Alec laying *Redshank* at a slight angle along the lock-wall and using the reverse motion to pull her straight. We followed neatly in at what seemed to me a truly alarming speed. Theory into practice again! I pulled the tiller out, laid it on the cabin roof, and then stepped off with the strap coiled in my hand. Three turns round the post and ease her in, don't snatch at it or the strap might break. I was sweating with nervousness and, out of the corner of my eye, noticed that Alec had stepped on to *Redshank* and then crossed over to *Greenshank* by the mast. Afterwards I realised that he could have used the mast line to stop *Greenshank* if I had fouled up, but nothing was ever said. The strap groaned under the strain as *Greenshank* slowed abruptly and came to a halt just short of the bottom gate. Nonchalantly, as if I had done it a thousand times, I coiled the line and laid it back on the boat before shutting my gate as Alec drew the bottom paddles. Inwardly, of course, I was positively bursting with pride at my progress and immensely grateful for the trust that was being placed in me.

At Denham we found Ronnie waiting and I swopped back to *Warbler* for the last bit. It was dark as we passed through Uxbridge and Cowley, going above the locks each time and starting them behind us for Alec. I didn't want to miss anything and sat on the cabin-top as we wound along the final pound to the Nestle's factory, Hayes Cocoa, our destination for the day. It felt as if I had been on the cut for weeks although it was actually only two and a half days. So much experience had been packed into this short time and I had learned a good deal very quickly. Especially I had learned to keep going, one of the many lessons from the cut which stood me in good stead in later life. Not yet hardened to the long hours and the busy outdoor life I found myself very tired that night at Hayes Cocoa. I had cycled miles that day down bumpy and uneven towpaths, drawn many many paddles and heaved on many gates. It had all been strange and, doubtless, I had also unknowingly expended a good deal of nervous energy in my determination to get everything right, and that was without taking *Greenshank* into a lock for the first time! I was so tired after the engine stopped that I decided that washing could wait until the morning; snuggling down on the side-bed I was asleep almost immediately and heard nothing of Ronnie returning from his supper on *Greenshank*.

The next day was a day of coal. No other pairs were in front of us at the factory and we were to unload immediately. Most of the work was done by Nestle's men operating a large grab which swung the coal out of the boats and dumped it into huge piles on the wharf. All we had to do was sweep up a bit behind them and shovel the little piles we created into the grab. This job fell to me whilst Ronnie busied himself in the engine-hole, checking and cleaning and leaving all the brass cocks and valves gleaming and winking in the morning light. *Warbler* was emptied first and by mid-morning I had got the hold all swept out, side-cloths re-furled nice and tightly in curved rolls along the gunwale, and all the planks and stands put back neatly with everything well mopped-off. It was then cup of tea time before cleaning and mopping-off the cabin top and refurbishing the outside brasses. Strangely enough, the more I worked on cleaning and straightening *Warbler* the more I felt I belonged and, by the time *Redshank* was emptied, I had cleaned the cabin and the inside brasses for good measure. *Warbler* looked a picture as she lay high out of the water, just beyond the unloading length. Feeling justly proud of her I wandered back to lend any sort of hand I could to the emptying of the pair. By early afternoon we were ready to go and waited anxiously whilst Alec phoned for orders. I, of course, wanted back-loading to Birmingham for the sheer experience of it, Ronnie and Alec wanted it for tonnage money!

"What are you looking so black about?" said Alec to me as he returned with the news. I had been unthinkingly wiping my brow with hands blackened with coal dust and looked, to everyone's evident amusement, like a chimney sweep!

I was soon put out of my misery. Our orders were to go down to Brentford and load for Birmingham the very next morning. No waiting about at all. This was the ideal with the boats fully employed, but it didn't always happen and long days could be spent hanging about waiting for lighters to appear up the river from the docks. Everything seemed to be going our way. By eight o'clock the next morning we had descended the Hanwell Locks and were swinging round in the broad loading reach at Brentford, before tying above the locks leading down onto the tideway. Brentford, in those days, was a busy transhipment depot and had largely superseded Regent's Canal Dock as the place from which back-loading to the Midlands was undertaken. Cargoes would come up the river from the docks, at both London and Tilbury, in strings of lighters towed by powerful tugs. These lighters would then be worked through the two entrance locks into the wide basin in which transhipment took place. Timber was loaded direct from lighter to narrowboat by the boat's crews but other cargoes, such as wheat for Wellingborough, various metals for Birmingham, barrels of tomato concentrate also for Birmingham, were handled by crane with the role of the boat crews happily reduced to that of helpers. Within the hour we were ordered across the other side to commence loading. Lil and the girls had gone off shopping but it was a simple matter for Alec and Ronnie to move the three boats over, using just *Redshank* as motive power with me once more watching and learning!

It was to be a mixed load for us that day. *Warbler* and *Redshank* were loaded with stacks of rectangular ingots of spelter for Tyseley, whereas *Greenshank* received a load of tomato concentrate in little wooden barrels. This was destined for the HP factory at Warwick Wharf, or Fazeley Street as it is also known, particularly by the boatmen of the northern canals who also traded there from Runcorn and Weston Point. The cargo was clean to handle and little effort on our part was needed with the actual loading which was done by means of a large crane and three muscular dockers who took over virtually the whole operation. Once more the boats lay low in the water and now I had to learn the whole complicated business of 'sheeting-up' for the first time. The top-planks came first, these were laid from the existing plank at the masthead back along the stands to the cabin top, where the final plank was held in place with a large metal pin. Lengths of wood, with 'vees' cut in each end, called uprights, were placed at intervals from gunwale to top-plank to support the planks in position. The side-cloths were then unrolled and secured into place by means of strings passed over the top-planks and then back up to be secured tightly with a special hitch. Once all the side-cloths were in position it would normally have been the practice to bring out the heavy top-cloths and cover over completely until the boat resembled a long tent, thus keeping the cargo secure and dry. Spelter, however, would not rust. There was little point in making work for ourselves and so the top-cloths remained folded up under *Warblers*' cratch. *Redshank*, also laden with spelter, was dealt with in the same fashion whilst *Greenshank*, her hold full of wooden barrels, was not clothed up at all, instead, the planks were laid as straight as possible through the barrels to ensure smooth access to the fore-end.

All was ready. A slight hold-up ensued as Alec and Ronnie went off for a pint, much to Lil's professed irritation, leaving the rest of us to put the finishing touches to the boats and devour a well-earned sandwich. The dock lay temporarily quiet in the midday sunshine and I pottered about on *Warbler*, indulging myself in a spot of desultory rubbing of outside brasses and setting up the tiller bar. A pair of British Waterways boats lay, half-loaded with wheat, ahead of us and the pair we had followed down from Croxley remained on the other side of the basin waiting for orders. Three other pairs of B.W. boats also lay peacefully alongside some empty lighters, presumably waiting for their cargoes to come up the river. It was hardly a scene of frenetic activity and reflected a certain lack of overall organisation that seemed to bedevil the swift turnaround of the boats. Mind you, we could hardly grumble!

Mid-afternoon found us emerging from the Hanwell flight, ready to settle down to the pound along to Cowley and the start of the long climb back up to Cowroast. We eased right down to pass the line of boats tied in the 'lay-by' at Bulls Bridge, the main GUCCCo base, now taken over by British Waterways. The lay-by had been cut back far enough to enable the waiting pairs to tie stern-on to the bank and here, as I had read in *Idle Women* and *Maidens Trip*, the crews waited for orders to load. By this time there were rather fewer pairs working and it had become the custom to send boats back empty direct from the Mills if no back-loading was imminent. The 'lay-by' was not completely out of use, however, and about a dozen pairs lay waiting that day as we stole past, acknowledging the waves from those who had emerged to see who was passing.

I was steering once more up this deep and straightforward pound and beginning to get to grips with the feel of a loaded boat although I had not been tested yet on anything like a 'big turn', nor had I done any steering in the locks with the exception of that one memorable effort with *Greenshank*. It would all come in time and I was very content that afternoon, proudly steering *Warbler* along and looking forward to the long journey up to Birmingham. 'Up' was the word to begin with! We reached Cowley to find the lock ready for us, this pleased me considerably as I got to steer up the next pound to Uxbridge where we tied up early enough for Ronnie to take Phyllis to the pictures. I was not invited! Having the cabin to myself was pleasant enough though and I fantasised about being captain of a single motor as I caught up with my diary. Diaries were all very well but there never seemed to be time, or crucially enough energy, at the end of the days to do it properly. Tonight at least was peaceful, the day had been an easy one, and so everything was brought up to date before I was asked over to *Greenshank* for a cheese sandwich and a last cup of tea.

The next day was bound to be harder, but I had not anticipated how hard it would become as I awoke to the sound of rain beating relentlessly onto the cabin top. I had been very lucky with the weather thus far but that day all was to change. Perhaps it'll stop, I thought, as I slopped around at Denham, getting *Warbler* through, and then setting the lock for the oncoming pair before cycling on to catch up. That day, as I became more experienced, I began to find myself lockwheeling for both ourselves and Alec, unless the locks were really close together. It was a reminder of early days on the Northampton Arm in that I was lockwheeling ahead, helping *Warbler* through, leaving a paddle up for the lock to drain off for Alec, and then pedalling off hard to overtake and get far enough ahead to have the next lock ready for *Warbler*. If anything the rain intensified as the day wore on, the towpath becoming a veritable morass of puddles and mud and my legs aching with the effort of forcing the machine through. It was all rather unfortunate. Boats from the Mills were ahead of us going back empty and, although we met the occasional south-bound pair from time to time, we were constantly faced with a 'bad road'. I was very soon soaked through, a reminder of that Thursday on *Canada Goose* the year before. Like then, I might be wet but, strange as it may seem, I was perfectly happy. Boots and socks filthy with mud, rain running in rivulets down my back, hands wet and grimy, I was fine! As we slogged steadily up that day not once did I wish I hadn't come, the thought never crossed my mind. This may have been the other less glamorous side of boating, but it was still boating and that was all that mattered.

A brief respite in *Warblers'* cabin for a welcome bowl of soup, with hunks of bread to dip in, and then it was back on the bike for the afternoon. Our climate may be much criticised but it doesn't actually very often rain from dawn to dusk, at least not in the south, but that day proved to be the exception. I found myself having to dig deeply into my reserves of energy as I slopped and sploshed along through Berko and the remaining few locks to Cowroast. The towpath was now so squidgy in places that it sometimes meant having to get off and push, at least it wasn't too windy I told myself with a wry grin. Everything comes to an end if you stick at it, so they tell us! A dank gloomy afternoon was merging into early evening as I drew off the final summit lock with a feeling of triumph, mixed together with the satisfaction of a hard job well done. Everyone had got horribly wet that day. Steering round the long pounds further north one can at least hunch up on the footboard, the cabin doors shut tight to protect the legs and the fire keeping your bottom half dry. But, in lock country, there's no respite from the constant movement on and off the boats, with the ever present danger of slippery locksides and treacherous gates to contend with. We waited above Cowroast for Alec to come up and make his intentions clear. This was quickly apparent, even before he reached the bridge below the lock under which I was sheltering. Picking up his stern rope he held it high whilst simultaneously miming a tying action and pointing a finger at the leaden sky as he did so. I passed this message on to Ronnie who proceeded to tie *Warbler* up, leaving me to help the pair through the final lock of the day. Alec ambled up the lockside and stood watching me tying the fore-ends together as the boats rose high in the lock. He grinned and wiped some water off one of my shoulders.

"Good lad today," he said, before stumping off to bring the pair out, with me walking along to the ring with the fore-end strap. It didn't sound much, but it was enough for me. I was proving myself as a willing and hard-working member of the crew and, in so doing, was becoming accepted.

One advantage of living on a motor boat was in the drying of wet clothes. The long rods, running just under the cabin ceiling, from the steerer to the engine-hole were ideally suited for hanging wet clothes on and, with a warm fire going, they dried so much more quickly than being hung up in the engine-hole. *Redshank* had only two rods, one for gears and one for speed, but *Warbler*, being an old-fashioned single Bolinder, was blessed with four for gears, clutch, speedwheel, and oil rod for extra speed. That night four rods proved themselves invaluable, to such an extent that we had Phyllis's wet clothes hanging in with ours due to the shortage of rod space on *Redshank*. Steam began to fill the cabin as Ronnie stoked up the fire and the wet clothes became drier. With red faces in the sauna-like conditions we were quite relieved when Lil called us over on to *Greenshank* for some tea and much-needed air!

Thankfully the next day dawned misty but with the promise of sun to come, according to Lil, as she sniffed the early morning air. Our clothes had dried overnight and were back on again, ready for whatever today might throw at us. The boats themselves remained very wet and my first job was mopping off and wiping down, as we churned across the short summit. What goes up must come down. The hard-won summit level was soon behind us as we moved into the first of the twenty-four downhill locks which would take us to 'Finney' and the valley of the Great Ouse beyond. We were lucky at Maffers, meeting a pair of Barlows on the summit who had started that morning from the bottom lock. This allowed me to start all the locks behind *Warbler* before catching up to help at the next lock; as we came through the wide turns in the attractive flight the sun appeared strongly and twinkled on the broad waters of the feeder reservoirs. Lil was right, we weren't going to get wet today! Below Maffers it was back on the bike for me, pedalling along down 'The Fields' to Grove Lock where I got back on, only to leap off again at Leighton Bridge and rocket along to fill the lock. I was well into the routine now, school and my life in Northampton seeming very far away as I spent the afternoon having some serious steering tuition around the 'Finney' pound, cheering myself hugely by rounding several of the quite big turns without any problems of sticking. I was getting there, and along the long aqueduct straight was encouraged to put *Warbler* into reverse for the first time.

On *Redshank* this was a matter of extreme simplicity. There the clutch rod was pushed in for ahead, centred for neutral, and pulled back for reverse, with nothing really to go wrong. On *Warbler* matters were rather different. The clutch rod, which had to be pushed in quite some distance, only served to engage whatever gear the boat was in. A brass speedwheel controlled a hit and miss governor and was wound in a clockwise direction to get the engine running steadily, winding back on the speedwheel producing that distinctive 'bomp-bomp ... bomp', so characteristic of the single Bolinder. The oil rod gave even more speed by changing the position of a spindle in relation to the jet it served; when the spindle was in the closed position, with the oil rod off, fuel would only emerge from the jet in a fine spray, but with the oil rod on and the spindle open the fuel would emerge in a steady and unbroken stream. It was a golden rule that the oil rod should not be pushed in until the speedwheel was fully on. The fourth rod was the reverse rod which changed the rotation of the flywheel, but it was a tricky manoeuvre. Reversing a Bolinder is an art which requires confidence and perfect timing or one of two things happens, either reverse gear is not actually engaged or the engine 'goes out' completely. The procedure was oil off, with the oil rod back, speed off on the speedwheel, clutch out, pull reverse rod back and now comes the awkward bit. As the reverse rod is pulled back the engine revs fall, almost to the point of stopping, before the direction of rotation on the flywheel changes. It is only too easy to panic at this stage, pushing the reverse rod back to its central position too early with the result that the engine continues to run forward. Not a problem if you are just 'chucking-back' to clear the blades of weeds, but distinctly difficult if you are just entering a lock. It was for this reason that Ronnie always kept a strap, attached to a dolly, coiled ready on the top, in order that he could jump off and check the boat round a stump if reverse gear was missed. If you get it right, then it's push the clutch rod in, speedwheel on, oil rod in, and an impressive boiling of water under the counter brings the boat to a standstill. It is an enormous amount of pulling, pushing, and twisting to go from full ahead to full astern, not to mention dealing with the tiller and ensuring that the long snubber leading back to the butty doesn't get caught in the blades.

On my first 'go' I predictably was too early and *Warbler* remained ignominiously in forward gear. I managed it the second time and again on the aqueduct itself, bringing us to a near standstill in the trough before Ronnie took over again to take us into the lock, which I certainly wasn't yet trusted to do. I had learned a bit more though, being told to practice reverse gear by 'chucking back' from time to time when I was steering tomorrow. This cheered me up, at least I would be steering tomorrow! We tied once more at Cosgrove, this time above the lock, and once more I went along for beer and skittles at the 'Barley Mow'. I was already a different boy from that first visit which seemed weeks ago, but was actually only a few days, such had been our progress. I felt stronger and more confident with the life, my hands were harder and my leg muscles, although accustomed to cycling at home, had nevertheless become like steel! Skittling that night with the others, a pint of beer to hand on the shelf above, I felt happy to bursting as my dreams became reality.

At the top of Stoke Sister Mary greeted us effusively, quickly ascertaining that I was alright before ushering me into her house where she absolutely insisted that I ring my mother at work in order that she would also know that all was well and that I was Brummagem bound! A light drizzle had set in as we emerged from the depths of Blisworth Tunnel which had been very wet from the heavy rain of two days ago. Ronnie decided that I could steer for a bit and that he would clean the cabin and make us some tea. If anything untoward occurred he was there to be called but I felt very confident along here. It was my home territory, I knew every twist and wrinkle along the pound and felt safe in the knowledge that the first 'big turn' was miles away, at High House beyond Heyford. We encountered a good deal of south-bound traffic that day, including two more pairs of Willow Wrens engaged on the long coal run from Cannock to Hayes Cocoa. Occasional 'chuck-backs', mostly successfully executed, punctuated our progress up through the Arm End and Bugbrooke. Although I 'missed' a couple of times I was generally learning to distinguish that slightly different engine beat, an indication that reverse gear had been successfully engaged. Ronnie was out and sitting on the cabin top for High House where, using my newly-taught techniques, I came round and through the bridge hole very neatly, adding a little more to my gradually growing stock of confidence. At the big Railway Turn beyond Weedon Ronnie steered, but talked me through it as he did so, promising me a crack at some more big turns on the morrow. I had recounted my problems at Shuckburgh on the way down to Hayes and wondered if he would remember this the next day. Shuckburgh was difficult and would definitely present me with a clear challenge!

Up Buckby we went, the rain long cleared away, and out along the long straights of the Braunston summit where once again I found myself entrusted with the tiller as Ronnie tinkered in the engine-hole. Through the last high bridge hole and the dark portal of Braunston Tunnel showed ahead as I began to ease off a little. He emerged and came along to stand on the counter, in such a position as would make it difficult for me to swing the tiller bar any distance.

"Keep it straight and steady," he commanded, and disappeared into the cabin, switching the headlight on as he did so.

I had done it on *Canada Goose*, but the loaded *Warbler* was a different proposition altogether. Pulling the oil rod back, I eased down and 'bomped' into the gloom determined at all costs not to get a touch. Once accustomed to the darkness I was pleasantly surprised to find that steering a loaded boat seemed to be somewhat easier than *Canada Goose*. Being much lower in the water meant that the yellow arc of the headlight gave greater visibility with the upraised mast providing a good focal point for keeping everything centred. Through the curving walls of the 'dog-leg' I felt my confidence growing and 'put some oil on', not all but about half the rod. The noise was tremendous, the 'bomp-bomping' hugely magnified in the confined space as we pressed on with *Redshank*'s light casting a long finger across the troubled waters behind. I emerged triumphant without a touch, lockwheeling Braunston with my feet about three inches off the ground! There was no-one to tell but myself, so tell myself I exultantly did, as the paddles rattled and the gates slammed and I ran around with all the vigour and exuberance of youth.

We tied by the Willow Wren yard at the bottom of Braunston and were greeted by Dennis Clarke, the foreman/fitter, who gave us news concerning *Teal*. *Teal* was an old Fellows Morton & Clayton butty, originally named *Minnie*, and was lying idle under the shed awaiting her turn on the dock. One of the earlier additions to the Willow Wren fleet, she had seen quite a bit of service and certainly needed the dock! Her cabin sides were very dilapidated with worn and peeling paint rendering her a sorry sight beside the resplendent *Redshank* and *Greenshank*. Ronnie and Alec were interested in working with *Teal* before she was docked. The broad plan was for Ronnie and Phyllis to work the pair together, but in company with the others, with Phyllis continuing to share *Redshank*'s cabin with Young Lily. This somewhat complicated arrangement did not unduly concern me, but I climbed about on *Teal* along with everybody else and noted what was needed to make her workable. She was a typical 'northern' boat, with fine lines at the fore-end and everything seeming slightly smaller when measured against the bluff bows and deep capacious hold of *Greenshank*. *Teal* was, despite her looks, essentially a sound boat. Her docking was needed for re-painting and general re-furbishment, but she had all her cloths and planks and the cabin had been left scrupulously clean, as was the custom. After the usual pattern of banter and deliberation had run its course it was agreed that we should return to Braunston after unloading and take on *Teal* for a while, prior to her eventual docking when Dennis hoped another butty would become available. Willow Wren was steadily adding boats to its fleet at this time and we were all optimistic about the company's future, there was not really any doubt that a change-boat would become available whilst *Teal* was on the dock.

Our evening was interrupted by the steady beat of a diesel in the twilight and we were joined for the night by Billy Wilson and his wife, Clara, with *Grebe* and *Snipe*, deeply-laden with coal for Hayes Cocoa and interested in our views about the chances of a back-load from Brentford. They were an oldish couple even then and I never really got to know them at all well, we were always seeming to pass them rather than tie up with them. Stalwarts of Willow Wren for a number of years the couple had done several unusual pioneering trips, including bicycles from Smethwick to Brentford for export to Iran, and a trip earlier that year up the river Kennet to Burghfield Lock to help publicise the problems of the Kennet & Avon. I would have liked to talk to the Wilsons about that trip of just a few months earlier, but the chance never came. Darkness had fallen and we all retreated to our respective cabins, tired after our days in the open. As the soft early light stole across the waters they were in the lock at six o'clock sharp, their engine beat serving as an alarm clock to spur our own departure.

In the event it was almost midday before we finally got going. The same problem that had dogged *Redshank* at Bulbourne on the way down had re-surfaced and it needed nearly three hours of work before Dennis pronounced the matter finally solved and we were free to move. Time was rarely totally wasted however in these situations. I was dispatched up the hill to the village with a shopping list, returning to find a pile of handwashing strung precariously along under the top-planks of both motors and all brasswork twinkling in the sun. The rain of the last few days had now vanished completely and the sky was clear blue with just a few cotton wool clouds occasionally drifting across to remind us that things could be different. Off we went down the beautiful Napton pound and Ronnie had not forgotten! After spending some time in the hold, wiping the bike down and oiling everything thoroughly, I climbed out and was promptly given the tiller on the pleasant winding section before Shuckburgh Bridge, scene of the biggest foul-up of my short canal career. Ronnie stood on the gunwale as we swung round into the wide '30s' bridge hole. Oil off, speed off. Don't get nervous! The bend disappeared round to my right behind that same huge bank of rushes. I edged gently over as instructed, but not as far as I had on *Canada Goose* when I had got badly caught along the middle of the boat. Steady! The fore-end drifted on towards the long curving length of unforgiving coping.

"Now!" said Ronnie.

Speed on, furiously turning the wheel. Oil on, ramming in the rod firmly and giving *Warbler* everything she'd got. Tiller hard over, juddering in my hand and muscles aching with the effort of keeping it there against the surging wash from the blades spraying out in a huge plume behind us. *Warbler* turned rapidly, almost in her own length, and the fore-end missed the concrete by a comfortable two yards as we swung on through and I straightened up hurriedly so as not to go too far the other way!

"Easy!" grinned Ronnie.

Easy it wasn't, at least not to me. However I was round and another important obstacle had been overcome. I would never go round Shuckburgh without remembering that first horrible mess, but I had now gone some way towards regaining my confidence about this particular 'big turn'. Would I have got round on my own? Done it without Ronnie standing there telling me exactly when to turn and when to wind it on? I was still dubious about this but I was learning all the time, next trip perhaps I really would make it on my own!

At Wigrams Three I encountered for the first time the worm-screw paddles of the 'new' locks, encased in their white tubular covers with a little window through which you had to look to ensure that the paddle was completely wound down before you drew at the other end. I didn't like the 'new' paddles much at all. Twenty-one turns of the windlass were needed to raise each one, with none of the merry clinking of the safety-catch to accompany your efforts. They were a dull spectacle with no great wall of water bouncing off the sill as I drew the top-gate paddles when lockwheeling, instead just a sluggish bubbling as the lock silently filled. All a little bit lacklustre. That night saw us at the bottom of Itchington Ten, snugly tied right outside the pub. We could have comfortably reached the bottom of Radford Ten, but Alec preferred the pub at Itchington and we would get to Birmingham just the same the next day, even if we did have to get up a bit earlier!

Starting *Redshank* was just a question of climbing into the engine-hole and pressing the starter button to be rewarded with a whining noise, followed by a steady 'chug-chug-chug' as the engine settled down. *Warbler* was a wholly different matter. The engine had first to be primed by means of a blow-lamp heating a hot bulb on top of the casing. Methylated spirits were lit under the blowlamp itself and then, rather like the primus, you pumped hard at the critical moment inducing a fierce flame which quickly turned the hot bulb cherry red. Once, and importantly not before, the lamp was really hot you then had to work various brass polished handles and levers to achieve oil on, three strokes of the fuel pump, oil off, another three strokes and then, with no more ado, pull out the spring-loaded pin on the flywheel. Foot on the pin and kick really hard, forcing the fly wheel over against the compression, and allowing your foot to slip off the pin as you did so. Sometimes it took a couple of kicks but success was rewarded with a great roar of noise and vibration as the engine caught, running at full revs for a few moments before you adjusted the controls, allowing everything to settle down to that familiar rhythmic 'bomp-bomp ... bomp' of a single Bolinder in neutral. All this took time and, on this particular morning, Alec had decided to have a lie in! Young Lily and Phyllis started *Redshank* whilst we were still messing about with methylated spirits, promptly disappearing off towards Radford and leaving us to work with *Greenshank*.

"Make a change for you!" grinned Phyllis, as she moved away.

I was perfectly happy to work with *Greenshank* that day as it would teach me more about the techniques of working with a pair as against a single motor. I was never entirely sure what Ronnie thought about it all!

By the time we had got going *Redshank* had disappeared and she was three locks ahead as I pedalled down Radford behind them. Phyllis was lockwheeling and I was getting nothing started for me as we followed on, dropping down the flight with *Redshank* still comfortably ahead and out of sight along the Leamington pound as I flung my bicycle down to fill the bottom lock. The Leamington pound found me on *Greenshank*'s tiller once more as Lil produced a belated breakfast and Alec, now restored to the land of the living, had first turn at eating it before relieving Ronnie. I enjoyed my spell of butty steering, no speed controls to consider for one thing and no suspicion that people might think you could be going marginally faster for another. Following happily on I diligently kept her lined up behind *Warbler*, as we ran through the backs of Leamington and ascended the two Cape Locks at Warwick. Hatton, the low or high spot of the day depending on your point of view, was just around the corner! For me it was very much a high spot. I had heard and read a lot about the famous flight of twenty-one locks, the 'stairway to heaven' as the top section where the locks cluster closely together is called, and was eager to get to grips with it.

With *Redshank* still ahead I knew what my task would be and was off with the bike at Junction Bridge, where the reeded blocked-up entrance to the short Warwick Arm went off to the left, having the bottom lock all ready as the pair approached. The girls had the good fortune to have the flight ready for them and were getting well on as I pedalled in pursuit, this time helped by Phyllis shutting the top gate behind *Redshank* each time but not actually starting the lock in case they met someone coming down. Up we went, past the Asylum Wharf where mooring rings and distinct traces of coal along the towpath served as a reminder of traffic sadly now gone, and on to where I saw 'the thick of Hatton' for the first time. It was as spectacular as it appeared on the various photographs I had seen, mostly taken from the spot where I now stood. *Redshank* was clearly visible ahead and my wave was acknowledged by the hard-working girls as they raced determinedly upwards, keen to spend the next week telling everyone how quickly they had gone up Hatton compared to that slow pair behind! As I wheeled over the bridge by the Depot, with just four locks to go, I saw that *Redshank* was in the top lock whereas the pair were two or even three locks behind me but then, as Ronnie and Alec would say repeatedly, single boats travel faster than a pair anyway! I reached the top lock to find *Redshank* ticking over above the top-gates and Phyllis offering me a mug of tea "while we wait!". They had done well, clearly revelling in the unusual situation of working alone together, and had been determined to prove themselves fast. In this they had undoubtedly succeeded, blushing and preening themselves in the light of the praise duly and fairly offered as the pair caught up.

'Normal service' was resumed beyond Hatton as we all swopped back. *Warbler* led once more as we rattled through the short Shrewley Tunnel, past the inviting junction with the Stratford Canal at Kingswood, up the five at Knowle with their especially stiff paddles, and off along the final long pound to Tyseley. The countryside points a long green finger into the city when approached along the Grand Union and we had scarcely emerged from the deep wooded cutting at Solihull before we were pulling alongside the wharf at Tyseley, ahead of us lay two pairs of BW boats also waiting to empty spelter and steel tubes respectively. My first complete beginning to end trip had been done and, as I snuggled down on the side-bed that night, I reflected on all that had been seen and learned since leaving Stoke at the beginning of the holidays. I was, in truth, having the time of my life but I only dimly perceived the significance of it all. The cut was changing me and continued to do so. Besides making me stronger, I became more determined to finish any job I had set my hand to and increasingly developed an independence of mind which, although it later made me uneasy with committees and such-like, was probably the most useful lesson of all. We would, with any luck, empty the next day, although *Greenshank* had to be somehow got down to Warwick Wharf which might mean a bit longer. Then it was back to Braunston to collect *Teal* before loading again. I fell asleep wondering vaguely what day it was. Strangely it didn't really seem to matter anymore.

*****

Chapter 5

Round Again

Without any previous experience to compare against I was only vaguely aware of the fact that we had done extremely well since leaving Stoke, managing to keep going with almost no interruptions to progress. Waiting about, either to load or unload, was often a major source of delay to the boatman and frequently seemed to be caused by inefficiences beyond his control. Sometimes factories regarded the boats as floating storage for their coal until they were ready to use it, instead of emptying the boats promptly and storing the coal on their wharf. Sometimes an uneven flow of traffic caused problems at both ends of the trip. This resolved itself in lighters full of cargo arriving at Brentford with boats being frantically diverted down from the Mills to deal with it, only for hold-ups to occur at the other end as pair after pair arrived putting an undue strain on the unloading facilities. Sometimes 'your' coal was in railway wagons somewhere in the system and you could find yourself hanging around at Sutton Stop for two or three days whilst it was located and matched up with you. And occasionally you could find yourself waiting about because no cargo was currently available, only for the system to produce more cargo than the boats could handle the following week. It could all be very frustrating and I had a small taste of this during our efforts to empty at Tyseley, which eventually finished up spreading over two and a half days.

Everyone was up and ready at eight o'clock when the unloading crews began work. There was a 'problem', we were told by the ganger, a large lugubrious looking man with a thin roll-up seemingly permanently in his mouth. The 'problem' continued until about ten o'clock when suddenly a gang of men descended and work began. The two pairs ahead of us had been waiting two days already and naturally they had priority, cranes manouevred, chains descended, and long steel tubes were lifted out of the first pair. At lunchtime we were told that we would be emptied tomorrow, apparently the gang was wanted at Sampson Road Wharf that afternoon and we weren't the priority! A phone call to Warwick Wharf elicited the information that *Greenshank* was earmarked for unloading tomorrow afternoon and for us to make sure that she was there by two o'clock. In the meantime the two empty BW pairs sorted themselves out and presently clattered off to begin their journey round the Birmingham & Fazeley

Canal, the notorious 'Bottom Road', to the Warwickshire coalfield leaving us alone at Tyseley, no other pairs having arrived that day.

Needless to say the time had not been entirely wasted. Lil had caught up with more handwashing and all three boats had been given a good 'going-over', a coat of black paint on our chimney, some fraying side-strings spliced on *Greenshank*, and the engine-hole given a really thorough clean on *Redshank*. There was nearly always something that needed doing, but I would much rather have been on the move! Even the next day did not go quite according to the proposed plan as further hold-ups ensued. *Redshank* was emptied promptly enough in the morning, her piles of spelter being lifted out and stacked with others on the wharf, from which they were being steadily removed by lorry to non-waterside factories. Spelter is an easy cargo to empty, with no sweeping up of loose bits and dust to complicate matters, and soon she was on her way, riding high out of the water and incongruously towing *Greenshank* on a short snatcher along to Warwick Wharf, just below the five narrow locks at Camp Hill.

Ronnie and I had a cheese sandwich and a cup of tea and then emerged to get *Warbler* ready for emptying. We should have known better!

"Sorry, mate!" intoned the foreman. "They've gone round to Sherborne Street."

Sherborne Street, Ronnie informed me, was yet another basin on the other side of the city, mostly used by 'northern Joshers' trading up from Runcorn and Weston Point. Doubtless the hard-pressed foreman had problems and pressures on him that we knew nothing about, but to say that we were not amused would be putting it politely! Alec returned that evening, this time with both boats riding high and intending to go on to Knowle, only to find us still tied in exactly the same position. He wasn't best pleased either! By nightfall five more pairs had piled in around us, gloomily deprecating the authorities as we recounted our efforts to empty. It was typical of the problems encountered at that time and, upon reflection, must surely have been a factor in the gradual drift of traffic away from the canals. We made absolutely sure that we were first in the length the next morning and had emptied in less than two hours, reaching the bottom of Radford that evening and Braunston the next.

Teal was all ready for us, even to the extent of being winded so that she was pointing in the right direction for the coalfields. Nothing could be done about her deplorable paintwork but her straps and lines were in order, battery topped-up, cratch and planks in place, and cans and tiller bar resting in the cabin. A further day was spent moving aboard and fitting out, but Phyllis had been forewarned and had many things ready, and others planned, for 'her' cabin. Alec made her a mop using old strips of felt underlay salvaged from a dump, and the traditional three brass bands were fixed to the chimney. From here a brass safety chain looped down and through the handles of the two cans thus preventing them from being swept overboard in the event of a chance encounter with willow branches or some other obstruction. Curtains were draped around the bed-space and some lace-edged plates were hung up. I, willing as ever, black-leaded the range! Black-leading seemed to have become my special department, I wonder why! Our new arrangements had Ronnie sleeping in *Teal* and Phyllis remaining on *Redshank* with Young Lily, leaving me with *Warbler*'s cabin all to myself! This was something I had not bargained for when we had left Stoke Bruerne and I took great pride in 'my' cabin, keeping all the brasses twinkling and everything swept out and clean. No criticisms of 'mucky cabin' were going to come my way!

I had expected that, following our return to Braunston, we would be sent to the stop lock at Hawkesbury Junction, Sutton's Stop or 'Sutton's' in boatman's parlance, there to await orders to load in the Warwickshire coalfield, but this proved not to be the case. The next morning I found myself assigned as porter to Lil on her shopping expedition up into the village and upon our return, heavily laden with bread, meat, tins and other essentials, we were greeted by the surprising news that it was to be Hayes Cocoa again. This meant loading at Cannock, well to the north of Birmingham, and there was a choice of routes available to us. We could either retrace to Birmingham, drop down to Salford Junction and round from there, or go round through Suttons and Atherstone and back up the 'Bottom Road' to Salford Junction. Retracing meant much heavier lockage, sixty-three in all as against thirty-one, but the locks were wide to the top of Camp Hill and the cut was deeper. I, naturally, fancied the 'Bottom Road' route as I hadn't been that way at all or worked through narrow locks yet this summer. Mind you, it wasn't for me to comment on choice of route and I could see the logic behind the decision to retrace the route we had just taken and then get into the narrow locks in Birmingham.

With nothing further to keep us we were soon off again, this time working as two pairs and agreeing to alternate the leading pair, dependent upon the state of the locks, from day to day. In the event, it mostly seemed to be *Warbler* and *Teal* which led with me running around and, when at all feasible, starting locks for the others. With *Teal* close-up on the cross-straps Phyllis was able to spend even more time getting her just as she wanted and, with Ronnie in the habit of dropping back to help especially on the easier pounds, I found myself entrusted with an increasing share of the steering, a responsibility I enjoyed hugely. After days of loaded boats the tiller seemed light and responsive and so much easier on the wrists! Round the Napton pound I went in the warm summer sunshine with the wash running and gurgling along the banks and popping up through holes in the coping. I could not have been happier as I attempted to become even more professional by cleaning the chimney brasses and tiller bar whilst going along, without conceding any unnecessary wobbles in *Warbler*'s progress. Shuckburgh 'big-turn' was rounded with Ronnie beside me, but this time allowing me to decide upon the exact moment to 'wind it on'. On the other hand we were empty and, until I had done it loaded and alone, I would not in my own mind have laid this particular ghost to rest. We had the luck that day as, approaching the big turn under the towpath bridge which would take us to Birmingham and not Oxford, we were surprised by the long low shapes of Albert Beechey's 'gas boats' on their regular run to Banbury. Their turn into the southern Oxford must have been a really difficult one, but I was far too busy frantically getting oil off, speed off, clutch out to take in the finer points. It was still potentially a very awkward situation and I was quite relieved when Ronnie ran along *Teal*'s planks and took over as we idled in mid-stream to let them through, with Phyllis urgently signalling *Redshank* to ease off behind her. All went well and round the turn we went as the receding Mrs Beechey signalled that twenty-three locks i.e. the bottom of Radford were ready for us. Very good!

The pair went down those locks in a way that would be strongly disapproved of today, but was common working practice then. I would be off with the bike and waiting ready by the bottom paddles as the pair swept in, engaging reverse in a crescendo of smoke and 'bomping'. At the signal I was already drawing a bottom paddle as the boats came in, Ronnie continuing to hold back hard until the pair halted just short of the bottom gates whereupon he and Phyllis pulled together on the top gates which, drawn by the increasing pull from the paddle, slammed together with a resounding crash. I was already across and drawing the other paddle, the boats sinking down quickly and we were through in three to four minutes. If we had been working alone I needn't have had the bike off at all but could have ridden down the pounds, leaping off from the mast beam as the pair surged in. However, with the others following, I had another job at each lock. Young Lily, lockwheeling ahead, would arrive whilst we were still in the lock and further practices, also frowned upon today, would occur. Phyllis and I would open the bottom gates, knocking off the paddle catches with the ends of our windlasses to send them spiralling downwards. Ronnie would immediately 'wind it on' with Young Lily drawing a top paddle to flush the pair out of the lock even faster, leaving Phyllis to jump aboard from the steps as they swept past. Down the lock came Young Lily at a steady trot and together we slammed the bottom gates to, before I pedalled furiously off to overtake the pair and be ready in position at the bottom paddle as they entered the next lock. This was real professional boating, with everyone reliant on everyone else to do their jobs properly, and all our energies bent to 'getting 'em ahead'. There is a certain exhilaration in boating at this speed and a pride in such fast but smooth progress which spurs you on to even greater efforts. If anything, the pressure on Young Lily to both help her own boats and still be down to play her part with the top paddle was greater than that on me, to overtake the pair and be ready at each lock. Certainly neither of us had much time to spare and our pedalling muscles received another good work-out, particularly in the longer pounds towards the bottom of Radford.

We made the Cape that night, changing positions with Alec the next morning as the whole of Hatton appeared to be ready. The uphill technique was rather different and again would be well beyond the pale today. I was catching up to *Redshank* and *Greenshank* at each lock and, upon Alec's signal, drawing half a paddle as they left the lock with Young Lily shutting one side and me running up to shut the other. Having completed getting the lock ready it was back up to the top paddle as the pair came bustling in, once again drawing upon signal to help stop the forward progress. Phyllis would be off *Teal* and running up the steps to pull on the heavy bottom gate, Ronnie would be up off the cabin top to do the same on his side as I continued to draw. Once more we would be through in three to four minutes, taking just one hour ten minutes for the flight. It will be seen that my task entailed drawing all four paddles at each of our locks, a total of eighty-four turns for each lock of the twenty-one in the flight, all good arm exercise for a growing lad! The pressure was very much on me that morning as I ran around the locks, wound paddles furiously, and pedalled hard to be there as Alec left the lock ahead. Panting and damp with sweat I felt that I had definitely earned my cup of tea as the boats rose in the top lock!

Empty boating is fast boating and we were pushing on hard with the aim of reaching Anglesey Basin at Cannock the next day. Beyond Tyseley everything was new to me again and, as we wound past the B.S.A. factory and on to Sampson Road, I was being prepared for my part in the narrow locks to come. I was to be the bow-hauler! I had seen this process at work on the Northampton Arm with the wheat boats, but I had always helped Meadows with the motor. There were to be no such luxuries now! It was once again a well-organised routine with each of us having our part to play. *Teal* was to go down ahead of *Warbler* and the technique would be the same for each lock. Young Lily, following *Greenshank* down, was 'starting' each lock for us and, with a whole paddle up, they would be full by the time I plodded up with the long line running back from my shoulder to *Teal*'s mast. I would open the top gate and then continue pulling *Teal* in, with Phyllis steering very carefully in order to keep straight and thus avoid any sudden jerks on the line as there would be if she skewed upon entry. Halting *Teal* with a turn round the stump, I would then draw the bottom paddles as she shut the top gate, before hanging the line between the gates and going down ready to take the strain leaving her to open up and drop paddles. Once more I would lean into my task, assisted by Phyllis who would draw a ground paddle to help *Teal* along before dropping back on to the cabin top and shoving on the balance beams of the bottom gates as she drifted out, causing them to close gently behind her. The lock would then begin to fill ready for Ronnie, 'bomping' along as he brought up the rear with 'Warbler'.

Down Camp Hill we went, turning right at the bottom and running along to the next locks at Saltley which must rank as one of the filthiest flights in the country. Everything was covered in a film of black grease, liberally mixed with coal dust and dung from the horses used in the extensive local trade carried on in day or 'joey' boats. In wet weather it was foul, but even today at the height of summer I found the towline, which necessarily had to be laid down somewhere, becoming soggy and leaving a black mark across my shoulder which found its way right through to the skin. My hands were filthy and the old habit of wiping my brow with them did not help my general appearance! Phyllis tiptoed about trying hard to avoid the worst, but her pinny was soon grimy from the gates and black thumb-prints adorned the cheese sandwich I got for tea halfway down the flight. And that was before my thumbprints got on it! Struggling through a long gloomy section, half buried under a large factory, I found myself becoming the target for ribaldry from the machinists, doubtless thankful to have something to take their minds off the boredom of their repetitive tasks.

"Lost your horse, mate!" was a particular favourite.

"Shot it!" became my usual response.

That night we tied at Salford Bridge and needed a kettle of hot water each to make ourselves respectable once more. Salford Bridge was the main base of T & S Element, one of the largest carriers on the Birmingham Canal Navigations or BCN. Nearly all of their trade was done with horse-drawn 'joey' boats, either cabin-less or with only a small day cabin to shelter in, and a number of these craft both empty and loaded were tied at their wharf on the Leamington Road. At that time I was rather disdainful of 'joey' boats, feeling that they could not hold a candle to the long distance world of which I was now a part, and so missed a chance that evening to go off with Alec and meet some of the men who worked them in the local pub. It was a chance that would not arise again, and now never will, as Salford Bridge is completely re-developed and the world of the 'joey' boats has become just another fading memory.

More grime was the order of the day as the next morning found us working steadily up the flight of thirteen narrow locks at Perry Barr, known colloquially as the New Thirteen or just 'the New Uns'. The New Thirteen, as seen from my point of view, was actually two locks to bow-haul, back on the cross-straps for towards a mile, four locks to bow-haul, back on the cross-straps for a quarter of a mile or so, and then bow-haul the final seven, before being confronted by the long wide straight reaches of the Tame Valley Canal, colloquially known as the New Cut, and a welcome breakfast eaten in *Teal*'s hatches. The factories and housing estates alternated with large areas of overgrown industrial wasteland and there were good views in both directions from the embankments which, along with the deep cuttings, enabled the New Cut to maintain its straight line. Occasional islands appeared with a channel on either side. These places were where the boats used to be gauged and a close track kept of their movements for the purposes of toll collection. Some of them had little brick huts built on the central island to house the toll keepers but these, where they still existed, were now derelict and overgrown and we passed through unchecked and unnoticed.

At Newtown Junction we had difficulty with the sharp right-angled turn into the Rushall Canal, which would take us on towards Cannock. The space available at the junction is little more than a boat's length, chips and paint marks on the copings around the turn indicated that we were not alone in our problem. Phyllis was still clearing up in her cabin as we approached the junction with me sitting idly for once in the hatches as, drawn up tightly on the cross-straps, *Teal* virtually steered herself. I had no real idea of where we were, only realising that we were going to make the turn when *Warbler* eased off and Ronnie indicated his intentions by pointing. Phyllis, alerted by the change of engine note, emerged to take in the situation. She had only done this trip once before, but she remembered this!

"Tricky," she opined. "Very tricky, especially coming back loaded."

Round swung *Warbler*, almost in her own length, and clouted the concrete with a resounding bang causing her to lurch and water to slop from full cans on to the cabin top. *Teal* followed round and Phyllis diplomatically made a cup of tea which she took along to Ronnie. He did not refer to the incident and we both knew better than to offer any unsolicited comments!

I bow-hauled the Ganzy Seven and after a further mile came the Mosses Two, above which we joined the Daw End branch of the Wyrley & Essington Canal which took us on a level pound, characterised by a number of sharp turns, to Catshill Junction. Here an easier turn saw us swing right on to the main line of the Wyrley & Essington before, after only a short distance, finally turning left up the Anglesey Arm, just above the top of the disused Ogley Locks. The Wyrley and Essington originally continued on down this long flight to link up with the Coventry Canal at Huddlesford Junction, the obvious route for the Hayes Cocoa traffic. From Anglesey Basin to Braunston was 60 miles and 47 locks via Huddlesford whilst the way we would go was 59 miles and 84 locks which meant considerably more labour, especially for the unfortunate bow-hauler struggling along the grimy towpaths of Birmingham and the Black Country. It was early afternoon when we arrived at the loading place in Anglesey Basin. 'Joey' boats lined the canal on both sides and only a narrow channel led through to the loading chute. Cannock, I had been assured, was a very efficient place for loading and it was supposedly possible to be in and out of the length in half an hour, all of which seemed rather improbable to me. Also long distance cabin boats, of which we appeared to be the only ones there, were normally given priority. Be that as it may, after two and a half days trying to empty at Tyseley I was not optimistic and viewed the assembled mass of 'joey' boats with considerable gloom. I worried needlessly!

"Hallo, my dooks," greeted the foreman with a beaming smile. "Heard you'm were coming. Two pair for Nestle's ain't it?"

This, by canal standards, was unbelievably efficient. *Warbler* was in the length and under the loading chute as Alec was still picking his way in. Coal poured down into the boat with us hurriedly pulling her along somewhat to fill the gaps. Out went *Warbler* and in went *Teal*. I now found myself with the task of trimming the motor's load with a Size 8 shovel in order to ensure that she would 'swim' well on our long journey south. Ronnie supervised *Teal* in the length whilst Phyllis and I, once trimming was completed, laid the top planks along the coal to the mast, checked her side cloths were still rolled tight, and mopped her off. It was interesting to see what a remarkably small amount of dust had accumulated here compared with some later experiences in the Warwickshire coalfield. Having winded first we pulled back and attended to *Teal* in similar fashion, as Ronnie helped Alec with the other pair. Phyllis was very particular about getting *Teal* trimmed just so, spending quite some time eyeing her up before pronouncing herself satisfied.

"Don't grumble," she insisted. "If she don't swim right she'll be twice as hard to steer, and you won't like that!"

Amazingly, not only had we loaded the same day but there was still some time in hand. Nobody particularly wanted to lay for the night at Anglesey so, with *Redshank* leading, we retraced back down the arm and stopped for the night by a pub called 'The Traveller's Rest', known on the cut simply as 'The Traveller'. Alec, especially, had a great fondness for beer and the comradeship of the public bar after his day's work was complete and I had come to realise that our stopping places nearly always coincided with the proximity of a pub approved of by him. I gave 'The Traveller' a miss that night and, with *Warbler*'s cabin all to myself, had a good wash-down and an early night as tomorrow looked likely to be a very hard day indeed. Boating could be very tiring and I was still only fifteen, not by any means fully grown. Yet I was keeping up with the others as well as I could, accepting whatever task was asked of me without demur. I still enjoyed it all and, with each day bringing fresh and vivid new experiences, remained as 'happy as Larry'. Gradually my body was hardening to the life and, as each day passed by, I grew stronger and more adept at my tasks. Given six months I would have been completely hardened, finishing days with plenty of energy left for beer and darts, but this process was still happening and that night I slept like the proverbial log.

The next day did indeed prove to be very hard, particularly for me as I continued in my role as bow-hauler. I was not yet considered skilled enough to work *Warbler* through the locks on my own which would have allowed Ronnie to take a turn on the line, but Phyllis and I knew our respective roles with *Teal* and things went well enough. The difference between bow-hauling *Teal* empty and getting her moving with twenty-seven tons of coal on board was rather greater than I had realised. Leaning resolutely into the line at the top of the Mosses, I proceeded to exert a fair degree of effort. Very little happened! *Teal* lay deep in the narrow lock and I had to get her on her way before Phyllis could draw her paddle to help 'flush' her out, drawing too early could cause a flush back which would hold her in against all my efforts. Gritting my teeth I took a fresh grip and strained every sinew, my reward was *Teal* slowly beginning to move, gathering pace as Phyllis 'flushed her', before once again banging the gates to for Ronnie. He, in turn, would start the lock for *Greenshank* and a similar procedure would facilitate 'Redshank'. Not all crews worked in this fashion, indeed 'motor first' seemed to be the common practice on the Northampton Arm. It was a matter of personal preference and the nature of the crew, with two-handed pairs having to adopt a much more rigorous and time consuming way of working. Mosses Two and the Ganzy Seven were followed, after both boats had bumped round the turn at Newtown Junction, by a most welcome respite along the New Cut. It was however something of a short-lived respite as all too soon the long line was out again for the New Thirteen. We were concentrating hard on our individual tasks and food took second-place that day, consisting of 'doorstep' cheese sandwiches, made with extra thick slices and followed by plenty of tea, all quickly prepared as the locks emptied and filled.

By Salford Junction I was already feeling tired and could now see only too clearly why the Hayes traffic used the Grand Union route south, rather than going straight on around the 'Bottom Road' and then along the northern Oxford to Braunston. Those lovely wide Grand Union locks began to look increasingly attractive as we arrived at the bottom of Saltley where it began to rain, deceptively gently at first but then quickly intensifying into a steady downpour that looked very much as if it was set in for the rest of the day. With coat collar turned up I glanced balefully at the oil-streaked and filthy chamber of the lock, reminding myself that I was on holiday and enjoying the cut! The life of the cut provided a constant series of contrasts, that journey up Saltley in the rain being something to set against the very different circumstances of bow-hauling in glorious sunshine down the exquisitely rural flight at Claydon on the southern Oxford. In a very short space of time we both became as filthy as our surroundings. The rain made it all so much worse, with the line dragging on the towpath and becoming impossible to handle without covering your hands in a sticky black mess. I trudged stoically upwards, harder now because Phyllis couldn't flush me out and the effort was all mine. Her timing, as she drew a short couple of turns of paddle and then ran up the lockside to start the topgate swinging, before scrambling aboard to steer and leaving the lock to empty behind her, had to be perfect. If it was'nt, then either I would be unable to get *Teal* out of the lock against the pull of the paddle or she would be too late to get back on board! Her boots were leaving a filthy mess in *Teal*'s hatches, despite the trick of putting old flat cardboard boxes down to catch the worst; it would be scrubbed off later, but that was yet another job and so it went on.

More ribaldry ensued at the factory as soon as my bedraggled figure trudged into view, the torrential rain still sheeting down from a leaden sky.

"Come on! Gee up!"

"You need two more legs, mate!"

"Faster! Faster!"

I was far too tired to even consider attempting any sort of response, trudging sourly past and reserving an occasional scowl for the most persistent of the grinning faces lining the open windows. Another brief respite along the intervening pound saw me drinking tea in *Teal*'s cabin, resting my aching shoulders and girding myself up for the final flight at Camp Hill, beyond which lay the welcome broad waters of the Grand Union. As *Teal* rose in the top lock my temporarily flagging spirits rose with her. Shunting yards on the left, Sampson Road Wharf on the right with a pair of BW boats waiting to empty alongside, and in the middle the wide oil-streaked and rain-spattered waters of the main line and its lovely wide locks! I pulled *Teal* out and unhooking the long line from her mast thankfully stowed it in the space below the fore-hatch. It would come back out again tomorrow in order to be towed behind for a while to get it clean, but there was no more bow-hauling on this trip!

I looked at Phyllis. She was soaked, her long corn-coloured hair plastered down with rain and her battered old coat begrimed from her efforts in the flights. We were both very tired but neither of us said so, there was after all such a thing as pride! I smiled ruefully at her, as the lock emptied behind us and *Warbler* could be heard 'bomping' up the last pound.

"Well done, John!"

"Well steered!" I responded, summoning up my last dregs of energy to go and draw for Ronnie.

Enough was enough! The rain was still bucketing down and there was a fair bit of necessary cleaning to do after the efforts of the day. Nobody argued when Alec suggested that a pint in the nearby 'Woodman' would not go amiss that night. What a good idea! A very good idea! We got ourselves tied up very quickly indeed before he could change his mind!

The next day, as so often happens in summer, was just as different. We got going at just after six with a warm sun already piercing the smoke and dust of the shunting yards opposite. *Warbler* led the way on the long three hour pound out to Knowle and my spirits rose as green fields appeared beyond Solihull, the pleasant prospect of several days of rural boating lay ahead. Different cuts appeal to different people. I am well aware that some canal aficionados are very keen on the industrial scene surrounding the BCN and it certainly has a grimy charm, but there are problems which I always found outweighed this attraction. The BCN often runs close to large housing estates and the passage through these can sometimes become rather hairy. Groups of youths had a nasty habit of collecting on bridges and pelting the boat crews with whatever came to hand and, when they weren't doing that, they were dumping all manner of rubbish into the cut which slowed us down, often resulting in a 'bladeful' which could take some time to clear. Prince offered us some defence, at least against the stone throwers. Alec had two dogs, Prince and Sally. Prince was a large black labrador who was highly effective at guarding the boats, allowing no-one whom he didn't know to even think about putting a foot aboard. He also thoroughly enjoyed chasing gangs of unpleasant youths! Alec would have him off and running free along the towpath in likely trouble spots and, on the word of command, he would bark and snarl in a most aggressive fashion offering an effective protection to the boats. Sally was a small Jack Russell bitch and a very good ratter. Woe betide any rat who considered making a home on our boats, their life expectancy was very short! She was often put 'off' in the evening and, having done 'her business', frequently returned with a rat, earning high praise for her efforts! She was Lil's especial favourite and lived a comfortable life in the butty cabin, unlike Prince who had a kennel under the cratch although he seemed happy enough with it. Coming back to my original point, I preferred the country canals, and breathed deeply in the clean air as yesterday's grime was furiously attacked and the boats were restored to their spotless glory. Looking back from scrubbing *Teal*'s white strings at the work going on behind us, I knew that both pairs would once again be a source of pride as we locked down together in the welcome broad locks at Knowle.

Two pairs of Willow Wrens were met near Shrewley. They confidently assured us of a 'good road' down Hatton, but this proved not to be the case when we arrived above the top lock only to find the chamber empty and one bottom gate open. Back in my now familiar role as lockwheeler I spotted the culprit from the top of the 'thick'. A small pleasure cruiser was happily descending about seven locks ahead of us and beyond them the locks were indeed ready. They had every right to be there and I could hardly ask them to give way to working boats when they were seven locks ahead. Besides, it was a lovely sunny day, there was no bow-hauling and only one bottom gate to close! Like them, I was happy enough as we descended towards the tall tower of Warwick Cathedral ahead, after four journeys through here inside a fortnight Hatton was really becoming quite familiar!

From the bottom of Itchington we reached Braunston by early afternoon and I began to wonder how the traditional stop at Cosgrove would be fitted in on this particular trip. I soon found out as, instead of going straight on into the bottom lock whose gates stood invitingly open, *Redshank* and *Greenshank* breasted-up and tied below the lock opposite the Willow Wren yard. We followed suit and engines coughed to a standstill. Was the day's work over so early?

"Don't you wander off, young John!" said Alec jocularly. "It's washing time!"

Because of our quick turn-arounds recently, and *Greenshank*'s diversion to Warwick Wharf, precious little washing of clothes had been achieved beyond handbowls full of socks, undies, and the odd shirt. I was as grubby as everyone else but had said nothing, there would be time enough for washing when we had stopped moving. However the situation had now reached the critical point where everybody was out of clothes and

Lil had decided on drastic measures. That afternoon we were to do the washing. We would also then be nicely back on course to tie at Cosgrove the following night! Neatly done all round! In these days of automatic washing machines, with launderettes in every suburb, doing the washing sounds easy enough, but for Lil it wasn't that simple.

Firstly Alec had to light the big old coal brazier. This was set up on the side of the towpath and was vital in maintaining a constant supply of hot water. The dolly tub was brought out for the pile of dirty clothes to be given a good pounding and an old hand mangle was set up for the wringing. Everything that needed washing from both pairs was piled in a big heap and Lil took charge of the situation. As usual each of us had our part to play. My bit seemed to consist of staggering backwards and forwards from the tap, which was adjacent to the bottom lock and at least fifty yards away, carrying enormous quantities of water both for washing and rinsing. Alec kept the brazier burning brightly, heating the tubs of water whilst Phyllis mangled and Young Lily hung out on long lines set up along both butties. Lil did the nitty-gritty. Scrubbing clothes on a board, pounding them furiously with the dolly, then a really thorough rinsing before finally passing them over to Phyllis on the mangle. And Ronnie? Ah, well! Ronnie seemed to have disappeared over to the yard on unknown business, obviously this couldn't possibly have waited, and unsurprisingly only reached a conclusion as the last clothes were being pegged out and all the equipment was being restowed under *Greenshank*'s cratch. All very convenient, as Phyllis tartly put it upon his return!

It was a gloriously warm summer's afternoon giving perfect conditions for drying clothes. By late evening all the washing had dried and been put away in the various drawers, except for a very few precious items that merited ironing. These were left in a neat pile in the corner of *Greenshank*'s side-bed and would be dealt with during the passage of the long pounds which awaited us tomorrow. One snag developed and it was entirely our own fault. The locks at Braunston were padlocked shut at 10pm, except for Sundays when a 6pm closure was the fashion. To ensure first passage in the morning it was the custom for boats arriving after 'the lock was on' to tie up with their fore-ends resting on the gates, thus making it impossible for anyone else to get ahead in the morning when the lock came off at 6am. Upon our return from the 'Admiral Nelson' at just after half past ten we found ourselves still alone at the bottom lock. It had been a warm evening and the smooth cool beer had made us mellow, so much so that nobody could be bothered to move the pairs up a few yards thereby blocking the bottom lock and guaranteeing a good road in the morning. No one else would come now surely? At just after midnight I was awoken by the steady beat of an Armstrong as it eased down before passing us and tying half-in and half-out of the empty bottom lock. Peeping through the door-holes in the gloom I could just make out 'Samuel Barlow Coal Co Ltd' as the butty drifted past. Our good road had been snaffled and serve us right for not moving! It wasn't too bad really because we were only going to Cosgrove and the Barlow pair would surely go further, making the most of the long summer evenings and pressing ahead. In any event, the plan was for us to go second tomorrow and so I would had to have lockwheeled the three flights anyway, but Young Lily wouldn't have needed to!

The weather was again glorious and I came in for a good deal of practice on *Teal* through the Blisworth pound as Phyllis, having dealt with all her domestics, joined Ronnie on the motor. I enjoyed being on the butty and zealously tracked along in *Warbler*'s wake, being especially pleased to go right round the outside of the big Railway Turn and never a touch! Phyllis dropped back at Candle Bridge, but I was allowed to continue through the tunnel whilst she prepared our tea ready to be eaten in the flight to come.

"No bumping about!" she grinned, as we disappeared into the darkness at an alarming speed with me concentrating for all I was worth as I buttied through for the first time. Two pairs of BW's headed back empty provided an extra test, but I was getting much better and, apart from the inevitable light brush against the wall as we passed, I came through cleanly enough and was happily eating my jam sandwich as we came abreast above the top of Stoke. The pattern from Stoke was much the same as that of the first trip, but the difference lay in myself. An awful lot had been learned in a short time and I was now much more at ease with the work, more knowledgeable about what to do and when to do it. I also felt markedly stronger, getting less tired as the days progressed and oddly proud of my calloused hands and the ingrained grime that soap alone would not move. In short I had become part of the scene and to a lay person would have been indistinguishable from the others. I was also completely and utterly happy with my lot.

From Cosgrove we made Berko and thence to Hayes Cocoa, arriving in the light this time after a smooth run down. Emptying the next day, we dropped down to Brentford and tied adjacent to the lock on the towpath side to await orders. My holiday was running on now, the end of August was rapidly approaching and the shadow of the schoolroom was falling across me once more. It was not a pleasant thought and I would much rather have stayed boating, but my parents quite rightly would never have countenanced this and it seemed likely that I would have to leave the boats at Stoke on their return journey to Birmingham. For two days we waited, having been promised our share of a lighter full of spelter which was supposed to be coming up from the docks, but obstinately refused to appear. Waiting around like this tended to become tedious. All the odd jobs could be done at leisure, but there weren't that many of those and very soon the boats were in pristine apple pie order with nothing really to do. I had even finished all my schoolwork for the holiday! Even more annoying was the arrival of a very large quantity of wheat for transhipment to Wellingborough on the river Nene. Pairs of BW boats coming down from the Mills were being loaded and turned round almost immediately, whilst we sat tucked up in our corner watching the busy scene from across the wide waters. It was all very frustrating, especially as I could sense my time running out ever more quickly.

I wandered off to explore Brentford, walking along from the tall bridge where the High Street crossed the canal. Durham Wharf, where the 'Gaffer', Leslie Morton, had his small office aided and abetted by Stanley, the clerk, lay down an alley on the left and opposite this was Alec's favourite pub hereabouts, 'The Six Bells', which I had yet to venture into. It was a popular haunt of the boating and river fraternity and I would, in time, spend a number of increasingly well lubricated evenings there, but that was all in the future and today I was more interested in the unusually high cables strung along above the roadway. Trolley buses still ran through here and I watched their silent progress with great fascination. They were restricted in their movements by the range of the side to side sweep of the pick-up bar located on their roof but, nevertheless, had the advantage over the trams of being able to move in to the side of the road to pick-up and discharge passengers without blocking the street. Like the trams I had seen in Birmingham they were quiet, efficient and non-polluting and were soon to vanish in the wave of modernisation and change which was about to engulf the country.

I did not realise at the time that I was living through a short golden period in history. The war was over and the years of austerity which had followed were now superseded by a simple prosperity, with low inflation and very little unemployment. The branch lines of England still rattled along in the twilight of the steam age, little knowing that the Beeching axe and dereliction would soon be the fate of so many of them. Traffic on the canals was still vigorous in many areas and, although fading in others, none of us realised in 1958 how little time there was left. Within five years everything would change, leaving only a forlorn remnant to struggle on for a few more years before long distance boating and the way of life became a memory. On that morning in Brentford, however, the cut still remained a peaceful world of its own, finely balanced between the old ways and what was to replace them. Slowly diminishing carrying fleets shared the waterways with a small number of pleasure craft and only a few hire boats, nearly all of which were crewed by serious canal enthusiasts. It was a brief halcyon time that I was living through, a time when my mother could sit on the steps of her cottage at Stoke Bruerne on a warm Saturday afternoon in July and be disturbed only by an occasional passing pair, or friendly villagers taking a stroll up the towpath in the sun. Peace and tranquillity reigned unchallenged, but as any reader who has visited Stoke Bruerne on a comparable day recently will attest, not for very much longer.

Other than shops there did not seem to be a great deal else of interest in the High Street and I drifted back to the boats to find we had received unexpected orders in my absence. The flow of BW boats down from the

ROUND AGAIN

Mills to load for Wellingborough had temporarily ceased. The BW fleet, though large, was widely scattered and there was a sudden shortage of carrying capacity, just when it was most needed with this large quantity of wheat for Whitworth's Mill. Leslie Morton, never slow to seize an opportunity for his burgeoning fleet, got us the sub-contract and, on the afternoon of our third day at Brentford, *Warbler* and *Teal* moved across the basin to load for the Nene river. This was truly a gift from the gods! Calculating the days left to me I happily discovered that if everything went without a hitch, then I would be able to complete this trip and return upstream to Northampton with the boats before the end of the month. Absolutely perfect! Loading was by grab leaving little for us to do, other than adjust the position of the boats and keep a weather eye open for any unforeseen problem that might develop. Over swung the grab into the lighter, alongside which we lay and, having bitten deep into it, would swing back across to us disgorging a golden flow of wheat directly into the hold. The lighter would rise fractionally higher and we would correspondingly drop an inch or two deeper in the water. Like coal, the wheat needed to be loaded evenly along the hold in order for the boat to lie level and straight with everything nicely distributed. Also, under no circumstances, was the wheat to get wet and we would sheet up fully for this trip, another new experience for me.

Once *Warbler* was loaded we swopped the boats round and, leaving Phyllis to watch *Teal*'s progress, Ronnie and I set about the business of sheeting up. As with the spelter, top planks were put up along the stands and secured in place in the same fashion with side cloths then unrolled and drawn up tight by means of the strings over the top planks. This much I had done before, but the wheat still lay open to the elements beneath me as I knelt on the top planks and tightened my last string, whilst Ronnie crawled along checking that I had got everything tight enough. It was now time for the top cloths to be pulled out from under the cratch and added to the jigsaw. Willow Wren had green side and top cloths, some adorned with the company's name, whilst the BW boats almost universally sported black top cloths also suitably emblazoned with their name in big white letters. Top cloths are essentially large pieces of tarpaulin and they were draped in equal measure over the top planks and down to overlap the side cloths, being secured in place by yet more strings, running through the little rings to be found neatly spaced along the gunwale and back up, and again knotted tightly into place. Any rain now descending would run down the top cloths, on to the side cloths and continue down over the gunwale and into the water, leaving the cargo snug and dry within. A deeply laden narrow boat, completely sheeted up, is a heart warming sight and *Warbler*, with her bright paintwork and polished brasses, looked an absolute picture as the afternoon sun shone down on the prosaic scene. *Teal* followed, but time was running out. Alec would load in the morning and his pair towered high above us, as we lay four-abreast in the tranquillity of the warm summer evening.

I found myself drafted in to help Alec sheet up the following morning. Young Lily had opted to accompany Ronnie and Phyllis up the Hanwell Locks, upon the clear understanding that they would wait for us at Cowley. It had been decided that extra loading and sheeting up would be good practice for me and, doubtless, the others enjoyed their bit of time together as they went ahead on their own. Lil had gone off shopping, leaving Alec and me working steadily together as first *Greenshank* and then *Redshank* went under the grab. Despite working as two pairs, I had spent most of the summer concerning myself primarily with getting *Warbler* and *Teal* ahead and this was the first appreciable amount of time that I had been alone with Alec. We worked happily side by side that morning, chatting about the cut as we sheeted up and prepared the pair for the journey ahead. All was ready for departure, but Lil had still not returned and so I prepared to polish the outside brasses whilst we waited.

"She's gossiping," announced Alec. "Always takes hours to shop when she's here."

This was very probably so. Boating was, in many ways, a solitary life with long hours spent steering along with the boats separated by a seventy foot line. Even in the locks the well oiled routine left little time for anything more than a casual remark. It was thus only natural that Lil should take the chance to catch up on all the news before the exigencies of travelling took over once more. Alec used the time to encourage my efforts and to find out more about me and my family, where I went to school, and what I wanted to do with myself. On the latter question I was vague, but only because I really had absolutely no idea! I knew deep down that boating on a permanent basis was unlikely ever to be possible. Much as I loved the way of life I already knew that the combination of family pressures and that kernel of ambition deep within myself would drive me in other directions. Nonetheless, I was determined to enjoy it all while the chance was there, for now tomorrow could look after itself.

I felt deeply grateful to Alec and his family for sharing their life with me and for their many small kindnesses and tolerant manner as I learned the finer points of boating, for my part I was always determined to 'do my bit' and went to some lengths to keep myself usefully busy. It was the first time I had been in *Redshank* as, at Alec's bidding, I descended into the cabin to find the rags and Brasso which were in one of the soap holes by the doors. The cabin was immaculate and remarkably tidy, the range gleamed with a glossy black sheen, lace-edged plates hung down the side of the table cupboard, and crocheting hung in neat folds along the tops of the bright flowered curtains shrouding the bed space. Patterned blue lino gleamed from floor and side bed and a circle of lacework adorned the porthole. The bed was up and stowed away in the bed cupboard and all was pristine. I sat briefly on the side bed and looked at the lovely castle, surrounded by clusters of roses, which adorned the outside of the table cupboard, twin brass rods with rosettes at one end shone above. Sticks and coal were neatly piled in the coal box and a small radio seemed to be the only concession to modern life. It was a sight to behold and a real credit to Young Lily whose home, currently shared by night with Phyllis, it was. I was still finishing off the large brass eagle, whose claws gripped the top of *Redshank*'s pigeon box, when Lil eventually returned, loaded down with bags in either hand and ignoring Alec's badinage about 'tittle-tattle' as she climbed aboard. She enjoyed a 'tattle' from time to time, it did her good and she was content as she unpacked her bags and stored everything neatly away, whilst the kettle was set to boil for a much-needed cup of tea.

We would travel abreast to the top of Hanwell and thus there was no actual need to wait for the kettle to come to the boil as the tea could be handed back and forth on the move. *Redshank* was started on the press of a button and quietly 'bonked-bonked' away, warming up as I untied the fore-ends and pushed off a little bit before running back down the side of the lighter to drop on to the counter. Alec and Lil were sitting comfortably in *Greenshank*'s hatches with their tea and my mug was passed over.

"Go ahead,then!" grinned Alec.

I needed no second bidding! *Redshank*'s clutch had only a short movement, compared with the long shove required on *Warbler*, and I quickly had her in gear and wound on the speed wheel to 'get 'em ahead'. We were off again! My spirits soared as the bubbling wash ran out behind us and the heavily laden pair passed under the high railway bridge and headed for the flight. I felt very proud steering this beautifully turned-out pair on such a warm summer's day, this was what I had long dreamed about and every minute was gratefully savoured! It was only destined to be a short steer with Alec taking charge as the bottom gates of the Hanwell flight loomed into view. A 'good road' ensued as we met an empty lighter, pulled from the towpath by a small tractor, just emerging from the bottom lock and so everything was easy. Lil got sandwiches ready up the locks, emerging only to step off and climb the steps to shut the bottom gate. On Alec's signal, I wound up a ground paddle to check the pair's forward progress before running down to close the gate on the motor's side. Lil didn't seem in any hurry and left it to me to run back up and draw the other ground paddle. Gate paddles, if drawn too early, would flood the fore-ends and so I watched and waited until the sill was covered, before inching up a bit of gate paddle and sending a gentle flush across the sill to swirl around the boats. Once they had risen high enough it was up with the rest of the paddle, cross over, up with the other side, and the lock would rapidly fill. Gate paddles have now become a memory on the Grand Union due to the dangers of inexperienced tyros flooding their boats and possibly sinking them, as could easily happen, especially at somewhere like Denham Deep. They did, however, speed things up very considerably and lockage today is a slow process compared to the roar of the incoming waters of yesteryear. Up we went, meeting two more empty lighters and a pair of BW's with orders for Wellingborough in the deep wide pounds between the locks.

At the top lock I dropped down on to the fore-ends as the boats rose and untied them, prior to laying the loop of the long snubber across *Greenshank*'s cratch in such a way as to make it easy for the motor steerer to take it as the boats singled out for the pound ahead. The motor steerer was to be me!

"Go ahead, John!" invited Alec, as I came back down the lockside and stowed my windlass half under the slide. "You be alright?"

It was a rhetorical question and we both knew it. I was only too eager! The pound was deep and easy and I was now experienced enough to be trusted alone on the motor, at least along this fairly straightforward section. Off I went out of the lock, nudging the gate open with the fore-end and picking up the line which I hooked on to the dolly on the counter, before 'holding back' as the line ran out. The trick is to be virtually stationary as the line tightens allowing the butty to respond with a slight jerk, a sudden hard jerk which might well snap the line is to be avoided being poor boating and incurring an extra splicing job. With both boats moving you can then steadily wind it on and 'get 'em ahead'. This manoeuvre successfully accomplished I settled down to enjoy the pound, looking back from time to time at the oncoming bluff bows of *Greenshank* brushing aside the motor's wash. The weather had remained very settled and the sun shone down as I eased off to pass the moored boats at Bull's Bridge, and then again to pass Jack Monk's pair of Willow Wrens emptying at Hayes Cocoa. I stood on the footboard in the sunshine, sleeves rolled up and the boat responding to every movement of the brass tiller bar clasped firmly in my hand. Feeling supremely content I could very happily have steered all day, however all too quickly we were passing the entrance to the long straight Slough Arm and easing off to enter Cowley Lock, beyond which I could see the waiting *Warbler* and 'Teal'. I had never steered the motor into an empty lock before, being still not entirely safe at getting *Warbler* into reverse every time, but it was clear from Alec taking up position on *Greenshank*'s fore-end ready to coil in the line that I was now expected to take *Redshank* in. Worse, the others had heard our engine and were clustered at the lockside to greet us. I concentrated hard and willed myself not to foul it up. Slowed down rather more than was strictly necessary I aimed the fore-end for the bricks about two thirds of the way up the chamber and then held back hard, thankfully she swung neatly across and laid herself perfectly along the wall leaving a clear run in for *Greenshank*.

"Good lad!" murmured Alec, as we all swopped round. We would go second today which meant Young Lily, with a good road ahead, would not have to lockwheel. I would, but then I enjoyed it!

As we were only planning to go to Ricky that night I did not find myself under undue pressure that afternoon. We went below Uxbridge and at Denham Deep I leapt off at the last bridge hole before it, pedalling along hard to empty the deepest of all the G.U. locks as Ronnie idled up. Having thus saved my legs a little I was content to pedal steadily ahead through that glorious summer's afternoon. Mostly I found myself catching up and helping Alec through his locks, before setting them for Ronnie. We climbed steadily on what turned out to be the hottest afternoon of the summer, the wooden lock beams warm to sit upon and the trees nodding drowsily above the dry and dusty towpath. I was feeling quite proud of my brown arms and face, but it was nothing when compared to Alec who seemed to have turned a rich mahogany, doubtless compounded by years of exposure to the elements. Sitting contentedly on the beam and watching Stockers Lock emptying out in a swirling bubbling surge, slowly diminishing as the levels began to equalise, I recalled the struggle up Saltley on the journey south. Filth, mud, rain and puddles had been our lot and now it was greenery, cracks in the earth, and hot sun. It was such contrasts as these which made up one element of the charm of the life, the struggles with the first enhancing and giving true weight to the warmth and beauty of the second. Philosophical musings were interrupted by the arrival of *Warbler*! I hurriedly opened the gates and dropped paddles, 'getting 'em ahead' remained the priority in sun, rain, hail or storm! We tied above Batchworth Lock at Ricky that night with the air hanging warm around us. Not often is an evening so comfortable in England and we made the most of it, eating dinner in the butty hatches and puttering gently at odd jobs until the darkness finally overtook us. Even then, we still stood around chatting and content, all reluctant to let go of such a beautiful day.

Needless to say it didn't last! England being what it is, a light breeze had got up in the morning and I felt the need of my old and rather oil-stained jacket as I lockwheeled up through Cassio Park and the Mills. Barlow pairs going back empty to Suttons had again given us a 'bad road' for the day. Nevertheless, our three-handed routine was well practiced now and steady incident-free progress saw us make good time that morning. School seemed to be another world inhabited by a different person, but I knew that this was not really the case. I was that person! I determined to squeeze every drop of enjoyment out of these last few days before the life of rules and restrictions claimed me again. Things improved through Boxmoor and jackets were soon off again, although still the light breeze persisted indicating a possible deterioration in the weather. Alec seemed to have little sense of urgency on this trip and our pace seemed almost relaxed, especially when compared to some of the earlier boating. Cosgrove was a factor, of course. By pushing on hard from Brentford we would have gone through there in the middle of the day, taking things just that little bit steadier meant an evening arrival became attainable. It wasn't always possible to so arrange things as to stop at Cosgrove on every trip, but we managed it that summer!

Crossing the summit we tied at the bottom of Maffers, early enough for me to explore the first mile or so of the narrow arm leading off to Aylesbury. The arm began in interesting fashion with a double staircase lock, similar to Botterham on the Staffs & Worcs, and then ran down fairly straight through a steady series of locks. The contrast in towpaths was immediately noticable. On the main line above the path was clearly defined by the bicycle wheels of the hurrying crews, the northbound chasing along to get the two below Maffers ready and the southbound heading for Maffers itself. Here on the arm the path was smooth and grassy. Few cycles passed this way and those that did were fishermen, the arm was very little used at that time and days would pass with no traffic disturbing the placid waters of the lock pounds. Ambling back up in the still summer's evening I thought of the narrow Northampton arm ahead and my meeting with my old friend, Meadows. What a surprise he would get when 'them old Willer-Wrens' turned up at the top lock! Bow-hauling again, of course. I eyed the Aylesbury arm speculatively with a bow-haulers gaze. Not too bad really. Straight pounds, a good grip for the feet, but how deep was it? You're never likely to find out, I told myself, nothing much comes down here now. In this I was later to be proved wrong, but it seemed unlikely at the time and I rejoined the main towpath as a few small bats came out to flicker along the hedges and swoop low across the quiet waters.

A very heavy dew presaged a fine day as I pedalled cheerfully along the next morning. Feet were soon wet in the soggy grass around the two below Maffers, or Peter's Two as they are sometimes known. Ignoring this minor discomfort I pedalled on to the swingbridge above the Nags Head Three, opening and closing it for the boats before hurrying on to set the locks. We were second that day and ahead Alec enjoyed a 'good road' which persisted all morning as we met a steady stream of southbound pairs working up through 'The Fields'. This was my fourth ride along here and I found myself increasingly getting to grips with the distances, timings, and other little details which make the lockwheeler's life just that little bit easier. By mid-morning the sun was well up and my feet had dried out nicely as we came down Horton Two, through Church and Grove, and on to Leighton Bridge where I was off again shopping. Phyllis had given me a list of mostly basic stuff such as bread, potatoes, sausages and so on, but I had to hurry as 'getting 'em ahead' did not include waiting about! By dint of some fierce pedalling and despite a full bag perched precariously on the handlebars I just managed to catch up as the pair was leaving Leighton Lock, at least avoiding having to ride part-way round the Jackdaw Pound for good measure.

Below Talbot's I was again entrusted with *Teal* as Phyllis joined Ronnie on the motor and, having done all *Teal*'s brasses down the pounds, she began a good polish all round on *Warbler*. At Finney I pleased myself by neatly bringing *Teal* to a halt with the strap in a most professional manner, the lock having been made ready for us by Bill Whitlock's pair of Barlows whom we had met just before the A5 bridge. Phyllis, much to my satisfaction, was inclined to stay on *Warbler* for a while longer and I was given stern warnings with regard to Finney Bridge which was notoriously tricky. Clearly I was becoming a more trusted member of the crew and I stood proudly on the footboard as *Teal* left the lock, excited at the prospect of further steering and looking out for the bridge turn ahead. Finney Bridge is a very tight 'S' bend and I remembered it well from *Canada Goose*. Ronnie eased *Warbler* through and I followed, concentrating hard and just avoiding the coping on the far side. It really was very tight and complicated by the narrow bridge hole in the middle, luckily I never had the misfortune to meet another pair there!

There are some big turns on the Finney pound and I found myself having to row the butty tiller hard in order to get *Teal* round. Just pushing the tiller over on the butty is not always enough to get her round a big turn, an extra 'kick' is needed, rather like 'winding it on' with the motor. This extra impetus is achieved by pushing the tiller out hard, back in, hard out and again, rowing the laden boat round with the big heavy rudder. It is surprisingly hard work, but my arms and wrists were much stronger now and with each turn successfully rounded my confidence and experience grew. Once beyond Black Horse Bridge the hard work of the Finney pound is done, the remainder being relatively easy for the steerer. Concentration is still needed, as to get stuck or hit the side along here would be highly embarrassing, but I could definitely relax a little, safe in the knowledge that careful steering would get me to Cosgrove with no problems. On we went, through the carriage works and over the aqueduct before breasting-up below the lock where *Redshank* and *Greenshank* were still lingering, more gossiping! Ronnie eased right down and I carefully laid *Teal* alongside, with *Warbler*'s engine note changing as he worked the rods to get reverse. Phyllis, on *Warbler*'s fore-end, looped a line around *Teal*'s stud and I accepted one from Ronnie at the same time. Together we eased *Teal* as *Warbler* held back, bringing the pair to a standstill in mid-channel, lines tightened and secured, with more clattering of rods leaving *Warbler* 'bomp-bomping' away in neutral. Eventually we locked through and tied on the big bend beyond the stop-place, looking forward to another evening of skittles at the 'Barley Mow'. A full moon illuminated our path back and the air was still warm, boding well for another hot day on the descent to the Nene river.

The next day promised to be an emotional one for me as, not only was it nearly the end of the holidays, but our route lay right through the very waters which I had haunted so assiduously in the early days of my fascination for the cut. I had come a long way since then and was now about to return as an integral part of a working pair, the dream had indeed become a reality. We led away that morning and I found myself on *Warbler*'s footboard from the beginning as Ronnie steered *Teal*, releasing Phyllis for her cabin chores and then enjoying his breakfast with her as we wound steadily up the easy pound leading to the bottom of Stoke. I knew it was the last sizeable pound before Wellingborough and I extracted every ounce of enjoyment from it, 'chucking-back' for practice and generally making the most of the time left to me before finally dropping back for breakfast at Grafton Bridge. Life had been good to us on this trip and the sun was shining down from another clear blue sky as we reached the top of Stoke, where I was promptly hailed by Sister Mary.

"Mr James told me you were due, dear," she began, her eagle eye looking me up and down to make sure I was still in one piece! "Have you enjoyed it?"

I assured her that I had loved it all, lavishly praising the kindness of everyone concerned, which pleased her enormously. Ronnie and Alec had been her choice for me, a marvellous choice and something for which I will always be grateful. In turn they grinned at Sister, insisted that they hadn't been working me too hard, but that I was 'a good lad' and welcome to come again!

It was Bank Holiday Monday and school began the following week. I knew this only too well, but was given a reminder just in case it should have slipped my mind!

"Your mother told me to tell you that you must come home on Saturday," continued Sister seriously. "You will make sure you do, won't you!"

I was surprised my family were not actually at Stoke, but Sister assured me all was well and that they were merely using the Bank Holiday to catch up on family visitations in the town, perhaps we would see each other as the boats passed through! Home now was only a bus ride away and I had already reluctantly worked out for myself that I would need Sunday for a bath and to get myself back into the school frame of mind. It was to be an important year, with GCEs at the end of it, and my love for the cut would have to be balanced against the demands of my future. After promising Sister faithfully that I would be home by Saturday without fail and having checked headlights in the lock, we waved goodbye and headed for the dripping gloom of the tunnel and the Northampton Arm beyond. It was surprisingly cold in the tunnel and Phyllis took refuge in the cabin, ostensibly to attack the breakfast washing up, leaving me to follow on behind *Warbler*. Once through Candle Bridge she took over again, dispatching me along the top planks to extract the long line from *Teal*'s fore-end, setting it up to run from the mast before rejoining her for the turn into the arm. This pound was so familiar to me from the towpath, but today was special. Today I belonged. Not simply a spectator, but part of the scene and therein lay the essential difference.

Ronnie held back with a great clattering of rods and noisy 'bomping', allowing *Teal* to drift past in the narrow waterway before I brought her to a halt with a couple of turns round the stump, her bows nudging against the top lock of the arm. For reasons which were never really clear to me we were again to go down first, which gave us quite a hard job. All the locks were empty, although at least the bottom gates were shut in most cases, and I would have to go down to draw paddles on these whilst *Teal*'s lock was emptying, before running back to pick up the towline. Phyllis would again be 'starting' the locks for *Warbler*, just as she had done in the Black Country. It promised to be a busy day, but it was pleasant enough. Green countryside, a sunny day, and most of the locks close together, it was a case of sleeves rolled up and off we go! Greatly to my disappointment there was no sign of Meadows that day, his cottage looked shut-up and no-one came out to greet us or lend a hand, which I had been sure would happen. I later found out that nothing untoward had occurred, he had merely been visiting his friend's allotment in Blisworth and, as is the way sometimes in life, we had simply missed each other. Down the Rothersthorpe Thirteen we went, our team work honed to a nicety by the experiences to and from Cannock. Little was said, we both knew our parts and the locks slowly succeeded one another, as the 'Blizzy Flyer' puffed past on the two coach shuttle service up and down the branch. It was certainly nicer than the last time we had worked *Teal* together. Grass was under my feet and birds chirped happily in the warm summer sun, the water running through the overflows was clean enough for me to wipe the sweat from my face, all a distinct improvement on the joys of Saltley in the rain! Pounds on the arm were surprisingly deep and bow-hauling, although tiring in the hot sun, was not bedevilled by problems with gruesome submerged objects, as had happened to us in the New Thirteen at Perry Barr. The flight curved downwards into the valley and, glancing back, I could see Ronnie running about with *Warbler* with, every now and then, a brief glimpse of *Redshank* following him down. In those days the Arm was much more rural than is now the case, the M1 had yet to be built and the huge dual carriageway of the Blisworth by-pass was not even a figment of a planner's imagination. Instead the locks descended with only the occasional passing train to break the peace before the cut curved round the side of the deeply wooded Hunsbury Hill and came finally into the town at Cotton End.

At least there were only thirteen of them, I grimaced, as we waited for *Warbler* below the bottom lock, with both of us taking copious cupfuls of water straight out of the top of the can. My, it was warm! On we went and I found it fascinating. Reeds stretched far out into the water beyond the Rothersthorpe Bridge Lock leaving only a very narrow channel for the boats, steering was easy enough given the lack of width but passing another pair would have been very tricky in places. I had cycled up the path on the other side of those reeds so many times, but the view from here was quite different. Lounging contentedly at *Teal*'s tiller, whilst Phyllis produced the inevitable cheese sandwiches, I saw the Nene valley with fresh eyes. Once through Duston Lock the tentacles of the town slowly began to close in and, at the next and penultimate lock, we found ourselves in the shadow of the main line railway bridge towering above, with the Cotton End marshalling yards spread out across the lower level beyond. A rather dilapidated house stood by the lock housing the family of a 'Company' man; his wife came out to speak to us and drop a paddle as the southbound 'Royal Scot' thundered past overhead. That particular cottage has long since been demolished and it really must have been a rather unpleasant place to live, with smoke and soot descending from above at very regular intervals. I had the bike off for the final length of the arm in order to get the last lock ready for *Warbler* and also to get the drawbridge, adjacent to the big corrugated tin warehouse with an overhang for the boats to unload under, up ready for the pair to pass straight through. This bridge, habitually used as a playground by the local children, was badly off balance as a result of being so regularly bounced up and down upon, and I found myself literally having to hang from the chain before it reluctantly rose before the oncoming boats. Drawing the bottom paddles on the final lock I sniffed the pungent scent of hops emanating from the Northampton Brewery Company alongside South Bridge, across which a very familiar red double-decker bus was passing.

This was my home town. I had known it all my life, but now I saw everything anew as our engine note echoed under the bridge and we began our journey down the river. Passing through the town lock we found Becket's Park, normally very quiet on a weekday, thronged with a Bank Holiday crowd. Cruisers were moored all the way along the blue brick wall, curving along under the arched iron bridge giving access to the island between the lock and weir channels. Weston Boat Club, whose base was at the fourth lock downstream, had come up to the town for their annual festival and the river was busy as canoes and dinghys windmilled about. *Warbler* bomped through on tickover, Phyllis followed with me sitting on *Teal*'s cabin top, my back to the throng and hoping not to see anyone I knew. Canals were my secret alternative life and attempting to explain at school what I was doing on *Teal* was something I could do without. We slipped through the multitude unscathed and rounded the double curve by the outdoor Midsummer Meadow Swimming Pool, the tall cooling towers of the power station throwing a long shadow across the river as we passed, drawing away from the town now and heading towards the second lock at Rush Mills.

The Nene locks were different again with big wooden top gates, often with rounded rather than square ends to the balance beams, and just a single gate paddle each side to admit water. Many of the locks had a small hand rail which stretched only part-distance across the gates. This made the cross-over in the middle – completely bereft of any support – a hazardous undertaking, exceeded only by the occasional lock with no hand rails at all. On a dry sunny day such as this it was an exercise in concentration to cross these gates, on a wet day it would not be a prudent move! You could, of course, always be sensible and play safe by crossing the small bridge built at the tail of every lock. At the bottom end, a huge steel structure supported a massive guillotine gate which was raised and lowered by means of a very large fixed handle secured by a lock, the key for which Ronnie had obtained at the 'Company' houses on the towpath near South Bridge. Twenty-one turns were needed to raise the guillotine and the same number to lower it, the same magic number as at Hatton! In most of the locks the gate went up and down in the conventional guillotine manner but at some, Northampton and Rush Mills for example, the gates were of bascule design and swung out and upwards to leave a passage for the boats beneath. Care had to be taken to ensure that the boats were not sucked forwards and downwards when the guillotine was raised, straps came off the fore-ends of both boats and we took turns around the large black stumps provided expressly for the purpose of holding the boats back. I knew, from watching pairs on the river, that some crews went down breasted-up to Wellingborough but this was far too slow a procedure for Ronnie to contemplate, instead we ran singled-out along the pounds and brought the boats together above every lock. Given the number of pairs ahead of us it was perhaps inevitable that all the locks would be empty with the guillotine gate locked in the 'up' position, the Bank Holiday also meant that we met no empty pairs returning up the river bound for Suttons. The Nene was very quiet and I got in further exercise for the arm muscles by firstly winding the massive guillotine gates down and then up for us, and then down again and a paddle up to start the lock for Alec, before leaping aboard *Teal* waiting just below the bottom gate. Lockwheeling would have been very difficult on the river with the towpath obstructed by stiles and gates and virtually non-existent in some places. You could, as I knew, just about force a bike through, but the enormous effort required rendered it pointless and Ronnie was content for me to ride down the pounds on *Teal*.

We had had a good day and tied below Cogenhoe Lock that night, leaving just a short run to Wellingborough in the morning. The evening was warm and the sun sank in the west behind us, sending a long golden path of light along the river above the lockgates where I sat soaking up the scene. Moorhens and ducks pottered about around the boats, hopeful of any scraps that might come their way and a last blackbird scuttered among the trees. The sun had been very kind to us all the way up from Brentford, helping to make this latter part of my summer truly memorable. I sat that night at peace with myself, not really tired after the day's efforts, comfortable with it all. Everything seemed in balance that evening and a state of harmony prevailed. A beautiful day had been enjoyed in the open doing something I loved, now in the sylvan peace of evening there was time to reflect and place everything in its true perspective. I looked back down the lock to where the boats lay basking in the evening light. Alec was sitting in the butty hatches smoking a thin roll-up and resplicing a line, Lil had the handbowl on the slide and was rinsing out some 'smalls', laughter came from *Teal*'s cabin where Young Lily could be seen sitting on the footboard looking in at the other two. In a few short weeks these people had become my friends and I felt an immense affection for them. They had accepted me unquestioningly on Sister Mary's recommendation and had taught me an enormous amount, both about boating and about life. In turn I had given of my best so as to be worthy of their trust and friendship. It had truly been a fabulous summer, a time from this world that I would never forget.

There was no rush the next morning and it was gone nine o'clock before we started down those last few miles to Wellingborough which was reached around lunchtime. Here the true nature of the situation was revealed to my disbelieving gaze. Winding down the guillotine I counted ten pairs altogether, all loaded and waiting on the towpath side, and an eleventh pair across by the towering Mill having her cargo sucked up into its bowels. Bicycles lay on the grass, dogs wandered, and washing lines had been set up along the bank. It looked like a long wait. So much for my private plan to empty and accompany the boats back to Northampton for Saturday. It looked a forlorn hope. We locked through and took our places at the end of the line. Dropping down into the engine-hole I gloomily shut *Warbler*'s engine off for what must surely be the last time, certainly for this summer anyway. It transpired that the Mill was full and could only take more wheat as existing stocks were used up. Basically the wheat would be stored in the boats until needed, the crews receiving only 'waiting money' and the boats unavailable for any other work. It was costly and inefficient, but not an unusual practice in many parts of the system. Today was Tuesday. The foreman at the Mill seemed to feel that perhaps two pairs a day might be emptied, with Sunday being a day off this left us with about a week to wait. Alec was not happy himself and he sensed my disappointment almost at once.

"Never mind," he consoled. "You've done well on the other turn-rounds."

It was true. I had done well. We had emptied almost immediately at Hayes Cocoa on both occasions, had experienced few real delays at Brentford and the turn-round at Cannock would remain my fastest ever. Only the two and a half days at Tyseley had been frustrating, until now of course. This sort of queue was a classic case of bad organisation and planning by the powers-that-be. Some of the BW pairs ahead of us had already been there a week and it really was a total waste of everyone's time. A boat travelling empty earns no money, but sometimes it was unavoidable. However boats hanging around for days on end being used as grain hoppers was a ridiculous situation and spoke volumes about the administration and organisation of the British Waterways fleet.

My summer was over. I left the boats the next day carrying just my bag, leaving mattress and blankets to be dropped off at Stoke next time *Warbler* passed through. Goodbyes were brief, we all expected to meet up again as the pairs came through Stoke that winter and I was already hoping for further trips next year. I had yet to learn that nothing ever stays quite the same. Reaching the bridge, after walking down the long line of moored boats, I turned and looked back upon the scene. My gaze ran down the long succession of blue and yellow cabin sides to the green cabins with the roundel of 'my' boats, tucked in at the very end of the line. Phyllis was standing in the hatches vigorously polishing her chimney brasses with proprietorial pride, she had evidently been following my progress for there instantly came a beaming smile and a final wave. Raising my hand in a last sad farewell I turned away, walking pensively up the slope into the town for the bus that would take me home.

It was not an end, of course. The cottage was still there and the cut would always remain, but there could never be another summer quite the same. Things had changed. If anything my love of the canals had deepened but now, although I always remained interested in their history and their features, it was the way of life of the boat people that became my passion. At a very impressionable age their values became mine, the way of life something to be treasured even as it ran to its end. I had truly become a boatman and the cut had put its stamp on me forever.

*****

Chapter 6

Welsh Interlude

Upon my return I began gloomily to adjust back to home life and the prospect of a new term at school. As I had arrived home during the week we were all able to spend what seemed like the last week-end of summer over at Stoke Bruerne. The sun still shone and my spirits lifted somewhat as I wandered about on the flight or up at Tunnel End. It was towards the end of the week-end, as school began to loom large, that my parents sprang their surprise.

"You know that aqueduct in Wales," began my father, as we all sat on the front steps on Sunday afternoon, drinking tea and watching the swans drifting along the edge of the reeds over by 'The Boat'.

"Pontcysyllte," I responded, wondering vaguely what was coming next.

"That's the feller!" he grinned. "We thought that'd be good to see, don't you think?"

Wales was miles away in another world. I had admired the photographs of the great aqueduct in my books but I knew no commercial traffic had passed that way for many years and that the whole waterway had been almost lost for ever in the late forties. My chances of seeing the aqueduct seemed very remote indeed.

"While you were away," he continued, "We thought that another week's boating wouldn't go amiss and so we've hired a little cruiser from Market Drayton. It says in the brochure that you can do Llangollen and back in a week. After *Canada Goose*, and all you've done this summer, I'm sure we could manage that, don't you think?"

"You've actually booked it!"

"First week in October! Couldn't get it any earlier, I'm afraid. You'll have to miss a week's school again, but I expect you'll survive that!"

I certainly would! The Welsh canal up to Llangollen was supposed to be one of the prettiest of waterways, as well as featuring the aqueducts at Chirk and Pontcysyllte which made the 'pig trough' at Wolverton look almost tiny.

"Thought you'd be pleased," said my mother, beginning to collect up cups and the bun plates.

Pleased I most certainly was! I had 'Edwards' out that evening and looked more closely at our route. Starting from Market Drayton had been an inspiration as it linked up neatly with our furthest point up the Shroppie on *Bredon Hill*. My finger traced the journey along the Shroppie main line, noting the fifteen locks at Audlem, to Hurleston Junction and the Welsh Canal. This then ran for forty-six miles before terminating at the Horseshoe Falls at Llantisilio, just beyond Llangollen. The total journey worked out at about 120 miles and 86 locks which seemed perfectly feasible in a week, even if the weather wasn't too good. The knowledge that some more boating was in prospect before the winter closed in helped enormously during that first week back at school. I adjusted more easily than I might have supposed by employing a new mental trick. Now, even if some of the pettiness of it really irritated me, I had no need to get cross. Instead I just mentally switched over and pictured myself steering *Warbler* round the Finney pound, or lockwheeling down 'The Fields', or any number of other happy memories. I was becoming more adept now at living the double life and, although my work at school prospered and my reports were good, my heart was on the cut.

On the first week-end of term I detoured round through Duston Mill and up the Arm as I cycled over to the cottage, my parents preferring to bus across. Meadows was at work in the Rothersthorpe flight doing some light hedge trimming and I learnt that the two pairs had returned up the Arm from Wellingborough on Wednesday, having waited a week to empty. They were headed for the Warwickshire coalfield and hoped to load without too much further delay. He was expecting one more pair back up from Wellingborough the next day, this would then leave the mill clear of boats and Meadows was of the opinion that "things'll settle down a bit". We had clearly been unlucky as far more wheat than normal had arrived at Brentford and there had naturally been pressure put on to get it out of the lighters which were wanted elsewhere. Unfortunately the mill had only a finite amount of storage space and so the later boats had finished up acting as granary stores. It had happened before and, such were the vagaries of the system, would doubtless do so again. As things turned out, the two pairs loaded in the Bedworth Arm for Croxley early the following week and passed through Stoke Bruerne before the week-end, I would not see them before the Welsh trip which was now tantalisingly close.

We travelled by train to Market Drayton on a bright and breezy Saturday in early October, changing at Birmingham New Street for Shrewsbury and finally up the branch line to our destination. The attractive little market town has its own short chapter in *Narrow Boat* where a description of an annual horse fair held in the town is given. No such splendid sight greeted us as we made our way from the station along to the wharf where the small boat-hiring business, then owned by John Haines, was based. Our boat was an old-fashioned centre cockpit cruiser with a narrow gunwale running round her curved sides and a single porthole giving a view forwards from the small front cabin. She was nowhere near as new as *Bredon Hill* and had almost completed a full season of hiring with dents and scratches to show for it. *Enid* was powered by a small petrol engine, located under a trapdoor in the centre cockpit, and this was still being worked on as we put down our bags on the wharfside.

"Just checking her over!" reassured John, as we were invited to make ourselves at home.

Enid was not, by any stretch of the imagination, the smartest hire boat then available on the system, but there were, no doubt, worse. She would get us up the Welsh Cut which was the main thing in my mind as I viewed her fully for the first time. The checking over was quickly completed and, once our experience had been established, it was clear that lock instructions would be superfluous. We were asked to be absolutely sure to shut the top gates up the Welsh. Very few boats moved up there at this time of the year, we were told, and a number of the bottom gates were notoriously leaky. The boatyard itself looked none too prosperous either but everyone was very friendly and, at about half past four, with the best of the day behind us, we were waved away as we set off northwards.

Enid was what could only be described as 'one-paced'. Her throttle was controlled by a small switch and I very soon learned that this was best put straight to maximum speed, as the differentials between this and tickover were remarkably slight. Top speed was nothing special either, being only slightly faster than a loaded pair and a good deal slower than *Bredon Hill*. On the long wide straights of the Shroppie main line this steady chug could seem a little too steady and I was glad that we were not heading off in the other direction, hour after hour along the pounds to Cut End. As it was we were soon busy at the first little flight of five locks at Adderley which came after about an hour's travelling. We were straight into our old routine, with mother steering down and finding it considerably easier than *Canada Goose*. Three handed with a small cruiser on a well maintained flight of narrow locks proved easy work after my experiences that summer and we came down smoothly, helped by the locks being largely full although all gates were closed, a paddle having to be raised on each just to top up and enable the top gate to be opened. It was already past six, and the early autumn evening was beginning to close in, as the gates swung open at the bottom lock. 'Edwards' informed us that it was just over a mile to the top of Audlem and we agreed that tying there would be just right on our first day. To have gone down Audlem would have entailed working the bottom half of the flight in the dark, rather pointless given the time at our disposal.

Working boats, of course, have no such compunctions and we had not been long at Audlem before the familiar 'bomp-bomp' of a single Bolinder was heard coming along from Adderley. *Enid* stirred at her moorings as an ex-Josher BW single motor, heading back empty, went above the top lock just beyond where we lay. Unfortunately we were on the brink of serving up dinner and any thoughts I might have had of 'lending a hand' to the lone steerer down the flight were very firmly squashed by my mother! Instead I simultaneously ate and watched through the forward porthole as the lock was filled. Top gate pushed open, and the young steerer scrambling back aboard by the mast beam, before running down the top planks to the cabin. I knew the sequence and proceeded to provide a running commentary to my long suffering parents! Clutch rod in, speedwheel on, oil rod in. In she goes. Oil rod out, speedwheel off, clutch out. Off with the strap and a couple of turns round the strapping post on the top gate, stopping the boat and shutting the gate in one smooth combined action. Coil strap and lay on the top. Clutch rod in, keeping her bows nudging against the bottom gates to avoid any danger of drifting back on to the sill. One bottom paddle up. Off he goes, running down to set the next lock. Back up and open the bottom gates of the now empty lock. Drop back on to the cabin top of the slowly moving boat. Regaining the footboard, it's speedwheel on, oil rod in, and drive her out. The rhythmic beat died away in the distance as three delicious pieces of Market Drayton bread pudding were devoured. We would have a 'bad road' in the morning!

A soft clinging autumn mist shrouded the cut as a good fried breakfast was 'put down' to fortify us for the day ahead, which had every promise of being an interesting one. That evening would find us 'up the Welsh', but we had to get there first. Wiping bread around my plate I listened hopefully for the sound that would tell us that boats, which had tied at the bottom of Audlem the previous night, were now working their way up the flight. Traffic on the Shroppie was quite light, by comparison with the relatively busy waters of the Grand Union, but there might be a chance that someone would present us with a 'good road' that morning. We were out of luck, but it didn't really matter as a 'bad road' simply meant more paddles and gates to work, and hence more enjoyment as we descended the long straight flight with the sun slowly burning off the mist as we went. Shroppie locks are light and easy to work and short work was made of the Audlem Fifteen, time enough for a stop near the bottom to pick up buns in the nearby town for 'elevens', before setting off on the hour long pound to the next two locks at Hack Green. These were the final locks for us on the main line and we pressed on eagerly, past the disused basin at Nantwich, to reach Hurleston and the junction with the Welsh Canal just nicely for lunch.

We were on holiday and trying hard not to be obsessed with 'getting 'em ahead'. So we tied by the bottom lock to eat our sandwiches and have a leisurely cup of tea, before embarking on the Welsh that afternoon. I inspected the four locks at Hurleston after we had eaten and it was clear that we were very much about to leave a main road for a country lane. The main-line Shroppie locks were neatly painted, with white-tipped beams and well oiled paddles, and bore the patina of regular use. The locks of the Hurleston flight were different. Gates were faded, the locksides grassy and little used by comparison. Ten years earlier this waterway had seen virtually no boats at all and was threatened with final closure. This situation had been averted through valiant work by individuals and groups fighting for its survival, but there was still a lot to do and traffic remained quite infrequent, especially out of the summer season. Ambling up to the top of the flight I surveyed the scene as the waterway stretched away into the distance. The channel appeared quite narrow, but seemingly free of weeds and with very clean water due to its use as a feeder channel from the river Dee at the Horseshoe Falls. I did not linger long, the unmistakeable sound of a single Bolinder had me running back down the flight, just in time to see a pair of Clayton 'gas boats' heading past bound for Oldbury.

Hurleston Locks were empty and, with the excited sense of another adventure just beginning, we locked upwards and set off along the winding reaches of the Welsh Canal. The plan was to get above the Grindley Brook locks that evening, in order to have plenty of time the next day to enjoy the long pounds and the two mighty aqueducts. Two locks at Swanley were followed by another three at Baddiley before we paused in the solitary lock at Marbury for a cup of tea and a chocolate digestive to which I then was, and indeed still am, very partial. The day was cool but pleasantly sunny and the surroundings unspectacularly pastoral, *Enid* went along at her steady pace meeting no other boats in a manner reminiscent of our time on the Staffs & Worcs. The indisputable highlights of the day were the three staircase locks situated at the top of the flight of six locks at Grindley Brook. The sides of the locks were covered by a wide expanse of bricks, with raised sections incorporated in places to give a good grip to boat horses and boatmen's boots alike. The wooden strapping posts were all still there with the grooves of many lines etched into them. All rather poignant, I thought, surveying the vista from the bottom lock in the knowledge that the chances of commercial traffic ever resuming through the flight were infinitesimal. The staircase was completely empty which meant water had to be run down from the top before we could begin our ascent, a minor inconvenience when compared to confronting an empty 'thick of Hatton'.

Soon the top gate was lurching open on to a twenty-mile pound, stretching away to where the sun was beginning to sink lower in the west. The weather was still dry and we decided to press on that evening until it got dark. Other traffic on the canal was not a problem and *Enid*'s draught was so shallow that we could tie anywhere, unlike *Canada Goose*. We passed the blocked up junction to the old Whitchurch branch and pushed on through pleasant countryside, passing Platt Lane to tie adjacent to the roving bridge at Whixall Moss where the short Prees Arm went off. Darkness fell as we made our lines fast which meant, much as I would have liked to, that a walk along the Arm was not possible. It was a surprisingly warm evening for early October and we stood in the cockpit for a while enjoying a cup of tea, the silence around us broken only by the occasional splash as moorhens and ducks settled down in the reeds. This silence was almost tangible and again I felt the spirit of the canals creeping over me and was truly content.

Silence. I had awoken and listened intently to it. All was very still, certainly no rain and very little wind. I was hoping desperately for a fine day in which to see the aqueducts and as I lay contentedly, snug and warm in the half-light, the silence seemed to promise just that. Once more a fine mist soaked the hedges and grass cloaking *Enid* in its dampness. The morning was windless and still, a repeat of yesterday looked to be on the cards with the sun forcing its way through and a pleasant day ensuing. Time, as usual, presented us with some problems. The Welsh Canal is a beautiful waterway and full of interest, ideally it needed at least a fortnight to do it justice and we had only a week. However, I surmised, as we wended our way through the 'Lake District', a series of shallow tree-shrouded meres near the town of Ellesmere, at least I was here and not sitting in a crowded classroom wrestling with theorems! It would have been splendid to have tied up and spent some time exploring here, but the aqueducts called and the weather was holding, so on we went. We did go into the deserted basin at Ellesmere where just two rather elderly cruisers were moored up, principally in order to get bread, buns, and chops for dinner. The basin was an impressive spread of water and it was easy to imagine the once busy scene, with boats unloading and horses clattering along the wharves. Now all was quiet in that short peaceful time before the explosion of the consumer society would bring more traffic to this canal than it had ever seen before. All this was in the future, that mysterious and unknown land. It was certainly unforeseen by us as we swung gleefully round the empty basin in a long arc before rejoining the main canal by Beech House, once the headquarters of the Ellesmere Canal Company and the maintenance yard for the whole system.

A few more miles brought us to Frankton Junction, from where the long line of the Montgomery Canal led down through Welshpool to a basin at Newtown. This also merited a stop, albeit a fairly brief one! It is astonishing how quickly decay can set in. Only twenty-two years earlier this waterway had been in regular commercial use. Traffic may have been light but it had been there, and the sadly derelict locks we now contemplated would have been trimly maintained, with the towpath showing clear signs of horsedrawn traffic. In 1936 a small burst occurred in the bank down below Frankton, it would have been a simple matter to remedy but the railway company, who then owned the waterway, used it as a convenient excuse to close the entire canal. One unfortunate boat was caught on the wrong side of the breach and for them there was to be no way out. The canal was then abandoned on the spurious grounds 'that there had been no traffic for some years past'. Few, at that time, seemed to care. We walked down the first few locks looking gloomily at the rotting gates, the reeds, nettles and weeds, and feeling the general air of ruination that hung over it all. It was very sad as the journey down here would also have been a beautiful experience, but could now never be undertaken. One of the very positive things to emerge from the great explosion of interest in the waterways which has occurred since that time has been the emergence of recovery groups, dedicated to attempting the restoration of waterways such as the Montgomery. At the time of writing it seems quite likely that I may yet see the long line to Newtown open once more, something which seemed utterly impossible as we stood looking at the ruins on that sunny autumn day back in 1958.

Frankton, although interesting, was depressing and it was good to be back on a navigable canal and to reach the final two locks at New Marton, above which a thirteen and a half mile level led to the river Dee at Llantisilio. The cut had been very pretty through Ellesmere and remained pleasantly rural past Frankton, but beyond the locks came something of a change. A brief and rather dull industrial section followed, unexpected signs of coal mining were evident as we passed through the St Martins area before a rapid improvement brought us along to the approach of the first of the two aqueducts at Chirk. Here the canal swings along a high bank looking down into the valley of the fast running and beautiful Ceirog, which at this point forms the boundary between Wales and England. The adjacent road descends into the valley bottom, crossing the river on a conventional bridge before running uphill again into the small border town of Chirk. We, however, clung to the contour and edged along the side of the hill before running out onto a splendid aqueduct of ten spans, striding high above the river and taking me into Wales for the first time. The aqueduct channel is only seven feet wide and I decided, on this occasion, that the odd bump along the side would not be counted as unprofessional! *Enid*, on tickover, drifted very slowly across, with the higher arches of the parallel railway viaduct looking down on us as we, in our turn, looked down on the rushing waters of the Ceirog below. This was a far bigger structure than either the Ouse aqueduct at Wolverton or the Avon aqueduct along the Leamington pound, both of which seemed very small beer when set alongside its splendour. Because of the proximity of its even bigger neighbour Chirk does not get the recognition it should, in fact the aqueduct is a major work of canal engineering and its setting, as you drift across with the tunnel entrance immediately ahead, truly memorable. All this merited a closer inspection and, with *Enid* moored adjacent to the mouth of the tunnel, we all re-enacted the experience by walking back across the aqueduct and soaking up the view below. Impressions count for a great deal when you are fifteen and I was enthralled. I had been born and bred in the relatively flat Midland shires and this was my first time in the hills, my first real experience of fast running rivers, high hills, and the grandeur and beauty of it all; to this day it remains vivid in the memory.

More was to come! We were surprised upon returning to the boat to see a headlight in the tunnel, only one boat had been encountered since Hurleston and we had become accustomed to having the cut all to ourselves. Chirk Tunnel was built complete with towpath and is only about eight feet wide and so it was necessary to wait until a small cruiser, powered by an outboard and crewed by a retired couple, emerged to exchange friendly greetings with us before moving out across the aqueduct as we, in our turn, steered into the narrow tunnel mouth. The tunnel was short, a mere 459 yards, and we then found ourselves in a wooded cutting at the end of which were unmistakeable signs of trade now gone. This was the North Wales coalfield and at Black Park was a substantial basin, now choked with reeds and grasses, but once the place where coal would have been loaded into narrowboats for distribution along the Ellesmere and Montgomery systems. Once again all was silent and derelict and, like Frankton, rather sad and poignant, another reminder of the life that had gone. Commercial traffic on the Staffs & Worcs was now only very spasmodic and we had seen none, although we might have done so as occasional cargoes still moved down the waterway. Here, for the first time, I was navigating a canal from which commercial traffic had long since departed and was never likely to return.

Rounding a gentle curve we were greeted by the sight of two magnificent structures as we looked down into the long anticipated valley of the Dee. Near at hand a long spectacular railway viaduct strode across the river, but our eyes were drawn further on to where the tall stone piers of the famous aqueduct carried the cut high across the valley. Along the side of the valley we went, lifting the tall white-painted wooden drawbridge at Vron before curving round on the high embankment leading us through tall trees to the long straight iron trough ahead. I had read about it and studied drawings and photographs of it, but nothing had quite prepared me for that feeling of surprise and exhilaration as *Enid* slid very slowly out onto the great aqueduct. On the eastern side was the towpath with its protective iron railings, but in the west was simply the narrow rim of the trough standing a few inches above water level and affording an uninterrupted view clear up the Vale of Llangollen. Immediately beneath was a small sports field and further across woods and trees shrouded the line of the canal clinging to its ledge along the valley, with the Ruabon to Llangollen railway line running just below it. The far end of the aqueduct looked a very long way ahead as we drifted gently across soaking in yet more marvellous vistas. Nowhere else on the system is there anything quite as spectacular as this and we all rightly saluted the genius of the engineer, Thomas Telford, for his stupendous achievement. When we finally reached the far side we found ourselves faced with another disused and reedy arm, long deserted by traffic, whilst to our left, a right-angled turn led through a narrow bridge and continued the route to Llangollen. Both aqueducts had now been crossed but this magnificent structure positively demanded further exploration. After making the tight turn through the bridge-hole we immediately tied for the night, a clear view of the aqueduct filling our cabin windows.

The walk back across the trough was memorable. Our steps were slow as we admired the views in all directions, almost reverently touching the black railings stretching reassuringly along beside us as we looked down well over a hundred feet into the churning rushing waters of the Dee. Clambering down to river level we viewed the magnificent stone pillars with awe, this was truly a wonder of the waterways. The canal was originally projected to run due north from Pontcysyllte, through the coal district around Wrexham before linking up with the main system again at Chester. Hence the line of the canal coming off the aqueduct led straight ahead into what we now discovered to be a short arm, completely derelict and weeded-up. This insignificant length was all that had been built of the line to Chester before the Ellesmere Canal Company had run into economic difficulties. The side arm to Llangollen and Llantisilio existed as a navigable feeder, designed to supply the system with water drawn from the river Dee and with the added potential for a small amount of traffic to Llangollen. We slept that night with the noise of the Dee in our ears and interrupted only by the occasional rattle of a passing train.

Morning brought a familiar but wholly unwelcome sound, the beating of rain on the cabin top, our first of the week. Welsh rain, we quickly discovered, was different from that experienced at home. The downpour was intensely heavy and drummed so hard on the top as to render conversation quite difficult as we ate breakfast. The day from Napton to Stoke Bruerne had been wet, but this was in a different league. Anyone venturing out would have been soaked in minutes and drying facilities on *Enid* were not easy. The prudent course was adopted and we waited to see if it would ease a bit. This proved to be a wise move as by the middle of the morning the rain had done more than ease, it had stopped and a weak sun had struggled fitfully through, although the westerly wind was still strong with further ominously black clouds being driven along in the distance. It was the harbinger of a day of sunshine punctuated by heavy showers and, after several of these, we simply learned to live with it and accept the pauses forced upon us by the more ferocious showers. Hiding under bridge holes became a feature of the day. This was not exactly very professional, but it kept us from becoming totally saturated with all the attendant problems of getting everything dry again. The cut between the aqueduct and Llangollen proved to be very narrow and constructed largely on a shelf cut into the side of the valley, *Enid* puttered gently along with the wooded hillside on our right and the railway line and river below us on our left. An hour brought us to the lovely little town of Llangollen which lay spread out below us beyond the railway station and river bridge. Above, a towering hill was topped by the ruins of Castell Dynas Bran. An attractive little wharf offered an excellent place to tie and we descended into the town returning with bread, sausages, and a Welsh cake which was different from anything I had encountered previously, it was also delicious! It was rather difficult to do justice to exploring the town as the heavens opened once more and fierce slanting rain had us cowering in doorways for twenty minutes or so as the shower spent its fury.

The canal does not actually end at Llangollen, despite the presence of a large winding-hole beyond the wharf which clearly indicated that most traffic would not have passed this point. Naturally I was keen to go to the very end and my enthusiastic arguments carried the day with my doubtful parents, *Enid* was of very shallow draught and she could be turned without the need for a seventy foot winding-hole, besides which we couldn't possibly come all this way and not see the Horseshoe Falls! The rain seemed to have moved elsewhere for a while as our lines were taken in and *Enid* continued westwards, under a large concrete roadbridge and then chugging along a shallow length of cut to a further bridge near the 'Chain Bridge Hotel'. Here the valley sides had become rocky and the swollen river roared as it descended under a narrow suspension bridge, whose construction clearly accounted for the name of the hotel. *Enid* was down to tickover and we were all anxiously studying the depth as she came alongside the back of the hotel, with the waterway narrowing right down and an unforgiving rocky bank looming on the side opposite the towpath.

"You can see the bottom clearly!" said my mother anxiously, as we looked forward to another slight curve taking the canal on.

"It can't be far now!"

Determined to reach the end so long as there was no hazard to the boat, I took *Enid* out of gear. The water was now very shallow with green weed streaming out just below the surface, fanned by the current flowing from the intake at Llantisilio. We could have just walked the last little bit, but I was young and obsessively determined! We would get there! So my father and I, with mother fending off, towed *Enid* along that final piece of towpath until her bows were resting on the concrete wall of the little pumping station built to take water from the nearby river. We had done it! We had literally reached the end of the system!

It was well worth it. Before us the Horseshoe Falls, so called because of the long curving sill built to help divert the waters of the river Dee for canal use, were a magnificent spectacle in the afternoon sunshine as the torrent of water churned over them and fell away towards Llangollen. The contrast with Northamptonshire was enormous and it was enough simply to drink it all in. *Enid* could go no further and her bows nudged against the pumphouse as the feeder waters bubbled out beneath her hull. A stroll along the beautiful banks of the Dee upstream from the falls was rudely interrupted by the approach of further dark clouds, driven along on the very fresh westerly wind, and the third or fourth really heavy shower of the day caught us out before we could regain the shelter of *Enid*. This time the shower seemed disinclined to stop and proceeded to turn itself into what the weathermen rejoice in calling a 'prolonged shower'. Already soaked from the banks of the Dee we became aware of passing time as a family conference was called to plan out the rest of the day. Staying where we were overnight with only a very few inches of water under the hull was not a sensible idea, instead we would disregard the torrential rain and drop back to Llangollen. The Horseshoe Falls may be the end of the system but there was no winding-hole and no space even to turn a boat as small as *Enid*. We got on the lines again and pulled her slowly back down the narrow weedy channel, past the hotel and through a narrow bridge hole until we had reached a place where the cut was just wide enough to turn her. Once round it was a simple matter to putter back through the by-now 'extremely prolonged' shower to tie thankfully for the night at Llangollen.

WINDLASS IN MY BELT

The rain seemed to set in with renewed fury after dark. We had already been soaked through and the cabins were festooned with clothes hanging off impromptu lines made from lengths of string. Fetching fish and chips was ruled out and we settled instead for an omelette and a lengthy game of scrabble. Oh, the joys of boating on a wet night in Wales! Sometime in the middle of the night I sensed the wind ease and the rain begin to lessen its drumming on the top, crossing my fingers I turned over and snuggled down to be awoken again by sunshine pouring into the cabin from a clear blue sky. The wind remained, but it was much lighter and the freshness of the morning was definitely promising. Clothes were still damp and, having taken my parents the luxury of tea in bed, I rigged up a clothes line from the boat to a tree in true boatman fashion and had everything out blowing in the air before anyone else was up. A hearty breakfast was followed by another walk around Llangollen with me spending some time on the bridge watching a couple of tank engines on the local push and pull service, the Welsh equivalent of the 'Blizzy Flyer'. A long line of mineral wagons loaded with stone chippings also came clanking through, presumably carrying from one of the many quarries in the area. The station at Llangollen was very attractive and beautifully sited alongside the turbulent waters of the Dee. Like many others the line became a casualty of the wholesale cuts of the 1960s, but the station still remains as the focal point of one of the many steam preservation societies without whom little of the past would remain. Cards were bought and sent to Ronnie and Phyllis, Alec, Lil and Young Lily, Sister Mary, Mr and Mrs James, and not forgetting Meadows. I was lucky in being able to buy cards showing both the canal at Llangollen and a view of the aqueduct at Pontcysyllte, such a contrast to their familiar Midland haunts.

Returning to *Enid* in mid-morning we found that the day had become surprisingly warm, our wet clothes had dried enough to be taken in and stowed as we busied ourselves with untying and looking our last on the little town below, No other boats had been seen on the move since Chirk, but we were surprised by one that morning in the narrows between Llangollen and the aqueduct. Passing even a small cruiser was not possible and we found ourselves having to pull back for nearly a quarter of a mile to one of the specially cut wide places provided for the purpose. It was really very narrow along the ledge and any appreciable volume of traffic would have turned passing into quite a frustrating exercise. However, we had no further worries on that score being destined not to meet another boat all day. A long stop was made in the very centre of the aqueduct. We shut off the engine and ate our sandwiches in peace, sitting on the cabin top and revelling in the views, another memory to conjure up when French verbs grew tiresome! Pontcysyllte is so spectacular that we were very reluctant to move on knowing that this was in all ways the high point of our journey. At last we managed to get going and with many lingering backward glances passed off the trough to wind along the side of the valley towards Vron and our last sight of the aqueduct before a bend in the canal hid it from view. All of us felt sad to be leaving the Vale of Llangollen where, in spite of the rain, we had spent two superb days and wished it could have been two weeks, such was the potential for exploration. Further wanderings up the Dee and around the Horseshoe Falls would surely have needed a day or two, and the ascent to Castell Dynas Bran above Llangollen simply begged to be undertaken, if only time had not been so pressing. Doubtless there was much more and I dreamed of returning on my own boat with unlimited time! Such dreams are the very stuff of youth and I drew a veil over how it was all to be financed, such was my optimism! One thing was certain, the grandeur of the upper end of the Welsh Canal would make the Northampton Arm, despite its comforting familiarity, seem very prosaic.

These were the thoughts that occupied me as *Enid* passed through the short 191-yard long Whitehouse Tunnel and approached Chirk once more. We had done only eight miles from Llangollen, a very short day with no locks at all to slow us down, but we were lingering, none of us wanted to leave Wales. *Enid* was gently chugging along at half-pace and, having stopped at Black Park for another look at the old wharf, we drifted on into the wooded cutting at the end of which could be seen the dark opening of Chirk Tunnel and the road back to England.

"Today being Wednesday ...." my mother began in ruminative fashion after consulting the distance tables in 'Edwards'. "We've actually got plenty of time."

"Don't want to get back too early," added my father.

I knew what was in their minds. If we pressed on in true 'getting 'em ahead' fashion for the rest of today and tomorrow we could be left with a very short day on Friday. The option of going a little beyond Market Drayton and back only took us along waters already covered in *Bredon Hill*. Turning left out of the Welsh to Barbridge Junction gave us a choice of the Middlewich New Cut or a bit more of the Shroppie in the direction of Chester. Neither of these alternatives seemed particularly inspiring after Pontcysylte and Llangollen.

"It's very nice around here," I ventured, letting it be known that I would be happy to stop.

"If we tied in that lovely little basin between the tunnel and the aqueduct," I continued, "We could go to Marbury Lock tomorrow and the top of Adderley for Friday night."

This suggestion was very rapidly agreed upon, I think that both my parents, like me, had become enchanted with the area and were wishing to prolong their stay as long as possible.

Professionalism was duly observed in the short Chirk Tunnel and *Enid* emerged without a touch despite the very narrow confines. A still pool of rather weedy water constituted the small basin between Tunnel End and the trough of the aqueduct. I recognised the scene from the beautiful photograph in Eric de Maré's *The Canals of England* and now here I was tied up in the middle of it, an idyllic spot and nicely sheltered from the persistent light breeze. It would be true to say that a loaded pair emerging from the tunnel and lining themselves up for the aqueduct might have grumbled at our position, but this was most certainly not going to happen and we were no problem to the very infrequent small cruisers which had been the only traffic encountered on the Welsh thus far. It was mid-afternoon and, after a cup of tea, we walked up into the small border town of Chirk through which ran the Holyhead Road, the A5, our old friend from home. I recall it, at this distance in time, as a pleasant enough little town with a castle and beautifully light jam doughnuts!

Being only fifteen I still loved scrambling about and exploring in odd corners, a love that has remained with me through the passing years. During the late afternoon and evening of that day I was to excel myself. Nothing would do but that I had to walk through the tunnel along the narrow towpath where, despite its short length, it became satisfyingly dark in the middle. I had noticed that the railway line, the old GWR Chester to Shrewsbury tracks, had run through Chirk Station on our left as we approached the tunnel but afterwards crossed the Ceirog on our right parallel with the aqueduct. Scrambling up above the tunnel I found the railway crossing over above the line of the canal tunnel, after recrossing it myself I made the short overland journey back to the basin where I stood admiring the spectacular view from on top of the tunnel mouth, the exact position from which one of my very favourite photographs had been taken. Of course, the aqueduct then had to be walked over and a scrambling descent on the other side enabled the spans to be viewed from the perspective of river level. More determined scrambling then took me under the aqueduct and upwards to stand cautiously on the railway viaduct, thereby gaining another unusual view of the aqueduct. It was very tempting to walk across the railway viaduct, but a number of trains had passed by that afternoon and prudence led me to draw the line at this point and recross the river by towpath to the waiting *Enid*. Standing in the cockpit that evening with a last cup of tea I looked up through the trees at a clear sky filled with the glitter of stars. A crescent moon illuminated the dark shadowy waters around us and that welcome sense of peace and ease crept over me once more.

Thursday dawned cool and breezy. A typical autumn morning threatened a day of sunshine and heavy showers, but happily the showers proved to be fairly short-lived and failed to spoil an interesting day's boating as we reluctantly left Wales, crossing the Ceirog and heading back into the pastoral scene of the border country. After an hour or so the windlasses were briefly out again for the New Marton Two before we settled down for the long twenty mile pound to Grindley Brook. *Enid* seemed to get slower that day although the engine looked fine when viewed through the hatch-cover, in any event we lacked both the tools and the knowledge to attempt any adjustments to this rather elderly petrol engine. It was actually possible to walk slightly faster than *Enid* and my parents did just that through the Ellesmere 'Lake District' as they strolled ahead of the boat, enjoying the views and leaving me to putter along behind picking them up at a bridge hole when they had had enough. There seemed no actual problem with the engine despite the lack of speed and so we simply continued on in stately fashion around that long and very peaceful pound. Sandwiches were eaten on the move and distances ticked off as we drifted past the Ellesmere Arm, through the short 87-yard Ellesmere Tunnel, noted the wharf at Hampton Bank as a future tying place, looked with interest at the peaty bogs of Whixall Moss, past the old Prees Arm where we had tied coming up, and on through green fields as another two hours brought the reward of sighting the top gate of the Grindley Brook flight.

Here we encountered an unexpected hold-up. All day we had travelled from Chirk and had barely seen a soul, not to mention another boat. My windlass was on the ground paddle at the top lock ready to draw when a familiar sound made me pause and wonder if I was hearing things.

'Boink! Boink! Boink!'

A narrow boat was entering the bottom lock of the three! Leaving *Enid* tied to the rail of the top gate we all descended the staircase to investigate this unexpected occurrence. A nicely converted ex-Josher, crewed by a kindly looking white-haired couple, was rising in the bottom lock as we approached and made our greetings. They hailed from Swarkestone, miles away on the eastern end of the Trent & Mersey Canal, and they actually lived on their boat. Naturally we all helped with the gates and chatted eagerly at the same time; one enthusiast soon recognises another! They were planning, lucky things, to winter up the Welsh, certainly as far up as the top end of Pontcysyllte and possibly, after an inspection of the depth, they would attempt to reach Llangollen itself. To say I was green with envy would not have been understating things at all, fancy spending all winter slowly and carefully exploring the Welsh instead of doing GCEs! My grinning father said I could do it when I retired, I remarked that the cut might have gone by then! As things have turned out I am now retired and the cut has most certainly not gone, although it has been transformed. Once derelict waterways are being restored all over the country and there are now so many boats that queues form during the summer at the popular flights. Much of the peace has fled the waterways, as it has fled the countryside in general, but I must admit that I could still be sorely tempted by a winter up the Welsh.

The old couple were tying at the top lock to facilitate shopping in nearby Whitchurch the next day and we found ourselves invited aboard for a cup of tea, to be followed by a tour of the boat of which they were rightly very proud. I looked with interest at the neat little oak bookshelves which held an assortment of novels and biographies and, of course, canal books. Their collection was similar to my own with one exception, there on the end of the shelf was a Bradshaw! I was allowed to look through this and examined with great interest some of the distance tables which were not in 'Edwards', such as those for the Thames & Severn and Grantham canals. It was clearly a treasured item and he had come across it in a small and unprepossessing second-hand bookshop in Tunstall, whilst passing through the Potteries a couple of years ago. His advice to me was simple, keep looking! Their original interest in the cut had stemmed from a reading of *Narrow Boat* upon its original publication in 1944. As my mother wryly remarked at the time, "That man has got a lot to answer for!" Eventually we tore ourselves away and got going again, descending the staircase and the three locks beyond which were more or less ready for us. More or less. The top gates were closed and, although barely an hour had passed, a foot or more of water had drained away through the fissures in the elderly bottom gates. What with *Enid*'s adoption of an even steadier version of 'one-paced' and our interesting and friendly encounter at Grindley Brook it was getting late, dusk came on as we hurried down the Willeymoor Three and it was dark as we moved through the final pound to tie above Marbury Lock as planned. Another glorious day for the memory with the long but never boring pounds, our interesting encounter at Grindley Brook, and then a few downhill locks to round it all off. What could be pleasanter?

Pleasantness could not really be claimed for our last full day of boating. How the time had flown! We had been awoken in the greyness of dawn by the incessant drumming of Welsh rain crossing the border. It was sheeting down as I crossed the centre cockpit bearing tea in bed, which now seemed to have become a regular part of the morning ritual afloat!

"Raining!" I remarked, rather stating the obvious. From the noise it sounded as if someone were hammering on the cabin top!

My parents drank their tea and looked out at the greyness, searching hopefully for any sign of a break. It didn't look at all good. This, of course, was before the age of transistor radios, Walkmans, and other such paraphenalia. We had no wireless on board and weather forecasting was done by noting the signs of wind direction, cloud layers, and that instinctive feel for the day that comes with living close to nature. Bearing all this in mind, it still didn't look good! The rain was heavy, angling in on a wind that seemed intent on increasing in strength. If we hadn't stayed at Chirk we would be out on the main line now and could have had a much shorter day, on the other hand Chirk had been a memorable afternoon and so no regrets there. Whilst mother was cooking breakfast I looked it all up in 'Edwards', coming up with the undeniable figures of nineteen miles and thirty-two locks to the top of Adderley which, with a ten o'clock finish the next day and a train to catch at quarter to eleven, was an inescapable destination.

With breakfast eaten and everything washed up there was no real excuse for not starting, except for the clatter of stair rods bouncing off the cabin roof. On the Grand Union I now worked out each day by time rather than by miles but here, on a strange cut with a doubtful engine and the old enemy of wind, it wasn't quite so easy to convert the figures from 'Edwards' into the number of hours required to reach Adderley. Six hours at 3mph, but then there was the odd drawbridge on the Welsh and all the locks, with possible delays in the two Shroppie flights if we met working boats. It could be nine hours I thought, maybe eight, or even ten! Come on! Gird up! Worse things happen on the Grand Union! I recalled bow-hauling *Teal* up Saltley and Camp Hill in similar conditions, at least our day was in the country. Coats on, collars up, and off we go! I climbed off on to the soaking towpath and began the day by filling Marmbury which had drained off completely overnight. It's only a drop of rain, as Young Lily used to say! *Enid* seemed even slower as I steered along to the drawbridge at Wrenbury, with my parents wisely staying below and saving their strength for the rigours to come. It was pretty along here, in spite of the rain, but a bit more power from *Enid* would have been very welcome that day as the wind began to catch her high cabin sides, pushing her across the cut and causing us to go along in a crab-like fashion on the more exposed pounds.

It is only eight miles from Marmbury to the main line at Hurleston but it seemed a long haul that morning as, first Baddiley Three and then Swanley Two were negotiated, before the final pound to the entrance locks. The rain had eased somewhat now, but the wind still seemed to be intent on working itself up into a veritable gale and was making it very difficult. We had a foretaste of what was to come when a particularly vicious gust blew *Enid* into the reeds and I was forced to take her out of gear to avoid weeds on the blades. Pinned helplessly to the reeds it was hard to get off and our lack of power didn't help at all. In the end I shafted the stern off whilst my father reversed her out and then, in a brief quieter spell, regained headway, thankfully descending the Hurleston Locks to turn right at the bottom on to the broad waters of the Shroppie main line. I had read in *Narrow Boat* about the difficulties posed by the wind along the open reaches of the Shroppie with its notoriously shallow edges and today I would learn the lesson at first hand. The older Brindley canals wandered around following the contour which resulted in plenty of bends and extra mileage, but no exposed embankments. The Shroppie, built much later, was a very straight waterway and this had been achieved by a succession of cuttings and embankments, cut and fill, the fore-runner in engineering techniques of the railway age.

The snag was wind. On a day like today the cuttings became a welcome refuge from the rigours of the west wind which was blowing fiercely across the canal, relentless in its ferocity. On the succeeding embankment there was nowhere to hide and life became a desperate struggle. *Enid* could not be 'wound on' as the power was simply not available and so, in the more exposed places, we found ourselves going along sideways. Several times I was forced to leap off and shaft her off the soft clinging mud, it was then a case of walking along holding her off with the shaft until welcome relief was afforded by the next cutting. It became particularly tricky at the tail of locks as any sudden unexpected gust was likely to skew *Enid*, making my mother's task of steering her smoothly into the lock chamber doubly difficult. Above Hack Green we pulled in, put some soup on and drew breath.

WINDLASS IN MY BELT

This was, by any standards, a hard day. I had experienced wet days in the summer, but not accompanied by such a strong and unrelenting wind. I recalled Lil saying that she could cope with hot suns, the rain, snow and ice, but that wind was the worst enemy and I realised now the truth of her words. Not only did it make getting the boat along much more difficult but it battered away at you until, in the end, you were driven to seek respite if only for a few precious minutes. We sat in the cabin with faces burning and ears tingling, savouring the shelter as we listened to the gusts pressing *Enid* against the bank in their fury.

"Hurricane!" grinned mother stoically, as we sipped welcome bowls of oxtail soup with hunks of Chirk cottage loaf to dip in.

"Strong anyway!" I returned. "Gives your head a good blow-out!"

Although not a hurricane it was nevertheless an unusually ferocious wind and the sensible thing to have done would have been to tie up and sit it out. Unfortunately this was the one option which was definitely not available to us, we had to get back. So, with the inner man satisfied, we donned coats once more and went out to do battle.

The rain had thankfully now largely eased, with the exception of the occasional vicious shower which lashed against us from time to time. These were invariably short and we took to stopping and retreating into the cabin for the ten minutes or so it took for them to pass. Audlem was reached at last and with only one further skirmish on the mud. Once on the mud it was surprisingly awkward to get going again. You tried desperately to shaft out and get underway again, a procedure considerably hindered by *Enid*'s lack of power, whilst the wind having got you out of the channel and stuck seemed to do its unforgiving best to keep you there. Locking up Audlem necessitated a change of routine. The locks were full with top gates standing open and paddles up, an absolute 'bad road'. This didn't help at all, in that for successful progress it was essential that the lock be ready and gates open as *Enid* approached. With *Warbler*, I expect we would have come in under full power and risked the last minute ferocious gust that would knock you sideways. With *Enid*, that sort of approach was just too risky. Progress was fairly crab-like anyway and, if mother approached as fast as she could, any sudden gust at the critical moment would have skewed her, banging her thin cabin sides unacceptably hard into the unforgiving lock wall. Instead we decided that my father would empty the locks and *Enid* would not leave one lock until the next was clearly ready for her. I then walked along the towpath carrying the shaft and, as mother eased off to enter the lock, I would rest it against the coaming of the centre cockpit and hold her out level with the correct line of approach. This may have looked amateurish to a narrowboatman but it had the merit of working; lock by lock we ascended Audlem, windblown but unscathed. With a certain sense of triumph we reached the top, remaining in the lock for a cup of tea and a well-earned bun from the bread shop near the bottom lock. Only one more short pound and then the five Adderley locks, we would do it now!

WELSH INTERLUDE

We met no working boats on the Shroppie that day and I commented on this to the lock-keeper who had come out to commiserate with us as we paused in the top lock.

"Empties can't move!" he replied. "Day like this, they'd be straight up the mud! They'll all be tied up keeping their heads down, like as not. This cut's a booger for wind!"

Loaded boats apparently could move in these conditions and a couple of single motors had been through that morning, hence the state of the flight. Trade was getting a bit slack though, he added gloomily. At last, as late afternoon began to give way to evening, the wind finally began to die away and we had the luxury of finishing the day by ascending Adderley in our normal manner with the shaft thankfully restored to the cabin top. It had been a tough day. Hardly a holiday in the conventional sense of the word, but a worthwhile experience for all that. Another contrast in a week packed full of them, stretching from the grandeur of the Vale of Llangollen to the damp bucolic scene at the top of Adderley that evening. Such contrasts, as I had learned to appreciate in the summer, are the very essence of boating and of life itself and we would be infinitely poorer in spirit without them. The next morning a final quiet hour under a blue sky flecked by white clouds scudding along in the breeze returned us to Market Drayton and the end of our trip 'up the Welsh'. Stourport to Llantisilio and back had been achieved, in two separate halves. It had been a fascinating journey giving us much to savour and reflect upon as the little tank engine, with it's three attendant coaches, took us along to Shrewsbury on the first leg of our journey home.

As things turned out this autumn trip up the Welsh Canal was to be the last of the three holidays we would have as a family on the cut, although none of us knew this at the time. My parents had enjoyed their trips in a different way to my own youthful fervour and I shall always remain grateful to them for the way in which they supported my passionate interest to the extent they did. The cottage at Stoke Bruerne was to give us all a number of years of happiness and the companionship of good friends, now sadly almost all dead. My parents willingness to go boating had led us down this road, without it none of this would ever have happened and a very great deal would have been missed. All of this can be said with the benefit of hindsight and I must confess was not at all in my thoughts at the time. Clambering aboard the bus at Northampton's Castle Station my reflections were concentrated upon the joys of a wonderful few weeks of boating, the memory of which would be more than enough to carry me through the dark days of the coming winter. It had been quite a year and my love for the cut and its people was deeper than ever. What next, I wondered, as I looked towards the following Spring.

*****

Chapter 7

Bits and Pieces

The cut, though never far from my thoughts, had to take something of a back seat through the winter of 1958 and on into the warm spring of 1959. This was the year of GCE 'O' Levels and, rather like the year leading up to the 11 Plus Examination, life had become rather serious. Exams, then as now, were hurdles which had to be jumped on the road through life and my parents expected me to pass and move on into the Sixth Form. It was also my expectation and I applied myself diligently to the task in hand. Both of my parents had left school at fourteen, as was the way in their day, and had made progress despite this, but the world was changing. Qualifications were what was needed if a life on the shoe factory floor was to be avoided. A small inner voice informed me that I could always be a boatman but, deep down and beyond my love for the way of life, I knew that that was not an option. The life of the narrow boats was almost certainly doomed in the long run and besides there was something else stirring deep inside me, a nagging core of ambition spurring me onwards. I had no idea at that time what I wanted to do with my life, but I did know that failure in the summer of 1959 would narrow my choices very considerably. These exams must be passed and then there would be two more years of 'A' level work by which time things might be somewhat clearer.

Week-ends during the autumn were still spent at Stoke Bruerne although now I had to discipline myself to spend several hours working on my homework. Mostly I worked in the early mornings and the evening in order to give myself the bulk of the day free for wandering or, if I was lucky, 'assisting' a pair through the flight. By now I had grown to become 6ft tall and, although not sixteen until the following spring, I had become used to enjoying pints of beer with Alec and Ronnie during the previous summer. My father enjoyed a pint also and that autumn I found myself discreetly introduced to the bar of 'The Boat'. Nothing was ever said about my age by any of the three members of the Woodward family who then ran the pub, but clearly an 'arrangement' about me had been reached between them and my father. From then on I became an accepted member of the small community which met most evenings in the quiet low ceilinged bar, often joined by the crews of any pairs which had tied above the lock for the night. Much has changed at 'The Boat' since those faraway autumnal days as the pub has striven to keep up with the mushrooming explosion of visitors to the village, but then it was really a very simple affair. Beer was served from a small black wooden bar located curiously in the centre of a single large room. Coming in to the pub from the canalside you would find yourself in a narrow passageway leading straight through to the other side of the building, from which another door gave access to the road via a narrow track which also served to accomodate the lorries which delivered from the two breweries in Northampton – Phipps and N.B.C. On the left a door gave into a sitting room, used by the family in the day but doubling as a kind of lounge bar at night. Some of the local farmers would use this room in preference to the public bar frequented by their workers and Emily Woodward, the white-haired licensee, would serve them whisky and water from a tray carried through. On the right was the door used by the rest of us as an entrance to the low-ceilinged country bar. The serving pantry stood in the middle of the room and four glass doors enabled service to be given in any direction by the two occupants. Emily's son, Jack, and his wife Zoe, worked with her in the pub in those days, but there was only ever room for two people at any one time in the tiny pantry. Beer, a choice of the two local brews, was the order of the day with a few spirits being available for the ladies. Crisps were the only food on offer although packets of nuts made an appearance the following year, quite an innovation for the late 1950s!

Going to the pub in the evening enabled us to become much more a part of the wider village, our distant links with the Gardiners of Shutlanger also forming the subject of much conversation and interest among the locals. Boat people, of course, also used the pub when they tied at Stoke for the night and this gave me the chance to widen still further my acquaintance with them as, due to my links with Ronnie and Alec, I was now an accepted member of their tight-knit little community. One character I became particularly friendly with was 'Old Charlie', then a sprightly eighty-three year old and living in a rented house in the bottom of the village. He did not emerge at night any more, but at around midday his burly figure would be seen on the bridge, waiting until the pub door was unlocked before making his way along. It would never do to be seen actually waiting outside for it to open! Charlie had his 'own' chair in a corner of the pub which he would make a beeline for, propping his stick up against the wall and settling himself down for a couple of hours of beer and, more importantly, chat. He was a kindly old man, universally popular, and after his initial draught he rarely bought a pint, it being a village tradition to get Charlie 'one in'. Sometimes he had more 'in' than he could cope with, but these were always carried forward to the next day and neither Charlie or Emily ever lost track of the correct number in hand! Charlie had spent most of his working life as a lengthman for both the Grand Junction Canal Company and its successor, the Grand Union Canal Company, working along the stretch between Stoke and Buckby, with occasional excursions down the Northampton Arm. We spent hours chatting about the horse boats of earlier in the century, of the old Grand Junction Company, of Joshers, Harvey-Taylors, Faulkners, and other companies now no longer carrying. He had very clear memories of the great changes of the 1930s and the construction of the large new fleet of narrow boats which were to revitalise trade on the waterway. Charlie was always interested in the life of the cut and seemed to take great pleasure in listening to the enthusiastic tales of my doings 'along the Junction' that summer. He was very vague about Llangollen however and had clearly never heard of Pontcysyllte, such was the narrowness of the old way of life. After attending the local village school and starting work at thirteen, he had, with the notable exception of his exploits in the Northamptonshire Regiment during the First World War, hardly ever left the area. He was an absolute mine of information on Stoke and the narrow strip surrounding the waterway northward, but had little knowledge or interest in the wider world beyond. Despite this, he was a very contented and amiable old man and sadly missed by us all when a few years later, at the grand old age of eighty-eight, he had to be admitted to the Old People's Hospital in Daventry where he died within the month.

From a totally different world came Teddy. He was a vet with a thriving practice in Northampton and had known my mother since they were both children. Teddy lived in a beautiful house fronting the small village green and opposite the school, his back garden running down to the canal just across from the Mill. Here a small landing stage had been constructed and a blue day cruiser called *Julia*, powered by an outboard engine, demonstrated Teddy's interest in the cut. I was always somewhat in awe of Teddy who assiduously cultivated the persona of a country squire both in dress and manner, a style which doubtless served him well in his profession. He was also keen on country pursuits, especially favouring the local shoots which were organised from time to time whenever it was felt that the pigeons or the crows had become too numerous. My mother and Teddy got along famously, we even got to borrow his boat one afternoon in late autumn when my great-aunt Vera took it into her head to visit us at the cottage. A boat trip would be just the thing to occupy her with, reasoned my mother, and Teddy seemed only too happy to oblige. I had no objections, especially as I was drafted in to serve as boatman, steering both ways through the tunnel on a trip to the Arm End and giving my elderly aunt a running commentary on the ways of the cut as I did so. Quite what my aunt made of all this I never really knew but suffice to say, with her curiousity satisfied, she never visited us at the cottage again!

Of 'my' boats I had still seen nothing as the late autumn drifted on towards winter and November came in quiet and misty. My mattress and so on had been dropped off at Sister Mary's in September and I had sent them all a card from Wales, but in the intervening week-ends since there had been no sign of the two pairs. Nothing was said to me by either Sister Mary or Mr James about them and I suppose I was too shy to ask. They'll come through one week-end, I reasoned and left it at that. Consequently I was completely unprepared for the change in circumstances which had overtaken my friends since the summer. It was the second week-end in November and I was doing English homework, my mind full of the machinations of Macbeth, when the steady beat of a diesel was heard coming from the direction of the tunnel. By now I had become reasonably good, but by no means infallible, at recognising the distinctive sound of the various makes of engine and mentally registered that the oncoming boat sounded very much like a twin-Bolinder. Having already firmly resolved that schoolwork would take priority that afternoon I resisted any temptation to set the lock, not even opening the door for a quick glance up the cut. Thus I was still dutifully scribing away at a table littered with books, with my parents reading comfortably in the armchairs situated on either side of the warm glowing fire, as the engine beat died away and an immaculate cratch, adorned with scrubbed whitestrings and canvas, drifted into view. Macbeth and all my resolutions to ignore boats and concentrate on schoolwork came to naught as I glanced up to see *Redshank* inscribed neatly on the bows. Homework might be critically important, but this was even more so! I emerged like a scalded cat to see Young Lily holding back, Alec on *Greenshank*'s fore-end coiling in the snubber, and Lil easing down the inside of *Redshank* prior to breasting-up above the empty lock.

"Hey up, young John!" grinned Alec, securing the two fore-ends and signalling Young Lily to hold back even harder as she brought the pair to a standstill with their cabins right outside the cottage door.

"Got your card! Lil's got it up in the cabin! Pride of place!"

My parents were out and everyone was smiling and chattering all at once, the more so as we found ourselves joined by Sister Mary. They were going to Cosgrove as usual that night and it was quickly agreed that I could help on the flight and then go down with them, returning to Stoke by bicycle despite the darkness. Just make sure you're very careful, my mother reminded me.

Young Lily was filling the lock as we gossiped and I fetched my coat and windlass, before wheeling my bike up the jetway from the cellar and laying it on the coal by the middle beam. She shouted to me that she would lockwheel so as to stretch her legs after steering the long Blisworth pound and, picking up the bike off *Greenshank*, disappeared over the bridge and down towards the second lock. I stood undecidedly on the towpath as the lock filled and looked back up the cut, perhaps I should lockwheel for *Warbler* and *Teal* who would surely be here in a minute. Lil, seeing me hesitate, got in first before I could ask.

"We're on our own now, John. I'll tell you down the locks."

Obviously whatever had happened would have to wait a minute and so, promising to be back by nine at the latest, I opened the top gate on the butty's side and got to work as Lil steered the pair in. It was straightaway into the old routine as they went down breasted up, with me attending to everything on *Greenshank*'s side of the locks. Down the long pound between the second and third locks Alec steered and I joined Lil in the cabin for a brief heart to heart. My Welsh card I noticed was indeed in pride of place, clipped to some lace above the table cupboard. It transpired that Ronnie and Phyllis had split up, naturally it was their personal business but the upshot was that Phyllis had left the cut for good and gone home, leaving Ronnie deciding to try and work ashore for a while in the Coventry area. I remembered that beaming smile and wave Phyllis had given me as I had reached the bridge at Wellingborough only a few weeks before, the rainwater running out of her hair at the top of Camp Hill, our efforts together with *Teal* in the narrow locks. She had been so proud of *Teal*, her own boat, and now it was all shattered to pieces. I could think of nothing to say beyond conventional commiserations and Lil seemed disinclined to discuss it further. We were probably both rather relieved when Alec eased for third lock and work took over once more. I never saw Phyllis again and have no idea what became of her, our lives had crossed during that brief summer and then uncrossed leaving us to move on in our separate ways. Of Ronnie I was also to see relatively little in the future. He returned to the cut in the summer of 1959, taking the newly painted Willow Wren motor *Egret* for a time, before eventually marrying a boat girl from a family largely unknown to me and settling ashore in the environs of Sutton Stop.

Working down the remaining five locks I assimilated the news gloomily. Everything had been so good in the summer, but those particular days were already past and all seemed uncertain once more. Reaching the bottom lock we were rejoined by Young Lily who grinned broadly at me and reminded me of my status by calling me 'Bachelor Boy', an old joke from the summer and linked to a hit record of the time by Cliff Richard. Her vivacity soon lightened my gloom as we shoved open the bottom gates together, she was only two or three years older than me and looked little different from the summer in her pinny, old coat, and black boots. I steered *Redshank* down the Cosgrove pound with Young Lily cleaning her cabin, puttering at odd jobs, and handing me a cup of tea near Yardley Bridge. Presently, with all jobs apparently completed, she climbed out to join me, declining my offer of the tiller and taking up position on the gunwale. We seemed to talk mostly about my various activities, including schoolwork and the forthcoming exams, as we ran on, past 'The Navigation' and the ornamental bridge, to find ourselves breasting-up once more above Cosgrove Lock. Young Lily had shared a cabin with Phyllis and must have known most of what had occurred, but it was private business and to her credit she hardly mentioned it, except to say that she missed her and that the cabin was now very quiet in the evening. Pedalling back to Stoke in the enveloping darkness I felt sad and rather subdued. Somehow I had thought that I would be boating on *Warbler* and *Teal* again the following year, but it was clearly not to be. An early lesson in the impermanence of all things had been learned and, though I would see both boats regularly in other hands, I was destined never to steer either of them again.

Christmas came and went and, with the demands of mock exams in February, I had little time for the cut. Indeed we only went to Stoke on alternate week-ends in those gloomy mid-winter months in order that I should have every chance in the exams. Winter passed, the mocks went reasonably successfully and at long last Spring was in the air again. We resumed our regular pattern of week-ends at Stoke and my thoughts returned with relief to the cut where life, compared to the competitive rigours of school, seemed fairly simple and straightforward. That Easter my father and I created a small allotment in the corner of Sister Mary's orchard, just about where people now park for the museum. The earth was black from years of deposited night-soil and our vegetables grew at an alarming rate. This patch, combined with my continued efforts in Sister's garden, was to provide ample vegetables for the canalside that summer with enough to spare for Old Charlie to find a pile on the corner of his doorstep from time to time. It was pleasant enough hewing and delving in the neglected orchard, but it merely burnt up energy that I would much rather have been expending on the boats. I would have loved to spend the Easter and Summer holidays aboard *Redshank* and *Greenshank*, as I would do in the future, but this was not possible at present as there was nowhere appropriate for me to sleep. Getting afloat again presented a bit of a problem and so for me 1959 would go down as the year of 'bits and pieces'.

It began with Wilfred one day towards the end of the Easter holidays. For years Wilfred had run a pair with the assistance of his Uncle Alf, who had once been an Oxford Canal 'Number One' and was getting on in years. I had, on a number of occasions, lockwheeled the flight for them and usually cadged a ride on the motor with Wilfred as far as Grafton Bridge. He had a particular friend in the village called Jack and he and his uncle frequently contrived to spend a night at Stoke in order for Wilfred and Jack to enjoy a pint together. I had sometimes sat with the three of them in 'The Boat' and liked Wilfred who had a great sense of humour and, because he had a small private source of income from his family in Abingdon, was never in such a rush to 'get 'em ahead' as most of the other crews. He tended to start a bit later and finish a bit earlier than most people and frequently tied in mid-afternoon at Stoke in order not to miss his evening with Jack.

This year Wilfred came up the flight with *Barnet* on his own and, having tied in his usual place just beyond the Mill, sauntered back for a chat which quickly led on to him coming in for a cup of tea. Uncle Alf, he told us, had fallen ill during the winter and after a lifetime of boating had been forced to give up the cut and retire to Abingdon, there to be looked after by the rest of the family. Wilfred had opted to continue with *Barnet* as a single motor for as long as he could, but he confessed to getting a bit lonely sometimes and fed up with 'talking to the chimney', as he put it. I needed no second bidding when he suggested that I might like to accompany him to Braunston the next day, putting the thought of the long ride home firmly to one side! I was more than happy in those days to trade a day's boating for a few miles on the bike, although I might think twice about it now! Once upon a time cycling to Braunston had been a really big adventure and had taken a whole day, now I was strong enough to contemplate the run from there back to Stoke as an evening's exercise after a full day's boating.

We left at about half past nine the next morning with Wilfred, as usual, in no hurry about getting up. He started *Barnet*'s National, mainly because I didn't know how to, undid the fore-end and then retired back into the cabin leaving me to get on with it, which I did with alacrity. Once again I was in my element and swept confidently into the tunnel at about twice the speed of my entry with *Canada Goose*. On this occasion pride did not come before a fall and we passed through quickly and without even coming near 'a touch'. An empty motor on a well maintained cut can eat up the miles and we had rounded Banbury Lane before Wilfred's trilby rose in the door-holes to "see how we'm a doing". He wouldn't hear of steering, insisting that I get on with it and enjoy myself on my day out. I was certainly doing that and the heavy swirling wash ran from bank to bank as *Barnet* churned through Bugbrooke, rounding the turns at High House and Stowe Hill before running out onto the long airy straight of the Weedon embankment.

"Fancy a pint?" asked Wilfred, as I eased her down for Weedon Bridge.

"Love one!" I responded. After all, it was my day out!

This was a very diferent kind of boating to that experienced with Ronnie and Alec. That Alec was fond of a pint of beer was undeniable, but his working practices did not in any way extend to a half past nine start followed by an early stop at Weedon for a beer. Most empty boats, in the normal way of things, went from either end of the Stoke flight directly to Sutton Stop in a day's work, but Wilfred was a law unto himself and did things his own way. We tied up on the bend above the filling station and went straight into the pub by the bridge, spending the next two hours playing skittles with a couple of local itinerants and sinking four pints of Phipps' apiece.

"Bread and cheese?" offered Wilfred, as we wandered happily back along the towpath to the waiting *Barnet*. We did not eat 'on the move' like everyone else, but instead remained tied whilst Wilfred rummaged in what was clearly his food drawer beneath the bed-cupboard. I sat on the end of the side-bed near the little row of books lined up on a small shelf situated just inside the door-holes. Books tended to be a rarity on the cut and a quick glance revealed that Wilfred had an evident fondness for detective fiction of the English variety. The cabin reflected its bachelor occupant and was considerably more spartan than most I had seen. There was only one brass rod above the range, no ornamental plates or lacework, and no curtains across the bed-space. Nevertheless it was all very clean and tidy, with the food drawer and the table-cupboard shelves lined with fresh paper and smart lino covering the floor and side-bed. The range was freshly black-leaded and his brass primus gleamed brightly in the sunlight pouring in through the open doors. Cheese and tomato chutney were accompanied by thick rounds of bread, this was apparently Wilfred's usual fare in the middle of the day and he seemed never to tire of it, although variations were allowed. He would ring the changes on the type of cheese and sometimes pickled onions were substituted for the tomato chutney, once later on we even had a pickled egg with it! Life could be so simple on the cut, I reflected. Wilfred steered his boat, lived in his tiny cabin with not even a wireless to listen to, read his second-hand books, and seemed to have few worries or concerns. He didn't even own a bike!

"Tasty cheese!" he said. "You can't beat a nice chunk of tasty!"

Wilfred was appalled that I had been on the cut all the previous summer and couldn't start a National! He accompanied me to the engine-hole and demonstrated his starting technique to me before stopping the engine, made me do it, stopped it once more, and then me again before he was satisfied.

"Got to be able to do it, John," he insisted. "Then, next time you come with me, I can have a nice lie-in and a read while you get on with it!"

An empty pair of Barlows had come past whilst we were tinkering in the engine-hole. This meant that Buckby would certainly be against us, but Wilfred was unconcerned.

"That's Arthur and Ernie," he grinned, watching their retreating sterns and raising a hand to Rosie in the butty hatches. "They goes too fast for me, any old how. We'd have only had to loose 'em by."

Keeping the National running after my last attempt, we got underway again on a particularly warm and spring-like afternoon, which enhanced a sense of well-being already considerably boosted by the intake of half a gallon of Phipps'. Wilfred sat on the top, his legs dangling down the side of the cabin, as I brought *Barnet* round the railway turn and headed on into the Spinnies. The peace was now disturbed by the noise of construction machines at work on the new road, a motorway to be called the M1, and destined to drive another and final nail into canal carrying. Wilfred leaned back on his elbows and grinned at me as we churned along through the trees, he seemed to have complete confidence in my abilities and was obviously relishing what he termed 'his holiday day'.

Upon our arrival at the bottom of Buckby he elected to walk ahead to set the locks leaving me to bring *Barnet* through on my own. This was the first time I had actually done this and felt quite honoured to be regarded as trustworthy to do so; this was real boating with a vengeance. Wilfred ambled away up the flight and I was simply expected to follow on. It was a bit tricky as the locks at Buckby are deep and, if I steered *Barnet* all the way in, I would find it very difficult, if not downright impossible, to clamber up to the lockside from her cabin top. A long strap ran from a shackle on the gunwale to where it presently lay coiled just in front of the slide, this was obviously what was needed. Wilfred had opened only one gate for me but it was the one on the same side as the shackle. I would stop

Barnet by strapping her in. Theory into practice again, but this time laced with much more experience. In we go, nice and steadily, take her out of gear and climb the adjacent steps drawing her to a halt with the strap on the stump provided expressly for this purpose. Gate shut, ground paddles up, check she isn't drifting back, and then up with the gate-paddles to the accompanying roar of the inrushing water. Coiling up the strap I stepped back on to the top and then dropped down on to the footboard, leaving the strap to hand on the slide. Once back on the footboard I engaged gear to keep her nudging against the gates, ready to 'wind it on' as the levels equalised and *Barnet*'s fore-end pushed its way through the top gates.

I was just nicely getting the hang of it all and thoroughly enjoying myself into the bargain when I met a south-bound pair of Willow Wrens, right under the railway bridge between the fourth and fifth locks up. I knew them and exchanged greetings and the inevitable joke about my position on *Barnet*'s footboard.

"Top lock's ready," was the parting shot, as the gap between us widened once more and we went our respective ways.

I fully expected to see Wilfred waiting for me at the next lock but there was no sign of him, although one gate had been considerably closed for me. As *Barnet* rose in the top lock there was still no sign of my missing captain and I began to feel just slightly anxious, where had he gone? I needn't have worried myself! As I peered hopefully around, the shop door suddenly opened and out he came carrying a small cardboard box of provisions.

"Swiss roll!" he grinned, brandishing one from his box as he dropped into the cabin and began to stow everything into his food drawer. The lock was full and I engaged gear once more, ready to head out across the summit.

"Hang on! Hang on!" exclaimed Wilfred. "Whoa! Got to take the box back first! Put the kettle on, we'll have us some tea before that old tunnel."

He disappeared back into the shop leaving me to get the primus going and boil up for tea. Wilfred never hurried and I had boiled a kettle, made the tea, and cut two thick slices of Swiss roll ready without any sign of his return. I didn't really want to interrupt, but stewed tea is not usually appreciated either, and so I tentatively stuck my head round the shop door where Wilfred was in animated conversation.

"Tea's ready!"

"Waiter Service!" he responded, with a wink at the shoplady. "My day for being spoilt!"

Off we went, with even larger second slices of roll accompanying second cups of tea. This saw us nicely along to the tunnel, whereupon Wilfred continued his 'holiday' by disappearing below once more for the duration of our journey underground. Lights ahead manifested themselves into a south-bound pair, all very handy and giving us a 'good road' down Braunston. A reversal of my usual role saw me steering down with Wilfred acting as the 'gate and paddle' man, the only exception being the closing of the top gate which remained my responsibility, once *Barnet* had come to a standstill. As we passed the 'Nelson' I began to be conscious of the westerly sun and passing time, it was going to be a long ride back. Time was pressing on me as we tied by the oiling place below the bottom lock and I thanked Wilfred for a marvellous day, resisting all suggestions of a pint in the 'Nelson' to help me on my way.

"Pleasure to have you!" he concluded. "I've really enjoyed my little holiday!"

The pleasures of the day gave me plenty to think about too, as I pedalled out of Braunston and settled to my journey. I was used to cycling, of course, and made surprisingly good time, aided by a nice breeze at my back. Darkness fell as I turned off the A5 at Stowe Hill and threaded through to Bugbrooke, but I knew the way and my trusty lamp played along the familiar lanes, through Gayton to Blisworth, and then finally over the top of the tunnel, before rattling down the long curving hill to the bridge and home.

The summer term began the next week and it was an anxious time. GCEs in May and June were one worry and the long summer holiday to follow was another. I had somehow assumed that this summer would follow on from the last but this scenario was looking increasingly unlikely. A close friendship had been built up with Alec and his family and I didn't really want to go boating with anyone else, but there was no space on the boats. Wilfred didn't do enough to need another pair of hands and, although I probably could have secured a spot with several other pairs, something inside me wanted to stick with the family I knew and trusted. I put the matter out of mind as much as possible in those last tightly-organised weeks of revision. Let's get this done first and then we'll see, went my reasoning, as the exam dates drew ever closer. We still spent every week-end at Stoke, of course, but my time was now strictly rationed between work and a walk, as May brought the deadline perilously close.

One afternoon I took my walk up above the tunnel and was surprised to see the S.M.J. line full of a mixture of old wooden coal wagons and the more modern steel mineral wagons. Clambering up on to the bridge I found that the line of trucks stretched as far as the eye could see in both directions – even by climbing on top of a wagon I could still see no end. This marked the end of the S.M.J. as a working line. The trucks remained unmoving and neglected all through the long hot summer which followed. By walking along at various times I was able to ascertain that the line of wagons began by the points near Towcester Station and extended out of sight beyond the the main line bridge at Roade. Birds nested in the axle boxes and I amused myself by scooping up the small amounts of surplus coal to be found in most of the wagons and transporting it by rucksack back to the cottage, there to be added to our small coal store in the cellar. The line from Blisworth to Towcester was not blocked in this way, but the turntable at Blisworth Station had been removed and the signs were ominous. Eventually the hundreds of wagons were shunted away to the scrap yards and, early in the following year, the last act began as the track was removed and the hedges began to close across. Today at Stoke it requires a good deal of imagination to picture the panting old locomotives, with their attendant long line of wagons, trundling across the bridge over the horse path on their solitary cross-country journeyings.

Half-term coincided with the midway point of the exams timetable, half completed and the other half still to come. It was a welcome few days break from the onslaught and I decided to stay over at Stoke that week, interspersing periods of revision with wanderings down the flight. It has been said that life deals the cards but we play them. Such was to be the case that week as suddenly, and without any previous hint, my problems with boating that summer were solved. Wilfred had tied at Stoke on the Tuesday night and I had decided to have a half-day off and accompany him down to Cosgrove the next morning. The strict revision timetable dictated a half-day only and I steadfastly resisted the temptation to go to Finney and make a day of it. We got away in the normal leisurely fashion at about half past eight and, with a good road down the locks, were soon chugging along in bright sunshine with me contentedly at the tiller and determinedly putting GCEs out of mind for a few hours at least. An uneventful morning took us along to Cosgrove where, after helping him through the lock, I again resisted all blandishments to go to Finney. The things you do for exams! Resist I did, however, waving Wilfred off along the embankment and inwardly praising my own self-discipline!

Wheeling my bicycle past the Beechey's cottage, which looked shut up and deserted for the day, I tucked trouser legs in my socks and prepared to mount up for the ride back.

"Hallo, John!"

A tall and very brown man with a salt and pepper beard, twinkling eyes and an infectious smile, was running a hosepipe from the tap to a tank on his boat. This was Mike Sloan, founder and proprietor of Sloan's New Way Holidays which largely consisted of a pair of hotel boats, converted from carrying craft, and appropriately named *Wanderer* and *Wayfarer*. His boats were based at Brownsover Wharf, up a little side-arm near Rugby, but they often spent a night at Stoke and I had chatted to him on several occasions and admired the single Bolinder which powered *Wanderer*. His boats had seemed very quiet as *Barnet* had passed and I had assumed that everyone was out exploring in the village or down looking at the aqueduct. Mike ran the pair with the assistance of his wife, Laura, who did the cooking in reputedly splendid fashion. He had a mate for the boating side of things and a girl to help Laura with the domestics, although I had never met either. There were two or three pairs of these hotel boats on the system at that time and they seemed to do a regular trade, mostly being patronised by older single people who didn't wish to hire their own boats.

"Hi, Mike!" I responded, with a smile.

"Shouldn't you be at school, then?"

I assured him it was half-term and that I was well within my rights to be there, not to mention my extensive programme of revision for the week.

"Revision?" he twinkled. "On *Barnet*!"

"Just a break," I countered firmly. "I shall get back and work solidly now."

"You can have a lift back with us if you like," he offered. "I'll bet you could do with some lunch!"

In that he was absolutely right. Wilfred had not yet got to his bread and cheese and I faced a six mile ride before I could satisfy the demands of my own inner man. It was tempting. Very tempting. The sun was shining. It might rain tomorrow. Bother GCEs!

"Laura!" called Mike.

A dark-haired woman, dressed in blue shorts and a short sleeved white top, stuck her head out of the double-doors on *Wayfarer*.

"Hallo, John," she smiled. "Shouldn't you be at school!"

Mike explained my position and elicited the information that lunch was fresh ham salad with apple pie to follow. Yes, there was more than enough for me, affirmed Laura. It was all very tempting and my steely resolve weakened, especially as I was very partial to apple pie! I gave way without further resistance, after all cycling in the mid-day sun might have given me a headache!

Climbing aboard I was introduced to the mate, a rather plump youth whose name I misremember and who was apparently leaving them at the end of June. The other crew member was a pretty girl in her mid-twenties known as Wheat. This I later learned was short for her surname, Wheatley, and she used it in preference to her long and rather old fashioned Christian name. Over lunch Mike, who had seen me with Ronnie and Alec last summer, asked me what I was up to these days and I explained about exams and my inability to follow up the spell of working boating I had done. Nothing further was said about this and, with my bike stowed in *Wanderer*'s engine-hole, we got underway and 'bomped' in leisurely fashion up the pound towards Stoke. I was allowed to steer *Wanderer* for a while along through Yardley and Grafton Bridge before Mike took over again for the flight, where I assisted happily on the motor's side of the lock. They tied up beyond the Mill and I hurried back to the cottage. It was already past five o'clock. So much for my half-day's boating and half-day's revision. I decided a boiled egg would do for tea and then the whole evening on English Economic History in order to catch up on the revision schedule.

At about eight o'clock I was deep into the intricacies of Victorian factory life when I was disturbed by a sudden and unexpected tap on the door, which turned out to be none other than Mike Sloan again. He looked at all my books spread out on the table and apologised for disturbing me, but could I spare a minute? I was ready for another cup of tea and we were soon comfortable in the easy chairs enjoying this along with one of my favourite digestive biscuits.

"How much time have you actually got off school this summer, John?"

I explained that once 'O' levels were finished we were not really needed in school again. Therefore, assuming success and a place on the 'A' level courses in September, I would have the unusual luxury of about ten weeks holiday this year instead of the more customary six, or occasionally seven. It was peaceful in the quiet cottage, the only sound seemed to be our old chiming clock ticking softly away on the mantelpiece, but the bookstrewn table served to remind me of reality and I wondered what Mike really wanted. We didn't know each other particularly well, not really well enough for him to come tapping on my door like this, surely there must be some other reason than just being sociable.

"Can I be straight with you, John? Strictly between ourselves, OK."

I assented readily enough to this and Mike went on to explain that his current mate, whom he clearly did not rate too highly, was leaving at the end of June but that he was so strapped for cash that he could not really afford to replace him. Bookings were down this year and his situation was very tight. I nodded sympathetically, wondering what this had got to do with me.

I very soon found out! He was offering me a deal, in essence the same as the conditions upon which I had worked the previous summer. Food and board and plenty of boating in exchange for my commitment and effort. I considered this over a second cup of tea. Hotel boats were most certainly not working boats, which was where my heart lay. However they were definitely better than nothing at all, which was also beginning to look a stronger and stronger possibility as the weeks slipped past. The actual travelling, of course, was much less than on the working boats but, looking on the positive side, there would be more time to explore places and, with passengers changing weekly, the chance to meet lots of different people. I hesitated slightly but then decided that beggars can't be choosers, a bird in the hand and all that stuff. With no more ado I agreed with Mike that I would start at Brownsover on the first Saturday in July and work with him until the end of August.

"Sure?" he persisted. "You won't change your mind?"

"No, no!" I retorted. "Let's shake on it. If you shake on it, you have to do it. A deal's a deal!"

We shook on it there and then and off he went, doubtless pleased to be able to tell Laura, whose suggestion it had been, that the problem of a mate and the finances had been solved for a few more weeks. I returned to my books fairly sure that I had done the right thing, at least I would be afloat.

The remainder of term passed in a torrent of revision followed by exams sitting in serried rows in the Gym or the Hall. I wrote for hours and my right hand ached with the effort of it all, not to mention my head! Finally on a warm day in mid-June I headed gleefully for the bike sheds, it was over! The results would not be known until mid-August, but you know yourself in an exam whether or not you have done well enough to pass. As I rode jubilantly home that day, picking up a celebratory cream cake on the way, I felt fairly confident that the amount of work I had put in would result in success and that this would open the door to the Sixth Form and two years of 'A' levels. That job was done. School could now be left behind for a few weeks and, with a clear conscience, I could once again turn my full attention to the cut.

The summer of 1959 turned out to be a regular thumper with a high pressure system blissfully stuck over the country. For once the weather became entirely predictable, every day was warm and sunny and rain became a memory. I took the train over to Rugby before walking down to the cut which, with the bag I was carrying, turned out to be further than I had bargained for in the hot sun.

The Brownsover Arm was a survival of the straightening process undertaken by Cubitt in order to shorten the distance between Hillmorton and Sutton Stop. This work was carried out between 1829 and 1834 and the total length of the Oxford was shortened from 91 miles to 77 miles. The redundant loops criss-cross the pound and the original tortuous course gave rise to the old boatman's saying that 'you could travel all day within the sound of Brinklow Church'. I never really had time to explore the line of these old loops which would have interested me greatly but I did manage, during one turn-around week-end at Brownsover, to cycle along the towpath to Newbold, pronounced 'Noble' on the cut, where the short tunnel, complete with towpath, carries the northern Oxford under a small hill on its way to Sutton Stop. Here the original line of the cut left the new line and ran past 'The Boat' inn before it also went into a tunnel that carried it under the road and the churchyard. There was no sign of a tunnel entrance at this end but, by walking through the churchyard, I followed a path dipping down into a field and found myself facing the old red-brick exit of the tunnel. It was bricked-in just inside which prevented further investigation, but the old line of the canal was clearly traceable meandering across the field.

The Brownsover Arm was one of the very few pieces of the original cut still navigable and it ran for just a quarter of a mile or so from the main line, a slight bend hid its termination amidst a tangle of brambles from the view of passing boats. Passing through a gate I walked up an earthen track, much scarred by pot-holes, to where I could see *Wanderer* and *Wayfarer* tied singled-out along the old towpath. Further along, just by where the water abruptly ended, was the small coal wharf where an occasional pair of Barlows still traded from the Warwickshire coalfield. Also of interest, and on the opposite side to the wharf, tied against a mass of brambles and surrounded by water lilies, was an old Josher butty with the Fellows, Morton & Clayton lettering, peeling but still clearly visible, on her red cabin side. Forward from *Wanderer* was a small hut, situated at the end of the wharf just by where the towpath hedge began, and this served as Mike's office, workshop, and store-room, all rolled into one. Here was located the phone, with an outside bell to summon us from the boats, Mike's desk cluttered with paperwork, a battered old upright typewriter, and a veritable mass of paintpots, ropes, off-cuts of wood, cans of oil, and all the other paraphernalia of a one man business.

WINDLASS IN MY BELT

It was just mid-day and the boats seemed deserted. The passengers would not arrive until about three o'clock and, although the cabin doors were wide open, there was no response to my tap. Having looked in windows and tapped on *Wayfarer*'s stern cabin all to no effect, I put my bag in the hatches and wandered along to the hut where a small sign proclaimed its owner. Mike was sitting at his desk dealing with correspondence and looked up as I knocked the open door.

"Oh, hello, John. Made it alright then."

I nodded and looked round curiously at the jumbled hut which didn't at all seem to match the clean and tidy pair outside.

"Laura and Wheat are up in Rugby provisioning and I'm, as you see, condemned to the paperwork."

Suddenly shy again, I murmured something inconsequential and stood there feeling a bit of a spare part.

"Look! Why don't you settle in. You're in the motor cabin. They won't be long but I simply must get this done and you can help them unpack when they come."

I realised later that turn-around time was deceptively busy and that, with only being at Rugby every other week, Mike was always frantically trying to deal with the correspondence. He was clearly busy now, so I did as bidden and took myself off back to the boats.

Retrieving my bag from *Wayfarer*'s hatches I walked down and stepped on to *Wanderer*'s counter. The white ash strakes around it looked freshly scrubbed, the three tip-cats were nice and tight and tiller pin and chimney brasses gleamed in the sun. Outwardly *Wanderer* looked fine and I felt quite pleased until I looked in the cabin. My predecessor had moved out the night before and had clearly never heard of the cut tradition of leaving a vacated cabin clean enough to eat your dinner off the floor. My floor was covered in bits of dried mud, dust, screwed up sweet papers, and other assorted debris. The small stove was rusty in places and badly in need of black-leading and the whole cabin wore an air of benign neglect. There was no-one around and the clink of the bell on Mike's typewriter assured me that he was busy. Time to investigate! I wondered what the rest of the pair looked like, surely not like this mess! I needn't have worried as I sauntered through *Wanderer*, looking in to each of the little cabins. Everything had been cleaned that day, sinks polished, and beds invitingly turned down, with *Wayfarer* exactly the same. It was just my bit! Alec would have a fit if he saw it, but cabins are only small and I resolved to set my own professional boatman standard to it as quickly as possible.

However cabin cleaning would have to wait as a rather well-used looking van turned in at the gate and bounced and swayed along the track before coming to a halt outside the hut. Laura and Wheat climbed out, both looking very hot and bothered, as I quickly hurried over to help unload. Both greeted me warmly and by the time I had moved a number of heavy boxfuls of food from the van to *Wayfarer*'s galley I began to feel more comfortable. There is nothing like a spot of work to make you feel a part of things. By evening, with eight passengers welcomed aboard and dinner eaten, I already felt quite at home. The capacity of the pair was twenty passengers and I could see why Mike's business was in trouble by there being only eight for this, my first trip. As an addition to the hotel boats Mike also had two very small cruisers for hire. One was an 'Otter', which could double as a caravan if loaded on to a specially designed trailer, and the other was an old wooden single-cabined craft that had clearly seen better days. Both these boats were powered by outboards and were a constant worry for Mike. There was no-one at Brownsover whilst we were away and thus turn-around of the cruisers had to be handled by a character who lived in nearby Hillmorton and knew a little bit about boats. Neither craft was out that week and both were tied rather forlornly by the shed, a mute testament to the problems of the business.

To everyone's amusement I spent two hours working on my cabin after dinner. Drawers were taken out and vigorously scrubbed, drying on the bank in the late evening sun. Everything was swept out very thoroughly and then the whole cabin washed over for good measure. Drawers were then retrieved and lined with newspaper, happily passed over by Laura, before finally I stowed my kit and sat on the side-bed looking round. The cabin was now reminiscent of *Barnet* in its clean and tidy bachelor style, the little bottle stove still needed black-leading but that could be done another day, I decided, as I straightened the coalbox and put my windlass to hand on a conveniently placed hook above the stove. Thus satisfied I snuggled into bed ready to begin my first full day as mate. Once again school, and especially GCE exams, seemed a very long way away.

Mike was running a choice of three trips that summer. It was important to have a turn-around point where the passengers had easy transport facilities available to them. South-bound on the Grand Union this meant the main railway line at Berkhamsted, on the Oxford it meant Kidlington and a bus to the main-line station in Oxford, and this week it meant Lapworth and a connecting train to Birmingham New Street. Over the ten weeks I would do one round trip to Lapworth and two each on the Grand Union and Oxford runs. That first day encapsulated the many that followed and, like the working boats, we also had our routines which ensured the job ran smoothly. One of my jobs, as mate, was to be responsible for the cleanliness of the outside of both boats. Each day through that hot summer I would rise early and, as a first task, mop out the sitting areas in the fore-ends in order that they would be dry when the passengers had breakfasted. Next would come outside brasses and rope work on both boats and the scrubbing of the ash strips on *Wanderer*'s counter and around *Wayfarer*'s hatches. Whilst everyone was safely at breakfast I would then mop off the full length of the roof and cabin sides before giving a final polish to the windows with a 'chammy' leather, after which I was ready for breakfast myself!

Wheat, besides assisting Laura in the galley, cleaned the inside of the boats and made up the beds. She also waited at table in the long dining saloon on *Wayfarer*, which doubled as a sitting area during the rest of the day. Laura did all the cooking, looked after the domestic organisation, and kept Wheat and myself up to the mark, if necessary! Mike steered, dealt with any major problems to do with the passengers, and generally oiled the wheels with a geniality that was hard to resist. Our main aim was to ensure that the passengers had a pleasant and comfortable holiday and, indeed, some of them were on their third or fourth trip with Mike and Laura. It is not difficult to be helpful and I very soon found myself part of the team, anticipating needs and lending a hand wherever it was needed.

The actual boating was also quite a contrast to that experienced on the carrying craft. There the over-riding object was to 'get 'em ahead', to get from one place to another in the shortest possible time. On the working boats payment by the trip meant long hours and strenuous efforts to keep the boats moving whatever the weather. Hotel boating was totally different, just like chalk and cheese. Distances travelled each day were quite short, with plenty of time being allocated to allow the passengers to enjoy their surroundings and not miss features of interest. We were very happy for the passengers, should they so wish, to help with the locks and passed through very sedately with no drawing of paddles early, banging of gates, or any other little tricks designed to save minutes. There was no need to save minutes. We had plenty of time and travelled slowly, giving everyone the chance to enjoy the sunshine of that glorious summer and to relax 'on England's peaceful waterways'. Tunnels were steered through on tickover to maximise the time spent underground and we always stopped on the aqueducts to savour the view and facilitate the taking of photographs. It was really quite simple. People were paying for service and a relaxing holiday, our task was to provide it.

We got going on that first Sunday morning at about a quarter past ten or so. Mike set off on *Wanderer* and I stood in the hatches of *Wayfarer*, tied up close on the cross-straps, as we travelled the very short distance to the junction with the main line. This section would become familiar to me over the next couple of years but, at that time, I had never been along the northern Oxford having, as will be remembered, gone to the Cannock coalfield the previous summer. There was no 'winding-hole' in the Brownsover Arm and so Mike always reversed in at the end of each trip. Even so, it was a tight turn out on to the main line and I found myself directed forward to shaft *Wanderer* off, before scurrying back to guide *Wayfarer* safely round. Steering what was, in effect, an empty butty on the cross-straps is a very easy occupation, mostly only requiring light touches on the tiller to avoid bumping in bridge-holes or on tight turns. Along the straights you can sit in the hatches and watch the world drift slowly by. On working boats, travelling empty means the boatwoman is very often to be found busy in the cabin catching up with the odd jobs and only emerging when required. I was under no such pressure and was able to spend that first morning drifting easily along to the bottom of Hillmorton, just simply enjoying the sun and the sensation of being underway once more. At Hillmorton the locks are double, that is to say side by side, to accommodate the heavy coal traffic heading south. Laura emerged briefly from the galley and asked me what I proposed to do when Mike 'loosed me off' and then, having satisfied herself that I had the right idea, left me to it and went back to preparing lunch. This was my first lock with the Sloan's and I gripped the tiller in determined fashion, it wouldn't do to start off with a complete shambles! We were helped by both locks being ready with the bottom gates standing open, having met two pairs of empty BW boats that morning on the short stretch from Brownsover. Mike eased off completely, unhooking the cross-straps and waving me to take the outside lock. *Wayfarer* swung slowly across as I lined her up for the lock, only too aware of the hot pans on the galley stove. She went in clean as a whistle, barely brushing the locksides as I took the tiller out and laid it on the cabin roof before climbing off with the strap. *Wayfarer* was by now moving so slowly that I hardly needed to strap her in but, still mindful of Laura and Wheat in the galley, I brought her to a halt in immaculate fashion just inches short of the sill. Feeling very pleased with myself I shut the bottom gates and walked sedately up the lockside to draw. Even here I remained mindful of the two cooks and just drew half a paddle, starting things off gently with no sudden surges to cause *Wayfarer* any untoward bumps. Of course, I soon found myself explaining the theory of lockage to the passengers, one of whom was a retired Colonel who became very keen to try his hand with the windlass at the next couple of locks. This was to be encouraged and so very easily and smoothly, without any banging of gates and crashing of paddles, we ascended the three locks and tied for lunch at the top. Our morning's boating was complete!

We usually tied for at least two hours at lunchtime but it was hardly an idle time for the crew. Lunch was mostly a cold collation, especially with the present hot weather, but after having been served out and collected up by Wheat, it then all had to be washed up in the confined little galley ready for the main meal that evening. With breakfast and afternoon tea as well there was an awful lot of washing up, mostly done by Wheat and Laura with the 'lads' helping out as much as they could. It is true to say that I became very adept with a tea towel as the weeks passed by! Having announced my familiarity with single Bolinders I was allowed to restart *Wanderer* that afternoon. After watching me 'kick her off', Mike grinningly said that was one job less for him every morning! I didn't mind as I relished all that messing about with the blowlamp and various levers entailed in generating the thunderous roar as the engine 'took' and the familiar 'bomp-bomp-bomp' began. I steered *Wanderer* for about an hour that afternoon down the long Barby straights before Mike took over for the approach to Braunston. Here we would tie for the night, nestled in snugly just round the junction and facing down the long wide straight to Wolfhamcote. I had no oil rod in that afternoon and the speedwheel was only half-on as we almost drifted down the pound in accordance with Mike's instructions. Achieving the sensation of slow meandering through the heart of England was at the core of his thinking and, despite being often sorely tempted to 'wind it on', I could see his point. Our trade was in carrying people in need of a leisurely and restful holiday and so it was a case of 'nice and steady' all the way, taking as long as was reasonably possible round the pounds. Later on I found myself almost timing it to see how slowly I could get round a pound, the exact opposite of my Willow Wren days.

Our normal practice was to try and tie up by about five o'clock, with Wheat having served afternoon tea about an hour earlier. This gave the passengers time to explore their new surroundings whilst we dealt with the tea things and prepared dinner for half past seven. Another of my regular tasks, usually undertaken if possible at this time of day, was keeping the water tanks on both boats topped up from the hosepipe. A surprising amount of water was used, especially when we were fully booked, and sometimes I would find myself topping the tanks off twice daily as it would be a very black mark indeed if we ever ran dry. Thus, although the actual boating was done in a leisurely fashion, our working day was quite long. I found that it was usually past nine o'clock at night before everything was finally squared away and we could snatch a little free time for ourselves.

Most of my first week was spent getting used to the routine of running a small hotel on a pair of boats, a routine totally different from the one I had become accustomed to the previous summer. It was overall much less demanding than the life of the working boats. We only lockwheeled in the flights and then in a very relaxed manner as I strolled ahead, often accompanied by a few passengers, to set the locks. Mike was in no hurry and the pair dawdled down the pounds giving me plenty of time to ensure that everything was ready for them. The hours of boating were much much shorter, of course, but conversely there was more in the way of cleaning and domestic chores to keep me occupied when we were tied up. There was normally a spare hour at lunchtime for a rest or a wander and on Wednesdays we always tied up for the remainder of the day, which gave me most of that afternoon free to follow my own inclinations. Without any doubt, I was to see much more of the towns and villages surrounding the cut during my summer with the Sloans than I ever did during my twelve to fifteen hour days on the working boats, where it seemed as if we only ever stopped to have a pint and sleep. The weather that summer was magnificent and contributed hugely to the pleasure of it all. Hotel boating during a dreary week of wind and squalls, interspersed with periods of continuous rain, must have been a very different proposition with tetchy passengers, mud carried aboard to be cleaned up, and the difficulties of wringing any enjoyment from such a situation. This was not to be my lot and, apart from one afternoon on the southern Oxford when it clouded and rain actually fell for a couple of hours, I was blessed with clear blue skies and sun, day after day and week after week.

My first week proceeded steadily enough and set the pattern for those that followed. Lunch stop at Shuckburgh and Monday night at the top of Itchington. Lunch at the bottom of Itchington and Tuesday night at the bottom of Radford. The half day naturally was allocated to Warwick and its castle and medieval buildings, with the boats tied at the Cape. A late start the next day offered more time in Warwick, lunch half-way up Hatton at the Asylum Wharf, and Thursday night spent a mile or so beyond the top lock giving a very gentle run into Lapworth for Friday, the return trip to Rugby being the same. The Lapworth trip had been put into the brochure for the first time that season by Mike as a variation, with Warwick as its highlight. Despite this it was poorly booked and cost him dearly in lost revenue with only four passengers aboard for the return trip. My, they got good service! The Grand Union and Oxford trips were much better booked with the boats at least three-quarters full, but only twice in my time with the pair did we have a full complement of passengers and this at the height of the season and in the midst of a glorious summer. The reasons for this shortage of passengers was not apparent to me, then or now. The boats were well appointed, food was excellent, and, dare I say it, the crew was friendly and obliging. But the passengers were not forthcoming and I became aware through the weeks that Sloan's New Way Holidays really was in financial trouble and that my presence, as unpaid mate, was genuinely welcome as a small factor in alleviating the growing pressure.

Having completed a Berko trip I was excited at the thought of the Oxford run as I had never seen the waterway below Banbury. Mike insisted that the last three or four miles into Oxford were shallow and difficult and accordingly stopped just beyond Thrupp at Langford Lane Wharf, Kidlington. From here it was possible to catch a bus into central Oxford, although this was quite a long journey for the passengers. Occasional pairs of boats still delivered coal to Juxon Street Wharf in the heart of Jericho and privately I reasoned that, if loaded boats could get through to Oxford, then we certainly should be able to. I thought at the time, and still see no reason to change my view, that Mike was putting his own convenience ahead of the passengers in not proceeding to tie by Isis Lock. Oxford could easily have been reached by Friday lunch-time and the passengers could have had a half-day, in place of Wednesday afternoon, to explore the beauties of the city with a similar half-day being taken on Sunday morning for the return trip. However, as a sixteen year old mate enjoying a working holiday, I kept such thoughts to myself and simply helped carry cases to and from the bus stop in Kidlington.

The southern Oxford was rather shallow in places, but absolutely brimming with quiet charm. Locks succeeded each other at regular intervals down the valley of the Cherwell, whose course we utilised for a short burst of deep water steering near the cement works at Enslow. Joe Skinner had retired the previous year and commercial traffic was becoming very scarce. On one occasion we encountered a pair of Barlows in the Napton flight returning empty from the Banbury Dairy run but, other than the 'gas' boats whom we met on both my trips, there was no other commercial traffic to be seen. Below Banbury the cut became very quiet with the still waters broken only by the leisurely passage of ourselves and other occasional pleasure craft. Coal to Oxford might still happen, but only very occasionally. It was gorgeous work chugging slowly along those beautiful tree-lined pounds down through Northbrook and Pigeons and I loved the peace and beauty of it all, storing away in my memory that marvellous succession of sun drenched days. Undoubtedly I saw it at just the right moment, with the subsequent huge increase in boats such a tranquil summer could not possibly be replicated today.

Slowly the weeks passed by. Gloriously sunny days followed each other with only small incidents to disturb our routine. One of the passengers somehow dislodged a pane of glass from a sliding window and very careful prodding with the shaft revealed it to be conveniently resting against the hull of *Wayfarer*. We were tied above Pigeons Lock at the time and naturally it fell to the mate to go in and carefully lift it out – at least the Oxford is clean! Wheat, sunbathing on the top of *Wayfarer* in the Cosgrove pound, rolled over the wrong way landing in the cut with a most enormous splash, but was otherwise quite unharmed. Grinning with amusement amidst our cheering she hauled herself out and ran dripping along to the next bridge hole – the Cosgrove pound is fairly clean too! My parents were on their fortnight's summer holiday at Stoke as we passed through on my last trip in late August. Mother, looking rather pleased, produced the little slip of paper which indicated GCEs passed and a place in the Sixth Form, another hurdle successfully jumped!

We had no sooner tied at Stoke that evening than Alec came past, heading as usual for Cosgrove. Amazingly it was the first time that I had seen the pair that summer and I speedily obtained a dispensation to go down the locks with them on the promise of extra work with the tea towel upon my return! They were pleased about my exams and had news of their own. Young Lily was to marry her Cliff the following year! I had met Cliff, who worked in a scrapyard near Sutton Stop, and had liked him instantly, my congratulations being rather breathless as Young Lily and I fast-walked the long pound together to set the third lock. She insisted on setting the rest of the flight on her own, giving me the chance to chat and exchange news with Alec and Lil who seemed as pleased to see me as I most certainly was to see them. Good friends are not easy to find and these two would prove to be some of the best I have ever had. At Bridge Lock I found myself bowled over!

"Thought you was coming with us this holiday!" grumbled Alec.

"There was nowhere I could sleep!" I protested. "You said so!"

"Ah, well," he continued, "We talked about that. Young Lily would have slept on our side-bed if you'd have come!"

There was nothing to be said or done. Much as I had enjoyed my summer on *Wanderer* and *Wayfarer*, it couldn't compare to a summer with Alec. Such are the misunderstandings that dog us through life. Still, at least I knew I was now welcome if I appeared and that, in any case, Young Lily would be married and living ashore the following year. With two years in the Sixth Form to come my boating future looked well assured, it was with this thought that I consoled myself as I waved them off from the bottom lock before walking back to my pile of drying-up!

The end of August drew near. School loomed ahead once more as I made the final return trip from Berko, being overtaken at Leighton by Alec returning empty to the coalfields, at least I wasn't missing an exotic Birmingham run! I arrived back at Brownsover for the last time, as brown as I have ever been in my life after almost ten weeks of unbroken sun. I saw the passengers off on the Saturday morning and helped with the change-over routine before, having said my goodbyes to Laura and Wheat, I was run up to the station by Mike. With only one more Berko trip to do in September before bookings ceased he faced an uncertain future. They had been very kind to me and I had worked hard and done my best for them, a fair exchange all round. Our goodbyes were brief as, with a characteristically firm handshake, Mike wished me the best of luck before driving quickly out of the station forecourt. I never saw any of them again. I was not surprised when Sloan's New Way Holidays ceased to trade at the end of the season, the boats were soon sold and Mike and Laura disappeared from the canal scene for ever. The summer had been an interesting experience and at least I had been afloat, but it had been so slow! I longed to be back on the working boats where I felt so much more at home and where it was expected that you would 'put your oil rod in' and quickly at that!

School resumed as if I had never been away and, rather to my surprise, I actually found myself enjoying the Sixth Form with its attractive combination of small classes and challenging work. Comments were made about my deeply tanned face and arms but I shrugged them off casually, the cut was still my secret world and kept separate from my day to day life in the town. On a drizzly afternoon in mid-September a small cruiser ascended the flight steered by a dark haired bearded man and his attractive fair haired wife. All this I observed from the table in our living room, where I was completing my English homework and feeling comforted by the warmth from the fire, for autumn had now arrived with a vengeance and the weeks of warmth were just a memory. Suddenly there was a loud splash followed by shrieks and we all rushed out in time to see the pretty wife being hauled out of the cold cut. Without hesitation my mother insisted that she be brought straight into the warm cottage, with my father and I finding ourselves banished briefly upstairs whilst towels and a change of clothes were effected. This was my first meeting with Janusz and Ruth who would also become good friends to both me, and ultimately my wife, as the years passed by. Janusz was another serious canal enthusiast and we all had a long animated chat that evening, they having been pressed to stay to tea in order to ensure that Ruth was really and truly dry. It was dark when we parted. They to return to their boat and we to catch the late bus back to Northampton and the week's work. Our paths were destined to cross and cross again as the years unfolded.

The year's boating was nearly over. The October half-term would lead on to the time of short days and long nights when the cut became more difficult for me. On the first week-end of the break Wilfred tied at Stoke at mid-day on Sunday and we went into 'The Boat' for a pint or two. He had hurt his wrist slipping on the lockside at Buckby and considered himself lucky not to have ended up sharing the lock with *Barnet*. It wasn't too bad an injury and Sister Mary, after a lot of poking and pulling, had strapped it up and told him not to put too much weight on it. Difficult advice to follow when you're working a single motor! Having ascertained he was destined for Croxley Mills I considered the situation. There was a whole week ahead for half-term, but 'A' levels were proving to be much more demanding and I had about three days work that simply had to be done before returning to school. I looked at Wilfred, sitting there drinking his pint and complaining about the latest change in tonnage rates.

"I could give you a hand, if you want," I offered cautiously, not wanting to presume.

"Oi could do wiv an hand to Cosgrove," he retorted. "Can't hardly draw a paddle like this."

'Seize a chance and you won't be sorry for a might have been' was a favourite saying in our family and I remembered it now.

"I could come to Croxley, if you like. Train home from Watford. Give you a couple of days rest for the old wrist!"

I wondered what my mother would say. She entirely approved of Alec and Ronnie and didn't mind me having days out with Wilfred, but going to Croxley with him?

"That'd be nice, boy!"

He seemed pleased and said he'd be glad to have me. I made it clear that I could only go to Croxley as schoolwork was pressing but, as Wilfred said, a couple of days relative rest followed by time waiting to empty should make all the difference.

We returned via the cottage and mother was persuaded, without too much difficulty, that all would be well and that I would be home on Tuesday night.

"Bit fast for me!" complained Wilfred, but accepted that it was perfectly feasible.

An early start was agreed for Monday morning and we took *Barnet* down the flight that afternoon to ensure a clear run the next day. It was agreed that 'if I'm not up' I should start *Barnet* and get going on the long pounds ahead. Half past five the next morning saw me walking excitedly down the flight. This trip was an unexpected bonus and as before I determined to squeeze every last drop of enjoyment from it. *Barnet* lay in the length below the bottom lock with, not surprisingly, no sign of life. Stepping on to her counter I felt the chimney which was re-assuringly warm to the touch. Good. That meant that Wilfred had put a 'banker' in his stove and the fire would be capable of resurrection, rather than having to go to all the trouble of relighting it. A 'banker' was a large piece of coal with the grain running horizontally which would, if placed on the stove correctly, 'bank' the fire in overnight, thus keeping you warm in bed and saving a fiddly job first thing in the morning. Most of the boat crews had a small store of 'bankers', kept separately from the other coal stored in the back-end and from which the cabin coal box was replenished. Opening the cabin doors I dropped my small bag on to the side-bed and peered at Wilfred who was snuggled into a pile of blankets on the cross-bed.

"Cor! What time is it, boy?"

"About sixish," I returned. "You stay there, I'll get us going like we said."

Both of us knew that there would be no question of further sleep once the engine had started, but at least Wilfred needn't hurry himself about.

"Early', he commented dourly.

"Buy you a pint at Maffers," I replied encouragingly, before fitting the tiller bar and getting *Barnet* underway.

I steered for the first hour with the cabin doors closed around me and, as the exhaust pipe echoed under Yardley Bridge, became aware of movement within the cabin. Smoke swirled from the chimney as Wilfred got the fire blazing and a kettle was passed up for me to fill, being eventually followed by a most welcome mug of tea. I was thoroughly enjoying myself and the slow burgeoning of the sun seemed to indicate a rather chilly, but essentially fine, day ahead for our journey south. Just before Cosgrove, which was ready for us, Wilfred climbed out and sniffed the air appreciatively.

"Gonna be a nice day, young John. Nice clean air," he announced, breathing deeply of a mixture of cabin smoke, exhaust smoke, and, it has to be said, fresh autumn air!

"How's the wrist?"

"Not too bad."

He eyed the strapping gloomily and winked at me.

"So long as I don't do too much with it!."

Mist lay along the Great Ouse as we crossed 'the pig trough' and turned along past the carriage works with the aroma of frying bacon rising up around me from the cabin. Presently Wilfred took over and I sat contentedly on the side-bed eating a bacon sandwich of doorstep dimensions and washing it down with that staple of the cut, tea. Another kettle was simmering for washing up but Wilfred, who said that he was in charge of light duties, insisted on doing that and cabin tidying. I was back on the tiller and assisted by doing the outside brasses as the glorious Finney pound unfolded before me in the bright morning sunshine. Wilfred had no bicycle and so lockwheeling, except for those close together, was not possible. However the luck ran with us that day as we met two pairs of Wellingborough-bound BW boats in the latter part of the pound.

"Leighton's ready!" said the steerer, giving us a good start on the climb up to the summit.

Pausing for bread at Finney I made more tea whilst Wilfred shopped. He loved a chat and even buying a loaf of bread would take him ten minutes and often longer. No one had tied at the top of Stoke the previous night and so there was no danger of anyone catching up to us and stealing our good road, pleasure boats being few and far between at that time of year. With nobody pressing we could relax and enjoy the day which was turning out to be a glorious late autumn extravaganza of reds and browns accompanied by gently fluttering leaves. I filled the water cans, checked the engine-hole, and generally fiddled about until Wilfred returned clutching bread and yet another of his favourite Swiss rolls.

"Wagons roll!," he grinned, as he climbed down into the cabin, leaving me to spin the gearwheel and get *Barnet* moving once more. On we went with the sunshine seemingly set for the day as I rounded the Jackdaw pound faultlessly and with great confidence, so much had been learned since those early tentative days of narrow boating on *Canada Goose*. I felt a deep inward glow of sheer happiness as I handed over to Wilfred and jumped off to do the work at Leighton Lock. It was thought that a pint would be in order at Leighton Bridge, but time was marching on as we hurriedly tied *Barnet* up and almost ran across the bridge. Closing time was desperately close as we scurried in, but we still managed a couple of pints apiece in the near deserted bar before the towel went up and we returned to *Barnet* for cheese and some of the fresh Finney bread. I came to the conclusion that since Uncle Alf had retired to Abingdon, Wilfred had got into the habit of sinking a pint at lunchtime in order to break up his long days of 'talking to the chimney' and that my presence, being only very temporary, had not served as any reason for him to break with this custom.

Lady Luck kept smiling on us that afternoon as we went up 'The Fields' and had the good fortune to meet four pairs of northbound boats spaced in such a way as to give us every lock ready. For the first time I had the experience of steering up the pounds through Horton and the Nags Head, instead of my usual view of them from the lockwheelers saddle. I had, of course, been afloat in those pounds that summer as Mike had made his leisurely way along, not the same thing I decided as *Barnet* left her wash racing along the banks and bubbling up in the holes along the towpath. We had done well that day and it was early evening as we passed the top of the Aylesbury Arm and tied, as planned, at the bottom of Maffers. Most people would have made the most of the good day and gone on to Cowroast, but Wilfred had been getting dinner ready since the top of the Nags Head and anyway preferred the pub here, 'The White Horse', to 'The Cowroast', so that settled it! Wilfred lived simply and dinner was hot corned beef and potatoes, with the Swiss roll as pudding, and very filling it was too! His wrist didn't seem to preclude him from throwing darts that evening and I wondered to myself how bad it really was, although he was adamant that darts were all part of 'light duties' only! I didn't mind in the least. Without the wrist I wouldn't be here and, despite the schoolwork waiting for me, I was relishing this short little bonus of boating before the winter closed in once more. We were joined in the bar that night by two other BW captains and I gloomily eyed their pairs, tied ahead of us and blocking the lock, as we picked our way down the pitch black towpath to *Barnet*.

"Don't matter, really," said Wilfred. "They'm about five-handed, what with all the kids and all. Without a bike we'd have had to 'loose 'em by', any old how."

On this note, and after putting in another 'banker', we went to bed. After a somewhat unsettled night curled up on the hard side-bed I was abruptly wrenched from my dreams by the steady growl of engines heralding six o'clock and the start of another working day.

Upon Wilfed's sleepy suggestion I stoked up the fire and made tea, as the paddles rattled and the gates swung together with a loud boom. We sat together sipping our tea appreciatively as the engine beats died away and a deep silence reigned once more. It was decided that Wilfred should steer whilst I walked ahead after working *Barnet*'s locks. This was inevitably going to be slower than normal but, given the weakness of his wrist, seemed the most prudent course of action. A blanket of fine mist shrouded both the cut and the reservoirs that morning, but you could sense that the sun was up there and getting to work on it and, with very little wind, it seemed another fine day was in prospect. Down from the Cowroast we had to go above most of the locks as the distances between them precluded lockwalking. From time to time we again met northbound traffic, both loaded and empty, but we only usually benefited from having one or two locks ready for us before once more being left with a 'bad road' by the two pairs ahead of us. We didn't really mind that much. The sun was well up by Gas Two, where another massive bacon sandwich was enjoyed, and we dropped easily down through the pounds past Berko with me thoroughly enjoying being once again in the locks last seen on *Warbler* and *Teal*. I recalled that first long pedal down here the previous summer and reflected on the chain of events since then. I was a much better boatman now and my enjoyment of the cut remained undiminished, indeed it had taken on new depths of meaning as I had become that little bit older and capable of immersing myself even more fully in the way of life. Down we went, eventually passing the two pairs ahead of us when they stopped at Apsley Mill. It proved thereafter to be a 'good road' for the last few locks and past the lovely red and brown autumn colours of Cassio Park, with long coppery branches hanging out across the wide waters. Croxley was finally reached in late afternoon if you were feeling charitable, or early evening if you were not! Wilfred insisted on buying me a pint before I walked up into Watford for the Northampton train but, as I assured him at the time, it was really for me to be grateful as yet again I had thoroughly enjoyed myself.

This was the final trip in what I later came to affectionately regard as the year of 'bits and pieces'. It had been a good year in many ways and the long hot weeks with Mike Sloan had broadened my knowledge of people and the wider world which would not go amiss in my overall development. My friendship with Alec and Lil had deepened over the year and I now knew that I was welcome on their pair whenever I could get away. This now seemed likely to include every holiday period as it was clear that no harm would come to me whilst under their benevolent eyes. As the train bore me away homewards through the darkness I was already looking forward gleefully to future adventures. I had two years in the Sixth Form stretching ahead of me before any other major changes would occur in my life and I pledged myself to work very hard in term time, with the obvious exception of an odd half-day with Alec if the pair happened to come through Stoke at an opportune moment, thus releasing the holidays for the cut with a clear conscience. With Young Lily getting married Alec and Lil would be working two-handed, a hard job and a situation that would enable me to give of my best on the cut I loved. So it was to be. In retrospect the next two years were a golden period. My schoolwork went as well as it had ever done as I enjoyed the greater depth of 'A' levels and the increased degree of freedom from petty rules that the Sixth Form offered. On the cut and at Stoke everything flourished and life was good. I was truly having 'the time of my life'.

*****

Chapter 8

Timber and Gravel

The long winter was finally over. The endless weeks of stuffy classrooms had given way to an extended Easter break and the cut beckoned with renewed urgency. By now I was able, through a combination of telephoning the Willow Wren office and utilising Mr James' list of phone numbers for the various locks, to pinpoint the location of the pair with a fair degree of accuracy. Thus it was that I emerged confidently from Watford Station and headed down the road to Croxley Mills where Alec, if my calculations were correct, should be waiting to empty after his journey south from Newdigate. The queue to unload usually lay between the road bridge and Cassio Lock where casual work could sometimes be obtained in the adjacent watercress beds, and it was from here that you would be called down to the mill when your turn to empty finally arrived. Leaning over the parapet a surprising sight greeted me. For the first time since I had come this way there were no boats at all in the waiting lengths. If Alec was here then he must be down at the mill or, and perish the thought, emptied and gone on. This I hoped was not going to be the case as it would involve still more phone calls and then a frantic chase by whatever transport seemed appropriate in order to catch up. Hurrying along the towpath to the mill I was greatly relieved to see the still-loaded *Greenshank* waiting to go under the 'jigger' in the length currently occupied by *Redshank*. She was very nearly empty and I waited for about quarter of an hour before Alec shafted her out of the length and let the high bows drift across enabling me to clamber aboard by the mast-beam thus saving an awkward journey through the mill itself. I had made it!

Little time was available for greetings as *Greenshank* was already being pulled into the length and *Redshank* needed sorting out! I was back and spirits soared as, dropping my bag on the side-bed, I began work immediately helping Lil to put her straight. The chains which ran across the boat to hold the sides together were hanging slackly down the inside of the hold where they had been unfastened to permit the passage of the 'jigger'. The first job was to hook them back together and then secure the correct degree of tension by winding the connecting worm-screw round with a thin metal bar. After this the cross-beams and planks were put back into place, beams first and then the planks running in a neat line alongside the stands from the mast-beam to the back-end. I then turned my attention to the hold, setting to with a thick brush and sweeping along the boards to get up the remaining coal dust and small pieces of slack, these were then swept on to the shovel and dumped unceremoniously over the side. Lil, in the meantime, had mopped the boat off from stem to stern and was now finishing off by checking that all the side-cloths were still neatly and tightly rolled along the gunwale. A place for everything and everything in its place! By the time I had helped Alec repeat the process on *Greenshank* I knew that I was well and truly back. My coat was hanging on the mast, my hands were grimy once more and my old habit of wiping my face had left the usual dark smudges, much to Alec's amusement as we lay abreast below the mill and enjoyed a well earnt cup of tea in *Greenshank's* hatches.

"What are you looking so black about! Thought you were pleased to be back!"

The bantering was familiar and we all grinned as I caught up on the news. I was pleased to be back and they seemed equally happy to see me. Now that they were two handed, my presence, coupled with my growing experience, meant that they could both take things just that little bit easier for a while.

To my great joy the pair had been ordered to Brentford to load timber for Great Bridge, near Tipton, in the heart of the Black Country. I had seen the Willow Wren pairs moving through Stoke that winter loaded for Tipton and had hoped then to do the trip myself, despite bow-hauling in the narrow locks of the Black Country. It was a new trip for me and infinitely better than 'back empty to Sutton's'. The lighters were apparently already at Brentford and so it looked like a quick turn round, which was even better news as the one thing about boating that I really disliked was hanging about waiting to load or empty when, after all the odd jobs had been done, life could get just a little tedious.

"Right!" said Alec. "Drink up then and we'll get down to the top of the locks."

I glanced down the cut to where the top gates of Croxley Lock could just be seen. The gates were closed. A 'bad road' on our journey to the top of Hanwell Locks. Pedalling again!

"Somebody might come up," Lil said optimistically, seeing my glance.

"Might do!" I replied. "I'll just check the tyre pressures!"

Somebody did come up! Abel's fore-end's were rising in Ricky Lock as I pedalled into view and presently laid the bike down at the lockside. Abel was a friend of Alec's and we had met before on several occasions

"How do, young John! Having an holiday from being a scholard then! You'm got Cowley ready!"

This was good news and I sat contentedly on the balance beam watching Abel, loaded for Wellingborough, clatter off and waiting for my own breasted-up pair to appear. Hopefully, with Cowley ready for us, I could put the bike back on board and be given a bit of steering that afternoon in place of pedalling. So it turned out and I found myself contentedly in place on *Redshank*'s footboard with the brass tiller bar firmly in my grasp. Yesterday had been the last day of term and now here I was, real life had begun again. We passed Hayes Cocoa on the long pound to the top of Hanwell Locks and it was sad to see the wharves still stacked with coal, but no longer canal-borne as the contract had ceased the previous year. I reflected on my good luck both in getting a Hayes run and in visiting the Cannock coalfield, even if it had been hard labour with *Teal* through the narrow locks. The chance of loading at Cannock would never come again for me, but at least I was spared from bow-hauling up Saltley again! However, melancholy thoughts about lost contracts did not trouble me for long on this particular afternoon as, easing past a few pairs in the lay-by at Bull's Bridge, we eventually tied with our bows rubbing against the top gates of Hanwell. There was absolutely no doubt about who would be first pair down in the morning!

By eight o'clock the next day we were swinging round in Brentford Basin and laying ourselves alongside the lighters stacked high with timber destined for the Midlands yard. My previous visits to Brentford had seen us loaded by crane but this time we were on our own. Our load had to be transhipped from lighter to narrowboat by hand, no mean task I thought as I considered the long empty holds awaiting their cargo. There were three of us and the trick, as always, was to be organised. Stands and cross-beams were taken out which, along with the planks and the unfastening of the chains, gave clear and unfettered access to the hold. The chains would be re-fastened as the timber level reached them but the top-planks, beams and stands would not be needed and were stored amongst the cargo. The timber had to be loaded in such a way that the boat was properly trimmed, that is to say that it lay level and balanced in the water. My job was in the lighter and I passed whatever sized piece I was asked for from floorboards to heavier gauges of timber up to 4'x4'. Alec loaded the pair in layers with plenty of heavy timber at the bottom in order to obviate any danger of being top-heavy. Lil pottered about stowing odd bits, helping me heave some of the heavier pieces out of the bottom of the lighter, making welcome cups of tea, and generally encouraging us to keep going. It was not especially heavy work, but it did need care and concentration with each piece having to be fitted properly into place and not just chucked in willy nilly.

Hour after hour we went on and it was the afternoon of the second day before both boats were fully laden and clothed up. The timber was a light cargo and we loaded to about eighteen inches above the gunwale before stretching the side-cloths up and over it, not to keep it dry but to prevent it from falling off the boat. The pair still had plenty of freeboard but to have loaded anymore would have presented an increasing danger of top-heaviness, as it was the boats rolled quite alarmingly if you climbed on board a little too enthusiastically. One big advantage, however, lay in moving about on the boats. The timber lay flat across the hold and you just walked about wherever you fancied, just like being on a pair of Thomas Claytons. The bicycle and the long shafts were just laid on the top and secured in place by an overlapping top string to prevent any possibility of losing them over the side. My hands had grown soft through the winter and felt decidedly sore after all the timber they had handled, indeed a closer inspection led to a needle being borrowed from Lil in order to extract several large splinters from my palm. Not to worry, by the time we'd completed the long trip to Great Bridge and off-loaded all the timber my hands would have got the message and become suitably hardened once more. A crate of sterilised milk was stowed in a small space by the back end of *Greenshank*'s cabin, loaves of bread were in the food drawer along with other supplies, including the much-favoured tins of stewed steak which, along with potatoes, made a quick and easy meal when we were pressing on late.

There was nothing really to wait about for and so, at about half past four, we 'got 'em ahead' and were soon ascending the flight once more. Every lock was conveniently ready for us after two pairs of BW boats had come down from the lay-by to load pulped tomatoes in little wooden barrels for Warwick Wharf. I always loved the first part of a long trip finding the prospect of several days continuous boating an intoxicating thought as I swung on gates and drew paddles on the first flight of the many, many locks on our journey to the Midlands. A slight argument developed at the top of Hanwell, with Alec wanting to stop at Bull's Bridge for a pint with some mates and Lil favouring pushing on to Uxbridge at the very least. I made a point of never getting into these sorts of discussions. Instead I happily took *Redshank* out of the lock and carefully, without any unnecessary jerks, picked up the tow and set off towards Birmingham. I was just getting nicely into my stride after realising that the lightness of the timber enabled the pair to go just that little bit faster when Alec ambled along the flat timber of *Greenshank*, manouevred himself carefully around the cratch and took up position on the deck We were on the approach to the pub which stood by the busy roadbridge just prior to the Bull's Bridge depot, 'winding off' the speed I pointed to the rings set into the concrete coping. Alec's nod of acknowledgement told me which way the decision had gone and I took her out of gear whilst he rapidly coiled up the snubber and *Greenshank* drew alongside. Accepting Lil's thrown line I looped it round the dolly and returned the end before getting ready to hold back once both Alec's line and hers were secure.

"Beer!" she grumbled. "All he ever thinks about!"

I prudently said nothing and drowned out any further possibilities of discussion by holding back noisily before gently laying the pair, with *Greenshank* on the inside, into the mooring length. We had had a long couple of days work with loading. If asked, I would have gone on happily enough but I was equally happy to stop a bit earlier and enjoy a pint or two after all our efforts. In short, I was remaining strictly neutral!

We were joined by a number of the crews from the depot that night and it was amusing to see the wives sitting all together on one side of the bar sipping their glasses of stout whilst the nobler, or ignobler depending upon your point of view, sex occupied itself with darts and chatter on the other side. Lil may not have favoured stopping early but she did not carry her objections so far as to refuse to come off that night, indeed she seemed to be thoroughly enjoying herself with the other boatwomen and, unusually for her, put away several bottles of stout not to mention a packet of crisps! A long journey lay ahead and who knows when we would all find ourselves together once more, it was very much a case of enjoy it while you can because tomorrow we won't be here! I was tired and a bit sleepy by closing time, but my efforts to slip off to *Redshank*'s cabin were quickly thwarted and I found myself accompanying a previously unknown boatman and his wife to share bread, cheese, and a cup of tea till well past midnight in the snug confines of their butty cabin. Bert, as he introduced himself, was related to Alec and Lil and there was a great deal of catching up to do as they had not been able to tie together for some time. Bert's pair were immaculate and he himself, as I later came to notice, nearly always wore neat blue overalls and invariably looked as if he had just got out of the bath. Paddle grease and dust, which seemed to stick happily to me, never affected Bert who, even at the end of a long day, always looked as if he had just begun it. It was past one o'clock and a million glittering stars promised a good day for the climb to Cowroast as I finally pulled the slide over and sank sleepily into bed.

Not for long it seemed! I was awoken by an insistent tapping on the slide at an unearthly hour which my watch confirmed to be half past five.

"Cup o' tea, John," murmured Lil. She passed the mug over and grinned at me as I took a first sleepy sip. She was, I noticed, fully dressed and had her coat on against the fresh spring morning; mist hung low along the waterway but traffic was already moving over the bridge leading into Central London.

"We'll be off when you're ready," she continued. "Gonna be a nice day so we'll crack on a bit."

"Right." It wasn't much of an answer but I was still half asleep. Of Alec there was no sign. Clearly I was being trusted to start *Redshank* up and get away up the pound and equally clearly 'when I was ready' meant now. I sipped tea and threw clothes on at the same time. I knew the signs and in less than two minutes I was descending into the engine-hole. Luckily *Redshank* was easy enough, just set a switch and press a button. Lovely! I don't think I'd have coped too well with the blowlamp and all that 'bomp-bomping' this morning. Clambering back out I found Lil busy loosing off the fore-ends, having already taken in our mooring lines. We were 'getting 'em ahead' with a vengeance this morning, I thought, as I fitted the tiller bar, shoved in the clutch, and moved off, 'bonking' gently past the still sleeping pairs in the lay-by. By six o'clock we were past Hayes Cocoa and settling to our task. Looking back to where the butty's bluff bows parted the bubbling wash I could see Lil resolutely steering, but still no sign of Alec. He would not be much longer, however, and emerged to take over *Greenshank* as we passed the turn for the Slough Arm. I had fingers crossed for a good road up but any such hopes were soon dashed, Cowley was full, top gates open and paddles up. Just what we didn't need. We couldn't quite work it out, but the lock-keeper at Denham put us straight. A pair had emptied down the Slough Arm and started back up the night before, I noticed that the lock walls were wet and dripping which indicated that they probably weren't that far ahead.

I lock-wheeled hopefully on, keeping an expectant eye open for any welcome downhill traffic. Eventually I managed to catch up with the empty pair ahead of us, they turned out to be none other than the ancient couple whom I had first encountered on *Canada Goose* and who I was in the habit of helping down Stoke if our paths happened to coincide.

"Whay ho, John boy! Alec behind us then!"

I grinned at them and accepted a mug of tea as their lock filled.

"We'm back empty again! They reckons we'm too old for Brummagem. You a-gooing to Tippon then?"

Confirming this I leaned on the handlebars and enjoyed my hot tea as the boats idled in the full lock. Anxiously I glanced back down the pound before handing my mug back with suitable comments as to how well the tea had gone down. My little glance however had not been missed!

"Don't worry! If you catches right up to us then we'll loose you by, but I reckons you won't quite catch us!"

It was an interesting situation. They were empty and travelling breasted-up with a 'good road', but they were also two handed and indubitably old. We, on the other hand, were three-handed, but slowed by being loaded with a 'bad road'. By every rule of the cut they had no need to even consider 'loosing us by', indeed if they had been Arthur, Rosie and Ernie, a very well known and fast Barlow pair, they would have spent the day drawing inexorably away from us.

As it was they stayed just ahead helped by the complicity of the unfortunate lock-wheeler. I found myself often getting to locks just as they were entering them and, well, what could you do? They had always been very friendly towards me in the past and so I found myself drawing paddles and shutting gates for them before finally drawing off the lock for ourselves. In this fashion we proceeded steadily upwards hour after hour, occasionally meeting south-bound pairs but never in such a way as to give us any advantage. Nevertheless, life seemed very pleasant. The sun was shining, a light breeze ruffled the water, and I was not at school. With cups of tea forthcoming from both pairs I was happy enough. Towards evening the old couple were clearly getting a bit tired and began asking about our intentions for that day. Lil had started the day in a very determined mood and, although

I was almost sure that we would tie at Cosgrove the following night, I had no real idea as to how far we might go tonight. At Berko they called it a day and tied just above the lock leaving us to continue on with a 'good road'.

"This'll do," they said. "Stoke tomorrer and then Sutton's. We'm alright!"

Redshank and *Greenshank* rose in the lock and I thankfully stowed the bicycle on top of the timber. It had been a lot of pedalling once again, but I was markedly stronger nowadays and nothing like as tired as my first trip down these locks with *Warbler*.

"Time they retired!" said Alec, observing that the old couple had finally tied up.

"Holding us up!"

Whether we would have caught up to them if I had dawdled a bit and deliberately not helped them will never be known, but I had felt myself caught between friends and held my counsel as we forged past and continued on. If we did stop at Cosgrove tomorrow then they would, according to their own plan, re-pass us anyway and so the question of who was fastest seemed an unnecessary one to get involved in. Darkness fell as we pressed on upwards through Gas Two, Northchurch, Dudswell and eventually to Cowroast. Four south-bound pairs were above the summit lock and I felt sure we would stop for another convivial pint, but not so. On we went, with me steering *Greenshank* through the gloomy Tring cuttings whilst Lil dealt with an accumulation of washing up.

"Gotta keep going, John," she remarked conversationally. "Catching up time from yesterday, see!"

I acknowledged this with a faint grin and wondered if this meant that we would not be stopping at Cosgrove this trip.

It did not! We found ourselves 'locked out' at Maffers that night but were away early in the morning and, after an smooth and uneventful day, reached Cosgrove at about half past four in the afternoon and promptly tied up. The old couple, who must have started very early from Berko, came past about an hour later with a good natured jibe about part-time boaters! In fact, what we were doing was not that unusual. Noel James often tied his pair of Barlows up at Stoke in mid-afternoon to see his family, and others, up and down the cut, did the same. The theory behind it was that you worked extra hard for the next couple of days to catch up the time and sometimes you might even find yourself doing so!

The next day was a Sunday and it began badly with rain falling heavily from a distinctly grey and leaden looking sky. Stoke were against us and I lock-wheeled upwards aware that my parents would be at the top lock and presumably knew from Mr James and the old couple that we were coming. It was bucketing down as I drew off the top lock and stood dripping on the cottage doorstep, declining an invitation to go in as I had to open the bottom gates for the pair. My mother glanced at me quizzically as we exchanged our news.

"Are you sure you want to do this?" she said, knowing full well what the answer would be!

"It's only a drop of rain," I protested. "Probably clear up later on. I'm fine!"

It was only too true. I was fine. In fact, as I steered *Redshank* out of the lock and picked up the tow, I could not have been happier. I waved to Sister Mary who greeted us from the surgery window, waved to Mrs James standing on her doorstep to see us pass, waved to my grinning parents and promised to be back for the start of term before 'winding it on' and disappearing into the welcome dryness of the tunnel. I was right about it clearing up too. By the Arm End it had stopped raining and the sun was out as we passed the signal box at the end of the Bugbrooke embankment. By High House it was really a pleasant spring day, a steady breeze had pushed the rain eastwards to leave us with a largely clear blue sky and fresh invigorating air. In the spinnies we met Wilfred, *Barnet* churning past with shouted greetings. He had come from the bottom of Braunston and would 'likely stop at Stoke for a pint' that night. He looked fine and we grinned at each other as he passed by with a joke about me steering a floating woodyard! Buckby was ready for us, albeit with only one gate open, and we made good time that day to tie by the yard at the bottom of Braunston with still a good hour of daylight left to us.

Braunston was another favourite stopping place for us. It was a reasonable day's boating from Cosgrove and to have gone further that day would have meant having to take on my old enemy of Shuckburgh Turn in the dark, always assuming that I was steering one or other of the pair. It would also have meant going to the top of Itchington if a pint was to be forthcoming, whereas the much favoured 'Admiral Nelson' was but a short step back up the flight from the bottom lock. Braunston would do us nicely that day and there was time for a spot of judicious cleaning and polishing in the cabin before being tempted by that short stroll. The 'Nelson', as run by Hubert and Thirza Clarke, was a boating pub in every sense of the word and the scene of many a memorable evening. That night, whilst not especially memorable, turned out pleasantly enough. Mark was also tied at the bottom lock whilst minor repairs were carried out to *Quail*'s single Bolinder, and he, along with a couple of retired boatmen from up in the village, made for a good evening of canal talk and banter punctuated by games of skittles at which I was definitely getting considerably better. A full moon gave a ghostly light for our amble back to the boats, the myriad stars glittering serenely above, offering the hope of a fine day to come.

The morning dawned bright and sunny with wonderfully clear and crisp air, just perfect for boating. I was up at half past five in the confident expectation that we would press on vigorously after our relatively easy couple of days. Mopping the dew off *Redshank*'s top and counter, I opened up the engine-hole doors, tidied up the cabin and then stood uncertainly on the footboard wondering what to do next as there was still no sign of life on

Greenshank. Surely Lil wouldn't have overslept? In my experience this seemed, to say the least, highly unlikely. The rising sun had by now dried the cabin sides and so, filling in time somewhat, I began work on the outside brasses and was busy polishing up the tiller pin when the slide was pulled back and Lil beckoned me over for a cup of tea. The delay was caused by our need to oil-up, a procedure which, as she caustically pointed out, could have been done the previous evening with a bit more fore-thought. The state of the diesel in the tanks was not one of my areas of responsibility and so, once again, it seemed prudent to take no sides in the discussion! Instead I was dispatched up the steep hill to the bakery to fetch bread and a treat of three buns to be eaten with a cup of tea round the Napton pound later in the morning. Hanging about like this to oil-up was not good boating practice, but Alec was clearly not in the mood to discuss his oversight when he eventually set off on *Redshank* with the sun well up in the fresh clear sky.

Thus I found myself unexpectedly steering *Greenshank* round the turn and down the initial long straight with Lil methodically busying herself with cabin chores below me. It was a gorgeous morning and it would have been hard indeed to stay grumpy for long. By Wolfhamcote Lil was already more cheerful, and we were not much further on before she climbed out and sent me up to the fore-end with Alec's mug of tea and bun. He grinned and eased off immediately allowing *Greenshank* to run up behind the motor's tipcats. I had the tea and bun balanced precariously on the cratch and busied myself coiling in the long snubber to avoid any danger of it catching in the blades as the boats came together. It was up to Alec to provide the necessary little adjustments of speed which meant that the two boats did not actually touch, but still came just close enough for me to hand over his sustenance without mishap.

"She still rabbiting on?" he asked with an exaggerated grimace.

"No!" I responded. "All sunny again."

"Can't remember everything, can I?" he returned as he gently increased speed, the gap between us widening once more as the snubber tightened and we were back on our way.

The little disagreement was soon forgotten as we basked in the sunshine round the beautiful pound. Between us we did *Greenshank*'s outside brasses and scrubbed off the white ash strips round the hatches followed by the ram's head and swan's neck for good measure. Everything was just so as I brought her under Shuckburgh Bridge. It was my first time round the turn with a butty and I 'rowed' hard with one eye on the looming concrete coping ahead. Lil sat in the cabin calmly peeling potatoes and seemingly trusting in my ability to manage. Hope I don't jolt her off the side-bed, I thought, as I forced *Greenshank* round. We made it, comfortably missing the coping by a good three feet and swinging away along the pound. It was silly really. Shuckburgh, although an awkward turn, was not, by any stretch of the imagination, the only challenging piece of steering on the Birmingham run, but for me, after my early experiences, it always remained the one to beat and spirits rose accordingly each time I did so. It was all very peaceful in the sunshine and we met with only one small cruiser all morning. Most of the traffic here went in the same direction as us and, after emptying in Brum, nearly everyone went round the 'Bottom Road', the Birmingham & Fazeley Canal, to load again in the Warwickshire coalfield. I had yet to sample the dubious joys of the 'Bottom Road', but knew that after emptying at Great Bridge this particular gap in my experience was likely to be filled. There was a very slight possibility of meeting an empty pair coming back from Banbury or even Oxford in the Napton pound and a somewhat greater chance of meeting the Thomas Clayton 'gas boats' on their Leamington to Banbury shuttle, once you had rounded the turn to Wigrams.

Sometimes the odd empty pair returned from Brum this way and even the occasional loaded pair carrying chocolate crumb from Bournville to London but even so, when working up to Birmingham, the oncoming traffic could never be relied upon to materialise and thus facilitate a 'good road'. One other trade to look out for were the 'cement boats' who emerged from a little side arm near the bottom of Itchington and delivered to Sampson Road. There seemed to be two or three pairs engaged on this contract at any one time and, in fact, it proved to be one of the last regular carrying contracts terminating eventually at Easter 1969, just one year before the final demise of long distance carrying. Given the workings of the Claytons and the BW cement pairs it was always difficult to be sure of the state of the road along here. A 'good road' down Itchington could suddenly turn into a 'bad road' at Radford if you were unlucky enough to have the cement boats emerge in front of you, other permutations were clearly possible not to mention the slowly growing possibility of a pleasure craft complicating the whole situation.

Wigrams Three were surprisingly ready for us that day, top gates open, paddles up. The 'gas boats'? Such was my conjecturing as I shut *Greenshank*'s gate and ran down to commence the twenty-one turns which would raise the bottom paddle. We were lucky that afternoon and the 'good road' continued down Itchington and Radford thereby saving me considerable energy which I put to good use in steering *Redshank* round the Leamington pound. There was no sign of the Clayton pair at the gasworks and so it did seem likely that we had just missed them that morning and that they were indeed responsible for the 'good road' we had enjoyed. Confirmation of this came when I arrived at Cape Two to find the lock against us. More practice in the art of breasting-up followed as we came snugly together in mid-stream below the lock before nudging gently up to the bottom gates. This allowed Alec and myself to jump off one on either side, running up the steps to draw and leaving Lil to bring the pair in. We knew that no long distance pairs were close ahead of us and yet the lock was full, top gates both open and paddles left up. Pleasure boats usually only left one gate open and often dropped the paddles. This looked like the cement boats which meant that Hatton would also be against us.

Muttering imprecations about cement boats in general I trotted up and drew off the top Cape lock, ascertaining from a small cruiser tied above it that the cement boats, 'a pair of British Waterways', had gone by about two hours previously. Given that we had had Radford ready for us they must have been tied along the Leamington pound for most of the day. Why? Breakdown? Shopping? It all seemed very odd but, whatever the reason, it meant Hatton against us unless we were very lucky and a pleasure boat came down. I relayed this information to Alec as the boats rose in the lock and was surprised by the decision to tie at the Cape that night. There was still a fair amount of daylight left and we could easily have got up Hatton and possibly gone on a bit more, even as far as Knowle. But my friends seemed to have had enough for one day and tied contentedly above the lock, just across from the 'Cape of Good Hope' which would be our venue for a pint that evening. Lil disappeared, ostensibly shopping, and returned in the deepening dusk full of news after spending some time chatting with an old friend, which probably went some way to explaining her benign acceptance of another fairly early finish.

That night we crossed the lock gates for an enjoyable evening in 'The Cape' where I spent quite some time talking to an old man who used to work through the heavily locked Worcester & Birmingham Canal and then down the Severn to Gloucester on a regular basis. He also knew Stourport and we were able to share our very different experiences of the Stour Cut where he had once traded coal behind a horse. Conversations like these made me realise just how much trade had been lost from the cut, even in the last few years, and this steady haemorrhaging was still continuing, with the wharves at Tyseley and Sampson Road handling less and less trade with each passing year. What I did not know was that, within only a very few more years, everything I was now doing and the boating world I was enjoying would become a memory as narrowboating passed into history. As things turned out we were to be made to suffer for not ascending Hatton on that pleasant dry evening. A breeze had got up as we returned from the pub and I was awoken the next morning at about half past four by the wholly unwelcome sound of rain drumming relentlessly on the cabin top. It was typical Spring weather. Two or three days fine and then this sudden change. The rain was very heavy and, as further sleep was out of the question, I got up and lit the fire in the range. It seemed likely that we would need it! A peep out of the doors showed a grey sombre cut with lashing rain pockmarking the surface with bubbles. Great! I stoked up the range which was now burning brightly, put my boots on and sorted out my thick donkey jacket and old hat as the rain showed absolutely no sign of relenting. A mug of tea was passed over at about half past five, but Lil with coat collar drawn-up and head-scarf pulled tight made no comment about the weather. If it rained, it rained. Nothing could be done and you just had to get on with it and remember it could be worse! Snow, ice, wind. Yes, it could always be worse so let's just 'get 'em ahead' and take what comes. What came that morning was memorably bad.

The rain was sheeting down as we reached the bottom lock which was, inevitably, against us. Leaving Alec and Lil to get through it I set off walking through the mud and puddles to draw the locks off. Alec had told me to draw each lock off, opening the gates and dropping the paddles, before moving on up leaving Lil and himself to bring the pair through. When I had drawn them all off I would return to lend a hand. Consequently by the time I reached the upper part of the flight, the 'thick of Hatton', the golden steps to heaven, I was some distance ahead of the boats trudging along with the rain stubbornly refusing to ease up even slightly. The sight which then greeted me was not a welcome one. The short intervening pounds in 'the thick' were virtually empty with hardly enough water to float a canoe through, never mind a loaded pair. Quite how this had happened I had no idea and, with the rain running down the inside of my collar and trickling down my back, I was in no mood to try and work it out. Not surprisingly there was no sign of the lock-keeper although it seemed unlikely, given that somebody had unlocked the flight that morning, that he could be unaware of the situation. On the other hand the rain was incessant and he could have been going to sort it out after breakfast, maybe! Water had to be run down from the top of the flight all through the locks to fill the pound at the bottom of 'the thick' before beginning the slow and laborious process of dropping paddles as each pound slowly filled up. To put it mildly, Alec was not a happy man as he spotted me dodging about amongst 'the thick' running water down, with the pair's progress dependent upon the time taken to fill the pounds. I had all four paddles up on every lock right back up to the top and the rain was adding its quota, but pounds will only fill so fast. Delay was unavoidable and it was nearly a quarter to eleven before the fore-ends were rising in the top lock. Thankfully the rain had finally had enough, easing to a drizzle with a small patch of blue giving hope of a day of sunshine and showers to come. I untied the fore-ends, put out the long snubber ready to pick up the tow, and wandered back down the lockside looking, doubtless, somewhat bedraggled and weary after my efforts. I could certainly do with some breakfast. The smell of frying bacon rose invitingly from *Greenshank*'s door holes as I stepped aboard the motor's counter and stowed my windlass on the hook near the soap holes.

Alec, standing in the butty hatches, grinned across at me as the water settled and the top gates opened an inch or two.

"Go ahead then,John! We're just going to have our breakfusses!"

I said nothing, dutifully putting *Redshank* into gear and feeling for the speedwheel.

"Oy! You've forgotten something!"

Alec beamed as my expression changed at the sight of two large 'doorstep' style bacon sandwiches and a steaming mug of tea being held out for me.

TIMBER AND GRAVEL

"Go ahead then!" he said. "Good lad! You did well this morning."

With that I 'got 'em ahead', munching contentedly and basking in the praise as I made my way along to Shrewley Tunnel. It had been a tough morning but it was all part of the game and things were improving. Bacon sandwiches were one improvement and a fitfully emerging sun was another. The range was giving off a good heat and rapidly drying my feet and trousers, as we passed Lapworth my donkey jacket had come off and by Knowle I felt virtually dry again, give or take the odd damp patch.

The original plan as espoused in 'The Cape' the previous evening had been to do a really long day and try to reach Great Bridge, so long as we were in time to get up the New Thirteen at Perry Barr. This was now clearly out of the question as it was getting on towards two o'clock as we left the top of Knowle with a three hour pound in front of us. The revised choice had us either at the top of Camp Hill or Salford Bridge and, as Lil considered that we had been a bit lazy at times on this trip, we were aiming for Salford Bridge. Our main meal was eaten in the middle of the afternoon along the pound as we would all be needed for the two flights of narrow locks to come. The old stand-by of stewed steak and taters went down well as I relaxed for a few minutes in *Greenshank*'s cabin as we passed through the long Solihull cutting, before taking over the steering again and allowing Lil to get everything straight prior to our arrival at Camp Hill. Past the 'Beezer', the BSA factory, we went and presently the railway sidings and Sampson Road Wharf framed the single top gate of the Camp Hill flight and I girded myself up ready for action.

It wouldn't be quite as tough as with *Teal*. *Greenshank* was a large Woolwich but she was only loaded with timber, whereas *Teal*, although a little smaller, had been deeply laden with coal making the bow-hauler's job just that bit more onerous. The routine was very much the same, except that this time Alec went ahead with *Redshank* and started the locks for us following on behind. This meant that the lock was full as I plodded up with the long line over my shoulder, allowing me to simply push open the gate before continuing on to pull *Greenshank* in. Different crews work in different ways in the narrow locks. In these downhill locks we developed a routine which meant that I drew *Greenshank* to a halt, taking a couple of turns around the strapping post situated two-thirds of the way down the lock, and then took the line on ready to take a turn around the paddle gear or handrail, so as to keep her forward and comfortably clear of the sill as the lock emptied. Lil steered carefully down the pounds to ensure no 'sticking', also taking responsibility for shutting the top gate and dropping the single paddle Alec had raised before regaining the boat as it sank down. Variations on this style included the butty steerer strapping the boat in with a turn around the end of the gate, thus shutting the gate and stopping the boat at the same time. Some energetic steerers took it upon themselves to open the bottom gates, saving perhaps a few seconds as this enabled the bow-hauler to take up the strain immediately.

I was not seemingly feeling the strain as much with *Greenshank* as I had with *Teal*. We had a lighter load, but the cut and passing time had combined to make me a stronger and more resilient person than my younger self.

Greenshank made smooth and steady progress down Camp Hill before we went back on the short 'snatcher' and bore right at the bottom along the short pound to Saltley. These locks were in their usual evil-smelling and oily state and once again my hands and coat became blackened by the towline as we sank down. It was well into the evening, sparing me the jokes and ribaldry from the factory as I plodded past its grimy windows, now all closed down for the night. It occurred to me that we were going down merely to go straight back up again at the New Thirteen and my mind played around with the alternatives as I dragged *Greenshank* through the filth of Saltley. Going straight on at the bottom of Camp Hill merely meant six more locks through the Digbeth Branch followed by a further thirteen at Farmers Bridge, then it was along the main line before turning off at Pudding Green Junction and going down the eight locks to Great Bridge. More locks, not less. Another alternative, and much more radical, would have been to use the northern Stratford from Lapworth, with the nineteen narrow locks there being followed by many miles of pound to Pudding Green and the descent to Great Bridge. Discounting the stop locks this meant twenty-seven locks against thirty on our route, although five of these at Knowle were wide locks. There was little in it and Alec was very dismissive of the state of the northern Stratford to cope with loaded boats. In time, as the southern end of the Stratford was being restored, these pounds were dredged allowing some timber to eventually flow this way before the final ending of the contract.

I missed Salford Bridge altogether that night! My only defence was tiredness as, feeling rather pleased with myself after successfully negotiating the big turn at the junction, I headed off with great aplomb to the bottom of the New Thirteen. Whether Lil, having equally successfully 'rowed' the butty round, was also sleepy or simply didn't wish to tie at Salford Bridge was unclear, but she certainly gave no indication that I should have stopped before the closed gates of the bottom lock forced me to do so. Alec was not best pleased and said so loudly as, after emerging all spruce and clean from his wash, he found himself faced with a fair walk back for his pint. I decided to make do without a pint that night and contented myself instead with a good hot water wash down in the cabin, drying my hair in front of the range and following up with a cup of tea and a few pages of Conrad's *The Rover*, one of my holiday tasks along with an essay on *Hamlet* which I completed sitting at the flap of *Redshank*'s table cupboard. We made relatively short work of the New Thirteen the next morning and I set off at a steady pace along the wide but shallow straights of the New Cut. As far as Newtown Junction I was on a cut which, if not familiar, I had experienced before but, once beyond that memorably awkward turn, I was in unknown waters. I continued straight ahead at the junction, the chips and scratches on the coping reminding me of our struggles to get round with *Warbler* and *Teal*, and found that the cut simply went on in much the same way as before with housing estates, factories, and derelict land providing the view. Eventually we reached a 'T' junction with the Walsall Canal, where I was directed to slow right down before turning left. We were nearly there now, a couple more bridge lengths were followed by a final right turn below a very low bridge to tie alongside the timber wharf at Great Bridge, it was journey's end.

There were no other pairs of Willow Wrens present and so, after a cup of tea to celebrate our arrival, we set about unloading the cargo. *Greenshank*, having taken the inside as we breasted up, would be emptied first, and cloths were untied and sleeves rolled up ready for action. A very large and smiling black man was produced by the yard, both to give us welcome help and to ensure that everything was stowed correctly on the wharfside and not just chucked willy-nilly into a big heap! We soon established a routine not dissimilar to the one used in loading. Alec took charge on *Greenshank* and laid the timber sideways on to the bank where the two of us picked it up and stowed it neatly on the correct pile. I was 'floorboard' man for much of the time, the pieces being long and floppy but not as heavy to handle as the larger gauge timber. Our new friend handled these as if they were matchsticks, although looking back on it with the benefit of hindsight, much of his apparent strength and dexterity came simply from long experience of handling the awkward lengths. Lil busied herself with domestic activities as we worked steadily on through the day. Drawers were taken out and scrubbed before being stacked in a line to dry in the warm spring sunshine, the range was blackleaded and our coats, which were still a bit damp from the rigours of Hatton, were draped over piles of timber to air off. Several kettles of hot water were boiled up and, after much scrubbing and rinsing in the hand bowl, a line of handwashing was strung incongruously across a corner of the yard. Corned beef sandwiches were produced at midday and several cups of tea went down well during the afternoon as *Greenshank* slowly rose higher in direct relation to the piles of timber rising on the wharf. Unloading was easier than loading as, in deference to our helper and director of timber piles, we only worked when he did! This meant the luxury of an early finish at five 'o clock and an hour for lunch, all very civilised as was the late start at half past seven in the morning! Timber work proved to be slow and steady and only about two thirds of the butty's cargo was dealt with on that first afternoon before the yard closed for the day, leaving us to enjoy the evening sunshine and the peace of the little side-arm. Mind you, I had my own jobs to attend to that evening. Not to be outdone, I had the motor's drawers scrubbed and out to dry and the range blackleaded, before being sent to get fish and chips at about seven o'clock.

Rain, especially if it had been of the Hatton stair-rod variety, would have been a problem with the unloading, but we were lucky as the next day dawned crisp and clear with a light breeze and plenty of blue sky visible between fairly innocent looking white clouds. Off we went on the dot of half past seven on the same routine of 'move it' and 'pick it up and stow it', working steadily on until by the mid-morning tea break *Greenshank* was empty and towering above her partner on the outside. Half of the job done. Slightly more than half actually, as the butty carried more timber than the motor, we were winning! The boats were swopped round and Lil began sweeping up the splinters and setting the hold to rights, enlisting a little bit of help from me when it came to the heavy planks and stands. With her brasses gleaming, white strings scrubbed, and all freshly mopped off and tidy, the butty stood proudly above the half empty *Redshank* and represented the very picture of all that was best about the cut. An hour off for lunch seemed most unusual to us. We couldn't really get to grips with it at all and pottered about most uncomfortably, eating our sandwiches and generally filling in time until our helper returned and we got stuck into the afternoon stint. He was in no great hurry, being somewhat naturally more concerned with getting the wharf stacked properly than with simply getting the timber out of the boats in the shortest possible time. We, on the other hand, were paid by the trip and were keen to get rid of our timber and get on. However the wharf dictated the pace and we obediently stopped work at five o'clock, even though another couple of hours concerted effort would have had *Redshank* empty that night, and we might even have got to the top of the New Thirteen!

As we had worked that day I had seen horse-drawn 'joey' boats passing across the entrance to the arm and heard the rattle of paddles from the bottom lock of the Ryders Green flight, or the West Bromwich Eight as Alec called it. Occasional 'bomp-bomping' was also heard as single Josher motors went through heading to and from the Cannock coalfield. I made my way up the Eight that evening and was not particularly impressed by the grime and dirt on the flight, not quite as bad as Saltley but still very grubby and sticky with dust. From the top lock an array of crumbling factories stretched ahead on both sides, some in use and some derelict. By the towpath several 'joey' boats were moored up, all empty and presumably waiting to go down the flight in the morning. The locks were still obviously busy as the patina of constant use was very evident on the shining paddle spindles and the rope-worn strapping posts, but trade was already in decline. Alec had told me stories of how there used to be long queues of boats here, all waiting to ascend and descend this notorious bottleneck on the direct route from Walsall and Cannock to the Birmingham Level. Nothing moved in the flight that evening as dirty water trickled softly across the oily sills and the warm evening light began to give way to the gloom of the approaching night. Sitting on the dusty balance beam of the top lock I recalled the sparkling waters of the river Dee and the leafy beauty of the Vale of Llangollen, all part of the same system but offering a very contrasting style of boating.

TIMBER AND GRAVEL

The pub that evening turned out to be a typically large Black Country bar with a little stage where, periodically, someone would ascend and sing to us. Their accompaniment came from an old upright piano played by a very large lady with a local accent so broad I could barely understand her. If the song was judged to be particularly dire, then howls of derision and volleys of skimmed beer mats brought proceedings to an untimely end. If not, then generous applause and cries for more were the order of the day. Alec enjoyed something of a reputation as a heavy drinker and a potentially fearsome fighter and he certainly enjoyed putting away pint after pint of beer, particularly the local Ansells Mild we were drinking that night. Of the fighting I had heard stories, some of which doubtless were true, but my experience only showed an essentially kind-hearted man who got on with most people and was invariably protective and supportive of his family and close friends. He was always exceptionally good to me, patiently teaching me an enormous amount about boating and, even more importantly, about life. In time he would become very proud that I had become a teacher and liked to take a degree of credit for my success. This he was absolutely right to do as my years on the cut undoubtedly strengthened my overall determination and fostered a pride in working hard and seeing a job through to a finish. We sat in a corner together that night at Tipton, talking boats quietly and drinking the tall dark glasses of mild in between occasional challenges on the dartboard, where Alec was very good and I was striving to improve. Lil joined us late on for her glass of stout and, with the towels going up, we wandered happily back together sharing a ninepenny bag of chips and seemingly without a worry in the world.

We were not quite so unruffled the next morning as a persistent seeping drizzle enveloped our smart boats in grime and soot from the nearby factories. It was cold and grey as we finished *Redshank* off, feeling pretty grey ourselves with the dankness of it all. The last floorboards were stowed and the boat was swept out as the drizzle turned into steady rain. It looked ominous but this time we were lucky. After drinking a cup of tea huddled in *Greenshank*s cabin the pattering ceased and it began to brighten up, lifting our spirits accordingly as it did so. Alec decided to leave forthwith and straighten *Redshank* up on the way along to the 'New Un's', but first we had the little problem of getting out of the arm. The entrance bridge was very low and, although we had got in easily enough, getting out constituted a bit of a problem. *Greenshank* was shafted back stern-first and, because she floated level, her cratch just passed under the brickwork of the bridge and we were able to carry on to wind her near the bottom lock. *Redshank* was a different proposition. The weight of the engine caused the cratch to stick up markedly higher than the butty's and it clearly would fail by about three to four inches to pass under the bridge. One solution would have been to dismantle the cratch and then re-erect it the other side, a complicated procedure which would have involved us in quite a lot of extra work and time. Instead we opted for the second and much simpler solution of bringing the fore-end down. Lumps of concrete block from the yard were put on the deck along with three full water cans, myself, and Lil. It was just enough. Very gently Alec eased *Redshank* back and we sat, legs dangling and anxiously watching the brickwork close above our heads, as she cleared with about half an inch to spare. Another problem solved! The only trouble was carrying the concrete blocks back across the road to the yard to be used by the next pair, my job that one!

Redshank looked a mess as we set off with side-cloths hanging loose, stands and planks scattered on the boards, and only the tightened cross-chains giving a semblance of normality. It was soon put to rights. Lil steered, with *Greenshank* trailing along behind on the cross-straps, as the stands and beams were inserted, planks laid along them over the empty hold, and the green side-cloths rolled up tightly along the gunwales. Vigorous work with both mops ensured we were soon our usual pristine selves as we chugged steadily down the long straights beyond Newtown Junction to the top of the New Thirteen. I was feeling particularly bouyant that morning given that our orders were to proceed round the 'Bottom Road' to load gravel chippings at Mancetter for delivery to West Drayton. This meant no waiting about in the coalfield and a good long run right down beyond Cowley to follow, couldn't be better! Lil and I got our act together well down the New Thirteen and we were soon passing Salford Bridge and setting out on what, for me, were the unknown waters of the Birmingham and Fazeley Canal, the 'Bottom Road', written about in *Maidens Trip* and *Idle Women* and now to be experienced at first hand. After instructions to 'go along steady and watch the bridge-holes' I was left to take *Redshank* along the first pound to the top of Minworth. It was unimpressive from the start with factories lining the cut and occasional 'clunks' as we encountered some hidden obstruction. Prudently I eased right off in every bridge-hole as the 'Bottom Road' had an awesome reputation for lurking submerged objects just waiting to wrap themselves round the blades.

However, nothing untoward occurred as we jogged steadily along before easing right down as the top gate of the first of the three Minworth locks appeared ahead. These are an awkward distance apart, some crews opting to bow-haul the butty whilst others stick to towing down on the cross-straps. It seemed to depend on your point of view and possibly how strong you were feeling! We towed down! I was sent on ahead to set the lock in order for *Redshank* to come straight in, waiting patiently by the strapping post to collect the thrown line before taking a couple of turns and preventing *Greenshank* from following. My next task was to shut the top gate as Alec had already gone down to draw the bottom paddles. This was yet another variation on the locking routine but I found myself managing well enough, being by now much more experienced at strapping boats into locks. It had been a procedure of which I had once been very nervous, always frightened of getting it wrong and losing control of the onrushing boat, but nowadays my worries were largely banished by successful practice and that day I gave myself over to enjoying my part in the butty work of the 'Bottom Road'.

Until recently there had been a fairly heavy trade in coal along this cut, mostly in the horse-drawn 'joey' boats of T & S Element or S.E. Barlow. A major part of this trade had been from the colliery at Pooley Hall to the General Electrical Company (GEC) at Witton just below the New Thirteen, but this now all seemed to be a thing of the past and we were to meet only one small pleasure cruiser in our day's journeying. By Curdworth Locks we had finally left the factories behind and were now proceeding through a rather unkempt succession of neglected pastures. The approach to Birmingham from this side does not compare at all favourably with that of the Grand Union main line from Knowle, a leafy finger of countryside running through 'Catty Barnes' and the deep wooded cuttings of Solihull, without question a much more attractive and gratifying route. Luckily the sun was shining for us again which always helps, on a dull day of grey cloud and seeping drizzle the 'Bottom Road' must look very dreary indeed. The eleven locks at Curdworth were awkwardly spaced for a pair, reminiscent in many ways of the New Thirteen. In some parts we worked down on the cross-straps, whilst elsewhere the locks were closer together and I was able to bow-haul *Greenshank* down, with Alec going on ahead and starting the locks for us. Passing the solitary 'Dog in a Doublet' pub at Bodymoor Heath we left the bottom lock to plod uneventfully along through a series of bridge holes before swinging hard round the big turn at Fazeley Junction and arriving at the first of the Coventry Canal locks at Glascote Two.

I looked with interest at the Glascote boatyards as we passed slowly by. Once the hub of S.E. Barlow's thriving coal business the Anchor Dock looked neglected and unwanted, yet another tangible reminder of the long decline in trade along these once busy waterways. Three pairs of BW boats snoozed in the sunshine above Glascote, idly waiting for orders having recently come round the 'Bottom Road' from Tyseley. Among them was Bert whom we had last seen at Bull's Bridge, he was as immaculate as ever and anticipated a bit of a wait before getting a load for the Mills.

"You're better off with that gravel, I reckon," he said. "Beats all the hanging about."

The cut from Great Bridge to Glascote could hardly be described as one of the great scenic routes of the waterways. There were a few points of interest along the way, but much of the journey could only really be described as dreary and so it was to continue for the remainder of the day. With further exhortations to 'go steady and watch them bridge holes' ringing in my ears I proceeded along past Polesworth and the steaming pipes of Pooley Hall to tie for the night at the bottom of the eleven locks at Atherstone.

Tomorrow would be time enough to ascend as we were not due to load at Mancetter until mid-morning. The loading wharf was to be found on the opposite side to the towpath and virtually in the middle of open fields, the actual business of loading being simplicity itself compared with heaving timber out of a lighter. The boats were laid alongside the wharf and large 'eight-wheeler' tipper lorries then arrived one after another from the nearby quarries, backing-up and smoothly and easily discharging their loads into the hold, clouds of fine white dust rising up and settling on everything. Our only tasks involved trimming the boats with the shovels to ensure they were level and would 'swim' nicely, mopping and sluicing all the dust off, and providing everyone with a cup of tea!

By early afternoon everything was neat and tidy once more, sandwiches had been eaten and we were all ready to begin the long run south. Open country beckoned tomorrow, a welcome change after many days in the Black Country, the dreariness of the 'Bottom Road', and now the unprepossessing cut through the Warwickshire coalfield. But all that was tomorrow and there was still work to be done today. We would go to Tushes Bridge that night and thus be nicely placed for a clear start in the morning. Steering *Greenshank* that afternoon, as Lil caught up with cabin chores, I viewed the backs of Nuneaton with considerable disfavour and then cheered up somewhat as things began to be more interesting on the approach towards Sutton Stop. Bill, with his pair of empty Barlows going up to load at Baddesley, was encountered and it was a tight squeeze past in the muddy rather shallow waterway before Alec was shouting "Hey-up" to two pairs of BWs waiting to load coal from Newdigate Colliery in the Bedworth Arm. We had been rather out of things for a while and it was nice to be back in the flow and seeing other pairs busy about their business. Swinging, with the necessary aid of the strap, round the enormous turn at Sutton Stop the boats drifted to a halt outside 'The Greyhound', waiting whilst I dealt with the stop lock controlling the three inch change in level between the Oxford and Coventry canals.

Suttons was one of the key hubs of the carrying trade. The office, where orders to load in the coalfield were collected, overlooked the junction and the bar of 'The Greyhound' was a meeting place for many canal folk, both working and retired. For once, though, we were not planning to stop here, but would instead go on to the pub at the next bridge hole, Tushes Bridge. Glancing through the iron footbridge as *Redshank* pushed into the lock, I became aware that many eyes were upon me. Pairs of boats were moored on both sides of the cut right back to the corner which took you round to Longford Power Station, known to all boatmen as Coventry Light, or alternatively just The Light. Trade from the coalfield seemed slack and I was glad we had come round for the gravel as I noticed three pairs of Willow Wrens and another pair of Barlows in amongst the line of waiting BW boats. The gap between these moored boats was left just wide enough to squeeze through singled-out and that afternoon I felt rather like being on stage in front of a critical audience. Strictly on tickover I edged *Redshank* forward past the waiting assembly, acknowledging a number of crews I knew well enough to talk to and solemnly greeting others whom I knew only by sight.

It would not do to make any sort of silly mistake here, not in full view of everyone. I found myself concentrating really hard to ensure no little bumps or nudges in that very narrow channel, making sure also not to get any unseemly jerks on the towline as I finally began to put on a little speed, rounding the turn towards The Light and away from those grave watchers!

We had tied at Tushes Bridge, rather than making the more customary stop at Suttons, in order to see the newly married Young Lily and Cliff. An especially jolly evening ensued with all the usual jokes from Young Lily about 'John, John, the Bachelor Boy' which she had not forgotten and was not going to let me forget either! Young Lily had been very kind to me on my first trip and I, in my turn, was very fond of her. Cliff also was very personable and friendly towards me and it was a real pleasure to see their undoubted happiness in each other. A rather large quantity of beer was consumed that night and I recall experiencing some difficulty in regaining the boat. The towpath at that time was very badly eroded on the edge of a wide turn which lay just beyond the bridge hole where we had tied. Not only were there several large watery holes to trap the unwary, but a further hazard was involved by the boats lying about six feet out from the bank with a narrow plank forming the only access. I got myself round the holes, helped by giggles and shouted warnings from the others, and then caused great amusement by having to have three attempts at the plank before finally landing unsteadily in *Greenshank*'s hatches. We sat on in the warm cabin, drinking tea and eating cheese sandwiches, making the very most of being together once again. It was well past midnight when Young Lily and Cliff said their 'Goodnight's' and I, to great mirth all round and shouted warnings about the sharks from Young Lily, stepped uncertainly across to *Redshank* and was asleep in minutes.

Needless to say we were late starting the next morning! The original plan had been to put in some really serious boating and go down to West Drayton in three days, but sometimes even the very best laid plans and intentions don't always work out. I awoke feeling distinctly bleary, but with an awareness that the cabin was unusually bright and that the morning traffic was moving in a steady flow across the bridge. Pushing the slide back I put my head out to glorious morning sunshine, clear blue sky and invigorating air, a few deep breaths of which made me feel considerably better. My watch said half past seven, so much for all those much discussed plans for a five o'clock start. Lil could normally always be relied upon in matters of getting us up and away, but even she had succumbed after the joyous night we had all had. A cold water wash in the handbowl revived me still further and put paid to most of the residual fuzziness – it had certainly been quite a night! The situation was a little awkward. There was no sign of life on *Greenshank* and, although I could start *Redshank* up, I couldn't get going without a butty steerer! Should I perhaps make them a cup of tea? I opened the engine-hole doors and let them bang rather noisily back before fitting the tiller bar and clinking about with the water can. My little dilemna was solved as *Greenshank*'s slide was pushed back and Lil appeared, still looking distinctly sleepy and dishevelled.

"Bit late, John."

"A bit," I agreed. "Good night, though."

"Lovely to see them," said Lil wistfully, seemingly unworried by the time and happy with her memories.

"Shall I 'er ..."

"When you've got your tea," she smiled. "No rush! I've got the kettle on for us."

It was an amazingly relaxed start to the day. No grumbling about the time, nothing about too much beer, or people being too lazy to get up. Instead, just sitting there quietly in the butty hatches soaking up the sunshine and watching the kettle boil up, and all the time chatting convivially about how well Young Lily and Cliff were doing and was I feeling all right after my escapades on the plank? It was most definitely not our normal morning routine!

Eventually we bestirred ourselves and, with a steaming second mug of tea on the slide in front of me, I puttered forward and picked up the tow before 'winding it on' and settling down happily for the long five and a half hour pound down to Hillmorton. Round past the muddy turn at Ansty and polishing the brasses in the long easy straights down to Stretton where I had a glorious view of an ex-LMS 4-6-2 roaring past in charge of the northbound express, 'The Mancunian'; passengers waving to me out of the windows and smiling as I waved back on this good-to-be-alive spring morning. We swopped over at the disused stop lock at Stretton and Alec, still making jokes about the plank, took over leaving me to drop back for a belated breakfast. This pound, although long, is always interesting with the old canal crossing and re-crossing our route as we headed south, our exhaust beat reverberating off the bricks in the short 'Noble' tunnel and bringing back memories of the previous summer and my cycle ride along from Brownsover to see the old disused tunnel behind the church. The occasional spring day in England can be absolutely glorious and this was proving to be one of them. The air was positively balmy and the sunlight glittered and sparkled off the water, lounging languorously at *Greenshank*'s tiller I glanced up the Brownsover Arm before heading round in familiar country once more to the bottom of Hillmorton. We had met five pairs between 'Noble' and 'Morton' coming up from Braunston to join the ever-lengthening queue at Suttons, they did not look at all pleased as Lil emerged each time to give them the unpleasant details. The coal trade might be in a slack patch, but we had our gravel and were grateful to be on the move.

Hillmorton, of course, were ready for us and we slid side by side into the bottom locks in a highly professional manner, all very slick and organised and feeling very at ease with life after the long quiet pound and the beautiful weather. It is the middle pair of locks at Hillmorton which are the tricky ones. There is a sharp bend below them and it's essential that both locks are ready if problems are to be avoided. Normally, even after five pairs had assured us that the flight was ready, I would have strolled up from the bottom lock just in case a pleasure boat had altered the situation. However, Alec chose this moment to disappear into the engine-hole leaving me to take *Redshank* on to the middle locks which we assumed were ready for us. I suppose it was just one of those things. The last pair we had met had confirmed that the flight was all ready for us, but had crucially omitted to mention the presence of a sixth empty pair coming along behind them. I was through the intermediate bridge hole and about to make the turn into the left-hand lock when I was surprised by a sudden flush of water as both locks started to empty at virtually the same time. It was a very awkward moment. Forced to pull out of gear, I found myself being pushed across the cut by the swirling surge of water flooding fiercely through the bottom paddles. Lil, in unenviable circumstances, did the best she could and turned into me, thereby effectively stopping the butty and leaving both boats blocking the entrance to the right-hand lock. By the time Alec, alerted by the thumps, had clambered out of the engine-hole the chaos was complete! It may have been undignified, but it was perfectly safe as the water on this turn is very deep. With a certain amount of good-natured grumbling we disentangled ourselves and pulled back slightly to let the grinning Ted and his wife through. Not the best place to meet, but then we were three-handed and so where was the lock-wheeler? There was nothing we could really say and so Ted was loosed by with shrugs and good grace, no doubt a suitably embellished version of the incident would go the rounds in 'The Greyhound' that evening.

We huffily sorted ourselves out and completed the flight before stowing our small windlasses behind the coalbox with some relief. Wide locks all the way now!

"Can you two manage to get ahead without getting tangled up in the hedge?" queried Alec, as we readied ourselves for the pound. I didn't quite catch Lil's reply to this particular quip! Whatever it was, he agreed that perhaps we might just about manage and I eased slowly ahead, picking up the long snubber and thankfully leaving the narrow locks behind for a while. The day remained fine as we jogged round under the railway and then on down the long Barby straight, chugging steadily along in no particular hurry as we were bound to tie at Braunston that night. It was remarkable how once again the situation had been contrived to include a night at Cosgrove, although to be fair the credit on this trip should really go to the after-effects of M & B Mild as our original plan for a three day journey had not included tying there. Braunston was reached in late afternoon and we squashed ourselves in alongside the various boats recently purchased by Willow Wren, all in various stages of being re-fitted. At this stage things still looked reasonably rosy. Leslie Morton, whilst losing some contracts, was still gaining others and also sub-contracting coal to the Mills. Seen from our particular angle the future still appeared quite promising, the disaster which lay just around the corner unforeseen by any of us. It was true that trade was shrinking in some areas, but conversely it was actually being revived elsewhere and new contracts developed. There seemed no reason to believe that commercial carrying was in any particular danger of collapse. After all, it was only two years earlier that *Raymond*, the last wooden butty to be built by Barlows, had been launched at the Braunston yard and we had all stood excitedly by the lockside at Stoke to watch Arthur and Rosie bring the beautifully fitted boat through on her first trip south. If boats were still being built, then surely the future couldn't be too bad. Thus I reasoned to myself, as I poked about the yard that evening and chatted to Dennis about the fortunes of Willow Wren.

It was back to another classic Spring day of sunshine and showers as we headed south the next morning through the familiar Northamptonshire countryside on one of my favourite sections. Two long tunnels, three flights, and the long intervening pounds made for a day of continual variation and interest. The only 'event' of the day occurred at the bottom of Buckby. I eased out of the bottom lock and picked up the tow as normal, holding back to minimise the jerk and then going ahead again and beginning to build up the revs. On this particular occasion *Greenshank* emerged from the dripping lock chamber and then, with her fore-end just clear of the steps, she suddenly stopped and listed slightly towards the inside. Luckily I had not, like some people, wound on the speedwheel furiously and was also fortuitously looking back at the time, spotting the problem immediately I was thus able to hold back hard and bring *Redshank* to a standstill with the snubber thankfully still intact. The butty must have been stuck on what was probably a metal barrel as she seemed to rock and move a little, but could not be induced forward. A little gentle tugging by *Redshank*, now backed close-up to the butty, accompanied by some hefty shafting, did nothing at all. She rocked and scraped, but stubbornly would still not move. *Greenshank*, Alec decided, had to be moved sideways off the barrel and a good flush would help! Lil was put in charge of *Redshank* whilst Alec braced himself with the long shaft resting against the coping ready to shove. At the signal I raised all the top paddles and a veritable roaring flush of water lifted *Greenshank*. Alec pushed. Lil, on *Redshank*, pulled. *Greenshank* rocked, but then stayed where she was. Paddles were dropped and another conference ensued with tempers beginning to fray and dark accusations about BW maintenance men who let barrels fall in the cut starting to fly about. I suggested that we tie *Redshank* up and leave her for a minute, that we then run a line from the butty's mast to the opposite lockside and then repeat the previous exercise, only this time it would be Lil on the paddles and Alec and I pulling. To my great satisfaction it worked! With water boiling past and the pound above nearly two-thirds empty, *Greenshank* rocked and then reluctantly, but with increasing momentum, slid sideways and floated free.

Paddles were hastily dropped and we were on our way again turning a blind eye to the near empty bottom pound.

Unfortunately we met a pair of our boats in the Spinnies! Mark, loaded with timber, slid past and, mindful of the empty pound awaiting him, I eased right down to give Alec, on the butty, time to explain and make his peace with him and Dolly. These things happen, although I still hadn't worked out how all those Hatton pounds had come to be empty that time. As for the barrel, it had disappeared by the time of my next trip, although whether shoved into the shallows by passing boats or actually removed by British Waterways I never knew. Other than this the day passed smoothly enough with only the occasional passing shower to irritate. At Stoke we found out that Sister Mary was selling up and moving to London in her final retirement. This was sad news indeed, as she had been a good friend to me over the short time we had known each other and would be a great loss to the canal scene. Alec and Lil were also rather subdued about it all, Sister had seemed to be such a permanent feature in their lives and who could replace her? A certain Colonel Ritchie, who owned a boat called *Lupin* and was reputedly keen on the cut, had purchased the property and the canalside at Stoke Bruerne would experience the first of the many changes which were to alter its character completely. All this was in an unknown and uncertain future. As the boats sank down in the lock, we could only wish Sister well and proceed on our way, digesting this momentous news as we did so.

From Cosgrove we went to Cowroast on another of those somewhat gloomy and uninspiring days where the sun never really breaks through for any worthwhile length of time. The blue boats of the Wyvern Shipping Company were returning to base for the changeover week-end and I was interested, when lockwheeling the Stoke Hammond Three, to find *Canada Goose* just about to enter the bottom lock. Many hirers in those far off days were, like I had been, very enthusiastic about the working boats and keen to do things properly and these people were no exception. Two families, with two vigorous boys who reminded me of myself, were all for coming out of the lock and giving us priority as they were told to do in all the books. However they were six handed and I had pedalled hard along from Talbots with the pair nowhere in sight. The locks were against us anyway, and they were only going to Leighton. I took it upon myself to insist that they continued on up ahead of us, which they did in a most efficient manner with one of the husbands staying back to help me draw off. It was all very friendly and pleasant and left a good feel on an otherwise grey day. There was much clicking of cameras as we passed *Canada Goose* at the Wyvern base and I like to think that our friendly exchange put the final gloss on their holiday, certainly the interest and enthusiasm of this unknown duo of families brightened my own day.

There often used to be pairs waiting at Cowroast to be allowed down to the Mills, but trade continued to be very slack indeed. Unusually we found ourselves alone there that night with our fore-ends pressed firmly against the top gates and ensuring first passage in the morning when the lock came off. No-one joined us from either direction and it was difficult to tell whether our road would be good or bad on the morrow. We had seen more pleasure boats than pairs in the last couple of days and their movements were far less predictable than those of the carrying trade. Getting away at six, on a somewhat brighter and more cheerful day, I began by lock-wheeling down along a muddy towpath as far as Gas Two where I met Ron and his BW pair, northbound for Wellingborough.

"You can stop sweating, young John!" he grinned. "Langley's ready!"

Langley was below Nash Mills which was excellent news indeed. I duly dropped the bike back on the gravel and worked happily downwards on *Greenshank*, thus releasing Lil to provide us all with a large traditional breakfast which went down a treat on the approach to Berko. However at Boxmoor Ron was proved wrong, as we had to go above the lock which was empty, still dripping with water and with only one bottom gate standing open. This, added to the fact that the bottom paddles had been dropped, seemed to indicate that a pleasure craft had started out after Ron had gone by and now had 'our' locks. This was annoying as I had been enjoying steering *Greenshank* down the pounds and proficiently strapping her into the locks. However, needs must, and I hauled the bike off once more and pedalled away, windlass in belt, to set the locks. Whoever it was could not be very far ahead, maybe they'd loose us by.

The lock chambers were very wet indeed which was always a giveaway. I drew a ground paddle before running down to shut the bottom gate and walking back to draw the remaining paddles. On the other hand whoever it was must be fairly efficient as I seemed unable, even with furious pedalling along the pounds, to actually catch up to them. At Nash Mills a pair, half empty under the grab, told me that I was chasing a converted narrowboat which was no less then ten handed! No wonder they were getting through the locks quickly! At Hunton Bridge, much to my relief, I found them tied up, but the locks remained against us until I reached Albert's Two in the Parks where I met a cruiser coming up. They were only leaving one gate open and could not remember how many locks they had left ready, but I thankfully seized the chance to rejoin the boats. Having only one gate open was of little significance as the surge of the incoming motor, coupled with a spot of judicious steering, pushed the errant gate open and gave *Greenshank* no problems.

It had been a reasonably sunny day with only one heavy shower and we were content as we dropped down through Ricky, only to encounter a bad road yet again at Springwell. Both bottom gates open, paddles up, signified someone going down empty from Croxley to Brentford. It had, in terms of the bicycle, been an on and off day, I thought to myself, as I remounted yet again and headed doggedly off towards Coppermill Lock. With the steady increase in pleasure craft this sort of day was to become a more normal state of affairs in those last years of trade and an uncertainty would creep in as to whether locks, said to be ready by an oncoming pair, would actually be ready when you reached them. There is very little more to add. West Drayton was reached that night and we were quickly unloaded by grab the next morning before reaching Brentford again the same night. Swinging round we tied alongside a lighter which was three-quarters full of timber. Destined for? You've guessed it! Tipton. Round trip completed, and now we could do it all over again!

*****

Chapter 9

Up the River

The Willow Wren Canal Carrying Company had a short life by comparison with the two old established Barlow concerns, or that of a large general carrier such as the old Fellows, Morton & Clayton. Despite this brief lifespan great credit must go to 'The Gaffer', Leslie Morton, who worked very hard and with much success to achieve new contracts for the firm and also to support some of the early efforts at canal restoration which were then beginning to get underway. It was a constant battle to keep the boats moving and sometimes a contract gained, such as the Hayes Cocoa run, could be inadvertently lost again as circumstances changed. Some work was to be had sub-contracting for British Waterways, such as our run to Wellingborough or the Mills runs, but this was always dependent upon the volume of trade and naturally they would put their own boats first. Having your own contracts was the best way forward for any carrying company but, in the years of decline that followed the Second World War, it became harder and harder to find new contracts and, above all, to trade profitably.

Many waterways were seeing little or no trade at all. The long line of the Leicester Cut from Norton Junction to the river Trent carried virtually nothing by the late 1950s and was distinctly weedy in a number of places, especially below Watford Locks. On the Oxford below Banbury a small amount of coal for Morrells still moved fitfully from time to time, but the contracts to Osberton Radiators, the Wolvercote Paper Mill, and all the other coal contracts to Oxford had been lost. No commercial traffic had moved for years on the Stratford Canal, and the Worcester & Birmingham Canal was in steep decline with only a very few pairs trading. The passage of loaded boats along the Birmingham & Fazeley Canal, the 'Bottom Road', and then round to Nottingham from Bourneville had ceased and the Trent & Mersey generally, east of the Potteries, saw little commercial traffic. Even the once busy 'Bottom Road' was becoming mostly a conduit for empty boats coming round from Birmingham, with the trade from the Warwickshire coalfield into the city now merely a shadow of its former self.

Once traffic had moved down the Oxford and out on to the Thames, both 'up west' towards Lechlade and south to Abingdon and Reading. John Knill had made those long runs with salt from Northwich to

Newbury as recently as 1950, but the trade was not sustained and, by the late 1950s, the river Thames was empty of narrowboats. It was thus with some surprise that I heard from Jack, a Willow Wren captain whom I was shutting a gate for at the top of Stoke, of a new contract involving the carrying of cattle cake and feed from Brentford up the Thames to Marsh Mill, just short of Marsh Lock at Henley. Being a Midlands youth I had absolutely no knowledge of this part of the world and rushed back into the cottage to trace the course of the river on my Stanford's map and look the distances up in 'Edwards'. This looked to be a trip with a difference. Jack had apparently been up the river in company with Alec's pair and hoped to do so again. So did I! However I was not counting on it. The Marsh Mills run obviously did not encompass the entire Willow Wren fleet at any one time and it seemed to be a matter of chance. Like many things in life, you needed to have the luck to be in the right place at the right time in order to find yourself ordered to Brentford to load for Henley. If you were at the southern end of the Grand Union when cattle cake arrived at Brentford you might get it, if you were elsewhere at the time then you missed it, all very much a question of luck.

The Sixth Form, in which I now found myself, was proving to be surprisingly hard work with 'A' levels being a big jump up from the 'O' levels which had preceded them. However I was coping and, by working long hours all week, was able to keep most of the week-ends and a good chunk of the holidays free for the cut. The chance to do this sort of boating would not necessarily come again, I reasoned, and so I determined to make the very most of it before the world of work and building a career closed around me. As things turned out I was proved to be absolutely correct in this approach as the demise of narrow boat carrying was only just around the corner although, at the time, I was confidently giving it another twenty years, such was the youthful optimism generated by the activities of the Willow Wren company in particular. Sometimes I would take work with me on the boats, books were read in all sorts of little bits of spare time and several essays completed whilst waiting around to load or empty. I had learned early the trick of compartmentalising and was perfectly able to cut myself off for an hour's school work before resuming once more the life of the boats. I also got much less tired. Older and tougher than when I first boarded *Warbler* I could now work long hours in all weathers without becoming, as I sometimes did on those first trips, virtually exhausted by the end of the day. Now, especially if we finished a bit early, I could snatch time for school work and still have enough energy left for skittles and a pint!

On this particular occasion a phone call ascertained that the boats were loading first thing tomorrow at Newdigate for Croxley. Given that today was conveniently the last day of term, I resolved without further hesitation to cycle out and join them at Braunston. This ploy would enable me to gain an extra day's boating and I could drop the bike off at Stoke on the journey south. I travelled very light in those days with just a change of clothes, washing gear, and my holiday work, stashed either in my capacious saddlebag or in the old RAF rucksack I had slung around my shoulders. Real life began again as I pedalled off on the now familiar road, the same route as that pioneering early trip undertaken with my father. Then it had seemed to me like an enormous expedition, but now cycling over to Braunston had become nothing out of the ordinary, a quite normal undertaking in fact. It was a gloriously warm summer's day, shirt sleeve weather with a vengeance, as I freewheeled down Whilton Hill and came to rest on the hump backed bridge below the second lock up on the Buckby flight. The locks were full, but there was no sign of any traffic. To save energy I elected to continue by road although it would have been perfectly possible, albeit rather slower, to have cycled up the locks and rejoined the road route at the second bridge-hole beyond Norton Junction. The lanes were quiet and leafy with the verges uncut and thick with cow parsley. There were also far fewer cars to bother about than would be the case today when it is difficult to cycle anywhere around Northamptonshire, even in the very smallest of lanes, without encountering a steady flow of motor traffic. All was peace as I passed silently through Welton, dozing sleepily in the sunshine, before reaching Braunston itself and turning down Dark Lane, a very appropriate name, towards the 'Admiral Nelson'. On a sharp bend I rattled through the gate and bumped down the field track to the bottom lock and the Willow Wren yard.

I had made good time and there was as yet no sign of the pair, but Dennis confirmed the loading pattern and said he expected Alec to arrive that night. If this proved not to be the case, then there were a couple of old butties I was welcome to doss down in! Hoping that it would not come to this I left my saddlebag and rucksack in his care and, feeling much lighter without the weight of books on my shoulders, pedalled off towards Suttons, optimistically expecting to meet the boats somewhere round the Hillmorton pound. A pair of loaded Barlows was tied at the Junction House, just outside their yard, but the cabins were all shut up and there seemed to be no-one about whom I could ask about the whereabouts of 'my' pair. Trundling over the double arched cast iron bridge at the triangular junction I considered the matter. Alec's pattern was well known to me by now. Surely I would meet the boats today if he did what he should do, that is to say, load in the Bedworth Arm, Tushes Bridge to see Cliff and Young Lily, then Braunston, on to Cosgrove, and thence, with one more stop somewhere, to Croxley. Passing under the busy A45 road bridge I rode slowly and carefully out along the little-used grassy towpath into the quiet fields towards Willoughby. A couple of bridge holes followed and then, as I was picking my way through a badly eroded length, I heard in the distance the faint beat of a diesel. I hurried on as best I could towards the next bridge hole, but had not yet reached it when I saw the fore-end of a deeply laden motor swing round a slight turn ahead of me. A blue and yellow fore-end told me that it was not *Redshank*, a fact which I should have deduced anyway from the beat of the engine. My disappointment changed when I saw it was none other than Bert, beaming at me and easing down as he came abreast.

"Hallo, young John! He's just behind us!"

This was the news I wanted and I smiled happily back at Bert, still as immaculate as ever, and told him I'd see him in the 'Nelson' later on. Exchanging greetings with the butty I pedalled on to the next bridge hole and stood under the arch waiting expectantly. Not long now!

'Just behind' could mean anything from a boats length to half an hour. In the event it was to be ten minutes or so before the eagerly awaited fore-ends came into view and waving arms indicated that I had been spotted. *Redshank* slid into the bridge hole and I threw my bike on to the coal before stepping on to the narrow gunwale. We grinned at each other and Alec stepped out of the door-holes, waving me towards the footboard with an extravagant flourish.

"Nice rest for me!" he grinned, as he hoisted himself on to the cabin top. "Get 'em ahead, John!"

I needed no second bidding and waved excitedly at Lil before twirling the speedwheel and feeling the surge under *Redshank*'s counter. Once again I was back in my element, steering into Braunston on what had become a deliciously balmy summer's evening. That first evening at the 'Nelson' turned out to be especially memorable, in more ways than one! Hubert had a custom of staying open after closing time on Fridays, but not for everyone. The favoured few, nearly all canal folk, would sit about after 'last orders' pretending to drink up until all the casual trade had gone, after which Hubert would bolt the door. Thirza would make sure that the curtains were pulled tight across and we would settle down for another couple of hours drinking. Hubert's only proviso was that you didn't go rolling down the lane afterwards and wake half the village up!

A well-lubricated group of us eventually left the pub and strolled along on a warm moonlit night, my watch indicating that it was nearly one o'clock. The most direct route back to the bottom lock was straight down the towpath, but a couple of the group lived in council houses at the top of the village and, so as to be sociable, everybody walked together along Dark Lane to the gate at the top of the field where, after exaggerated whispers of 'Goodnight', we went our separate ways. At the bottom of the field was another five-barred gate giving access to the dry dock on the left and the Willow Wren yard on the right. Full of beer, I was enthusiastically extolling my prowess at gate vaults in the school gym as we approached and, in view of my rather merry state, was challenged to perform one there and then by a young boatman who was with us and who shall remain unnamed. This I successfully did, landing with a slight splash in the edge of the large muddy puddle which stretched out on the other side. Not to be outdone, he then claimed that he had no need to vault gates. Why, he just jumped straight over them! This boast was, of course, seized upon by all present and, in order not to lose face, he elected to demonstrate this prodigious leap without further ado. It has to be said, before going any further, that he was very unlucky! He took a good run up and could certainly jump and jump well, unfortunately he just caught his leading toe on the top edge of the gate. His momentum took him over the top, but not in quite the fashion he had intended. To howls of laughter he landed face down squarely in the middle of the puddle! Soaked and muddy he staggered to his feet to find that, other than a graze or two, he was unhurt and we were able to deliver him back over the bridge to where his young wife awaited on their northbound empty pair. She was not best pleased at his dripping muddy state and had very choice words for us for allowing him to get like it, if only that gate had been an inch lower! After all the excitement it turned out to be nearly two o'clock before I blearily found my way under the blankets and fell soundly asleep. I was now seventeen, but still at that very impressionable age and revelling in the cut as much as ever. Yesterday I had sat in class working at 'A' levels and that was one world. Today I had cycled out and was blissfully content to be back in my other world which I regarded as much the better place to be, a view that has not changed with the passing of the years.

In the morning the lock came off as usual at six but, as can be imagined, we were not exactly bursting with energy! It was nearly half past six when, very strongly chivvied up by a determined Lil, I steered the pair into the bottom of the flight. Our friend of the previous evening was also starting up, singling-out to go to Sutton Stop, with his wife grimly supervising matters from the butty hatches. We put our hands to our heads and grinned knowingly at each other, it had been an evening to remember and we would do it again given half a chance! Fortunately it was another beautiful summer's day and, by the middle of the flight, the three of us were working efficiently together once more, although there was no sign whatsover of Hubert as we passed through the 'Nelson' lock! The sunshine followed us down to our customary stop at Cosgrove where, rather later than usual, we slipped off to the 'Barley Mow' under very strict instructions from Lil not to be back late tonight. As it turned out we spent most of the evening skittling, an activity which necessarily involved somewhat less beer than might have been put away sitting down.

I came across another interesting story that night which presumably was true as it was vehemently corroborated by at least four of those present. A few years back a pair of boats had stopped for the night and the boatman had got to boasting of his prowess at dancing along the top planks of his craft after sinking a gallon or more of whatever local beer was available. His claim was that he could always walk a straight line, no matter how much beer he had consumed, and he would become quite aggressive when challenged about this. At the end of this particular evening he had partaken of rather more than a gallon of Phipps' bitter, but was still persisting in his claims. Claim and counter-claim escalated until he found himself wagering to push a wheelbarrow across the outside rim of the nearby Wolverton Aqueduct. Seen when cold sober and in daylight this is a task that I, for one, would not even consider as the considerable drop into the shallow waters of the Great Ouse below could well be fatal. At closing time our worthy friend found himself escorted down the outside bank of the cut to the edge of the aqueduct, with the wheelbarrow clanking merrily along behind them.

Nobody seriously expected him to even consider the walk, they were simply there to collect their winnings when he realised the impossibility of the bet. However, upon reaching the aqueduct, our hero seized the barrow and threatened violence on anyone who tried to stop him which, at that instant, they were all belatedly trying to do. Without turning a hair he proceeded to wheel the barrow straight across the rim, his only difficulty coming when he had to lift the barrow, which was preceding him, off the far end of the aqueduct. With the bet achieved he descended the slope, went through the footpath tunnel under the cut, and emerged in triumph on the towpath opposite his vanquished opponents. Having then collected a sizable sum in winnings at the lock and returned the barrow to its owner, he retired to his cabin. The following morning a couple of the eye-witnesses, cycling to work at the carriage works in Wolverton, tapped on his top to offer further congratulations. To their surprise our hero had absolutely no recollection of his feat and veritably blanched at the suggestion that he might care to repeat it. Only their faithful assurances that he had definitely done it, coupled with the unusual number of ten shilling notes in his pocket, convinced him of the truth. He was so shaken that he couldn't even manage any breakfast for thinking about what might have befallen him, and his wife's comments on his behaviour nearly blistered the paint off the table cupboard door! There were to be no such heroics for us that night. All was serene as we ambled contentedly back for our customary cheese sandwich at the lock cottage and a relatively early night.

From Cosgrove it proved to be a fairly routine run southwards. With high pressure predominating the weather remained set fair. After a little early mist had cleared it was shirt sleeve boating all the way round the pounds and up through 'The Fields', with a succession of pairs returning empty to Suttons giving us very largely a good road through the locks. Of northbound loaded boats there seemed no sign and it began to look, as we began the descent to Croxley, as if this time it would be a case of 'back empty to Suttons' for us also. As was the custom we found ourselves held for a day below Cassio Lock whilst pairs ahead of us were emptied and, as I was enthusiastically polishing the chimney brasses, we were hailed by a small scruffy-looking gentleman who had appeared opposite us. He was offering two pounds for a day's work in the nearby watercress beds and, after some hesitation, I agreed to go. Alec claimed that he had to give the engine a good going over or otherwise he would also have come! It was to be a very hard-earned two pounds. The beds were rectangular in shape and each was about a foot deep in beautifully clear water siphoned off from the nearby river. It was here that the watercress grew in great profusion before being harvested and sent to Covent Garden. At the end of each cycle each bed had to be thoroughly cleared out in readiness for the whole business to begin all over again. A large rake was thrust into my hand and, suitably clad in large borrowed waders, I set to work raking out the old watercress plants and dumping them in large dripping piles on the side. A hot sun burnt down and the wet lumps of cress were surprisingly heavy as I laboured on. A princely break of exactly half an hour, 'and not a minute more, mind', was awarded for lunch and I staggered back over the lockgates, amidst general hilarity from all concerned, for my sandwich and half a pot of tea. It was unremittingly hard and hot work, but I had been well trained on the boats and most certainly would not give up. All through the long sun-drenched afternoon I doggedly persevered, triumphantly clearing one bed only to be sent straight off to start work on another. At last half past five came and, clutching my two pounds, I made my slow aching way back to the boats, at least someone had done *Redshank*'s outside brasses for me!

My resolve was not tested further the next day as, thankfully, we were called down to the Mill and spent the morning under the 'jigger' emptying out. After putting the holds straight and mopping everything down Alec went off to phone Brentford for orders. Lil and I sat in the hatches with a mug of tea, making gloomy remarks about getting the boats winded and ready to go back empty even before he had returned. However our natural optimism prevailed and we decided to leave the boats where they were, there just might be a load for us even if nobody else seemed to be getting one. Alec came slowly back with a face as long as the Moira Cut! Back empty, I thought, and very probably a long wait at Suttons when we got there just for good measure. He climbed gloomily aboard with much muttering, accompanied by exaggerated puffing and blowing, before suddenly breaking out into an enormous grin.

"Cheer up, John. What a long miserable face! We'm going to Henley!"

He had fooled us completely! Mentally I had already winded the pair and was back to Boxmoor before he had even climbed aboard, such had been his hangdog expression.

"Seriously?" I retorted, hardly able to believe my luck.

"Aye. Gaffer wants us down there tomorrow morning to start loading and then its Marsh Mill, here we come!"

Watercress beds were quickly forgotten as the news of this completely new trip was digested. The Thames was totally unknown territory to me and I had little or no idea what to expect. I had been told that it was much prettier than the only river I really knew, the prosaic Nene down to Wellingborough. This, as I was shortly to find out, was to be very much of an understatement.

Although we had been the first pair to empty at Croxley that morning, the time was now marching on and it was almost midday. If we were wanted in the morning, then we'd better get on with it. Bull's Bridge tonight for a jar and then down the Hanwell flight to Brentford, all ready to commence loading at eight o'clock the next morning. I had done this before and knew the routine, but this time I was so excited by the prospect of the river trip that I might even have seriously considered bow-hauling them to Brentford! We had a 'bad road' once more that afternoon. I didn't mind! I positively flew down the towpath on the bike buoyed up by thoughts of the days ahead and sublimely happy in the lovely warm sunshine. At Brentford a lighter full of locust bean meal awaited us as we arrived alongside, dead on time as the clocks were striking eight. Investigating, I discovered that the locust bean lay under a precautionary canvas in sacks, or bags as we called them, weighing about $1^{1}/_{2}$cwt each. Loading would be the same as with the timber, that is to say by dint of our muscle power. We were to load fifty tons.

Dealing with bags was another new experience for me and I awaited instructions from Alec who had done the river trip before and knew exactly what was needed. The initial plan was for me to drop the bags off the top of the lighter and into our hold where he would stack them. Lil would keep us supplied with tea and moral support as the weight of the bags precluded any attempt by her to lift one alone. The trick was to pull the corners of the bag out into two 'ears' which could then be gripped and the bag lifted up and across. The day was once again a very hot one and sweat poured off me as I laboured manfully at what was a formidable task. These bags were indisputably heavy. At first, taking them from the top of the load, it wasn't too bad a task but, as the lighter emptied, it would become increasingly hard to heave the bags up and over from one hold to another. In the end, standing deep in the bowels of the lighter, we would resort to both of us heaving bags together, up on to the gunwale of the lighter and then dropping them off from there. Ideally four strong men were needed for the job, but you have to make do with what you've got and we worked doggedly on that morning under an increasingly fierce sun. By lunchtime my hands were red and sore, with knuckles and finger joints in particular suffering from the constant rubbing against the rough sacking as I grasped my 'ears'.

Three pints and a pork pie at the 'Six Bells' restored us somewhat and we slogged on through the long afternoon, finishing *Redshank* off as the sun sank in the western sky and the evening shadows began to draw on. Many people would have called it a day at this point, but psychologically it would be good to have *Greenshank* partially loaded in the morning. So, leaving Lil to patiently tie up the side cloths on the motor, we swopped the boats round and spent a further half an hour dropping bags into *Greenshank* before finally covering them with a top cloth and completing the sheeting up of *Redshank*. There was not the faintest sign of rain but, if you didn't take the trouble to sheet up, then doubtless it would surely appear and sopping wet sacks of locust bean meal are not a good idea! It had been another very hard day and I slumped down on the side-bed almost too exhausted to move, yet still happy enough for all that. Other people holidayed at Skegness or Hunstanton, I did this and would not have changed places with my class mates for a second. A good wash-down, followed by bumper portions of shop-bought fish and chips, did much to restore me. Indeed I even found the strength to mop *Redshank* off, though remarkably little dust had accumulated during loading, before following Alec along to the 'Bells' for a well earned pint, or two, or three, or … !

A few new aches were to be found the next morning and my hands, especially, had not taken kindly to the relentless clenching and lifting of the previous day. I decided to simply ignore their protestations. They would harden up eventually as they had done before, it was just a matter of time. Bacon sandwiches and tea were enjoyed sitting on *Greenshank*'s footboard with the sun once more streaming into the cabin and promising another splendid day. This was a point in our favour, being hot was considerably better than trying to load on one of those classic days of sunshine punctuated by heavy squally showers; such uncertainty can be more irritating than steady rain. The plan for the day was simplicity itself. We needed to complete the loading of *Greenshank*, check the tides for our departure time, and get enough shopping in for the run up to Henley. I accepted a third cup of tea and drank it down quickly, the moment could be delayed no longer and we climbed stiffly on to the lighter, spat on our hands, and began heaving. The first twenty minutes or so were by far the worst as hands and assorted other muscles protested at the further imposition, but then I began to warm to the task and get into my stride finding a steady rhythm which took me nicely through the morning, with Lil providing a very welcome cup of tea about half way through. The cut seemed to be getting back to something like normal again after the recent slack period and several other pairs had arrived that morning to load spelter and steel strips for Tyseley. I watched enviously as the cranes transferred their loads from wharfside to boat with the crews largely spectators, as I had been myself in the same situation with *Warbler*. Still, we were getting on and the piles of bags mounted in *Greenshank* as she sank lower and lower in the water. It was a very hot day and the beer at lunchtime was almost physiologically necessary to replace lost liquid, that was my excuse anyway! It also made for a welcome break, taking us over the bridge and away from the boats to indulge in a spot of relaxation in the company of Jumbo, Porkchop and the other lightermen who frequented the bar.

By early afternoon *Greenshank* could take no more and the lighter was sheeted up to await the arrival of the next lucky pair. Another lighter was due up from the docks and at least one more load would be available for Marsh Mill. Once *Greenshank* was sheeted up the pair were tied very securely together as we would travel 'breasted-up' on the river, virtually a holiday cruise in terms of the effort required. But first we had to get up the tideway, a stretch of water I had yet to see despite several previous visits to

Brentford. You could not get out of Brentford Creek and up to the first lock at Teddington unless the tide was running in your favour. It certainly could not be done at night either and, upon making enquiries, we found that our 'slot' would be at about three o'clock the following afternoon. This was fine as it gave us plenty of time to have a little rest, get the boats immaculate for the journey upstream, and also to do all the shopping without pressure. In the late afternoon I made my way through the tangle of little streets, alleys, and wharves to stand at last beside the Thames at the mouth of Brentford Creek. To eyes accustomed only to the canals and the Nene, which were of much the same size, the river looked enormous. The tide was half out and soft wet mud showed at the edges, but the sheer width remained most impressive. I sat and gazed for quite a while savouring the prospect ahead, this was going to be totally different from anything which had gone before and the next day was awaited with eager anticipation.

Time passed very slowly indeed the following morning. Everything was ready and we spent an apparently desultory couple of hours puttering away at odd jobs, by lunchtime this seemingly casual effort resulted in both boats being well scrubbed, every piece of brasswork polished, the paintwork mopped off, and tidied until they looked second to none. Each individual sidestring was tight, the range was newly blackleaded and the brass cocks and levers in the engine-hole twinkled in the sunlight pouring in at the open doors. The Tyseley-bound boats pulled away in late morning and another couple of pairs were busy loading for the same destination whereas we, unlike every other pair in the basin, were pointing in the opposite direction and waiting impatiently for the tide. Lil wandered off after breakfast and returned quite some time later with the shopping and various bits of news gleaned from her several gossips along the way. At last it got to midday and Alec and I drifted off to the 'Six Bells' to while away an hour with a couple of pints of mild. The 'Bells' was unusually quiet this particular lunchtime as most of the lightermen were still out on the tideway, making their way slowly up on the flood from the various docks downriver.

It was very much a case of kicking our heels and even Alec seemed to feel it as we demolished a packet of crisps between us.

"Bloomin' tide! Why couldn't it be here in the morning? Save all this 'anging about!"

"It's all to do with the pull of the moon," I announced. Not for nothing was I doing 'A' level Geography!

"Huh! Bloomin' moon's fault then!"

My piece of information had not been joyously received, but the challenge of a game of darts was accepted with better grace and we found our minds diverted from the waiting by a particularly venomous struggle against a couple of deceptively decrepit looking pensioners. Our cup of joy was complete when we finished up buying the beer after a comprehensive defeat which Alec blamed on "all this 'anging about putting me off me stroke!". Passing back over the High Street bridge we espied a welcome sight. There are two entrance locks at Brentford. One, the second up from the river, gives access to the large basin in which the narrowboats normally loaded. Between there and the final lock is a semi-tidal section of waterway running between high walls and hemmed in by cranes, wharves, and high buildings. It was into this section that we were looking and the welcome sight to greet us was the brown turgid water flooding up and refloating the many barges and lighters which had spent the morning resting on their flat bottoms amidst the soft mud. It was time to make a start!

The tedium was immediately forgotten as *Redshank* came to life and the mooring lines were withdrawn from the lighter. We moved slowly into the large entrance lock with my excitement mounting by the minute. Another new trip begun and most certainly one with a difference. Emerging from the lock I sat with Lil in the butty hatches as we crept under the High Street Bridge and threaded our way through the long lines of lighters towards the final river lock and the waiting Thames. Little could be seen as the banks towered above us, but the lighters were of interest with their familiar names of 'General' or 'Charrington' or other more obscure firms, some of whom I had never heard of. Trade on the river was slackening even at that time and, looking carefully, it was clear that some of these empty lighters had not moved for quite some time, indeed one or two even had tufts of grass growing along their gunwales and seemed, to use an old wartime expression, to have been parked for the duration. At the entrance lock we had to wait again until the water in the creek below had made up sufficiently to float us safely out into the main stream. We sat in the full lock sharing a pot of tea with the lock-keeper and looking ahead down the narrow walled in creek to the wide swirling waters of the Thames beyond. Out there was another world with tugs drawing trains of lighters up-river and, further downstream, specially designed coal 'flats' bringing cargoes from the north-east up under the bridges to the enormous power station at Battersea.

"Right!" said the lock-keeper, draining his mug. "You ready then, mate?"

Ready we most certainly were as we sank down in the lock. The gates slowly opened allowing Alec to steer us steadily down the creek and out past the huge GWR depot into the main river.

Seen from water level, and the loaded pair did lie very low indeed, the river looked even bigger than it had the night before. With a surprisingly stiffish breeze blowing, the boats began to rock in a most unaccustomed fashion as we turned upstream. There was certainly no problem here about depth of water and, with *Redshank* flat-out and the tide surging under us, we forged ahead at quite a pace for a breasted-up pair, whose progress through the water can sometimes be quite sluggish. Spray rose up from our fore-ends, splashing back the full length of the pair on occasions, leaving us all grinning and wiping our faces as the breeze carried the fine droplets over us. The top sheets were soaked as far back as the mast and middle beam area with even the cabin tops getting a bit damp, the overall effect was exhilarating and a complete contrast to our normal steady chugging up the Hanwell Locks! It is about five miles up the tideway to Teddington Lock and, as a child of the narrow streets of a provincial Midland boot and shoe town, I simply drank it all in. The wide span of Richmond Bridge, the high walls as we went straight through the Half Tide Lock at Richmond, the fascination of Eel Pie Island, and above all the sheer width and splendour of the river. Alec steered and we just lapped it all up, yet another contrast to set against the much maligned Saltley Locks! All too soon we found ourselves approaching Teddington and the limits of the tideway. The lockgates swung open on our approach and we eased majestically into the long 132ft chamber, nearly room for two pairs at once. There was, I noticed, another much smaller lock at the side and rollers for the rowing boats, truly we were entering a different world.

It was also the world of the Thames Conservancy and not British Waterways. In the great scramble of waterways nationalisation in 1947 some waterways had been missed, my home river, the Nene, was one and the Thames was another. Lists of rules and regulations were posted at the locks and every lock had its own lock-keeper to enforce them. As on the Nene tolls were charged and we paid by the lock. *Redshank* was classified as a tug and paid the sum of 8d per lock, in exchange for which we were given a ticket, the complete collection of which I still have in my possession. Above Teddington we entered an environment far different from anything I had ever previously experienced. Enormous houses flanked the river which now ran placidly between grassy tree-shrouded banks with long manicured lawns rolling down to sumptuous boathouses in which nestled low beautifully varnished wooden launches. We plodded on, with the side-cloths long dried by the sun, under Kingston Bridge and eventually past Hampton Court Palace to the next lock at Molesey, above which we tied for the night. That day I learned that huge changes can happen in a relatively short distance. We had begun the day in the working atmosphere of Brentford Dock, essentially an integral part of the canal world with which I was so familiar, and ended it ten miles or so away in another world of trim locks and rich houses in which the boats scarcely seemed to belong at all. An enormous cruiser, more nearly resembling a floating palace, was tied just up from us. In the calm of evening I sat on *Redshank*'s slide and contemplated this extravaganza, all chrome and leather seats. It was crewed by a very pleasant couple who were equally curious about us, eventually strolling along to introduce themselves and seek Alec's permission to take a photograph. Their craft was normal here and it was we who were out of place. Smoke and the distinctive smell of East Midlands coal drifted through the trees from *Greenshank* as Lil busied herself with dinner; the Thames did not change us and sausages, potatoes, and thick gravy went down very nicely indeed.

I had not steered on the tideway and so was pleased to be back at the tiller the next morning as we pressed on up the broad winding reaches with a lock coming along every few miles to give a variation. All the locks were superbly trim with edged lawns and bright flower beds, life belts hung at the sides and kedges with long grey handles were available for raking out anything dropped in. No windlasses were needed as large round handles with spokes on them, rather like ship's wheels, stood at the four corners of the locks ready to be wound round by hand to operate the paddles. The lock-keepers would work the lock for you, but as often as not we would step ashore and turn one of the wheels, just to keep our hand in! Unusually for us we found ourselves having to take a turn round a post in the locks in order to prevent the pair from swinging across and fouling the cruisers and other light craft who often shared the lock with us. Everywhere we became the objects of much curiosity and attention. Working narrowboats were a very rare sight on the river and cameras clicked at every lock as we went about our business. Naturally we played our part to the full with brasses proudly polished, white strings gleaming, and everything just so about the boats; a floating advertisement for the virtues of the Willow Wren Canal Carrying Company. With lock-keepers to hand at each lock the bicycle became redundant and lay stowed under the canvas, a welcome break from pedalling for me! It became almost like a holiday cruise, with only the callouses on my hands serving as a reminder of the intense physical effort needed to load the cargo hidden away in our holds.

On up the broad stream we went with the sun glinting off the ruffled water. Past Shepperton where the river Wey disappeared off on its journey to Guildford and Godalming, with the Basingstoke Canal only two or three miles away down there too. Maybe one day, I thought. It was not very likely to be with Willow Wren, however, as the Basingstoke was reputedly in an awful mess with mud, weeds, and water problems making navigation hazardous, to say the least. For us there was no hazard at all as I jogged on through Chertsey and Staines with Alec and Lil lounging in the hatches, revelling in the sunshine and the unaccustomed rest from any sort of hard work. Steering was very easy. There were no big turns to worry about and the river was deep and wide throughout, all very simple! The only real problem came when we occasionally had to hang about in midstream whilst a lockful of cruisers debouched out ahead of us, otherwise it was speedwheel on and straight up the middle of the river with ample time to admire the fascinating panorama unfolding on either side of us.

Everything was going swimmingly until just below Egham Lock. I could see that a pause was inevitable as the lock was full of assorted craft about to be emptied out in our direction. Our choice was either to stop and just 'hang about' in midstream, or to go on in and tie to the length of piling provided for this purpose below each lock. Being highly experienced narrowboaters we elected as usual to 'hang' in midstream so as not to look like amateurs by tying up! Accordingly I eased right down, disengaged the clutch, and then decided that a touch of reverse was needed to stop the pair completely. Back came the clutch and nothing happened! Clutch in and try again. Same result! We drifted gently on as Alec hurried into the engine-hole and engaged reverse gear manually. Creeping in to the lock on absolute tick over we managed to strap the pair to a halt without hitting anyone else, a rapid inspection revealing broken linkage and a need for a new part. To proceed up the river reliant on someone standing in the engine-hole, taking instructions from the steerer by sticking a head out of the doors in order to get reverse was not good and The Gaffer, whom Alec telephoned from the lock, agreed. He most certainly didn't fancy any insurance claim caused by us hitting someone's gin palace through failure to stop, given a known mechanical fault. We were instructed to proceed to Windsor, exercising the utmost care, and await the part which he, living at Epsom, would bring out to us.

Alec took over and we crept up through Old Windsor Lock, wound around the edge of the Great Park, through Romney Lock, and tied outside 'The Donkeyman', just below the bridge and just about opposite the boathouses of Eton College. It was quite early, but our situation left us with no choice but to tie up. The Gaffer assured us, when Alec reported our safe arrival, that he hoped to bring the part, which we could fit, on the following afternoon. In the meantime there was nothing to do but wait. There are much worse places to be broken down than Windsor, as I was to discover on an exploratory expedition the following morning. Under instructions to get bread and sausage rolls for lunchtime I wandered up the hill, taking in the castle and the motionless guardsmen, the smart shops, and the general southern feel of it all. Having plenty of time at my disposal I crossed over the bridge, gazing down at the patiently waiting pair with Lil doing a bowlful of handwashing in the hatches, and found myself in the world of Eton. This was a very far cry from Northampton and, although the school was on holiday, it was not hard to see its dominance as the road passed down the High Street and ran through the various College buildings, flanked by the magnificent chapel which gazed across those famous playing fields. I looked at it all dispassionately, it was like gazing into another world, all very interesting to observe, but far removed from mine. Better get back, I said to myself. Picking up two loaves of bread and six large sausage rolls from an excellent bread shop in Eton High Street, I retraced my steps back over the bridge before descending to the riverside and the familiarity of the better half of my own two worlds. The afternoon was spent usefully enough in *Redshank*'s cabin, wrestling with the intricacies of Hamlet's fatal flaw upon which an essay had to be produced as part of my holiday tasks.

At about half past four I was interrupted by a loud hail from the bank and emerged to see Alec talking to 'The Gaffer' who was handing over a brown paper parcel containing our small, but essential, part. I have read and heard many tales about Leslie Morton since that day at Windsor but, at that time, I only knew him very slightly and, as 'The Gaffer', he was mentally bracketed with the Headmaster of my Grammar School. He was friendly enough though that afternoon, acknowledging me by name, and even evincing an interest in Hamlet after seeing the fountain pen still clutched in my hand. Accepting Lil's offer of a cup of tea, the three of us sat together in *Greenshank*'s hatches whilst he made sure that Alec had satisfactorily fitted the part. I was too young to fully appreciate the remarkable contribution which Leslie Morton had made to the Willow Wren company, and to the waterways in general, but I can still see him enjoying his tea in the sunshine on that faraway afternoon, and I would like this simple memory to serve as my own small tribute to a resilient and generous man. All was well and we could have moved on that evening, but it was hot! Henley lay comfortably within our reach tomorrow, and 'The Donkeyman' was a good pub, so why move? Instead, after a final check round in the engine-hole, we settled down to enjoy cold sausage rolls and tomatoes as the swallows swooped across the warm waters. This was washed down with a few pints of warm beer and a couple of bottles of stout for Lil, sitting together in the window seat of the pub and keeping half an eye on the boats which once again were proving to be the object of considerable interest.

The next day was a Saturday and consequently the river became even more crowded with cruisers, rowing boats, canoes, and other assorted craft, all enjoying the continuation of the long settled spell of hot weather. There was no great hurry as Marsh Mill was only twenty-three miles upstream. We could even, if we had felt so inclined, take two days over the journey as unloading at the Mill would not begin until Monday morning. However old habits cannot easily be broken and we were on our way at about seven, with the warm sunlight making it feel much later than that. It was clearly going to be yet another hot day, shirtsleeves from the very beginning with coats hanging half-forgotten in the cabin. I was very lucky on this river trip. If it had been grey and wet I would doubtless still have enjoyed it, but not in the same way as this. Day after day of unbroken sunshine ensured that the Thames looked at its very best, and I remained fascinated by it all, as each turn of the river brought new vistas of beauty. At Boulter's Lock the crowds were out and an ice-cream seller was doing a roaring trade as we picked our way through a host of light craft and entered the lock, with cruisers packed all around to keep us company. Cameras clicked as the water rose and I chuckled at another contrast. In and around Birmingham and London there was always the possibility of being abused from the bank or, a favourite trick of our tormentors, spat upon as you went under bridge holes. Cries of 'dirty bargees' or 'gippoes' usually accompanied the gobbets of spittle and the sight of any group of youngsters, leaning on a bridge parapet as the boats approached, was always sufficient to put you on your guard. Here we were very much a novelty, to be admired and photographed from every angle, with absolutely no hint of unpleasantness encountered anywhere. People wanted to know where we had come from, where we were going, what were we carrying, did we live on the boats, why did we have three brass rings around the chimneys? The pair created an enormous amount of very genuine interest and talking to these friendly and well-meaning people at the locks further enhanced my already very positive view of life on the Thames.

Travelling breasted-up was also an unusual experience for us. Instead of spending most of the day in splendid isolation, separated by a seventy foot line and then a further seventy feet of boat, we were all close together and sandwiches and cups of tea could be easily passed about without all the changing of steerers normally entailed. Mostly I steered. It was my favourite occupation, along with working the locks, and Alec and Lil were happy to indulge me as they sat together and enjoyed a sun bath in the butty hatches . Everything about the Thames was completely unknown to me at that time. I had not, due to considerations of weight on the cycle, got my 'Edwards' with me and consequently had little idea of which lock was next, or how far it was. I was a child of the East Midlands, my rare journeys to London being on the Euston route of the old LMS, the vivid splendours of the Thames Valley were GWR country and might just as well have been a foreign land. Other than the Embankment in London and the dock at Brentford, the nearest I had previously been to the Thames had been the two visits to Kidlington with Mike Sloan during the previous summer. It is difficult nowadays, when European and world travel is quite common, to remember what a narrow and constrained view of life my generation had. Money was scarce and our expectations were low, but we were happy enough in our own way, probably because we had little real idea of what we were missing My canal journeyings had got me away from Northampton, but they had mostly been either through the pastoral Midland shires or the industrial landscapes of the Black Country, this was something entirely different. The top end of the Welsh Cut from Chirk to the Horseshoe Falls had given me a glimpse of a different physical world of mountains and rushing streams, the Thames gave me a realisation of another way of life with its expensive cruisers and the houses and gardens littered along its elegant banks.

Above Boulter's Lock was one of the most beautiful reaches of them all. I had no premonition of what lay ahead as I steered up the lock cut and emerged on to the wider river, noting several long thin islands dotted about ahead of us. On my right were high woods reaching up from the waters edge and, on the other side, the towpath snaked sinuously through bushes and more trees, hemming us in on both sides. I had seen nothing like this before and gazed in awe at the sheer majesty of it all, but even more was about to come. An enormous house, which I later discovered to be Cliveden, stared down at us from high above the water and presently we passed a boathouse and cottage, an impressive flight of ornamental steps, and two more riverside cottages which, later still, I would identify as the scene of some very naughty goings on amongst the set who frequented the great house. I was innocent of all such matters then and simply steered past, amazed at the grandeur of it all. It wasn't like this in

Northampton! Cookham was followed by Marlow, with its beautiful white suspension bridge spanning the river in a single leap. Crowds of spectators gathered as we passed beneath without giving a thought to anything nasty descending from above, that sort of thing didn't seem to happen here! Past hotels and yet more crowds on the towpath to Temple and Hurley Locks, closer together than is normally the case, before another long curving pound swung past more large houses and a long stretch of meadow to reach Hambledon Lock, with its old mill and a splendidly long weir, it's waters sparkling in the afternoon sunshine.

This was the last lock of our journey but the final pound was also to be very beautiful and full of interest. Our course lay up the long straight past Temple Island, where each year the famous Henley Regatta took place, and where, as Alec proudly told me, the pair had had to stop for the best part of an afternoon on a previous run due to the rowing taking place ahead of them.

"They made it worth my while!" he reminisced. "Gave me a tenner for me trouble!" The long wide straight was now empty of eights and sculls, but bare patches on the grass showed where the marquees and refreshment tents erected to serve the champagne and strawberries had been, all so very essential to make the event go with a swing. The week-end crowds were again out in considerable force as we approached the beautiful many-arched bridge at Henley. Hired rowing boats windmilled about all around us and a steamer lay by the boathouses taking on passengers for a two hour 'there and back' trip up the river. Our very appearance caused an apparent sensation, with picnickers in the park leaving their chairs or blankets and flocking down to the waters edge to watch 'them old Willer-Wren's' go by. I was down almost to tick over, so as not to run any unwary boat down, and people had ample time for photographs as the pair drifted past the islands. "Nearly there now," said Alec, as we chugged up the final length with wooded hills on one side, the park on the other, and the bottom gates of Marsh Lock straight ahead. The mill, our destination, was up a backwater running off to the left shortly before the lock. We drifted in under a high wooden footbridge before turning sideways across the mill pool and coming to rest below the high gable end, from which the chains to haul up the sacks would descend. With lines secure and the engine silent I sat in the door holes and marvelled. This was truly a beautiful haven of peace. Just off the main river and overhung by willow trees, private gardens, and the silent mill we lay snugly in the pool after a really memorable day, boating at its very best.

Sunday was a day of almost total indolence. The sun shone down from a cloudless sky and we lay in our pool hidden from the busy main river and comfortable in the knowledge that there really was very little to do. Brasses remained clean in this weather and only needed a very brief buff-up to be gleaming once more, neither was there a need for cabin fires and the mess that accompanied them. We hadn't really got dirty on our 'cruise' upriver and so there were only 'smalls' to rinse out in the handbowl and they very quickly dried in the heat. Life was most unaccustomedly easy. I spent the morning in the cabin and, feeling remarkably clear-headed, polished off my essay on poor old Hamlet and all his problems. Other than some reading, I had now completed my holiday tasks and, feeling rather at a loose end, decided to follow a narrow private path to the lock, there I could cross over and amble back through the park to take a closer look at a Thames-side town, Henley.

The very name, Henley-on-Thames, has a resonance of quintessential Englishness about it and it was certainly rather different from the Midlands towns which had so far formed the bulk of my experience. The riverside path wound past wooden benches along the edge of a beautifully maintained park to the tall white boathouses which, on this hot summer Sunday, were doing an excellent trade in the hire of rowing boats and the sale of ice cream and pop. Resisting the lure of my favourite, a vanilla cone, I passed along a side road to the bridge where a large metal plate, prominently affixed to an abutment, warned traction engine drivers about the amount of weight permitted to cross. From there my stroll took me up into the town, past a most attractive church and along a broad main street, prosperous but quiet on this Sunday afternoon. At a crossroads I turned left down another street of closed shops, leading me back again to the river which seemed to be the main attraction that afternoon for the people of Henley. The town was small, but the nature of the shops exuded money, and I will confess to feeling somewhat out of place in my worn jeans and workshirt, sleeves rolled up to reveal fore-arms nicely browned by the summer heat. Sitting on a bench in the park I watched the river traffic for a while. There were a surprising number of gin palaces, large flashy cruisers, positively bristling with chrome-plated fittings, and crewed by beings from a world far removed from my experience. Wine glasses clinked and young shapely women lay around in shorts and even swimsuits, something never seen on the working boats. Looking upstream I could just catch a glimpse of a green cabin side lying half hidden by the overhanging willows of the mill channel, suddenly I grew tired of all the noisy bustle and the alien crowds and headed quickly back to the sunlit peace of that tranquil pool. That evening bats flittered around the boats in the soft balmy air. The clear sky slowly darkened, becoming spangled with stars and presaging yet another fine day in this remarkable spell of weather.

Sunday may have been a warm relaxed day of laziness and indolence, but on Monday reality dawned with a vengeance! Promptly at 7.30 the hatches on a gable end high above us were opened as were the double doors giving access to the mill floor just below. Emptying would not be quite as hard as loading, but in the full unrelenting glare of the sun it promised to be hard enough. Two chains were lowered down from the gable end and the trick was to loop one of these around the 'ear' of a bag and then, when both chains were fixed, shout "Right!" to the millworker above. He would use water power to lift them up to the double doors where two other workers would pull them in and unhook. We, in the meantime, would have two more bags prepared, with their 'ears' nicely pulled out ready to attach the returning chains. No mistakes were permissable with the chains, as if one came adrift halfway up, then it was Alec and I who were in the line of fire from a free-falling 1½cwt bag. Not to be recommended!

There was more fascination as the great wheel began to turn and the water churned out against the side of *Greenshank*, before bubbling round the ends of the pair and swirling out into the pool. Inside the mill was the unforgettable spectacle of massive wooden cogs, interacting tirelessly one with another, as they drove rods and pulleys, and thick canvas belting whirred silently around. Every piece of machinery in the building was water-powered and the activation of the mill wheel was akin to the awakening of a sleeping giant. Tea breaks and the short lunch break saw me clambering about all over the mill, absolutely entranced by the smooth almost silent movement and the various levers which, if pushed or sometimes pulled, brought the individual items of machinery into action. Once, not long ago, the mill had ground flour for bread-making, but this had now become uneconomic. Instead the mighty stones ground our cargoes up into cattle cake and other products for the agricultural market of Oxfordshire and Berkshire.

Emptying was hard but pleasant, working as we did in the beauty of the tree-shrouded pool. Bit by bit *Greenshank* rose higher and higher in the water until, with a cheer from us, the last two bags disappeared upwards and the boats were swopped round. My hands were suffering once more and they ached badly with all the heaving and twisting of the heavy bags. Like everything else on the cut there was a knack to it, another case of learning the hard way as I slowly and painfully grew more adept. No fuss, just keep going! On we went until work stopped promptly at five o'clock. The great wheel shut off and the churning waters fell still. *Redshank* still had about two-thirds of her load to go but we had cracked the back of the job, it had been a good day's work and everyone felt justifiably content. I was caked with sweat and dust, but a very simple solution was to hand! The water was so clean that I sluiced off by swimming naked around the mill pool, confident that I was not being overlooked and feeling much fresher as a result. Alec and I strolled into Henley for a well earned pint that evening, but it was all very quiet. I recall we had several pints in several different pubs, but they were all virtually empty and singularly lacking in atmosphere, not a patch on Braunston!

By Tuesday lunch-time we had sent up the last bag from *Redshank* and were busy putting the pair to rights whilst Alec checked our next move with 'The Gaffer'. How I would now have welcomed orders to go 'back empty to Suttons' involving, as it would have done, a continuation of our journey up-river to Oxford and then the full length of the Oxford Canal. It was very unlikely and I was not surprised by our actual orders to return empty to Brentford, there to take whatever load was forthcoming. Let's hope that something was ready for us when we got there, rather than just a long indeterminate spell of waiting hopefully about. Alec wanted, if the tides permitted, to get back by tomorrow night. It was a journey of just over fifty miles by water, considerably greater than the flight of the crow and reflecting the winding and twisting nature of the river. We were permitted, if the lock-keepers had gone to lunch or finished for the day, to work the locks for ourselves, so no problem there. Mind you, in summertime, the keepers seemed to work longer hours and be around until late into the evening, which would enable us to have a good run at it today. Without more ado we started up, shafted ourselves round, waved our farewells to the millers, and rather reluctantly left the idyllic tranquillity of the pool to rejoin the main river.

We remained breasted-up, but where coming up we had been loaded and forging against the stream, now we were empty and had the water with us. Consequently we 'got 'em ahead' with a vengeance, running down Regatta Straight with the speedwheel full on at a pace never normally possible. This was exhilarating boating, there were few bridges to worry about and they all had spans so wide that easing down was not even a consideration. The only hold-ups occurred at the locks. Sometimes there would be a delay upon entering, caused by upstream traffic in the lock which left us boxing about impatiently in midstream, on other occasions we found ourselves having to wait about whilst the keeper packed the lock around us with cruisers, before drawing off and releasing us for the pound ahead. On and on we went as the long afternoon gave way to the shadows of evening. Surging under Marlow Bridge we charged round past Bourne End to Cookham and the start of that most exquisite pound down to Boulter's. The great woods cascading right down to the water's edge looked almost enchanting on the return leg and the magical beauty of it all left a very deep and lasting impression on me. I did not know it at the time, steering down the long wide straight past those ornate cottages and the paths leading tantalisingly into the trees, but it was to be a quarter of a century before I would see this spot again.

Life took me on, as it has a habit of doing, and the time came when I secured a Headship in Oxford, something I would not have dreamed possible as I steered along that day. I returned then to Cookham and walked the length down to Boulter's and back, it was still just as beautiful as I had remembered it. Later we would find our way into Cliveden, now a National Trust property, and walk past the cottages and along the river before climbing to return along one of the paths I had glimpsed running tantalisingly through the trees above the river. Coming back to a place fragrant in the memory is not always a good idea, but the pound was still as magical as ever and it remains my favourite Thames-side walk. Sometimes as I stroll along and look out across the broad waters I remember that day, once again in my mind's eye I picture the high riding pair surging past, a young lad relishing the steering and his old friends basking in the butty's hatches, all of them supremely content with their lot.

Inwardly content we may have been, but there was still work to be done. All too soon the beautiful long straight was over and we dropped through Boulter's Lock, before surging on under the wide arch of Maidenhead Bridge. It had turned into one of those warm still summer evenings that occur more often in fiction than in reality. On we pressed through Bray Lock, past the hotels and grand houses, which became more and more evident as we came further down the river, and arrived at Boveny Lock. We could easily have tied here, but 'The Donkeyman' served a good pint and so we pushed on, under the tall arch of the railway bridge before easing right down through Windsor Bridge and making fast our lines in the gathering gloom to the same rings used on our outward journey. Soaked in sun we did not even feel tired and sat on the benches outside the pub, a very rare thing for Alec to do as he was very much a 'bar' man, sipping our pints and contemplatively watching the darkness stealing across the still waters. With an early start the next day it seemed likely that we would be able to cover the remaining twenty-five miles down to Teddington and then have enough water in late afternoon to get into Brentford Creek. Fingers crossed for another fine day!

A slight mist lay across the river as I pushed the slide off and took the proferred cup of tea. It was just after six and the air was very still, amazingly it seemed our run of weather was set to continue. All of us had become used to the sunshine and even began to take it rather for granted, a very rude awakening indeed was to be our lot when this tremendous spell of weather finally broke. There was no reason for delay and, in exuberant mood and already in shirt-sleeves, we set off downstream, working ourselves through Romney Lock and settling down to the long curve around the Great Park. The light mist very soon lifted and dispersed and by eight o'clock the sun was pouring down as we ate our favourite bacon sandwiches, chugging along and watching the world going to work on the busy roads around us. Aware of the time, but not overly concerned by it, we descended briskly downstream, the locks coming and going with predictable regularity. Chertsey, Shepperton, Sunbury, until we passed our first night's mooring at Molesey, where the lock-keeper informed us that we were well up to time and not to worry. We were not worried. It was all too idyllic to be worrying. The sun glinted on the clear waters and we were making the most of what felt more like a pleasure trip than work. The reason for our presence, the delivery of fifty tons of locust bean meal, seemed to fade into the background as we enjoyed the sunlit moment, working and living had become as one. Hampton Court was followed by Kingston Bridge and, almost before we knew it, the gates of Teddington Lock lay ahead, our odyssey was nearly over. Tying above the lock we discussed the situation with the lock-keeper. Not surprisingly we were slightly too early and the tide was still on the flood. Best, we were told, to wait a little while and then leave with it on the turn, giving optimum conditions for the short run down to Brentford Creek.

We waited. A good opportunity for me to explore the lock and its associated islands, enjoying the novelty of the rollers on the far side and watching with interest for the precise moment of high water. Luckily it was not for me to judge that moment, it was all precisely written down in the tide tables in the lock hut. Our moment of departure was done by watch rather than by eye. At last it was adjudged to be the optimum time.

"Better to be too early than too late," Lil had said, upon learning of the delay.

"You wanted to start at five!" rejoined Alec caustically.

"She would!" I laughed. Lil was always a great one for 'getting 'em ahead' and her idea of an early start was often fearsomely so, unless we had the luxury of facing a lock which didn't open until six o'clock! We restarted and eased into the huge lock, the calm waters of the river were now behind us and the tideway was serious business. Alec steered us out on to the swirling ebb and immediately the dual effect of tide and current became evident as we moved faster than ever down the five miles or so to Brent Creek. It didn't seem to take very long as we curved round past Twickenham, shot through the tide lock at Richmond, and presently picked up the twin landmarks of the GWR depot and the gasholder flanking the entrance to the creek. At what seemed an alarming speed Alec turned the pair slightly early, as he allowed for the sideways drift caused by the pull of the tide, and we shot into the creek to find ourselves roaring along between the high walls with the very solid lockgates dead ahead. Winding hard back on the speed wheel we returned to normality as the gates of Thames Lock swung open to receive us. We were back, or almost so.

"How do!" said Alec.

"Whay-up, mate!" returned the lock-keeper.

Oh, those dulcet tones! We were indeed back!

Up the short length between the old lighters we went and under the High Street Bridge, a red trolley bus whining plaintively overhead. Nothing much had changed in our absence. Several pairs of empty BW boats were waiting to load, their washing flapping softly in the light breeze, and ahead an empty lighter was drifting down upon the current with just a light touch of the shaft from the lighterman to keep her straight. She would arrive just nicely in time to nose into the full lock as we moved out. Further up still I espied the familiar roundels of a pair of Willow Wrens, it looked very much like Ray and Margaret, in the midst of the long process of loading timber from a lighter. There were, as I looked more closely, two lighters brimming with timber which looked promising. It seemed as if we might be in luck again as I reported this to Alec.

"We'll have us some of that!" was the enthusiastic response.

Back in the basin we were in our own familiar workaday world and it felt like coming home. Tractors passed by on the towpath as they moved the lighter traffic up and down the Hanwell Locks and beyond. Pairs came down, loaded and went back. Trains passed over the high bridge at the far end of the loading lengths, the familiar oil stains gleamed fluorescently on the dirty water. This was home, it was the river that was different with its trim locks and its emphasis on pleasure and relaxation. There we were the intruders, a novelty to be stared at and photographed, but somehow not belonging, not an integral part of the scene. Nevertheless it had been a wonderful experience and a complete contrast to our normal runs. The pound along under the Cliveden Woods and that beautiful Sunday of heat and peace in the pool at Marsh Mill would live long in the memory. I was never to return up the river and now consider myself extremely fortunate to have had the chance I did, most definitely a case of being in the right place at the right time. The Marsh Mill contract was to be lost shortly afterwards and I had not long been back at school when I heard that the last load had been delivered up the river, appropriately enough by *Redshank* and *Greenshank*. The mill itself has also faded into the past, having been turned into a rather attractive block of flats. But the mill pool and the overhanging willows are still there and so, on a warm and langourous summer afternoon, is that essential feeling of peace and harmony.

*****

Chapter 10

Aylesbury Duck

The chapter titles of this book neatly encompass the variety of trips I was lucky enough to make in those days just before the end of regular commercial carrying. 'Round Again' takes in the wheat run to Wellingborough, the runs to Birmingham and Tipton, the summer with MIke Sloan, and the Thames trip. But for many boatmen it was much more of a case of mostly or wholly 'Up and Down' from the Warwickshire coalfield to the London area. By the late 1950s the staple trade for the British Waterways crews was coal to the paper mills at Apsley, Nash, and Croxley and any back-loading, primarily to Birmingham or Wellingborough, that they might obtain was a bonus. At slack times, or as trade lessened into the 1960s, it became more and more normal to be sent 'back empty to Suttons' for more coal. For Barlow's it had always been very much an 'up and down' life from the coalfields to the Mills or various other destinations at the southern end of the Grand Union, such as the Kearly & Tonge factory just inside the Paddington Arm at Southall, popularly known as 'the jam 'ole'. Their only variant on this was sand from Leighton Buzzard to Paddington, another case of 'up and down'. Barlow's had once operated many other contracts, to Home Park Mill near Kings Langley, the Ovaltine factory, where they supplemented the work of the firm's own pairs, the Morrells contract to Oxford and the run to Wolvercote Paper Mills, to mention just a few. But trade was dwindling and in those final years, before the takeover of their last six pairs and the Braunston Yard by Blue Line in 1962, their crews were more and more restricted to the 'up and down' lifestyle.

I was fortunate in that, other than brief sorties with Wilfred, all my boating experience was with the Willow Wren Company which probably had the greatest variety of contracts of any carrier operating at that time. Consequently I had avoided much of the empty boating inevitably associated with the 'up and down' contracts. My luck had usually held with back-loading, but like everyone else Willow Wren crews did from time to time get caught up in the 'back empty to Suttons' syndrome. Indeed, on occasions in August when the collieries were shut for their annual fortnight's holiday, the boats had been known to work empty from Great Bridge to Brentford in order to keep the timber traffic moving. This particular trip started with a four day stoppage at Stoke Bruerne to enable new bottom gates to be fitted on the fourth lock down from the top, sometimes referred to as 'the middle of the thick'. The stoppage was timed to coincide with the Warwickshire coalfield's annual fortnight's holiday and this resulted in the curious situation of only one pair of BW boats, bound for Croxley, being caught at the top lock. There they remained, tied in splendid isolation outside the cottage with, as the collieries were closed, no-one else arriving to keep them company. However they had plenty of company at 'The Boat' in the evenings as empty pairs, returning from the mills, began to pile up at the bottom lock. Eventually a floating village of no less than seventeen pairs stretched back down the long straight, giving a superb view from the wooden footbridge spanning the tail of the bottom lock. The weather was set fair and the crews gossiped and chatted together, with some pairs angled across the cut and others tied side by side. They were sociable, but always mindful of one another's precious privacy. If crossing other people's craft was unavoidable, then it was always done behind the cabin by use of the back beam and never straight across the door-holes. Invariably you asked permission before boarding, the questioning shout of 'coming on' and then the wait for consent was universal even on your own pair; I naturally did this whenever stepping from *Redshank* over to the butty, as did Alec and Lil if moving in the opposite direction. This thought and consideration for others was a vital part of life afloat, the cabins were tiny and sound carried. In a situation like this where seventeen pairs were tied closely together, such scrupulousness was essential for the harmony of the community.

Twelfth down the line came Alec and Lil, with Bert two pairs further back. For once they too were empty, nothing having been available for them at Brentford after they had emptied gravel at West Drayton. It seemed to be a case of back empty for everyone, I thought, as I surveyed the long line, with not a loaded pair to be seen. Impromptu games of football were played in the adjacent field and everybody caught up with absolutely the last scrap of washing, ironing, and odd jobs around the boats. It was not a time for working furiously, but more one of fiddling about in the sunshine, alternately working, chatting, or just indulging in a spot of unashamed lying about. Evenings at 'The Boat' could best be described as lively, especially the last one when most people turned out to celebrate their impending release the next morning. A brand new gate, redolent with tar and creosote, had been lifted into place and all was complete. The tall tripod which had done the lifting had been removed and a variety of tools and equipment were lying in a couple of BW 'flats', moored well out of the way on the outside, from where would be collected by tug and returned to the Arm End after the melee of the following morning was over. I was to travel north with the pair the next morning and, not wishing to miss a single minute of the fun, had moved my bag aboard during the afternoon and would sleep on *Redshank* that night. How much actual boating I would get was problematical as, with eleven pairs immediately ahead of us, we could well face another lengthy wait at Suttons, nevertheless I remained illogically optimistic about our chances. Perhaps we could jump the queue by loading gravel again!

Such a crowd of boats all moving together was unusual. The prospects for the next day looked to be quite exciting with seventeen pairs poised to go straight through to Suttons, and all of us mindful that any pause would cost you places in the line. To avoid any unnecessary complications in the flight the pair waiting at the top lock were 'loosed away' by Mr James an hour early and proceeded down the flight in solitary splendour, ready to be released from the bottom lock around the normal unlocking time of six o'clock. Pairs were moved around below the lock to enable them to pick their way through and resume their journey to the Mills. I watched from the door-holes as they crept very slowly towards us through the narrow gaps created for them.

"How do, young John!"

"How do," I responded, as they slipped smoothly by.

I could see the first pair, Barlows as it happened, moving into the lock and a couple of pairs behind them starting up. Not long now, but first we had to endure a bit of a wait while those ahead of us got away into the lock. Lil, ever thoughtful, produced a large pot of tea to wake us all up nicely while we did so.

"Breakfusses round the Blisworth," she announced, as the jam of boats ahead of us began to break up and head for the lock.

It was time to be going. Alec started *Redshank* easily enough and we edged slowly forward awaiting our turn. There was no real question of overtaking anybody that day but the crews would all be on their mettle, determined to work as fast as possible and not be outdone by anyone else. Even the two-handed pairs should be alright as, with the locks in flights and the pairs breasted-up, lock-wheeling would be considerably easier for them. At last there was only one pair ahead and I got off to help as everybody else seemed to have been doing. Through they went, helpfully shutting a gate and leaving me furiously winding up the bottom paddles. At last we were on our way!

I walked up Stoke behind the preceding BW pair, who had very kindly detailed their eight year old daughter to assist me by shutting one gate as they left each lock. Losing no time in drawing off the locks, I looked back to where the pair were being shadowed by young Violet, lock-wheeling energetically behind us for the redoubtable Boswell family. At the top lock my parents took over the job of shutting the gates as I wound paddles, before once more being told to be careful and be back for the start of school! They were used to my disappearances by now and were happy enough about it, after all I was in very safe hands! There was little enough time for goodbyes as the boats rose in the lock, with Violet already there and waiting to draw off behind us. My parents, ever helpful, shut the top gates for her too as we pulled away, not forgetting a last wave before the slight bend cut the lock off from sight.

I was entrusted with *Redshank* for the tunnel having received clear and unequivocal instructions from Alec.

"No overtaking and no being overtaken!"

It was a fascinating sight inside the tunnel with several sets of lights glowing ahead of me and then, as time went on, several sets glowing behind me too. Luckily it was a warm and sunny morning and cabin fires were not adding to the diesel fumes swirling slowly along to the vents; remembering the dense acrid smoke encountered in Braunston Tunnel on *Canada Goose* this was very much something to be grateful for. Back into daylight we began the long pull along the Blisworth pound to Buckby. I had the pair ahead in view along the long straights, although they would disappear from time to time as bends intervened. Astern the blue and yellow fore-ends of our pursuers showed clearly on the straights, but I found myself similarly losing sight of them as the pound wound its way along. It was simply a question of steering as well as possible and maintaining station, above all the pair behind must not encroach too closely. I steered with even greater concentration than usual helped by the fact that up to Heyford, at least, this is a relatively easy pound. Along the Bugbrooke embankment we changed over and I was sent back for breakfast feeling very pleased with myself as Alec's comment rang in my ears.

"Well steered, John! You're keeping 'em back!"

Clambering back over *Greenshank*'s cabin top I looked astern to where the Boswell's were just emerging from the bridge-hole by the signal box which led out on to the embankment. They had gained nothing and lost nothing. Everyone would be happy. I stayed on *Greenshank* for the rest of the pound as Lil puttered away at her cabin chores and, in particular, a very large apple pie for which the range was presently lit. This pie was to go down very well indeed later on that afternoon around the long pounds beyond Braunston. We 'kept 'em back' that day with our pride intact, lock-wheeling Buckby on the bike as the locks are rather spread out, and then walking happily down the shorter pounds at Braunston. The pair ahead also worked steadily and efficiently and we never really got any closer to them than when we had started. It was a matter of honour being satisfied and it certainly was as we eventually tied, still twelfth, in the long line at Suttons. As always the pairs were tied closely together on both sides of the cut with just a narrow channel intervening to permit the passage of south-bound traffic. It looked likely to be a bit of a wait although hopefully, with a dearth of boats in the coalfield due to the stoppage, it wouldn't be too long.

For two days Alec reported to the office near the cast iron overbridge spanning the junction of the two canals, but there was nothing doing. Gradually the boats ahead of us cleared and returned laden with coal, sliding easily between the waiting pairs before disappearing southwards.

AYLESBURY DUCK

Sutton Stop, although a great meeting place for the carrying trade, was not my favourite place to be waiting. The great bulk of Longford Power Station, 'the Light', hummed away just behind us and, between ourselves and the parallel waters of the Coventry Canal, the view was of the slowly revolving arms of the sewerage tanks set between the two waterways. On the positive side there were usually some boats on the move to watch, particularly from the vantage point of the arched bridge which offered a grandstand view of pairs negotiating the very awkward turn into the Oxford, and furthermore a walk could be taken along the towpath in three directions. *Friendship*, with Joe and Rose Skinner living aboard in retirement, was tied just beyond the turn along the length of cut leading eventually into Coventry Basin. Seeing her I remembered that morning up Napton when I was still very new to the cut, at least I could treasure the memory of having seen an Oxford Canal horse-drawn (mule-drawn actually) Number One, as most certainly that chance would never come again either.

On the third morning I sat on the slide with my legs dangling down into the cabin and watched the steam rising from the giant cooling towers opposite. Alec had wandered off pessimistically to the office and I resolved to bike into Coventry itself if we were in for yet another day of waiting about.

"Cheer up, misery! We got our orders!"

It was Alec back with the precious slip of paper clutched in his hand. I must have been really drifting off not to have heard his return.

"Load at Baddesley. First pair tomorrow afternoon."

A mills run, I thought to myself. It would probably mean yet another wait, this time to empty, given all the pairs which had gone down ahead of us. If it was a Croxley run, then we would have to wait at Cassio Bridge again and I made a mental resolve to avoid the watercress beds if at all possible. Hard work was one thing, but they were something else! Alec climbed aboard and grinned quizzically across at me.

"Aren't you going to ask me where?" he persisted.

"Go on then," I returned. "Which mill is it?"

"Aylesbury!"

Aylesbury was somewhere I had not even considered. In fact, I had almost forgotten the existence of this contract which had rescued the Arm from total commercial disuse. I brightened up considerably. This was very good news as I had never been down there, another new piece of cut.

"You won't like it when we get there," Alec informed me. "Shovelling-out job this is."

I had shifted timber and humped sacks of locust meal, but had so far avoided emptying coal by hand. Another new experience to be relished!

"Firm up the muscles!" I joshed.

"So will bow-hauling down the Arm!" was the grinning riposte.

We had all had enough of waiting about at Sutton Stop. We were not ordered to load until about two o'clock the following day and could have gone up the next morning, but a change of scene would be very welcome. Lil nipped off for some last-minute shopping and then we got underway once more with an eye on spending the night at the top of Atherstone.

"After all," reasoned Lil, "It might rain in the morning and then we'd look silly enough."

This was perfectly true and, besides, I'd had my fill of stewing at the Stop! It felt great to be moving again as I steered steadily along past Charity Dock and then looked through the open gates of the stop lock at the waters of the Ashby Canal, or Moira Cut, stretching away on their long lock-free journey to Donisthorpe. Later on Willow Wren would load coal for Croxley up there in the last days of carrying, but it was not a cut I ever visited in those busier and still hopeful times. The grubby lengths around Nuneaton, which had us crawling through the bridge holes in fear and trepidation of lurking submerged hazards, were followed by scrubby fields and the gravel wharf at Mancetter before a final bridge hole framed the top lock of the Atherstone flight. The loading length at Baddesley I knew to be half-way down the flight, time enough to go down there in the morning. That afternoon we lay peacefully in the length above the top lock, being twice disturbed by pairs returning from loading at Baddesley and further on at Pooley Hall. Our turn tomorrow, I thought, as the deeply laden boats slipped cautiously past and through the bridge hole before steadily 'winding it on' for the first stage of their journey south.

A lie-in was in order the next day and it was mid-morning before we finally bestirred ourselves. Alec led down on *Redshank*, starting the locks and leaving us to follow on behind with the long line stretching back to the butty's mast . You get used to the wide locks and it came as rather a shock to the system to be back in the bow-hauling routine again, even with the relative ease of an empty butty. There was absolutely no hurry and Lil and I drifted down the few locks, having to wait at one point to permit a loaded pair to come up, still mopping-off and putting themselves together as they did so. By the time we arrived at the colliery basin *Redshank* was already tied up and her captain was catching up on the news with the loaders.

"Nice mule you've got there, Alec," was the predictable comment as I hove into view with the long towline draped over my shoulder. Jokes like that I didn't really need, but I played my required part and 'brayed' loudly whilst using my hands to simulate the tall pricked ears of a faithful donkey!

As promised we were first pair to load after the lunch-time break and the coal cascaded amidst clouds of dust into the empty holds, causing the boats to settle deep into the water with just 'trimming' required on our part. We loaded fifty-two tons which led Lil to query the depth of water on the Aylesbury Arm.

AYLESBURY DUCK

"It's fine," insisted Alec. "Harvey-Taylors went down there all the time!"

So they had, but not for some years. It'll probably be alright, I thought, mentally equating the Aylesbury Arm with the Northampton Arm which carried regular wheat traffic through on to the River Nene. As we would find out, the dead-end Aylesbury Arm, one mile longer and one lock fewer than my old haunt, was not quite the same thing at all. By five o'clock we had everything squared away and had given the boats an exceptionally thorough mopping off to get rid of the pervasive coal dust which seemed to get in everywhere, despite keeping doors and slide firmly closed whilst the coal was flowing. The outside of the boats came first, the film of dust in the cabins could be dealt with later on that evening.

Alec had a liking for the pub by the top lock and had already decided that we could lie there for the night. To my great joy he sent me on ahead with *Redshank*, with strict instructions to be careful about not slipping on the locksides in my efforts to do all that was required. As the locks were full with the top gates standing open, this was going to be quite a lot. I revelled in being in charge of *Redshank* and wished the flight was much longer. Like Tardebigge? Why not! As the lock was filling on one paddle I tore up to the next one on the bike and set it emptying, also on one paddle, before returning and throwing the bike back on the coal. With *Redshank* moving slowly ahead out of the lock I then emulated Meadows, in those early days on the Arm, by drawing half a bottom paddle before holding back just above the lock and setting the top gate swinging to. The water would pull it shut and, by the time Alec arrived with *Greenshank*, the lock would have emptied for him. Up I went, feeling very professional and not missing the bow-hauling one little bit! At the top lock I secured *Redshank* to the stump above the gate and showed willing by walking back down to assist with the butty.

"You haven't sunk her?" enquired Alec, as I arrived to help pull.

"No, just banged her about a bit!" I joked in return, but still feeling very proud of my efforts, Truly I was coming on!

After a good evening on Ansells Mild I agreed with Alec on something else. The pub at the top lock was a very good one and well worth having to start a bit earlier the next morning in order to catch up the time. At least that's what I thought as I went to bed. The idea did not seem quite so impressive when Lil, very determined to get us moving after all the hanging about, was tapping on the slide at just turned five. I took the tea as usual and grimaced in the early morning light.

"Braunston tonight!" she stated firmly, in a tone of voice which brooked absolutely no contradiction.

"Right!'

"You get going! Alec'll be up in a bit."

"Right!"

"Nice and steady. Remember all the rubbish."

"Right!'

I was a little bleary, but happy enough for all that. The long pounds stretched ahead with, doubtless, plenty of steering for me and skittles at 'The Nelson' to look forward to that night. Besides I was supposed to be the one who was young and an enthusiast for the canal life. So, off we go!

The pound from Atherstone to Sutton Stop could never be described as beautiful, although some would say it provided an interesting journey through the coalfield. On a grey and rather cloudy morning we jogged along steadily but always easing right down for the bridge holes which, particularly through the backs of Nuneaton, were notorious for harbouring all manner of rubbish. An unplanned halt with a 'bladeful' was definitely something we could do without. Brown muddy water swirled and bubbled up around us as we edged along the pound with occasional scrunches as *Redshank* rode over some obstruction on the bottom. Theoretically the pair could have loaded over sixty tons, but we would never have got along here if we had done so, and I wondered what the position would be like in ten years time if nothing was done in the way of dredging. It was slow and rather tedious progress, but I remained patient as we passed Marston Junction and the Moira Cut, secure in the knowledge that things would get better once we were through the Stop and into deeper water with a steadily improving pastoral scene. Presently Alec took over and I dropped back for breakfast and a further very welcome cup of tea. It had been a chilly start to the day but, by the time I re-emerged to steer *Greenshank* along to the Stop, a weak but improving sun was forcing a way through the gloom. Cars were beginning to cross above us as the rest of the world made their way to another day of work in factory and office, whilst I leaned happily on the curved wooden tiller bar and contemplated the green fields to come along the Hillmorton pound.

It seemed very unusual to be going straight through Sutton Stop. During all my previous trips with the pair we had invariably been in the habit of stopping there, or alternatively at Tushes Bridge only a little further on. However, today we pressed on without hesitation, pausing only to re-fill the water cans, before, with me once again happily in place on *Redshank*'s footboard, we threaded our way through the waiting pairs and set off round the long pound to Hillmorton. The clouds had cleared away now and the sun poured down as I 'got 'em ahead' through the Ansty bends and along the long straights to Stretton. Once again I was in my element. Steering the long pounds could be thought to be boring, but I never found it to be so. The placid Midland countryside slowly unrolled around you and there was always something of interest ahead enabling a long pound to be mentally broken up into shorter sections. On this pound, for example, there were the big turns around Ansty, the old stop lock at Stretton, the closed-up entrances to the old loops, Newbold Tunnel, the Brownsover Arm, the view of the old Cosford loop, and finally the anticipation of the likely state of the locks at Hillmorton. Also you could not let concentration waver too much as the deeply laden boat had to be kept in the channel at all times and would soon veer off course if the steering was neglected, even along the very straightest of sections. Nothing happened particularly fast but it was, as Emma Smith famously remarked in *Maiden's Trip*, 'an absorbing life and we were absorbed by it'.

Abel was encountered near Brownsover, heading back empty to the Stop, and he gave us the gratifying news that the Hillmorton Three were all nicely ready for us. As it turned out this was again not strictly accurate as we arrived to find one lock ready and one lock not so, a small cruiser having made its way up the flight since Abel's descent. *Greenshank* drifted on into the empty lock leaving me to leap off the motor's fore-end and rush about setting the other one. Memories of our little contretemps at the middle locks came back as I walked up the flight to draw off the other two locks, but this time all was serene as we smoothly ascended with no downhill traffic to impede our progress. The cruiser, needless to say, was tied up just above the top lock! After our early start Braunston was reached easily by late afternoon and Lil was even talking about going up the flight, a suggestion quickly vetoed by Alec who greatly preferred tying at the bottom lock. It had been a quiet day of long pounds and hour after hour of uneventful steering. Nothing much had happened. We had not got stuck anywhere, not met somebody in an awkward bridge hole, nothing had wrapped itself around the blades, and the sun had shone down keeping us warm and content. For all that it had been a satisfying day with everything carried out according to plan, not always the case on the cut! I went to sleep that night in the knowledge of a good day's work done and comfortable with our plan for the morrow, our usual run to Cosgrove which should prove to be no problem at all. I should, of course, have known better! Just when all is going well the cut has a nasty habit of making life difficult, even on my favourite 'easy' section to Cosgrove.

The day did not start well as I woke to the unwelcome drumming of rain on the cabin top. A quick glance out of a half-opened door revealed a grey morning with the rain beating down steadily and creating little bubbles of foam along the cut. "Perhaps it'll stop," I muttered to myself, as I dressed and tidied away the bed. There was no sign of life on *Greenshank*, although it was already nearly half past six. Probably hoping it'll stop too, I thought, whilst debating the fire. Pointless to go to all the trouble of lighting it if the rain then stopped, as it brightened up the cabin would become far too hot. Best to wait a bit and see how the weather went. Lil soon appeared and passed over a mug of tea, which she accompanied with a grimace and a upward rolling of eyes at the grey clouds above.

"Shall we get going?" I queried, sipping the welcome brew and pretending to ignore the rain.

"It'll be dry in the tunnel," she replied, pulling her headscarf tightly round her face.

This I took to be a signal to start up. Hurriedly sinking my tea, I donned my donkey jacket and old hat and made my way carefully along the wet gunwale to the engine-hole. At least the flight's ready for us, I thought, as I went through the starting procedure. *Redshank* refused to start! The engine whined, but she wouldn't catch. After several fruitless attempts I clambered back out of the engine-hole and went to report on my difficulties. Alec and Lil needless to say had already heard the abortive whining which had accompanied my efforts and questioning eyebrows met me as I peered into the cabin. It was unusual. *Redshank*, in my experience, was normally very reliable and I had never had any sort of trouble with starting her up before this. Alec mumbled some imprecations and climbed out to deal with it, leaving me to resignedly await the steady rhythmic beat as she started up. More whining could be heard, but no engine beat. I felt somewhat mollified at this, at least it wasn't just me being incompetent! The problem was methodically tracked down to a blocked fuel line and then took nearly three-quarters of an hour to fix, the eventual culprit being a very small piece of grit.

The rain, far from petering out, was still pouring down relentlessly from an unforgiving sky as we finally entered the bottom lock at nearly half past eight. The flight may have been ready for us, but we found the pound below the second lock from the top mysteriously half empty with nowhere near enough water to float us through. The lock-keeper must have seen this when he had unlocked that morning but, doubtless because of the rain, had chosen to do absolutely nothing about it. Cursing this particular individual I slopped my way up the muddy towpath to run water down from the summit, with the whole business costing us a further half an hour or so. This was not proving to be a good day and my watch told me it was virtually ten o'clock as I steered *Redshank* steadily into the dark mouth of the tunnel. At least it would be dry, or dryish anyway, in there! With the bad start to the morning and the heavy rain it was a relief to be chugging steadily through the darkness with a bit of time to draw breath. Braunston, unlike Blisworth, is a fairly dry tunnel and respite from the rain, as Lil had predicted, was very welcome. Everything was going nicely and I was concentrating on steering a precise course down the middle of the tunnel, keeping the cratch perfectly centred in the halo of light, when *Redshank*'s engine slowed, coughed, resumed running briefly, and then cut out leaving us drifting forwards in an uncanny silence. I estimated that we were approximately half-way through the tunnel, just about the worst place for it to happen.

Experience came to my aid. I immediately put the tiller string on to prevent the long brass bar from drifting outwards and fouling the tunnel wall and then, stepping back on to the counter, began coiling in the long dripping snubber by the faint light emanating from the cabin.

"What's up now?" came an echoing voice from *Greenshank*.

I indicated that she had just died on me and continued to pull *Greenshank* up until her fore-end came abreast of the cabin allowing Alec, who had precariously edged around the cratch, to scramble aboard and disappear into the engine-hole leaving me to secure the boats closely together. No other lights were to be seen which was something to be thankful for, any additional problems with other boats coming through we could happily do without. Some really quite choice language emanated from the engine-hole as Alec dismantled fuel lines and I gave moral support, silently handing over spanners and wrenches as needed. Another piece of grit was found and, after a second re-assembly, *Redshank* coughed into life once more with dire threats from her captain if she should dare to stop again! More time had passed and it was just about midday when I swept past the weedy mouth of the Leicester Cut to be confronted with a loaded pair of BW's in the top of Buckby. The top lock here, which possessed only ground paddles, was notoriously slow-filling and a further delay developed whilst we waited, idling about in mid-stream, for the boatwoman to emerge from the shop with her much needed purchases. Eventually they got going with many profuse apologies for the delay, these had simply to be accepted with good grace and we headed for the lock-chamber with another ten minutes lost.

"They're all ready, mate" said the boatman, who I did not really know other than by sight. "Two more pair behind us, though."

"How do!" came gravely from his wife.

With two more pairs in the offing I was dispatched down the flight on the bike in order to try and prevent any unnecessary drawing off of locks which were ready for us. At third lock I met another Tyseley-bound pair just coming through. This was very useful as I could wait and hold the lock until our own fore-ends were clearly visible in the pound above. Alec had a fierce reputation on the cut and, with other crews knowing who I was working with, I never encountered any problems when engaged in this entirely legitimate task of cycling ahead to 'keep our locks'. The same rules applied as with any other sort of lock-wheeling. You had to be sure not to get too far ahead of your boats, otherwise the locks would cease to be 'yours' if the oncoming pair were able to draw off and get through before your own boats appeared. On the other hand, if you inadvertently let the oncoming pair draw off and your boats then found themselves being held up, you were at fault the other way and found yourself being very roundly abused for not standing firm and 'holding the lock'. It could be a bit of a difficult balancing act and I was relieved to encounter the second pair in the short pound above the next lock, with the rest of the flight open and ready for us. Things were looking up. The rain had eased to a drizzle and was promising to stop altogether as gaps began to appear in the greyness overhead. It was, nevertheless, gone one o'clock when we cleared the bottom lock without, thankfully, any further encounters with submerged barrels. Five hours would be needed to reach the top of Stoke, but the incipient sunshine which began to appear as we passed through the Spinnies cheered us all up, with Alec busy in the engine-hole giving everything a good clean and check-over in the hope of avoiding any further trouble. At a rough estimate we were about three to four hours behind our normal time on this run, but 'three' things had gone wrong and so perhaps we had had our quota for the day.

Avocet and *Dabchick* were met near the railway turn with Jack, their steerer, loudly bemoaning the lack of back-loading, even though we had just passed three loaded BW pairs. Our own Willow Wren contracts seemed to be drying up, but Alec remained philosophical about the prospects, trade waxed and waned and that was just the way it was, no sense in wasting energy worrying about it. Spirits rose as the boats surged out along the breezy Weedon Embankment with cabin tops now dry in the warm sun and the Brasso rags hard at work smartening us up once more. Life always felt better in the sun and the trials and tribulations of the morning faded away as the pair swung this way and that along the long familiar pound. At Arm End I was forced to slow right down in the length between the two bridge holes in order to permit two pairs of BW boats, travelling closely together, to make the tight turn into the Northampton Arm on their way to Wellingborough. They waved their acknowledgements and we waved back, cheerfully ignoring the loss of a further few minutes – everything felt better in the sun! In the darkness of Blisworth Tunnel, sometimes ducking under the slide to avoid the downpours which were particularly heavy today following the rain, I pictured them locking down the Rothersthorpe Flight, scene of my first encounters with the boats. I had come a long way since those early days, but I still loved every minute of the life, even during a 'difficult' time like this morning. Stoke, thanks to the wheat boats, were all ready for us and Alec and I worked the pair down breasted-up, whilst Lil busied herself getting dinner ready and sorting out one or two other cabin chores. We were all quite equable again now, the lost time simply an accepted fact of life. These things happened sometimes and just had to be dealt with, besides we would still reach Cosgrove that night even if rather later than intended.

The final pound was memorable in the soft warmth of evening with the shadows lengthening around us as we wound steadily south, the tall needle of Hanslope Church gleaming in the low glare of the setting sun. The wind had dropped and the rain had vanished as if it had never been, it had truly been a day of contrasting halves with, as is always best in these things, the better half coming second. Our late arrival at Cosgrove was greeted with some amusement and jokes about me 'putting the pair in the field' were rife. I denied this with exaggerated vehemence, but took it all in good part as such ribald badinage was all part of my acceptance in the closed world of the cut. Our engine problems were ascribed to dirty fuel and were thankfully never repeated during my time with the pair. The experience of breaking down in Braunston Tunnel, however, was definitely one for the memory and I never passed through there again without thinking of it with wry amusement, it had just been one of those mornings.

Quite a different dawn greeted us as in bright sunshine, accompanied by a bracing and invigorating breeze, I passed southwards over the aqueduct at just after six o'clock. We were very much 'getting 'em ahead' and heading for Aylesbury that night. At half past four I had been rudely awoken by Arthur coming past with his empty Barlows, the pair were famous for their long runs and had come from Linford that morning. They would reach Stoke just as Mr James took the lock off and would doubtless be at Sutton Stop that evening. Further sleep didn't seem to be forthcoming in the early morning light and I was up and dressed, with half an hour of *Pride and Prejudice* read, before Lil's tap on the half open slide indicated a cup of tea and the start of the working day. The 'Finney' pound was its usual beautiful self that morning and, after a pleasurable hour's steering, I changed over with Alec for my breakfast, before continuing on with *Greenshank*. Herons paraded along the bank in front of us, before eventually reaching the end of their territory and flying back in a great half-circle to alight once more behind our swirling wake. Hares, with their huge ears erect, cocked their heads at our approach before lolloping away across the dewy fields leaving a dark trail in the grass behind them. Life was quieter on the butty and the sheer charm and sylvan peace of the twisting pound made your heart sing on such a lovely morning as this. It is a world which has vanished forever. Milton Keynes has buried those fields beneath a sea of roads, houses, and the dubious attractions of a 'planned' environment. The 'Finney' has become just a pound to be got through in order to reach the green country on either side, it's original solitary appeal now merely a memory, such is progress.

Our plan that day was to reach Aylesbury and I was eagerly anticipating the latter part of the day's work which would add another, hitherto unknown, piece of waterway to my experience. At Finney we paused briefly to enable Lil to get bread and three chops for dinner. She must have been put into an excellent frame of mind by the beauties of the pound, coupled with the morning sunshine, as she also bought a jam roll for us to share with a pot of tea whilst the next lock, Talbot's, was being worked through. Such luxuries! Truly we were being spoilt that morning! The afternoon looked likely to be the harder part of the day and so very sensibly Lil reversed her usual pattern of meals and served up dinner, the chops, carrots and potatoes, just beyond Leighton. Eating was still done on the move, of course, and the hungriest came last as I ate sitting in the cabin for the longish pound above Church Lock. From Horton the locks turned against us and I found myself pedalling my familiar way 'up the Fields'. It was a pleasant afternoon, dry and warm with the towpath firm beneath my wheels, life was a whole lot easier without puddles and clinging mud! Up we went, through the Nags Head Three and the swingbridge, before pedalling on past the pair to get our final wide locks, the two below Maffers, ready. Alec and Lil did not seem at all enamoured with the idea of the narrow Aylesbury Arm, and Dickinson's Mills seemed to be finding much favour in their conversation as we approached the top of the arm. Conversely, I was perfectly happy not to be going to the Mills and was only too keen to add to my experience by venturing down the Aylesbury Arm, despite the labour of the narrow locks and the joys of shovelling-out when we got there.

I pedalled on along the familiar towpath but this time, instead of crossing the bridge by the the arm and going on to set the bottom of Maffers, I picked my way through the maintenance yard, explaining myself to the foreman who had already told me to 'clear off out of it' before apologising when he realised my presence was legitimate, and drew the top paddles of the arm. The top lock, or two locks to be accurate, is a 'riser' and set very neatly between the maintenance yard on one side and a very attractive cottage on the other. Glancing down the arm I noted a veritable sea of white and black gates stretching down into the Vale of Aylesbury, the hard work of the day was about to begin. *Redshank* came slowly through the bridge hole and turned into the waiting lock, with Alec throwing the strap across for me to check *Greenshank* on the post. We had already agreed that *Redshank* would go first and that I would bow-haul down until the pounds lengthened out, it was also understood that Alec should not get too far ahead, just in case we had problems. As things turned out, this was proved to be a very wise move. Whilst *Redshank* dropped through the 'riser' I fastened the long towing line to *Greenshank*'s mast, adjusted the windlass in my belt, dumped the bike back on the coal, and girded myself up for action.

Fifty-two tons, whilst fine for the main line, is pushing it on the Aylesbury Arm and, with the benefit of hindsight, we would have had a lot less trouble if we had kept it to about forty-five tons or so. Hindsight can be a wonderful thing, but it doesn't help at the time, even though we did learn a salutary lesson on the amount to load from our experiences that afternoon. It was getting towards four o'clock and we had six miles and sixteen locks to go, it looked as if we would do it fairly comfortably for about seven o'clock or so. At last the lock was full for us and the moment could be put off no longer, here we go again! With an exaggerated grimace at the watching foreman, I spat on my hands before picking up the line and heaving *Greenshank* in. I had been spared the bow-hauling up Atherstone and had rather forgotten the sheer effort required to get a loaded boat moving. Never mind, I would soon get into the rhythm of it! At least the towpath was clean and grassy and provided a good grip for my feet, however very little commercial traffic had been down the arm in recent years and the distinctive patina bestowed on the locks by regular usage was conspicuously absent. Here there were no marks from the cycles of lock-wheelers, the strapping posts were dull rather than shiny, and the locks themselves all stood empty with gates closed at both ends in case of leakage.

Initially all went well as we dropped through the 'riser' and down the first short pound. Alec had 'started' the lock in the time-honoured manner and I had only to lean on the gate with my bottom to push it open before continuing to bring *Greenshank* in. The flight stretched ahead in a manner very reminiscent of the Northampton Arm, the only real difference being that the Rothersthorpe Locks curved their way downhill, whereas here we descended almost in a straight line. It was after the third lock that our troubles began. Heaving hard on the line I got her moving out of the empty chamber with Lil taking great care to steer a course exactly down the centre of the cut. Twenty yards below the lock, and right in the middle of the channel, *Greenshank* stuck, slewed slightly, and became stationary. It is not easy for a bow-hauler to 'wind it on' when hauling a loaded butty. I dug my heels in, wrapped the line around my shoulders, and heaved fit to bust. A few muddy bubbles came up around the butty, but she barely moved an inch.

"Run water down," suggested Lil, stranded as she was in midstream and powerless to help. After a final abortive heave I dropped the line on to the grassy towpath and walked, panting with the sheer effort of it all, back to the lock to draw both ground paddles. A steady surge of water flooded into the pound as I recovered the line, drawing breath for a minute or two, before beginning to heave as hard as I could. Very slowly and reluctantly she began to move, but we could both feel her constantly catching on the bottom as she made the short journey to the next lock. If the rest of the arm was like this, then we were in for a struggle.

I walked back up to drop the paddles noting that the top pound was now nearly two feet down. We had enough problems at the moment and I turned a blind eye to this. Hopefully the lock-keeper would rectify it or, failing all else, we would have to sort it out ourselves on the way back up. The next pound yielded much the same result with *Greenshank* obstinately stuck in mid-channel. She just kept catching on the bottom here and there, probably on little mud bars thrown up by the overflows, the problem being exacerbated by the irregular use of the waterway. Both ground paddles left up provided me with the necessary lift and flush to get her into the next lock, but it was immensely hard work as well as again draining half the pound above. We were definitely 'bringing our water with us'! Lil had had enough. With dark mutterings about too great a load and the state of the Aylesbury Arm generally she walked on ahead to confer with Alec, leaving me to lock the butty through and then sit patiently on the grass awaiting developments. Presently I saw them both returning having left *Redshank* on tick over below the next lock. In view of our problems they had decided to tow down rather than bow-haul. Logically enough, Alec did not wish to bring the motor back as this would have meant taking another lockful off the short pound rendering our progress even more difficult. Both ground paddles were drawn and *Greenshank* fairly surged out of the lock with both of us pulling for all we were worth on the long swaying line. A couple of small 'sticks' were overcome by sheer brute force, laced with a number of very fruity expletives from the captain, and the boats were re-united once more at the next lock, leaving me to run back and drop paddles with yet another pound half-empty behind us. The top pounds of the flight had been left in a real mess, but needs must and nobody was following us. Perhaps British Waterways would dredge the arm to facilitate the Willow Wren traffic. Pigs might also be seen to fly, but we lived in hope!

Towing down meant yet another technique being adopted. A long 140ft line ran from the stud on *Greenshank*'s fore-end to the dolly on *Redshank*'s counter. My job was to go ahead and prepare the lock for Alec who brought the motor in leaving the butty drifting along behind. With *Redshank* dropping in the lock we ensured that the butty's fore-end was snugly resting against the top gate. Leaving her out in mid-channel could be disastrous as when the lock was being refilled the water in the short pound would drop, with the strong possibility of her getting well and truly stuck. Bottom gates were opened and out went *Redshank*, with the long line trailing over the hand rail of the top gate and down the dripping lock chamber. For the motor steerer it was very important to go nice and steady, holding back in good time and avoiding any sudden jerks which could well snap the line. We were having enough difficulty without Alec being landed with an avoidable splicing job! I shut the bottom gates, carefully reaching down to flick the line up so that it did not jam between them, and Lil then drew the ground paddles. Once the lock was full, and the butty pulled back slightly to allow for the opening of the top gate, Alec was given a wave and he went ahead to draw *Greenshank* in. While the lock was emptying I pedalled down to draw a ground paddle and start the next lock filling. This could not be done any earlier as the pound would have dropped leaving *Redshank* stuck and unable to draw the butty into the lock. With Lil already back on board I then returned to open the bottom gates, the long line dropped free, and the boats resumed their journey.

It was a laborious and fiddly progression down the flight and the level of skill and timing required not to get stuck or snap the towline was quite high. But we each knew our role and, working closely together with the boats quite literally brushing along the bottom, we made our way down with no further hitches. Once clear of the thick of the locks the long straight cut seemed a little deeper and, back on *Redshank*'s footboard again, I made slow uneventful progress through that warm summer's evening. At the tail of the last lock was an unusually long and narrow bridge hole, which, as we were now very much in the town, the local populace had seen fit to use as a convenient rubbish tip. The infrequent flushes from the little-used lock had obviously not been enough to keep it clear as I emerged from the lock chamber with the motor and came to an abrupt standstill. Winding her on to full revs she inched her way forward amid clouds of exhaust smoke and a rattling reverberating echo bouncing off the brickwork on the underside of the bridge. Halfway through she stopped completely with the engine still full ahead. Alec, watching progress or lack of it from the lockside, signalled me to wind it off and put her into neutral. More waves instructed me to reverse back into the lock which, although chary of collecting a real 'bladeful', I achieved without further mishap.

"Right!" said Alec. "Both paddles are going up and you charge it from here! Take the line off so you don't have to worry about holding back."

Both ground paddles created a good flush of water and, amidst clouds of exhaust smoke and with a deafening noise, I charged flat-out down the lock and into the bridge hole. A marked slowing was accompanied by horrible scrunching noises, but we were through and apparently unscathed as I held back quickly on the other side so as not to disappear rapidly out of sight! *Greenshank* would be another problem. A short and very thick strap was attached from the motor to her fore-end stud, with another line off from her mast for bow-hauling assistance from the towpath. We swopped over for this tricky manouevre and, when all was ready, I raised the ground paddles and flushed her. With *Redshank* pulling and my contribution from the towpath she floated through surprisingly easily, perhaps a sign that the charge of the motor had pushed some of the rubbish out of the way.

Rapidly coiling the long line I hurled it into the coal before going back yet again to drop ground paddles. By now it was nearly ten o'clock and it had been quite an afternoon and evening. I had learned a lot and the basin was now only just ahead, surely nothing else could go wrong now? Thankfully it didn't. Reduced to walking alongside the pair I made my way around the end of the basin to the coal wharf, standing there in near darkness to receive a line as *Greenshank* bumped gently alongside. Another trip completed and a new bit of cut completed too! The Aylesbury Arm had been pleasant enough in its quietly rural way and I'm sure that with a smaller load we would have viewed it in a far less baleful light. On the other hand, when the deteriorating state of the cut meant that boats could not be loaded to anywhere near their capacity, then the decline of commercial carrying seemed even more inevitable. Our struggles down the arm, six hours for six miles, were an indication of the problems faced by those who sought new contracts over waterways which had seen little recent commercial use. The deep water of the Thames trip was one thing, the shallowness of the Aylesbury Arm was quite another. With being so late in arriving at Cosgrove I had not had a pint since Braunston, but I felt that I had earned a couple that night in Aylesbury. Only a couple, mind. It was all we had time for before the towel went up! In the morning I was to be introduced to another old canal tradition, the art of shovelling out. I could hardly wait!

Upon awakening I listened intently. The faint buzz of a few distant cars, but thankfully nothing else. Shovelling out sounded bad enough on its own without doing it in the pouring rain. The wharf was quite wide and, as part of the contract, the coal merchant had arranged with 'The Gaffer' that we would put the coal wherever he wanted it. In practice, this seemed to mean that *Greenshank*'s load would have to be initially barrowed to the very back of the wharf, the piles of coal then getting steadily nearer with the last part of *Redshank*'s load able to be thrown directly out on to the wharfside. For us all it was to be a day of quiet unremitting toil. Lil had decided to do the washing and was already hard at work setting up the brazier, the boiling pans, and the dolly tub in a corner of the wharf just along a bit from the boats and their coal dust, but as near as possible to the all-important tap. Alec had set up a long clothes line for her, safely upwind from the boats, and she busied herself with the task, leaving us to gloomily contemplate the coal.

"No good looking at it!" said Alec. "It ain't gonna jump out!"

Top planks and beams were dumped on the wharf out of harm's way and the bracing chains would be undone as we reached them. Two barrows were fetched in order to maintain a sort of shuttle service and ensure that there was no hanging about. Alec started by the middle beam, filling the first barrow standing next to him on the wharfside and using a Size 8 shovel for the purpose. I then had the task of wheeling the barrow to the back of the wharf and tipping its contents out against the wall, before returning to find the second barrow already filled and awaiting my attention.

We had started. Alec dug straight down into the coal, seeking the floorboards at the bottom of the boat which would give him a much more secure footing than standing in the loose shifting coal. I wheeled backwards and forwards and soon had quite a sizable pile of coal building up against the wall, although the amount in the boat hardly seemed to have diminished at all. Doggedly I filled in all along the back of the wall between the chalk marks placed there by the coal merchant, and then it was time to swop over. The amount of energy expended in 'shovelling and filling' or 'wheeling and emptying' is probably much the same, but the boredom factor is something else. It was primarily for this reason that, every half an hour or so, we would change over roles. The changeover itself was something to look forward to and the subsequent variation in task undoubtedly helped in keeping us going. Despite having to reach up with the shovel I found standing on the floors a good deal easier and worked with a will towards the butty's back end. Lil, with a lineful of washing blowing happily away across the other side of the wharf, produced tea for us all at about eleven. Between us we drank two pots bone dry!

A small cruiser came down the arm shortly afterwards. The crew turned out to be real canal enthusiasts and had obligingly topped up all the pounds which somebody had left half empty! Some time was spent photographing our various activities in return for a pint each at lunchtime, a promise effortlessly extracted from them by the genial Alec. With Lil having disappeared shopping, we took the chance to collect upon this promise, adding in a couple more pints of our own before returning hurriedly to the boats where corned beef sandwiches and a jam doughnut were waiting for us.

"You two been on the beer?" queried Lil, whose gimlet eye had noticed the abandoned shovels and barrows.

"Just filling up what's sweated out," I grinned, wincing at my own lack of grammar.

"And me!" added Alec.

AYLESBURY DUCK

Nothing more was said about our little excursion, but it had done us good and we set to work with renewed vigour that afternoon. The job had got a bit harder as a plank had now been laid up the coal pile, with loaded barrows having to be pushed aloft prior to emptying. The object of this was to increase the height of the pile and thus ensure that all of our cargo would indeed fit into the space allocated for it. By mid-afternoon *Greenshank* was empty. As a break from the monotony of shovel and barrow we put all her beams and planks back in, swept her out, and then changed the boats round leaving Lil to mop-off and give her a final tidy. An unexpected bonus was a mug of tea each and a slice of fruitcake from our new friends on the cruiser. Lil, always ready for a gossip and relatively spruce in her floral 'pinny', ate hers sitting comfortably on their boat, leaving us perched alongside on upturned wheelbarrows holding our cake in blackened hands.

Late afternoon saw us begin to empty *Redshank*. With the butty's coal piled high on the back of the wharf there was now not so far to barrow and Alec reckoned that we would soon be able to employ two shovels, throwing the coal directly out on to the side. All the washing had dried and a few special items, such as Lil's best blouse, had been given a press by means of a flat iron heated up on the primus. Our working clothes were never ironed as they very soon became crumpled in our efforts to 'get 'em ahead'. Work ceased at around seven with about a third of *Redshank*'s coal ashore and the boat tilted inelegantly at a slight angle. The remainder of the load should now be capable of being thrown directly out, ever the optimist I returned the barrows to a corner of the wharf in the hope that we would not need them again. Shop-bought fish and chips went down a treat that night with a portion of extra chips shared round between us. It had been a hard day's work, but we had established a comfortable rhythm and were satisfied with our efforts. Lost sweat could be replaced in the pub that night with a clear conscience.

Next morning it rained! It just had to! We waited till nearly nine o'clock to see if it would stop, but no such luck. Very reluctantly we got at it, throwing shovel for shovel on to the wharf and getting progressively more and more filthy with the clinging grit. Needless to say, just as we were nearly finished it eased to a fine drizzle and then stopped as Alec swept the remaining bits on to my shovel for a final triumphant heave up on to the wharf. *Redshank* was re-assembled and the pair rode high in the water, all ready for the next job. There was nothing keeping us and it was just a question of 'empty to Suttons' or 'empty to Brentford' for our next load. Alec went off to phone the office whilst Lil washed out our coal-stained clothes and I hung them to dry along a line stretching from *Greenshank*'s mast to her cabin top. Our piles of coal stood high on the wharf next to us and, with a few days left before school re-started, I wondered what came next. Timber for Tipton was one possibiity, perhaps steel for Birmingham, or even maybe another sub-contract run to Wellingborough.

I was soon disillusioned of all such conjectures as Alec gloomily returned with the news that it was 'back empty to Suttons'. It was 'up and down' work again. Coal south would be our next job, just possibly to Aylesbury again, but far more likely to the Mills. We sat in the hatches, ate a sandwich, drank some tea, and then started up. Going back empty up the arm was a simple matter when compared to the effort required to get down it loaded. The boats floated high and free and, with our routine well-polished, it seemed no time at all before we were back on the wide and deep waters of the main line. Shutting the top gate of the arm behind us I pedalled furiously on to investigate the state of the two below Maffers. Would it be a 'good road' or not? Scurrying along ahead I was doubly heartened to find both locks full and all ready for us. A good road and the chance of steering instead of pedalling, what more could you ask!

Empty boating I always found to be a considerably easier business than its loaded counterpart. High out of the water, the boats were much lighter to steer and less concentration was needed as a less exact adherence to the channel was possible. Flights of locks, or individual locks reasonably close together such as those met with down 'The Fields', could be taken breasted-up as a matter of course thus relieving the pressure on the butty steerer. Similarly, round the long pounds the butty was towed close up behind the motor on a short pair of ropes known as the cross-straps. Both straps led from a stud on the butty's fore-end to the twin dollies on the motor's counter, but they passed on either side of the butty's stem post to the opposite dolly. As viewed from the butty's deck the strap passing round the right-hand side of the stem post led to the left hand dolly and vice-versa, hence 'cross-straps' as they crossed over each other on the way to the two dollies. This crossover nature of the straps prevented the butty from swinging about unduly as would have been the case if a single strap, however short, had been employed.

One result of this simple but effective arrangement was that the butty needed little steering in the long pounds. She would trail happily along behind with the steerer only really being needed to prevent possible bumps in bridge holes, or to keep her off the rough rock-strewn edges of the cut when negotiating a big turn. The fortunate butty steerer could thus get on with all the various chores in a much more leisured fashion. Better meals appeared when travelling empty, it was also just a matter of clambering back and forth to change steerers or to pass over mugs of tea, sometimes even accompanied by snacks! Light washing and ironing could all be done on the move, sewing and mending were simpler too than when responsible for the heavy tiller of a loaded boat, the brasses could be polished and white strings and ash strips thoroughly scrubbed. You could even, if you managed to get everything completely up to date, sit in the hatches in the sun and watch the world go by, or on a cold day snuggle up in front of the range and make another pot of tea. The down side to all this spare time was money, or more accurately the lack of it. Boatmen were paid by the ton carried and our orders of 'back empty to Suttons' were far less lucrative than a load of spelter for Tyseley. A flat rate was paid for running empty and, as the boats earnt nothing during this time, it was hardly a princely sum.

Our good road lasted for precisely four locks as the bottom of the Nags Head was against us. Two pairs, or maybe more, must have passed one another along here whilst we were working up through the last few locks on the arm. Just to rub it in the weather had again turned cloudy and dull with occasional bits and pieces of light drizzle, as I pedalled through the wet grass towards Horton, Church, and Grove. It was along here that I had first lockwheeled for Ronnie and *Warbler*, worried about getting it wrong and either not having the lock ready in time or drawing-off in front of somebody else and getting an earful as a result. Experience in boating, as in life, is a hard won thing. Much more confident and proficient, I trundled along recalling those early anxieties, still mindful of errors but far less likely to make one.

A fellow Willow Wren pair, *Crane* and *Heron*, were in Church Lock as I appeared. Ray and Margaret were headed for the Mills and were not surprised to see me as apparently 'back empty' was getting a bit too common for comfort. He was confident that Leslie Morton would soon sort it out and before much longer we would all be going to Brentford again for back-loading. An empty BW pair was up ahead of us, Ray informed me, but we had the top of the three locks ready. Assuring him of a good road, at least to the top of the Aylesbury Arm, we parted and I perched myself on the beam watching him pull away and awaiting the arrival of my own pair.

That night we stopped at Leighton Bridge. Having always run south from Cosgrove I had only previously spent a night here when working with Mike Sloan. There was still a certain amount of daylight in hand and I was surprised at the early finish. Apparently Alec did not like the pub at the Stoke Hammond Three and going on to Finney would have made serious inroads into the time available for sinking pints, hence it was Leighton Bridge. Alec claimed, with some justification, that we had earned a few pints with all our shovelling and I certainly wasn't about to argue with that! Lil was not especially unhappy either with the stop as she could shop for fresh bread and then spend a quiet evening in the cabin, secure in the knowledge that Alec had promised to reach Braunston the next day. We made doubly sure of keeping in her good books by bringing back a bag of nice hot chips and a bottle of stout for her supper, even though we did sneak a couple of chips each on the way!

The morning dawned misty with a very heavy dew saturating the boats with fine droplets of moisture. Such conditions often presaged a fine day to come and I consoled myself with the hope of sun as we slid into Leighton Lock at about quarter past five. Lil had got us moving! We had said we would go to Braunston, and an early start, she reasoned, would make it certain. Lock country was being left behind now and we were entering the world of long pounds and flights, so much easier for the lock-wheelers legs! Ray's information was absolutely right. The top lock of the three was ready, but I had to set the other two before pedalling along through the wet grass to do the same at Talbot's. Along by Water Eaton we met two pairs of BW's who had spent the night at Finney, the last lock of the descent was thus ready for us and the long pounds lay ahead. As we threaded through the tricky Finney Bridge the sun began to emerge slowly from the mists and it looked a fine day in prospect for the long run northwards.

It felt very strange to be at Cosgrove in mid-morning. There was plenty of time and we lay comfortably in the lock, chatting for a quarter of an hour or so before pressing on with promises of 'we'll try to stop next time' hanging in the air behind us. The familiar landmark of Hanslope Church welcomed me back into 'home' territory as I contentedly steered *Redshank* up the pound, leaning on the tiller bar and watching our heavy wash rushing and gurgling along the broken banks on either side. I just managed to squeeze through Grafton Bridge in front of the oncoming Mark and Dolly, like Ray and Margaret they were also heading for Croxley and assured me that Stoke were ready which was pleasing news. Dolly informed me that they hadn't emptied the pounds for us either! Memories are long on the cut! When we got there, they weren't ready at all! Presumably a pleasure boat must have gone up in front of us, although all was quiet as I scrambled ashore to empty the bottom lock. By now it had turned into such a gloriously sunny day that I must confess that I didn't really mind whether the flight was ready or not, lock-wheeling would be a pleasant enough occupation after several hours on the footboard steering the long pounds from Finney.

At the top lock occurred an incident which was amusing at the time, but becomes even more so with the passing of the years. The pleasure boat, crewed by another very pleasant couple, was just leaving the top lock when I arrived behind them. They had already offered to let us through at the top of the thick, but I had waved them on through the last two locks on the understanding that we would go first into the tunnel. Lying abreast and idling in midstream by the Mill were a pair of Barlows whom I really only knew by sight. The crew consisted of an old, rather traditionally dressed, couple with their three younger children who seemed to do most of the work. The lock was clearly their's and so, leaning the bike on the fence, I strolled up to the top gate to socialise with the old man who was standing by the ground paddle and waving at his pair to come in.

"How do!" I said, grinning at the faded blue eyes set deep in his weathered countenance.

"Hey up! Alec coming then!" He clearly knew who I was even if, to the very best of my recollection, we had never spoken before. "You bin to Aylesbury then?"

I confirmed this and he began talking of how he used to horse-boat down there as a boy working for Faulkners of Leighton Buzzard. Suddenly he broke off what had been an increasingly interesting conversation, pointing up the cut to where an exceedingly large insect was flying an uneven course towards us.

"Look at him! He's a big 'un, ain't he!"

"What is it? I asked uncertainly.

"Damn great horse fly that is, boy! That'd give you a fair nip!"

We stood there, side by side in the warm sunshine, watching the insect dip and weave its way along above the water. It was certainly big, I thought, as it passed our cottage door and headed inexorably straight at us.

"Whooaah!"

Suddenly my companion was hopping madly around on the lockside. The horsefly had kept coming and we had both simply assumed it would fly straight past. Instead, at the very last second and for reasons best known to itself, it had suddenly veered and gone straight up his trouser leg!

"Whoooaaah! Get it out! Aaaah!"

He may have been old, but he could certainly jump around a bit and had very good reasons to be doing so! There was really very little choice in the matter, undignified it may have been, but it was either that or be horribly eaten! Cursing most horribly he undid his brass belt buckle and pulled his trousers down, eventually freeing the horsefly which evaded his vengeful boots and flew on its way leaving him nursing, at a preliminary count, three gruesome bites. His family meanwhile drifted in towards the lock, grinning broadly and not at all put out by his unfortunate predicament.

"You'll have to wear bike clips!" observed his young attractive daughter as she steered the pair in. This witticism was not entirely appreciated by her father who scowled ferociously at her and then disappeared down into the butty cabin, doubtless to make a thorough inspection of the damage. Just think, it could have been me!

A hastily scribbled note was left on the table in the cottage, where my parents were living during the summer months, although I knew that Mr James, who had come out during the horse fly fracas, would also be bound to tell them that I'd been through that day. On the spur of the moment I picked a little bouquet of roses from the tree around the door, supplemented it with flowers and greenery from our little garden, and presented the whole thing to Lil who seemed surprisingly touched by this innocent gesture. Stoke, basking that day in sunshine and its customary peace, was on the brink of momentous changes, although no-one would have predicted its present-day state at that time. Mrs James had recently died, suddenly and without any real hint of ill-health, leaving a bereft Mr James to start developing a small museum of cans, handbowls, lace and photographs in his tiny lock-keeper's hut next door to 'The Boat'. He was lonely and it gave him what appeared to be a harmless interest to go with winning and retaining the cup for best-kept lockside gardens. However, with the departure of Sister Mary and the arrival of the well-intentioned Colonel Ritchie, things were to change dramatically. The ground floor of the old Mill was opened up for use as a larger museum and this, coupled with the lockside gardens and the beautiful setting, began to attract people in ever-increasing numbers. Eventually the museum would grow to occupy all three floors of the Mill and have a shop built adjacent to it, Sister Mary's house would become a restaurant, the apple orchard would transform itself into a car park, the narrow green path up to the tunnel would be tarmaced all the way up, the old farm by the bridge would become a second and larger pub, coach parties would arrive and double yellow lines sprout up in what had once been a quiet and unassuming Northamptonshire village. These sad days were still some years ahead, today Stoke lay drowsy and sleepy in the sunshine as we scurried about our business, filling water cans and checking the headlight as the pair rose in the lock and the roar from the gate paddles died away as the waters equalised.

Working boats would have no part in the canal's future either. With the exception of a few surviving craft, crewed by enthusiasts and ghosting along with the odd special cargo or selling bags of coal to local villages, they were soon to disappear from the scene to exist only in memory and old photographs. However all this was in the future and completely unanticipated by us as I picked up the cross-straps and 'got 'em ahead'. Lil's bouquet stood proudly in its jam pot by the chimney as the pair swept on into the tunnel, my steering was as enthusiastic as ever and, looking back on those happy times, it seems I had already learned the invaluable knack of trying to enjoy each day as it comes. On we went around the familiar Blisworth pound, up Buckby which were all ready for us, across the short summit level and then down Braunston, arriving in good time at the bottom lock in the early evening light. The story of the horse fly went the rounds that night in 'The Nelson' and skittles flew as I made 'overs' on a number of occasions, my impending 'A' levels seemingly in another world, such was my absorption in this one.

With only having to reach Sutton Stop the next day there was no great urgency to be gone in the morning. We hung around for a while, allowing Lil to go gossiping and shopping, looking at the boats Willow Wren were currently refurbishing and discussing the general state of affairs with Dennis. We were all in positive mood as we surveyed the newly painted craft, surely a sign that further new contracts would be won by 'The Gaffer'. These would serve to keep the Company healthy and able to take on yet more pairs to compete with the much larger British Waterways fleet. None of us, as we entered the new decade of the 1960s, had any real thoughts that the death throes of commercial carrying were now very close indeed. On the surface all appeared to be reasonably well. The three carrying fleets moved up and down the cut with over a hundred pairs of boats in trade and the future surely seemed promising enough to ensure survival for some time to come. We got ourselves moving at about eleven o'clock on another remarkably pleasant day, easing past the clutter of old narrow boats and assorted pleasure craft tied outside Barlow's yard, before settling down for the first of the two long pounds round to the Stop. Several pairs coming up from the coalfield were met with that day and each of them told us that the queue at Suttons was quite short. This boded well for a quick turn-around, more good news which lifted our buoyant spirits even higher. Running on steadily through the afternoon we tied fifth in line at the Stop which did seem to indicate only a short wait before the next load. The Aylesbury 'up and down' was behind us and it had been hugely enjoyable. The journey down the arm had made a very welcome change from the more usual round trip to the Mills and the problems with lack of depth, although very irritating at the time, were partly our own fault for loading just that little bit too much. Shovelling out made for harder work than going under the 'jigger', but it had been another new experience to set alongside all the others and had hardened my muscles still further! Of course it had! Where to now, I wondered? With any sort of luck we should know the next job in the morning. Aylesbury again? Well, why not!

*****

Chapter 11

Banbury Bun

Back in the spring of 1957 when we had met *Friendship* in the Napton Locks, Joe Skinner had been returning to the coalfield after delivering a load of coal, either to the Co-op at Banbury or United Dairy. Obviously at the time we had not been in a position to ascertain which. Trade on the southern Oxford had been in decline for years and this had steepened after the war. Joe Skinner had become the sole survivor of that brave company of Oxford Number Ones so eloquently described in *Narrow Boat* by L.T.C. Rolt and, as mentioned earlier, a little coal still found its way down to Juxon Street Wharf in Oxford for Morrells Brewery with the very occasional load elsewhere. Upon Joe Skinner's retirement the Banbury Dairy contract had been taken over by Barlows and I had seen their boats in the Napton flight whilst working with Mike Sloan. Later still, following the take-over of Barlows by Blue Line Cruisers, the contract had been acquired by Leslie Morton, and Willow Wren had become responsible for keeping the dairy's boilers supplied with coal. The company had already run odd loads to Cropredy and even taken roadstone to Enslow, but nothing permanent had emerged from these pioneering attempts to find new trade.

I had enjoyed my experiences on the southern Oxford, both on *Canada Goose* and with *Wanderer* and *Wayfarer*, but had long ago decided that with so little traffic I was never realistically likely to be involved in any commercial runs down that way. I had turned nineteen and my schooldays were behind me as was the freedom bestowed by the long holidays. Nowadays I worked in an office learning the intricacies of an early punched card computing system and the cut was strictly for week-ends and, of course, for my annual two weeks holiday. It was this which at long last gave me the chance of a coal run on the southern Oxford. Although blissfully unaware of it at the time, this was also to be my last working trip with Alec and Lil. We still week-ended at Stoke Bruerne which, with Sister Mary gone, was beginning the period of change which would transform it from a quiet Northamptonshire canal-side village to its present-day ambience of a noisy and crowded theme park. Several week-ends had been enjoyed with the pair, south to Berko, north to Sutton Stop, and once along as far as Warwick, but on each occasion I had felt sad as Sunday night came and I had to look for the train home so as to be ready

240

for the office on Monday morning. It seemed as if my boating days were perforce drawing to a close, but the late summer of 1962 was to bring one final flourish for me, another nugget of memory to store alongside all the rest, before times changed for ever.

You always need a bit of luck in life and it was running for me that year as a still hot summer began to slowly shade towards the autumn. A clandestine call from the office to Willow Wren on Friday morning informed me that Alec was heading back empty from Croxley and should be in the Cosgrove or Stoke Bruerne area that night. Stanley further added that he was sure that Alec would tie at Braunston on Saturday night as nothing could happen in the coalfields until Monday at the earliest. Thanking him for all his help I softly replaced the receiver and grinned at my luck. My annual holidays started that evening and I had already arranged to spend them with Alec and Lil, wherever they might be. This particular scenario couldn't have been laid on any better if I'd ordered it specially. Alec would undoubtedly follow his usual routine of stopping at Cosgrove that night which meant that I could join them at Stoke the following morning, with no chasing round the country in trains and buses involved at all. The only snag was the possibility of finding myself sitting around at Suttons waiting for orders and watching the precious days trickle away. Worry about that when it happens, I told myself firmly, knowing that with the unpredictability of canal life anything was possible.

The next morning felt just like that first morning, several years before, when I had waited rather nervously at the bottom of Stoke for *Warbler* and *Redshank & Greenshank*. Leaning again on the wooden footbridge I watched the sunshine glinting off the familiar waters which were being gently ruffled by the light breeze. It wasn't the same, of course. We had all changed as life had moved on. Ronnie and Phyllis had gone their separate ways and Young Lily was now a mother and living contentedly ashore with Cliff, her years on the cut behind her. Alec and Lil had become a little older and now found themselves subjected to the rigours of two-handed working which I knew was putting a strain on them as their health was not as robust as might appear at a first glance. As for me, the boy had become the young man. I had come down against going on to University, after enjoying considerable success at 'A' levels, and was taking my first uncertain steps into the great world of work. Again, looking back on it now, this was probably a wrong decision on life's journey, but that's another story. Everything was different, but for a few minutes that morning, the years rolled back and I saw myself once more as the nervous eager youth desperate to enter the mysterious world of the narrowboats. I was so much more experienced now as I leaned on the rail, windlass in belt and listening for the first faint sound of the engine beat. Why, I'd even slept through the previous night!

At last, above the quiet chatter of the birdsong and the gentle rustle of the breeze, I heard it and pictured the pair swinging round the long curve below

Grafton Regis before making their way along the final section of water meadows and overflow weirs. The sound grew steadily louder and at last the high fore-end of *Redshank* appeared and we were exchanging waves. The paper and fuss of the office had gone and it was back to real life again.

"Hey up!" said Alec. "Expected you in the "Barley Mow' last night!"

"Didn't get over until nine," I replied, waving and smiling at Lil as I pulled on *Redshank*'s gate. "I'll skittle you in 'The Nelson'!"

"You will 'an all!" he grinned, as the two of them tied the boats abreast leaving me to cross the bridge, shut the other gate, and draw the paddles. It was just like I had never been away as we all immediately fell straight back into our well worn three-handed working routine. I slung my old bag aboard at the top lock whilst my parents chatted to Alec and Lil who had, by now, become part of the family and I certainly felt I had become part of theirs, such was the closeness and trust of our friendship.

"Go ahead then, John!" invited Alec, after checking the headlight and laying the cross-straps ready for the pick-up.

Aware of my parents and Mr James' eyes on me I eased forward and confidently picked up the straps without any embarrassing mishaps. As I began to pull away I was once again reminded by my mother to get back in time! Not for school now, but for work! I had never in all the years of boating not got back in time, indeed the whole thing was now beginning to become something of a family joke, I was nineteen after all! After the customary final wave at the corner I wound her on a little more, the engine beat singing in my heart as we surged happily through the cutting and disappeared into the darkness. There were now noticably more pleasure craft and distinctly less commercial traffic than had been the case when I had first become acquainted with this, my 'home' pound. Several hire firms had blossomed and I encountered quite a number of assorted craft that morning as we wound along towards Weedon, besides a couple of pairs of south-bound BW boats with the inevitable coal for the Mills. The sun shone and I positively glowed, this was still very much the life!

Braunston also showed changes that night. It was a warm evening in late summer and 'The Nelson' was crowded with villagers, people in cars, people off cruisers, and us, a little knot of canal folk sitting up the corner. Hubert always gave us preference at the bar, but on that Saturday evening we were very much outnumbered by the crowds. It was a foretaste of what was just around the corner. The cut was on the very brink of an enormous change, over the next few years it became very much a part of the leisure industry and the precious but fragile way of life of the boatpeople was swept away for ever. Unusually, our orders were forthcoming at Braunston. We were to load in the Bedworth Arm for Banbury Dairy on Monday morning. From a purely selfish point of view this simply couldn't get any better, no hanging about at Sutton Stop and a trip I had long since given up hope of ever doing. Even if the Oxford Cut was not entirely new it promised to be much more interesting than another trip 'down the Junction'. Alec and Lil were understandably not quite so ecstatic, for them the novelty of the narrow locks, the bow-hauling and shovelling out, and the Oxford generally simply represented a much harder trip than a routine run to the Mills.

Sunday was a relatively short day of boating and so the opportunity was taken for a bit of a lie-in, followed by a leisurely breakfast together in *Greenshank*, before finally setting off around mid-morning. Summer might be shading into Autumn but the weather remained very pleasant giving people the chance to indulge in a little more warmth before the days began to shorten and winter closed in. Cruisers were moving in the flight and villagers were wandering happily along the towpath looking with quiet interest at the world of the cut as we started off, chugging slowly past the long line of moored boats which was now beginning to fill the lengths between the bottom lock and the A45 road-bridge, and even beginning to encroach beyond it. A glance down the Napton pound was irresistible as we passed the Triangle and headed on round to the quiet fields beyond the main road bridge. We would be going down there in a couple of days, I told myself, with genuine excitement. Lady Luck seemed to have taken quite a shine to me and, not content with handing over a Banbury run, she further proceeded to lavish a beautiful warm Sunday on us for the long pounds up to Suttons. I was on top of the world, steering *Redshank* for most of the day, with Alec and Lil happy just to rest in the sunshine, dabbling with an occasional spot of brasswork, a bit of necessary splicing, or any other odd jobs that merited their attention. Through Tushes Bridge and round by The Light I ran before easing for the final turn and edging past the usual queue of boats waiting for orders at the Stop. Alec had already decided that we would go straight through the actual lock and tie round the corner in the Coventry Canal. This would enable a few pints to be put away in 'The Greyhound' that evening, before making the final very short run up to the arm so as to be ready to load first thing the next morning.

As I eased *Redshank* into the narrow channel between the waiting pairs heads popped up out of cabins to see what was going on. Queue jumping was an activity which just did not happen! Drifting gently through we explained our position to all concerned, calming any problems before they began! However, it was a very nice feeling to squeeze past Arthur, in his usual position at the head of the line, but still awaiting orders. Unlike some of us! Locking through I attempted, in full view of an interested knot of spectators, the huge one hundred and eighty degree turn into the Coventry. Hard over, wind it on and trust your judgement! All went well and, passing through the narrow stop place on the other side, we tied up for the evening. Alec and Lil went off to see Young Lily leaving me in charge of the pair which I always enjoyed immensely. It was a still windless evening with the boats reflected perfectly in the dark waters. I pottered about, mopping bits off that didn't really need it, coiling straps to perfection, and generally enjoying myself in the gathering twilight before eventually joining Alec, Cliff and some of the other crews for a pint or two in the cosy surroundings of the old pub.

The next morning we found ourselves first pair in the length. The Dairy had been promised that the coal would be unloaded by the following week-end without fail, a busy week lay ahead but blissfully not in the office! The Bedworth Arm was just a short length off the main cut served by a railway which ran down from the nearby Newdigate Colliery. Coal arrived in railway wagons and the boats were manouevred under the chutes and into position before the chocks were knocked out of the wagon doors. In a long rushing stream the coal cascaded down amid clouds of dust causing the boat to rock and sink deeper into the water. Two men then got into the wagon and shovelled the remaining coal out in practiced fashion before a second wagon was unleashed. It was simple but effective. We were very soon loaded and drifting about in the main channel putting our beams and planks correctly into position, trimming the boats as necessary to achieve the good balance so vital for the steerers, and then the general routine of mopping off and setting everything to rights for the journey ahead. We all worked assiduously at sorting ourselves out as quickly as possible, time was important now as Alec aimed to return to Braunston that same evening.

At the Stop I was kept busy filling water cans whilst Lil disappeared briefly for bread and a few fresh provisions as we would be very much 'out in the wilds' on our journey up and over the Oxford summit. *Redshank* lay ticking over beyond the lock with Alec at the tiller and the long wet snubber lying in the water and running back to *Greenshank*, half-in and half-out of the stop lock. Having dealt with the cans I stood in the butty's hatches, put the tiller into place and looked back along the path, aware of growing impatience on the motor.

"Can you see her?" shouted back Alec.

I shook my head and shrugged helplessly, aware of the waiting crews watching and grinning at the situation. Shopping had to be done and we did have to eat but, on the other hand, it was already mid-morning and time was ticking remorselessly on.

"Go and fetch her!" came from the motor. "She's yacking again!"

Somewhat reluctantly, and feeling very much like 'piggy in the middle', I climbed ashore and prepared to do as bidden, but then, thankfully for me, her bobbing figure came into view carrying two bulky bags and looking distinctly harassed. I trotted along and took what looked to be the heavier of the bags.

"He's getting a bit grumpy," I said, as we hurried towards the waiting boats.

"Huh! He'll still be wanting his dinner I expect!" she replied, as we clambered aboard with the butty beginning to move forward as we did so. I took the tiller and guided us through the assembled throng whilst passing the heavy bags down into the cabin for unpacking

"We'm all right!" she insisted stubbornly. "Don't matter if we don't get there till ten. 'Cept he won't get his beer!"

BANBURY BUN

I steered and kept my counsel. Least said, soonest mended!

A mug of tea accompanied by a slice of jam roll was passed over at Ansty and, suitably mollified, the Captain and his ever-willing mate steered on towards Stretton. Lil sat in the cabin, embroiling herself in her handwashing, and seemingly in an unusually benign mood, reminiscing to me about her childhood and the horse boats she had worked with in those far off days. Warming to her story she told me of how she had first met Alec whilst waiting to empty somewhere down the Junction. Alec, always a strong swimmer, had made the unusual approach of swimming up to her boat and hanging on to talk to her. She was just getting into the details of his courtship when Stretton was reached and a change of steerers took place. Alec slowed *Redshank* almost to a standstill in the old stop lock, I stepped off the fore-end and got her going again before the oncoming butty caught up. All very neatly done, and allowing Alec to drop back for his sandwich before presently changing again for me to have mine, thereafter steering *Greenshank* through to Hillmorton. Unfortunately the moment had passed when I regained the butty and Lil, now busily peeling potatoes, told me instead all about Young Lily's baby with the intricacies of Alec's courtship left hanging in the air, a tantalising glimpse into a past she rarely talked of.

We were fortunate at Hillmorton in encountering John Henry whose pair was in the bottom lock as we approached. All very handy. He assured us that the flight was ready, with no pleasure boats about, as we drifted slowly past before sliding side by side into the dripping locks. I wandered up the flight anyway, just to be on the safe side, but John Henry had got it right. All was quiet and we locked upwards effortlessly before facing the last pound of the day. I seemed to have spent most of my time that day on the butty, but this all changed that evening as I took charge of *Redshank* for that final fairly easy pound. As the late afternoon stretched on into early evening the sun sank down across the flat Midland landscape casting long shadows from the west. There was little or no wind and the tall trees were reflected in the still waters ahead of *Redshank*, their shadows lengthening into the fields on the opposite side. This was idyllic boating weather and we savoured every minute of it, something to be held on to when the rains came again. Comfortable in our shirtsleeves we wound along before arriving in the hush of evening at the triangular junction where, most unusually, we would turn right instead of carrying straight on to go down the Junction. It felt very strange to be going this way and tying in the short bridge length just around the turn, with the long flare path of the setting sun shining directly along the wide straight from Wolfhamcote. The engine died and the resultant peace enhanced the timeless scene. Greatly to Lil's surprise Alec decided that he couldn't be bothered to walk along to 'The Nelson' that evening, instead we all finished up sitting in the hatches enjoying the evening tranquillity, sipping our tea, and discussing the trip ahead.

Timing was the real problem. It was easy to plan a trip on the main line, when we knew to the nearest five minutes how long it took to get around a pound or up a flight. But the Oxford was different. It was shallow for one thing and we would have to tow up the Napton Flight, so how long there? How long for that twisting wriggling summit? Eleven and three-quarter miles in four hours? Sounded alright in theory, but the turns were notoriously huge and the mud was plentiful. If that summit level was even three inches low then all our timings would have to be revised accordingly. Inches can make a marked difference to the time taken to go round a pound, so just how long would that summit take? We could only estimate timings on the basis of previous experience but, without a shadow of a doubt, the conditions on the Oxford had worsened over the years and journeys were taking markedly longer, even for the 'gas boats' who knew it like the back of their hands. We sat there in the gathering gloom, with the air still warm around us, and decided on the only practical approach. Get an early start and then just bash on with the added help of the light summer evening. Push on as far as we could in the light and then call it a day, as none of us fancied travelling in the dark with loaded boats on the Oxford.

I was awoken by the now familiar sound of the slide being pushed back on *Greenshank*. It was a clear bright morning as Lil passed over the steaming mug of tea.

"Nice morning," she observed, with a soft smile wrinkling the lines of her brown weathered face. "Looks like we're going to have a good day for it."

"What's the time," I asked, "My watch has stopped in the night." I sipped the scalding tea gingerly. Mmmm, it tasted like nectar. That first cup in the morning, drunk just before we got underway, always seemed to taste better than any of the later ones.

"Just gone half past five. Alec's still thinking about getting up, but we can get started and get along to Napton."

She was right, as always. An early start would make all the difference on a day like this. A good run today would see us in Banbury tomorrow with time in hand to begin shovelling out. Finishing the tea, I sploshed cold water round my face and then started her up. Lil was untying the fore-ends and loosing us off as I emerged from the engine-hole, all ready to fit the tiller bar and coil in the last strap. Shoving in the clutch I put her ahead with a feeling of gleeful anticipation at what promised to be a really good day's boating. Down the length of the butty slid the motor at little more than tickover speed. Leaning across I collected the end of the long snubber, draped ready for me across the cratch, and, after dropping the loop on to the dolly, drifted ahead into the bridge hole. Holding back slightly to minimise the jerk brought *Redshank* almost to a halt as the line tightened between us. We were off. Winding on the speedwheel, with the wash bubbling and swirling out behind, the boats passed under the roving bridge and moved away down that first long straight towards Napton.

This was still a familiar piece of cut. The excitement would come when we went straight on at Napton Junction, instead of making our more usual right turn for Birmingham. It had all the signs of being another splendid day with a hot sun rising steadily into a clear blue sky, I had actually started in shirtsleeves such was the warmth and beauty of the morning. We made good time down that pound, which was always a favourite of mine, with its rolling fields and hills, the rabbits scampering in the fresh early light and the odd heron catching his breakfast. Alec was very soon up and we swopped over for 'breakfusses' just before my old enemy, the big turn at Shuckburgh. The long grass of the little used towpath was soaked with dew and there seemed little point in Alec getting wet feet walking between bridge holes to make the change. Instead I just eased off and allowed *Greenshank* to creep up behind. The correct procedure in doing this is to use the engine in such a way as to allow the butty to close right up, thus enabling both people to step across, but without the two boats actually touching. The person waiting on the butty's fore-end is helpfully coiling in the long snubber as the gap narrows, a 'bladeful' would not be at all welcome just when breakfast is ready! The changeover went perfectly and I retired below for a very welcome boiled egg leaving Alec to press on around the big turn.

Lil liked to have a tidy-out after breakfast and so I found myself steering the butty as we came up to the reedy entrance of the southern Oxford. Once again the banks closed in on us and the piling disappeared to be replaced by grass and reeds. It was certainly shallower and the engine note changed as Alec eased her down somewhat. The motor's wash told its own story. Normally clean and bubbly, it now revealed the brown mud swirling up from the bottom. Plainly we would have to be content to jog along steadily and try and avoid getting stuck anywhere. I found being on the butty a different experience in this situation. The cabin acted like an echo chamber magnifying all the little scratching and scrunching noises as she scraped against the bottom. A veritable symphony of stones, bricks, and other assorted old rubbish! Through Napton Bridge, a favourite stopping place for the Clayton 'gas boats', and the derelict windmill on the summit of Napton Hill was clearly in view above us. It was a familiar landmark, almost like an old friend really. First visible along the pound from Braunston, it could be seen down the locks on the Birmingham road and for much of the way around the Oxford Summit. I knew, as I glanced up the grassy slope, that it's broken sails would overlook our progress for several hours to come. Very slowly and carefully we edged round the tricky turns at the base of the hill, eased through the last bridge hole and entered the bottom lock of the flight of nine which would take us up to the summit at Marston Doles.

The flight is really a case of seven locks and then two more, with nearly a mile separating the final pair of locks from the rest of the flight. The first few locks of the flight are encouragingly close together. Close enough to have bow-hauled the butty if the interrmediary pounds had been deep enough. For us, three-handed as we were, this would have been the easiest answer to this flight, but the pounds were shallow and it was simply not feasible for me to attempt to drag *Greenshank* along the bottom. Thus it was to be the Aylesbury Arm routine all over again, the motor and the long

long line. As before we would need to work closely together in order to avoid such unwanted occurrences as a broken line or a badly stuck butty. A good start was made as the bottom lock was empty and Alec was able to nudge the gates open and enter before we arrived behind him. Lil brought the butty in at a slight angle allowing me to leap off the fore-end, check her round a stump, and bring her neatly to rest with her bows just short of the bottom gates. By the time *Greenshank* was properly secured below the lock Alec had got both ground paddles up and the motor was rising steadily up. This time it was decided that I should take the motor up, leaving Alec to look after the lines and the ground paddles, whilst Lil would steer the butty and deal with the bottom gates.

The very long 140ft line was fastened to *Greenshank*'s mast with the other end looped over a dolly on *Redshank*'s counter. It was the same procedure at every lock and success was very reliant on good careful boating from us all. The motor would leave the full lock at a steady pace, trailing out the long line behind her with Alec ensuring that it was running smoothly across the middle of the two bottom gates. It was important that the line did not catch or snag in any way, if it snapped there would be an inevitable loss of time whilst it was being respliced. I watched all this from *Redshank*'s footboard and, when I judged myself to be about 50ft out from the lock, held back to avoid any abrupt tightening of the line between the two boats. By now Alec would also have shut the top gate, the ground paddles having been dropped by me as *Redshank* moved forward, and drawn the bottom paddles. We thus had the situation of the motor idling out of gear in mid-channel about twenty yards above the lock, with the long line running back over the handrail of the top gate, down the middle of the emptying lock, before disappearing over the bottom gates to the mast of the waiting *Greenshank*. As soon as the lock was empty I engaged gear and began to pull the butty into the lock, each of us watching the other to ensure a smooth passage.

Alec would give me the wave when the butty was about two-thirds of the way in and I held back again to preserve the line from those unwanted jerks, silky smooth boating being the essential requirement. In the meantime Alec would partially draw a ground paddle ensuring just enough of a flush to stop *Greenshank*, mere inches short of the sill, and enable Lil, aided by the flush of water, to bang the bottom gates to. As they did so Alec had the rest of the paddle up and was crossing over to draw the other side. For my part, as I saw the gates closing, I would engage gear again and keep her ticking very gently ahead, the taut line holding the butty firmly against the top gate preventing her from drifting back and damaging her 'elum'. With the lock full, I steered up the short pound to the next one where we repeated the whole business again. It was slow work, but also surprisingly hard work. You had to be constantly watching the boats with hardly any time to relax as the locks emptied and filled. It wasn't at all like the wide locks on the Junction where you could usually spend a contemplative minute or two sitting on the balance beam, idly watching the water rushing through the paddles, and feeling no need to move until the steadying of the water indicated that the lock was nearly ready. At Napton there were few opportunities for sitting about. I was constantly aware of the need to maintain *Redshank*'s position, both in order that she should not get stuck in the shallow pounds and to avoid putting any unnecessary strain on that long rather thin line. A mistake, a sudden heavy jerk, could so easily snap it causing aggravation and annoyance all round, not to mention the time loss whilst the whole thing was sorted out. The same concentration was demanded of Alec and Lil. Both kept a constant watch on that line to make doubly sure that it was running smoothly as it passed over the two sets of gates. They also had the working of the locks themselves, double-locking all the time, as well as producing a cup of tea halfway up! It was amusing to me, the perennial lockwheeler, to see Alec careering up the towpath on the bike so as to be ready to check *Greenshank* at the next lock whilst I got on with shutting the bottom gates and drawing paddles.

Most of the morning was spent getting up Napton and it was well past eleven o'clock by the time that *Greenshank* was rising in the final lock at Marston Doles. The long line was coiled in and stowed by the mast ready for use at Claydon, the snubber was readied and we prepared to set out on the long solitary journey around that beautiful winding summit level. The lock-keeper, who had lent us a hand for the last two locks, assured Alec that the water level on the summit was well up before kindly indicating that he would shut the top gate for us. So, with no more ado, I engaged gear once more and, with a highly satisfying plume of water spraying out behind me, turned *Redshank* hard round before picking up the tow and setting off in glorious sunshine round the 'Eleven mile pound'. Working up the Napton flight had been hugely enjoyable and I couldn't help comparing my present position with that of the week before. Then I had been beavering away at costings in a hot stuffy office, now I was in shirtsleeves ensconced on *Redshank*'s footboard with the whole of the Oxford Summit before me. What could be more perfect?

We jogged on steadily for about an hour, easing down for the turns and the bridge holes and careful to avoid any problems. This pound was famous throughout the system for its big turns, but I was confident nowadays and pleased with my ability to keep the deeply laden motor safely within the confines of the narrow channel. There were a few pleasure boats about, but they all gave us a respectful wide-berth and so far I hadn't met any of them on an awkward turn or in a bridge hole which might have proved tricky. The lonely Northamptonshire Uplands ran away in every direction with the waterway twisting and turning on its tortuous course along the contour, no roads could be seen and no habitation either, all was peace. Drifting along in the warmth we noted the little things. The overgrown towpath hedge now no longer cut back for Joe Skinner's mule, the tall sentinel of a heron silent amid the long grass on the outside, a crow flapping purposefully across the fields to settle in a small copse lost among the rolling hedgerows. At lunch-time we swopped over steerers with *Greenshank* drifting up behind for another smooth change, as I stepped back on to the butty I reflected how well everything seemed to be going today, the sort of idyllic boating that filled your dreams on cold winter afternoons.

It was as I was sitting comfortably on the side-bed in *Greenshank*'s cabin, with a corned beef sandwich in one hand and a cup of tea in the other, that it happened. We were coming up to the infamous 'Cabbage Turn' and Alec was just in the process of swinging *Redshank* comfortably round it when something pretty nasty wrapped itself around the motor's blades. It couldn't really have happened in a worse place as, in an effort to prevent whatever it was tightening on the blades, Alec was forced to pull her out of gear. The motor was more or less through the turn but Lil, at the end of a seventy foot line, was only just beginning to swing the butty round. In this sort of situation the butty steerer relies on the tug of the line from the fore-end to help get round the turn. Thus, the moment the motor was put out of gear and the line went slack, Lil was in trouble. On a smaller turn she might have got away with it, but this was 'Cabbage Turn' and they don't come any bigger. It was not a good time to be eating a sandwich! All I could see of Lil was her legs from about the knee down as she leaned far out in a gallant attempt to 'row' the butty round. All I could hear was her ripe comments as she endeavoured to will the heavy butty to turn almost in its own length. By the time I was standing on the coalbox step the die was cast. One glance forward was enough to show that no amount of effort from Lil would suffice. Without the crucial pull from *Redshank* she was never going to get round that turn. Scrambling on to the footboard I held on to cans, kettle, and mop and awaited the inevitable. Concrete piling would have been a help, at least we'd have just bounced off, but this was the Oxford and piling of any sort was a rarity. We were heading instead for the worst possible thing. The cows had been down to drink, breaking the bank down and creating a well trodden mess of soft clinging mud. Despite all the desperate efforts of her steerer it was into this sticky morass that the fore-end came to rest.

It is prudent to draw a veil over what was said in those first few anxious moments, sufficient to say that the pleasant summer air was filled with the most unprintable remarks! Still eating my sandwich I walked down to *Greenshank*'s fore-end and gloomily surveyed the situation. She was dug well in, no doubt at all about that. Cramming in the last remnant of sandwich I gave a preliminary and optimistic shove with the long shaft which had no discernible effect at all. She looked well and truly jammed and would probably need the pull of the motor and all our strength to get her free. Alec switched off the engine and shafted *Redshank* back alongside, standing in the coal and carefully prodding about under the counter with the short cabin shaft, trying to feel what was round the blades. The sharp scratching noise that resulted only made matters worse.

"Wire."

"Much?"

'A great lump of it."

After a few minutes of poking and twisting about Alec succeeded in getting the hook of the shaft round a bit of the wire. All three of us took a firm grip on the shaft.

"Ready? Pull!"

I had a sudden comical vision of the wire suddenly giving way and us all falling backwards off *Greenshank* into the cut. I needn't have worried, absolutely nothing happened!

"Come on! Pull!"

Whatever it was we had got hold of gave about three inches and then stubbornly refused to budge any further. No amount of pulling and heaving would shift it and, after about twenty minutes of growing frustration, we stopped for a conference. My watch told me that forty minutes had already ticked past and still nothing tangible had been achieved. Our original hopes of reaching Cropredy that night were beginning to fade.

"It's wrapped round solid," said Alec. This was rather stating the obvious, but now would not have been a good moment to tell him so!

"Keep hold of it with the hook," suggested Lil. "Then you two pull while I ease the shaft round with the handle. Perhaps we'll be able to unwind it off."

This was, in theory, a good idea and might very well bring results. We resumed with renewed enthusiasm, pulling hard, whilst Lil just eased the blade round by turning the starting handle. It didn't work! Absolutely nothing happened! Despite a supreme effort on our part it simply wouldn't move an inch! We seemed to have arrived at a complete impasse. Very sensibly Lil made a cup of tea and we sat together in the butty's hatches, sipping slowly and considering the situation. It felt almost surreal sitting there in the sunshine amidst the silence of this solitary countryside, a silence so deep that it could almost be felt. No engine noise of any kind could be heard, just the quiet buzzing of bees and the chatter of a high-flying lark. Without doubt, it was an absolutely beautiful summer's day but we were in no mood to contemplate the subtler pleasures of life, we had coal to deliver! No boats had passed by and already we had been stuck for nearly two hours. Help arriving could certainly not be counted upon. Commercial traffic on the Oxford was now minimal and the few pleasure boat crews could do nothing to assist us, no matter how kindly disposed they might be. It was our problem and somehow we had to deal with it.

Everyone now knew what would have to be done and no-one, least of all me, was particularly looking forward to it.

"Wire cutters," pronounced Alec, emptying his dregs into the cut. "We'll just have to go in and cut it off."

I was young and knew what was expected!

"I'll have a go! Good job it's summer!"

This job couldn't be done by leaning down into the water from the butty as the motor's blade was too deep in the water. If we had been empty then I might have been able to reach, but if we had been empty it might never have happened. I stripped down to my underpants, sitting in the hatches as Lil tied rags round my feet to protect them from anything sharp. Standing on the counter of the motor I peered down into the murky brown water and prepared to experience another of the pleasures of boating! Sliding in gingerly I found that I was able to stand on the bottom at the stern of the motor. There was a tangle of thick wire round the blade which was going to take quite a bit of shifting. The whole thing would have to be done by feel as it was impossible to see anything through the muddy water. Standing on a solid surface in a dry dock I could very probably have cleared the blade in ten minutes, instead I was up to my neck in water with a none too firm footing. It took me nearly three-quarters of an hour of patient snipping and pulling before I was finally satisfied that the blade was completely clear. Despite the hot sun I was cold when I eventually climbed out on to the butty back-end, it was not a job I'd wish to repeat too often and I shuddered to think what it would have been like in winter.

"Well done!" said Lil encouragingly. "Kettle's on!"

Dried and dressed and warming up in the sunshine, I joined the others in the hatches for another very welcome brew and contemplated the other half of our problem, the butty. All three of us had given up hope of getting much further today and we sipped our hot tea appreciatively, quite content to have a break before attempting to free *Greenshank*.

"We'll still be there tomorrow," said Alec.

"And shovelled out by Friday!" added Lil.

I drank tea, warmed up, and said nothing. At this precise moment the joys of shovelling out were something I preferred not to consider! We all wondered how such a length of thick wire came to be in the cut at such a remote and unfrequented spot. It was always a possibility anywhere near a road bridge, but here? In the back of beyond? Strange to think that anyone should have brought the wire here and then presumably thrown it in. Most odd! Mind you, some people are most odd!

Thankfully *Greenshank*, to great relief all round, gave far less trouble than might have been imagined. Lil took the motor back and tied her fore-end to the butty's back stud with the strongest piece of line we possessed. Then, with *Redshank* hard astern and Alec and I pushing for all we were worth with the long shafts, the butty slowly eased herself free of the clinging mud and drifted out into the channel. Nearly five hours had been lost due to a length of wire that had no business being there in the first place. Ten minutes later we were 'getting 'em ahead' once more although, to be honest, no one felt like going much further that day. All of us were tired and dirty from sweat and treading about in the coal, it had become an intense physical and mental effort to get clear of this piece of bad luck and even Lil felt we had done our share for one day. With Alec steering she started to put the dinner together as I moved ahead with *Redshank*. I needed no telling to 'keep it nice and steady' along to Fenny Compton where we intended to tie for the night and recover our spirits in the 'George & Dragon'. It was the only pub along 'Eleven mile pound' and the next practical one was 'The Red Lion' at Cropredy, now too far for us to contemplate reaching. We had earned a pint and so Fenny Compton it had to be!

What had started so well that day had, through no fault of our own, gone rather pear-shaped. The morning had gone smoothly enough with a precise and steady ascent of Napton being followed by shirtsleeve weather around the summit, then had come the wire and the whole day had changed. Leaving Marston Doles we had been confident of reaching Cropredy, but here we were instead pulling into the grassy length at Fenny Compton and glad to be doing so. Enough was enough for one day! Life is full of ups and downs and our spirits, which had taken a bit of a dive on 'Cabbage Turn', were well and truly lifted in the 'George & Dragon'. There weren't many of us in the solitary pub, but somehow it managed to turn into one of those nights. The best sort of night. The sort that changes a routine evening of a few pints and a bag of crisps into a memorable one. There were a couple of old canal workers in there, some very friendly people from a cruiser tied just ahead, and us. Everything just jelled together perfectly. There was lively chatter and well-intentioned banter and everyone finished up merrily bellowing out songs at the tops of their voices. it was great, especially after our day of contrasting halves. Nights like that can't be planned. They just happen from time to time, often in the most unexpected places, and we must be thankful when they do. It gave an uplifting end to a day of contrasting fortunes.

At just after six, and feeling a little fragile from our exertions of the night before, I found myself steering steadily along Tunnel Straight. No matter how much you had to drink, or how late you were going to bed, Lil could always be relied upon to get you up and going if there was work to be done. Looking back over our bubbling wash I watched her slight figure, stoically steering in the early morning light whilst filling a kettle and getting another pot of tea going at the same time. In the bright shadows of the long narrow straight I suddenly felt a great wash of affection for this quiet, but determined, woman who had been so kind to me over the last few years. I was almost impulsive enough to wave back to her but restrained myself, theatrical gestures were not her style. Instead I pointed to the clear sky and mimed a warm sun, she responded in like fashion by wiping her brow and grinning at me, before ducking down to check on the kettle and leaving me to concentrate on my steering. Tunnel Straight was a curious feature. It was quite narrow with a fair amount of overhanging vegetation, but it was still easy to imagine it as a tunnel. It had been a very shallow tunnel, hence the decision to open it up, and nowhere through the straight is the cutting particularly deep, no more than forty feet or so. It offers an interesting comparison to the very deep cuttings on the Shroppie, such as 'The Rocket near Tyrley, reflecting the advances made in engineering techniques between the construction of the two canals.

When south-bound, the tricky steering on the Oxford Summit is over by Fenny Compton and I had a fairly easy start to the day, chugging along to the top of Claydon with only a couple of interesting features to break up the pastoral scene. Firstly there is the entrance to the feeder channel which ran in to the pound from the summit reservoirs, lost from view somewhere in the rolling uplands. Joining the summit under an attractive little bridge carrying the towpath across, it then stretches tantalising away out of sight. Of course it was a very narrow feeder but I always fancied trying to get up it in a small canoe, another unfulfilled dream! The other point of interest is the first encounter with the drawbridges of the Oxford Canal. This one was locked permanently in the 'up' position but *Redshank* still had to be eased right down, passing through the narrow opening with just inches of clearance on either side. These Oxford drawbridges were much lighter and easier to handle than the 'gallows' type on the Northampton Arm. Here the balance beam went up from ground level at a forty-five degree angle and you simply had to pull upon a chain to bring the beam down and the bridge up, it then being a simple matter to sit on the end of it whilst the boats passed through.

By a happy coincidence it was just about time for a bacon sandwich and another cup of tea as I brought *Redshank* through Bridge 144 and saw the top gate of the lonely Claydon flight of five immediately ahead. The eventful journey around 'Eleven mile pound' was over. The wire had been sheer bad luck which could happen to anyone. Other than that we had come round well and were now about to embark on the first downhill locks of our journey. Despite the early promise it was actually rather cloudier today which, with the prospect of double-locking, was probably a better thing to have than the baking sunshine of yesterday. The Claydon flight were all empty, as we had expected they would be, and jobs were rotated for the downhill locks. Now it was Lil taking *Redshank* down, with the butty still on the long line and steered by Alec. I, being young and fit, had the bike off. My task was to pedal furiously down to the next lock and start it filling. Ride back immediately, leaving it to fill on its own, and help with getting the pair through the previous lock. Then it was pedalling hard to get the next top gate open ready for Lil to come straight in. On short pounds, such as those at Claydon, you had to be quick about it, whilst still being careful not to put your front wheel down a rat hole! Team work remained the essence of it and we dropped smoothly down the pretty flight with no problems at all. Three-handed and well organised it was hard work but not difficult, two-handed would have been a much tougher undertaking and one that Alec and Lil would meet with on several occasions in the next few months.

BANBURY BUN

More tea followed in the short pound down to the next locks of Elkington's, Varney's, and Broadmoor. These three locks are close together and, although each has its own name, really constitute another small flight. The routine was the same as at Claydon and everything went well until the last of the three, Broadmoor. Following the pattern I had pedalled hard down to it, drawn one ground paddle to start it filling, and then nipped back to help the pair through Varney's. When I got back someone had unhelpfully dropped the paddle leaving the lock only half full! I arrived at full pelt and got both ground paddles up, glaring balefully about as I did so, but there was not a soul to be seen. It slowed Lil just a little, which was annoying, but I never did find out who dropped that paddle . . . perhaps the lock is aptly named! In the end I didn't get back on the boats until we tied at Banbury, a very enthusiastic lock-wheeler! The sun had broken through again and it had become a very pleasant day for a ride along the grassy towpath. The remaining locks occurred about every mile or so which gave me plenty of time to help the pair through and pedal easily along to get the next one ready. I could, as Alec pointed out to me, have ridden some of the way on the boats, but I was happy enough and to have each lock ready was a tremendous help. Boxing about above the locks with a loaded pair is not a good idea on the Oxford, it really is far too shallow at the edges for that sort of thing. I ambled along, savouring the sun and the peace. The cut was very quiet that day, there were no other pairs about and only two small cruisers were met with as we dropped down to Banbury, an enormous contrast to the Oxford on a summer's day now! At last we were through Salmon's Lock and easing our way gingerly along the notoriously shallow Banbury pound with three drawbridges for me to pull up before the final town lock in Banbury. Up with the drawbridge below the lock and then biking on again to lift the final drawbridge adjacent to our destination, the Dairy. Once through the drawbridge we breasted up and laid the boats under the hatches through which our coal must pass. We had brought our coal to Banbury, all we had to do now was get rid of it!

Time was getting on a bit and we were rather tired, although no-one actually was prepared to admit to this, least of all me! Nevertheless, Alec decided to make a start on emptying *Redshank*. It was sound thinking. We would wake up the next morning with the job begun and not feeling that we had the whole pair to shovel out. It all turned out to be a lot easier than at Aylesbury. Here the coal was shovelled through square hatchways straight into the boiler room of the dairy, just a case of dig and throw with none of the paraphrenalia of wheelbarrows and planks perched precariously up piles of coal to negotiate. 'Easier' is a relative term in this context, of course. Shovelling forty-five tons of coal through a hatchway is a simple enough job on the face of it. Start at the beginning and go on until you get to the end. Simple. Also jolly hard graft in the warm summer sun. It was Aylesbury all over again as Alec and I started off in great style, digging our way determinedly down to the bottom boards and giving ourselves a firm surface to stand upon. By the time we had actually dug ourselves a hole and reached the boards our pace had slowed a little in the hot sun, but then came second wind and the establishing of that steady rhythmic action which is the hallmark of efficient working. Dig in, lift up, throw it squarely through the hatchway with a little twist at the end of the throw to ensure that all the coal leaves the shovel. Then repeat and repeat, ad infinitum, with the boat very slowly rising higher in the water as, throw after throw, the cargo diminishes. We only did a couple of hours that afternoon, but it was a start and in this particular game every little bit helps.

Eight o'clock the next morning found us standing amongst the coal, shovels gripped ready to begin and the sun climbing into a clear blue sky, it was going to be very hot! Our original hole had been dug down by the back stand in order that all three of us could work in the hold without getting in each other's way Lil was to clear out towards the back end whilst Alec and I would dig forwards up the hold. There were several hatches leading into the dairy coal bunker and so it was quite easy to throw through a couple of them at the same time. We had one big advantage. There had been no rain at all on our journey from the coalfield and the coal was fairly dry. Dusty, but dry, which is a big help when shovelling-out. True, you get dust in your hair, in your ears, up your nose, and just about everywhere else too. On the other hand, wet coal is significantly heavier than dry and so for us the actual effort of lifting and throwing the shovelfuls was not as great as it might have been. All through that long morning we worked doggedly on as the sun rose higher and higher, causing rivulets of sweat to carve channels down our dusty faces. We found ourselves being photographed from the occasional passing cruisers, their crews basking in the hot sun and enjoying the glorious weather, lovely for boating but just a bit hot for shovels! Still, we really mustn't grumble, after all it might be raining!

At about half past twelve the shovels were thrown down and we took ourselves off for a couple of much needed pints. Rarely has a pint of beer gone down better! I felt exhausted already. It was much hotter than it had been during my previous shovel-out at Aylesbury. My hands were aching from the constant gripping of the shovel and my back from the relentless bending and lifting. I seemed to be covered in dust and grime and all of it was nicely intermingling with a sticky layer of sweat. One thing I had learned, I did not wish to be a coal miner! Alec and Lil were in much the same state but, in accordance with the tradition of the cut, nobody complained. It could, after all, have been very much worse. How would you fancy having sixty tons to chuck out in an icy sleet driven on by a bitter easterly wind? Two pints only was our ration and we took Lil a bottle of stout back which also went down a treat! Sitting in *Greenshank*'s hatches we looked like three chimney sweeps, nice black thumbprints adorned our potted meat sandwiches and the teapot was drunk dry as we contemplated the afternoon ahead.

"No point in sitting there looking at it!"

Lil was right, as always. The boats wouldn't empty themselves. Besides *Redshank* was nearly finished, so let's get at it! There was very little spare energy left for talking that afternoon. Each of us concentrated on the sheer physical effort of shovelling. Dig, lift, throw. Dig, lift, throw. At long last *Redshank* was empty, half the job was done. Lil produced another huge pot of tea and a surprise hunk of Swiss roll whilst we swopped the boats around so that *Greenshank* now lay below the hatches with the motor towering alongside her. *Redshank* was dusty and badly in need of a good clean-off, but all that would have to wait until the butty had been emptied, until the whole job was done.

We swallowed our tea, accepted 'seconds' of the roll, and then Alec and I spat on our hands and stepped out on to the top of *Greenshank*'s coal. The first shovelful each went through the hatch. It was symbolic, we were now more than halfway there. Once more the pattern repeated itself as I forced my aching muscles on. Down to the floorboards by the first stand and no pauses until you've got your feet firmly on them. Up to your ankles in loose coal, filthy dirty and spitting black, but don't stop. Just get yourself down to those boards! This time I dug my way towards the back end leaving Alec to confront the mountain of coal stretching away towards the cratch. Lil was taking a break by doing the pile of accumulated washing up and starting to cook the dinner, not many people's idea of a break but I'm sure she preferred it to shovelling. We dug on grimly as the sun sank down in the western sky and shadows began to lengthen across the still waters. It was almost over for today. Considering the heat we had done tolerably well and were now comfortable with the thought that it would all be finished the next morning. Dig, lift, throw. Dig, lift, throw. Come on, Lil, it must be ready soon!

"Dinner in about ten minutes, you two!"

Alec grunted and threw a last dozen or so shovelfuls. I said nothing, but carried doggedly on, and waited for him to call a halt.

"That'll do! We'll knock it off in the morning!"

We threw the shovels down and climbed stiffly out of the hold. It seemed to have been a very long day.

Alec sat in the hatches, blew out a long breath, and then grinned across to where I was drinking water by the cupful from the can.

"What are you looking so black about then?"

It was the classic question and this time I could justifiably respond with the classic answer.

"Same thing that you are!"

I was so tired that I cut a few corners that evening and contented myself with just a quick 'face and hands'. Ater all, I reasoned, I was only going to get to get filthy again tomorrow morning. Every muscle seemed to ache and I simply hadn't got the necessary energy to light the primus and boil up a couple of pans of water for a wash-down in the engine-hole. I'll have one tomorrow, I promised myself, a really good one when it's all finished. There was only one thing to do that night and we did it! My, we were thirsty! The first pint went down like a glass of water and we didn't really slow down until the third or fourth. It was a strange dreamy sort of evening, I suppose it was because we were a bit drained, but suddenly it was enough to do nothing except sip our pints and chat. No darts nor even dominoes, just quiet chat about the cut and times past. Lil, similarly tired, stayed on the boat and listened to the radio with another pot of tea and the remnant of the roll. For us all it was a quiet and restful ending to an exhausting day.

It was well past eight before we resumed the next morning, even Lil was feeling the pace a bit! It was decided that Alec and I should finish clearing the butty leaving Lil to take *Redshank* across the cut away from all the swirling dust and give her a really good clean-off as we were aiming to get back up to Cropredy that same night. Things didn't seem to take so long that morning and the pile of coal steadily disappeared as we dug our way along the boat. Soon we were beyond the mast and the last little bit seemed to vanish very quickly indeed. I swept the dust and fragments into little piles and thence on to Alec's shovel, suddenly the last throw went through the hatch and it was all over. We stood there holding brush and shovel and grinned at each other. We were dirty and aching, but we had finished. The job was done and soon we would be able to laugh about it. Not quite yet, but perhaps tonight at Cropredy the jokes about shovelling out and John's black looks would start.

There was nothing in Banbury to keep us. Lil had finished the motor which now appeared immaculate alongside the grubby butty, but that was no particular problem. The butty could be sorted out on the way up to Cropredy that afternoon. With a bit of shopping still to do in the town it was arranged that we would meet Lil opposite Tooley's Yard, all winded and ready to go.

"See you again," said the boilerman, by way of farewell.

"Hope not!" was Alec's bantering riposte.

I knew what he meant. The Banbury run was a change and I had throroughly enjoyed the new trip. But, for Alec and Lil, working two-handed, it represented a much harder way to earn a living than the bread and butter runs to the Mills. After all the dust and shovelling it was an absolute joy to be travelling again, for me steering *Redshank* out of Banbury and back into the green countryside of the upper Cherwell valley was as refreshing as a hot bath and a good dinner. Alec had the bike off as far as Salmon's Lock because of getting the drawbridges up, but after this we didn't bother any more with lock-wheeling ahead. With any luck the locks would be empty, but if not it was easy enough to go below them now that we were empty. It was another truly fabulous afternoon, one among many in a long summer, now drifting on towards autumn, that had really done us proud. Hot sun with a very light breeze, just sufficient to move the air around and prevent sultriness developing. I steered happily up the pounds looking back occasionally to where Alec and Lil were straightening and cleaning *Greenshank*. Already the shovelling out seemed a long way away and really quite painless!

By the time Slatt Mill Lock was reached the butty was her usual pristine self and, by Cropredy, the only dirty thing on the pair was me! Alec and Lil having taken the chance to get a good wash-down on the way up the last couple of pounds, one advantage of butty steering when you're empty. It was by no means late when we locked through at Cropredy and we could easily have gone on, but we had achieved our target for the day and sometimes enough was very definitely enough. Tying breasted-up above the lock we settled down to enjoy the summer's evening and a well earned rest. Last, but not least, I had my wash-down in the engine-hole. Washing all over is perfectly possible in the cabin and distinctly preferable when the fire is lit and the rain is lashing down. But in warm weather I quite favoured using the engine-hole as any worries about splashing water about in the close confines of the cabin were eliminated. My, it was nice to be clean again! Not to have that persisting taste of coal in your mouth was the best thing. I washed my hair in the handbowl and you could have used the water to fill your pen up with. When I emptied the bowl into the cut the black stain lingered in dark swirls in the clear water, very mucky duck!

Sitting all fresh and clean on *Redshank*'s slide I soaked up the evening sunshine, blissfully content just to live for the moment. Cropredy is a very pretty place to tie up, with overhanging trees and the classic canal scene of whitewashed lock cottage, white-tipped lock gates, and hump-backed bridge, over which a gorgeous narrow street led to the low eaves of 'The Red Lion' with the church tower looming opposite. Glancing across I smiled at Alec and Lil sitting side by side in the butty hatches and similarly basking in the warmth and tranquillity which enfolded us. Time was running out and I knew even then that my chances of spending many more evenings in such idyllic fashion were inexorably diminishing. The following year I was planning to go to St Peter's College in Birmingham to undertake a teacher training course which would at least give me more holiday time for the cut, if nothing else changed in the meantime. Alec and Lil were, I knew, finding life quite hard as a two-handed pair and very much welcomed my assistance whenever I could manage it. Lil's health was not good and she was finding the daily round increasingly onerous although, true to character, she never complained. Alec, outwardly strong and tough, was not quite the force he once was and, as I knew from personal experience, frequently spent the first ten minutes of most days coughing and spluttering in the engine-hole or cabin. In the event, as we shall see, the fickleness of fate took a hand and things ended rather more quickly than any of us would have thought possible on that warm balmy evening in the long lost summer of 1962.

Boating could be a life of great contrasts. Yesterday we were sweating away shovelling coal with a nice view of the gasworks for company and now here we were just a few miles away enjoying the rural peace of this beautiful spot. It was the same later on as we drifted over the bridge for a pint, leaning for a moment on the warm parapet to admire the boats lying quietly and forming an intrinsic part of the scene. Yesterday a rather grubby and very ordinary pub in a Banbury backstreet and tonight the old low-beamed bar of 'The Red Lion', snug and comfortable. Three or four pints, a bag of crisps, and a game of darts in this quiet bar rounded off a perfect afternoon and evening in which everything had taken its place in essential peace and harmony. It was still pleasantly warm as we ambled contentedly back to the boats in the soft moonlight, watching a pair of bats skimming along the hedge and listening to the soft hooting of owls as they sought their suppers.

At just turned six the next morning, with the customary mug of tea before me on the slide, I took the butty on the cross-straps and set off for Braunston. The sun had already been up for a couple of hours promising yet another very hot day. I felt extraordinarily happy that morning, almost tingling with joyful anticipation. A hot sun and a long day's boating ahead, what more could you ask for! On *Greenshank* it promised to be a nice easy day, except for the passage of the locks. The butty would need occasional guidance in the bridge holes or on big turns, but otherwise people could just sit back and get brown. Or cook the dinner, clean the brasses, do some hand washing, splice a broken line, black-lead the range, or a few other little jobs that might come to hand! We kept the butty on the cross-straps through Broadmoor, Varney's, and Elkington's, but decided that bow-hauling would be the easiest approach at Claydon. A cruiser had met us on the straight below the bottom lock and the whole flight lay ready for us. Alec went ahead with *Redshank*, starting the locks for me in the usual manner, whilst I trundled along with the long line drawing the relatively light butty smoothly up the flight leaving top gates standing open behind us as was the normal method of working in those days. All went easily enough and it didn't seem long before I was rounding the bend above the penultimate lock to see Alec lying along the balance beam at the top lock and pretending to be asleep!

"Where've you been all this time?" he protested, with a twinkle in his eyes. "I thought you'd sunk!"

"Oh go on!" I grinned. "You've not been here that long!"

As the butty rose in the top lock I coiled the long line and laid it by the mast where it would be needed again at Napton.

"Get 'em ahead, Alec!" said Lil. "John's earned himself a cup of tea!"

The top gate of the summit lock was always traditionally left closed, my final task before running along and scrambling aboard *Greenshank* at the first bridge hole which is conveniently close. I could certainly do with that cup of tea and leaned on the tiller whilst Lil took one along to Alec who also claimed to be gasping with thirst. We sat opposite each other in the hatches when she returned and talked a little more of her childhood, reminiscing about a young thin girl in a long skirt and black lace-up boots walking behind the horse all the way round this summit, a much harder task than our pleasant idling today. Steerers were exchanged at Fenny Compton and I was just getting into my stride when we met a very slow moving narrowboat conversion right on the big turn at Griffins Bridge, Wormleighton. He passed on the right taking the deep water on the outside of the turn which made it an even tighter turn for me, but we squeezed round without sticking . . . just! With loaded boats it would have been a very interesting situation indeed! At Cabbage Turn I eased right down before swinging through, eyeing the depths suspiciously for any lurking balls of wire just waiting for the chance to entangle themselves around our blades, needless to say nothing of the sort happened. A further glorious couple of hours of sun-drenched steering, winding this way and that through fields slumbering in the heat, brought us to Marston Doles where we had to drift about in mid-stream whilst a small pontoon conversion seemed to take an absolute age to get through the lock, I even had to hoot to stop them shutting the top gate behind them!

The intervening pound between the top two locks was bow-hauled before resuming on the cross-straps for the run down to the top of the remaining seven. Alec took a turn on the line from there and I revelled in being sent ahead with *Redshank*. Inevitably the pontoon had shut all the top gates which gave me some extra running and jumping to do, but I didn't really mind! Some of the locks had leaked away a little and needed topping up and in any event the motor had to be brought in above each lock, giving me the task of leaping off the fore-end to open the gate before scrambling back aboard to drive her in. Then, after working her through, there was all the business of 'starting the lock' for the butty. Exercise is good for you, they say, and I certainly enjoyed mine at Napton. *Greenshank* followed on smoothly enough and presently we were reunited below the bottom lock and the long line stowed away in the butty's deck. No more bow-hauling for a while as a Mills run seemed to be the most likely next trip, hopefully I would just about get there before it was time to go back to work. This time it was Alec who claimed the bow-hauler's cup of tea leaving me to set off around the base of Napton Hill on the last pound of the day. The forlorn windmill with its broken sail leaning drunkenly to one side stared mutely down on our passing whilst I, like generations of boatmen before me, leaned on the tiller and contemplated the gaunt ruin above.

Soon we were back out on to the deeper waters of the main line and the speedwheel could be given an extra turn. I had become accustomed to the narrowness of the Oxford with its grassy reed-strewn banks and now it was the wide and deep main-line, with its long lengths of concrete piling dated 1934 or so, that seemed a little strange. Mind you, it was quite nice to be able to 'wind her on' again and we fairly surged up the pound, our high wash stretching right across the cut. This fierce wash, unheard of in the horse age, eroded and damaged the banks, but it was very much a feature of empty boating with all the crews, paid by the trip as they were, deeming every little extra bit of speed important. On we went, sweeping confidently round Shuckburgh Turn, comfortable enough nowadays but always to be remembered for that early struggle with *Canada Goose*, and along through the peaceful fields of one of my favourite pounds to Braunston, tying up once more just short of the turn to Coventry. That evening Alec and Lil went up into the village to see some old friends whilst I remained aboard and enjoyed another gloriously spectacular sunset. Bats flittered around the old bridge as the great red ball sank inexorably behind us in the west giving a long dazzling reflection off the placid waters of the long straight. Sitting in the lengthening shadows on the motor's slide I felt the perfect stillness of the scene permeating to the very core of my being. In this busy world we sometimes need to be alone and still, at one with ourselves. That evening provided me with the intangible rewards of being so, a strange and memorable sense of peace and unity, a one-ness with the cut and the world around me.

The next day was a Sunday. Like the previous week we had only to get ourselves up to Sutton Stop and so again the day began with everyone being downright lazy. It was gone nine before a cup of tea was forthcoming and nearly ten by the time I found myself dispatched along to the bottom lock to pick up a newly painted handbowl which was waiting for Lil. The day was much cooler and cloudier as I cycled along the familiar towpath, pausing on the centre of the overbridge to take in the scene below. Barlows had recently been taken over by Blue Line, a hire-boat company which had now taken occupancy of the boatyard and control of the remaining six pairs and their coal contracts. Michael Streat was the man responsible and, in the view of a number of captains, would never be able to keep things going. It is well documented that this was very much a mistaken viewpoint, in fact the last three Blue Line pairs were destined to see out the conclusion of regular long-distance carrying in the autumn of 1970, the boats being maintained in exemplary order until the end. The old yard had been considerably tidied up since my father and I had first seen it, dozing in the sunshine and looking very much as if it had seen better days. The Barlow colours were being replaced by the blue cabin-sides and ships-wheel emblem of the Blue Line Company and most of the dock was beginning its changeover over to the needs of the pleasure boat industry which was to dominate completely in the years ahead. On that particular morning all was fairly quiet and, after an appraising glance at the changes underway, I continued along to Bottom Lock where I was given our new handbowl. It still smelt of fresh paint and shone brightly in the sunlight, covered in roses on a green background it had a little ring at the end of the handle to hang it up with. Trundling slowly back with the handbowl held on my handlebars I was at great pains not to scratch it as I bounced along the uneven towpath. A few boats were tied by the Willow Wren yard awaiting refurbishment, but no working pairs were present either there or at Blue Line, it seemed we would be able to get to Suttons without getting caught up in any sort of race. Lil, who had learned of her bowl's readiness the previous evening, was pleased to receive it on board and her old one, which was beginning to show signs of rust and wearing through, was relegated to the back end, there to be hauled out if clothes wanted soaking or a bowl was needed for a particularly mucky job. Nothing was ever thrown away unless it had finally become totally and irrevocably unservicable.

The day continued overcast as we headed for Hillmorton and on the Barby straight a fine drizzle began to fall. At the locks everything was slippery and the lines became wet and gritty to handle. Coats and wet feet again! We had been thoroughly spoiled by the long spell of hot and settled weather and it was quite an adjustment to face up to the wet once more. It seemed a long steer from the bottom of Hillmorton to the Stop with the rain steadily intensifying as the afternoon wore on. I huddled up in the old duffel coat with the hood up and the cabin doors shut tightly around me in order to give my legs some protection. It could always have been worse, after all we could have been shovelling coal! Sutton Stop was strangely quiet that evening with only four pairs waiting in the lengths prior to the lock with, as usually seemed to be the case, Arthur's Blue Line pair lying snugly at the head of the queue after his round trip. One other pair of Willow Wrens, Ray and Margaret, were in the length and we tied in snugly behind them, exchanging gossip and snippets of news as we did so, before hurrying down into the cabins to escape the continuing unrelenting downpour.

The Banbury trip was over and I knew, in my heart of hearts, that I was not likely to get the chance to repeat it. Once more I had been lucky in extending my experience of working on the system a little further before the looming tidal wave of change put an end to it all. It had been hard work, but there were many compensations. The southern part of the Oxford Canal is possessed of a quiet beauty which can take a couple of days to impinge upon your consciousness and it was only really upon the return from Banbury that this peaceful charm fully exerted its grip upon me. Its appeal is quite different from that of the wide reaches of the Grand Union, here on the Oxford everything is on a smaller and more intimate scale. Because of the late survival of horse-drawn traffic and latterly the steady decline of all trade there was much less need for piling, consequently it was possible to experience mile after mile of grassy banks covered with a profusion of wild plants and flowers, especially attractive amidst the solitude of 'Eleven Mile Pound'. Given our gloriously sunny weather, everything had been pleasant on the eye with idyllic flights at Napton and Claydon and Cropredy a perfect gem. Even Banbury was interesting from the waterside with five drawbridges, the old basin and lock, and the fine old fashioned boatyard of Tooley's nestling by the Factory Street drawbridge and still very much as described by L.T.C. Rolt. There was also still a very good market to be found in Banbury with fascinating little side alleys to explore running between the Market Place and the famous Cross, not to mention Banbury buns! Like much else it has changed enormously over the last few years. The secretive passage of the cut through the town has been lost for ever as demolition and the construction of a huge unsightly shopping centre and new bridge has overshadowed the whole area. Of the five drawbridges then in use, only a modern replica on the site of Factory Street is to be seen today and the dairy, where once we shovelled, has vanished completely. Just up from the distinctive narrow place marking where the dairy drawbridge used to be, a discerning eye can still spot the black marks of tar on the piling where the Claytons once emptied. Little else remains except litter and graffiti amidst the triumph of planned progress.

That night we rounded off the trip with a visit to 'The Greyhound' and toasted with tall glasses of cool beer the hot summer of 1962. Within twelve months so much was to change. Perhaps it is a good thing that the future is hidden from us, that no shadows fell across our simple happiness that evening as we celebrated together at the Stop for what was to be the last time.

*****

Chapter 12

Towards an End

Life does not stand still and, during the summer of 1962, I began to experience an inexorable period of transition from the narrow world of the canal obsessive, which had gripped me for so long, into the wider world beyond. With the enthusiasm of youth I became the first member of my family to learn to drive and, sharing in the general affluence now burgeoning across the country, my parents bought, with some assistance from my small office wage, a blue second-hand Hillman Minx. My father baulked at this new challenge but my mother, determined not to be outdone, also now embarked on driving lessons, and wider worlds began to open up. My bicycle, a faithful servant which had carried me so many miles through the local lanes, began to gather a certain amount of dust in the shed as the car now took us back and forth to Stoke Bruerne at week-ends. By now, having become fully trained, I was working morning (7am to 2.40pm) and afternoon/evening (2.20pm to 10.00pm) shifts at the office as the company tried to squeeze full value from its new and expensive machinery. However, office life, despite the pay, was proving rather tedious and I was already looking towards my three year teacher training course due to commence the following autumn, my place in Birmingham having already been secured.

Inevitably, I suppose, with full time work and the future to be planned and worked for, the canals began to occupy less of my life and thoughts. I still went boating and spent a happy couple of week-ends on the pair that autumn, picking them up at Stoke and enjoying trips to Berko with coal destined for Croxley and an empty run to Sutton Stop before work put me on the train back to Northampton. That winter I found myself playing Town League football on most Saturday afternoons, a commitment which cut further into the time available at week-ends, but at least I could now drive in from Stoke for the matches, returning mudstained and thirsty for an evening in 'The Boat'. The canal scene as 1962 drew to a close appeared largely unchanged. The three carrying companies still plied their trade, the boats still moved up and down as regularly as ever, although it was apparent that the British Waterways fleet was slowly shrinking and the Barlow/Blue Line fleet numbers had halved since I first went with Ronnie and Alec. Willow Wren, to all outward appearances, was holding steady and still seeking fresh contracts, despite the occasional gloomy rumours that the company was losing money on its operations. A casual observer on the Stoke Bruerne canalside would have noticed less traffic than a few years before, but there was still enough moving to create the impression that carrying would go on in much the same way for quite a few years yet. Single motors had become a thing of the past, Wilfred having retired to join his family in Abingdon, and more craft than ever seemed to be going 'back empty to Suttons' which placed an even greater reliance on the coal contracts.

However all these seemed at the time to be only small matters, all part and parcel of the long slow decline which had been underway since the coming of the railways in the last century. It was nothing too much to worry about and, as December came in and thoughts began to turn towards Christmas, there were no obvious signs of the disaster that was about to overwhelm the life of the cut. On a more personal level Lil was finding it increasingly hard to keep going in their two-handed state, indeed her deteriorating health was beginning to cause Alec such concern that he intimated to me that he might have to think seriously about packing it all in sooner than he had intended. They were very reluctant to do this as they both loved the life with its essential element of freedom, life ashore and a job in a factory held no appeal. That autumn, as I steered *Greenshank* round the lonely fields of the Finney pound, Lil told me that she thought she might be able to manage another two or three years. It was not to be.

Playing football in Abington Park on the last Saturday before Christmas, the mild rather wet conditions gave no hint of what was about to befall us all. By December 23rd it had turned much colder and a heavy frost greeted the dawning of Christmas Eve. The air remained very cold that day and a deep penetrating frost gripped the country as Christmas Day dawned. It was the beginning of the great freeze of 1962–63. Over the next few days ferocious blizzards swept across the country with the inevitable disruptions to road and rail links. I was untroubled in Northampton, walking to work and my only real complaint being the total absence of local football as every park pitch was treacherous with snow and ice. A visit to Stoke revealed that, whilst all was all was well with the cottage, the canal was in dire straits. Ice stretched right across in the cutting up towards the tunnel and also in the lock pounds further down, although clear water was still visible by the cottages and the Mill. A pair of Willow Wrens, *Tern* and *Dunlin* loaded with cocoa waste from Birmingham, were the only sign of traffic. They were an unfamiliar pair and Mr James informed me that a couple of young lads, real enthusiasts by the name of Bill and Dave were in charge. The two of them had gone home for Christmas and he was keeping an eye on the pair until their return which was doubtless being delayed by the bad weather.

Boats were stranded up and down the cut and most people had contrived to put themselves in places where a long ice-up could be sat out in reasonable comfort, but Alec and Lil were the unlucky ones. After emptying at Banbury they had left early on the morning of Christmas Eve with the intention of spending Christmas Day at Braunston. This was a longish run at this time of the year, with darkness closing in so early, but not by any means an insuperable task for such experienced boatpeople. It was, nevertheless, a bitterly cold day and, upon arrival at Marston Doles, both of them had had about enough and a fateful decision was made. In the dark and cold, immediately below the second of the two locks, they tied for the night. With the light of morning it would be a simple matter to press on to Braunston, still arriving in plenty of time for Christmas Dinner. After a good night's rest in the warm cabin, with a 'banker' keeping the fire in, they awoke to find the boats gripped by the ice and all their plans gone awry. They were trapped and would not move again until mid-March. At the time, of course, a freeze of this length seemed unlikely and, although there was some talk of the great winter of 1947, most people were content to sit out the Christmas period. The thaw would surely not be long in coming.

In fact, things got worse. More heavy blizzards fell and the countryside groaned under the burden of week after week of unremitting frost. The roads were soon cleared and ran like black threads through a white landscape accompanied by the railways, also soon functioning normally again with just the usual problems of frozen points. For the cut there was no respite. The ice was anything up to three feet thick and walking, or even cycling, along the pounds was perfectly feasible. All traffic was at a total standstill and, if the weathermen were to be believed, seemed likely to remain so for quite some time yet. Getting to Alec and Lil proved in the early days to be quite tricky. The roads along to Marston Doles were only by-lanes and were not a priority in the first bout of snow clearance but, in early January, I was able to slither along to the bridge by the summit lock and offer some succour to my old friends. Leaving the car squeezed into the snow at the side of the road I walked straight down the middle of the pound to where I had been told the pair were trapped. In terms of heat they were well provided for with a back-end full of coal, including a good supply of 'bankers', and plenty of meths and paraffin for the primus. Food was more of a problem with either a long walk or a very perilous cycle ride to the nearest shop, in Napton village or further still at Southam. Worse for Alec the nearest pub was two miles away at Priors Marston along a treacherously icy and narrow lane. One very good thing was the supply of water which was readily available from the cottage by the lock. The whole situation could actually have been even worse if, as Lil had typically wanted in the freezing darkness of Christmas Eve, they had gone on a further mile to stop above the next lock down. Even so, by any standards it was still a remote spot in which to spend such a prolonged freeze-up.

I made myself as useful as I could during those relentlessly cold weeks, running Lil to the shops in Southam from time to time and taking them both over to Braunston on a number of Friday nights, where they were able to stay before being ferried back the next day. It was not the best spot and they were a bit short of company, however people rallied round and they enjoyed regular visitations from many old friends, all of whom sympathised with their predicament. That winter saw the end of the old established order of things on the cut. The long cold spell and the total cessation of traffic for virtually three months was the last straw. Such cold spells had happened before, but this time the parlous financial state of the carrying companies could withstand it no more. British Waterways, whose large fleet was the mainstay of commercial carrying, announced that it intended to cease trading that Spring. This announcement from the largest carrier was the death knell for the old life of the cut. Willow Wren was also sorely taxed by the freeze-up and news filtered through that their main backer could no longer fund the mounting losses and that the company was effectively bankrupt. Only the tiny fleet of Blue Line boats with their sand and 'jam 'ole' contracts remained relatively unaffected by the debacle. For Alec enough was enough. He was unattracted by the new plan to lease his pair and thereby be responsible for maintenance whilst relying on 'the Gaffer' to continue to get contracts.

"Boats'll fall to bits in five years," he predicted bitterly.

In this prediction he was absolutely right. Many fine skippers left and those that remained were unable satisfactorily to maintain their boats. Some pairs were crewed by young lads and driven recklessly into disrepair with a careless abandon that once had no place on the cut, whilst a diminishing hard core of older crews fought a losing battle as trade shrank to a shadow of its former self. The great freeze had proven to be the end of the cut in terms of its old life and ways, although a steadily decreasing amount of long distance carrying lingered on until the last contracts were lost in 1970. Odd loads would move even after that, but the efforts of the well-meaning enthusiasts meant little beyond preserving the boats. The old way of life which had tenaciously survived so much had finally gone and the transformation of the cut from commercial carrying to its present day place in the leisure industry gathered pace.

By March Alec had decided to do a final couple of trips and then take up an offer he had received to run a pair of hotel boats that summer. It was a very pensive John who ran my old friends back from Braunston early one Monday morning with the ice now thin enough for them to recommence their interrupted journey. I had to be at work for the afternoon shift, but had allowed myself enough time to help with the Napton flight. Depositing them at the top lock I quickly ran the car down the back lane and parked adjacent to the bridge leading to the old 'Bull and Butcher'. I was determined to wring the most from the morning and proceeded up the flight at a fast walk interspersed with the occasional trot to meet Alec at the third lock down. It was a poignant moment and I think we all knew that after that day nothing would ever be the same again. In true stoical tradition, however, nothing was said and I was given free rein to take *Redshank* down to the bottom lock with Alec bow-hauling along behind with *Greenshank*. It was a dull rather cheerless morning with occasional pieces of ice still floating about in the short pounds and the sombre sky reflected my mood as I got *Redshank* ahead. Down we went in the time-honoured fashion, with paddles clattering down and gates banging shut behind us as I started each lock for Alec.

At the bottom lock I steered her very slowly and sadly out of the lock for what I knew was highly likely to be the last time. Past the bottom gates, out of gear and then hold back for a moment before finally securing her to an old stump at the tail of the lock. Putting the tiller string on I shut the cabin doors and pulled the slide half over, leaving her as comfortable as I could before gloomily stepping off to start the lock and wander back to help with the butty. In no time at all it seemed *Greenshank* was sinking down in the bottom lock and presently Alec was picking her up on the cross-straps and 'getting 'em ahead' for the pound up to Braunston. I shut the bottom gate behind them, even though this was not strictly necessary, and then stood on the bridge with a lump in my throat for a last wave as they disappeared round the turn. An immense sadness washed over me as I walked to the waiting car knowing that my carrying days were over, that this time it really was the end.

Nothing was ever really the same again as the late Spring gave way to a pleasantly warm Summer and the memory of the cold and ice began to fade. Alec was true to his word and left Willow Wren in early summer to take on a pair of hotel boats, very similar to the pair I had worked on with Mike Sloan. I was to see them only once that summer. In mid-August I had given my notice in so as to have a month off before departing for my course at St Peter's College, ironically located in the dubious surroundings of Saltley, in mid-September. Most of that month was spent over at Stoke Bruerne and one Thursday morning Mr James informed me that Alec's pair would be coming up that same afternoon. It was a gloriously warm and sunny day as I walked down to Grafton Bridge to meet them. Commercial traffic had already very considerably dwindled and I saw only a couple of cruisers as I wandered down the flight and along the familiar towpath, the tall grasses yellowing now as summer drew on. It was all a far cry from that morning of great excitement and anticipation as I had waited at Bottom Lock for Ronnie and the family to appear for the first time, now it seemed that I was waiting for what might well be the last time.

I sat in the shade at Grafton Bridge and watched the still green murky water. Presently it began to move, almost imperceptibly at first, but then more strongly as an approaching pair disturbed the tranquillity. Here they come, I thought, and stood up with an ear cocked. Soon the steady beat of the diesel could be heard and then the fore-end of an immaculate hotel boat came into view and we were smiling and waving at each other once again. I stepped aboard in the bridge-hole and was instantly ushered on to the footboard by a beaming Alec who shook my hand vigorously before telling me to watch my steering! Exchanging further waves with Lil I happily clasped the gleaming tiller bar and guided the unfamiliar pair round the short couple of bridge lengths to the bottom of Stoke. All the latest news was gleaned from Alec during that short steer and none of it was good. Willow Wren were taking over some of the redundant BW boats and their contracts, the crews that remained becoming self-employed with Leslie Morton continuing as overall manager. Alec was very pessimistic about the whole set-up and clearly felt that it was not for him. Even I, enthusiastic as I was, could not see a real future in it and gloomily felt that the final epilogue of long distance carrying was in the process of being written. As often happens the end came not with a spectacular bang, but with a fading whimper. Over the next few years trade declined almost to nothing with eventually three pairs of Willow Wren and three pairs of Blue Line finally coming to a standstill as their last contracts ceased in the late summer of 1970.

We breasted-up at the bottom lock and I clambered over on to the butty where I was given a hug by a smiling Lil who was clearly as happy to see me as I was to see her. They were both as pleased as punch that I was set to become a teacher and clearly felt that, as my 'second' family, some credit for my success should go to them. With this prognosis I was in full agreement. At a very formative and impressionable age they had shown me unfailing loyalty and friendship, encouraging in me the virtues of hard work, taking a pride in yourself and your boats, and the importance of completing the job in hand to the best of your ability. We locked slowly and easily up Stoke with the passengers already well-trained by Alec in the business of shutting gates. He was admirably suited to the job of Skipper, having an enormous fund of stories to draw upon and a genuine liking for the passengers although, as he whispered conspiritorially to me, he would much rather have been on *Redshank* and *Greenshank* and working in the old ways, before the Great Freeze changed it all. However time can never be wound back, those days had gone forever and we both knew it. We sank a few pints together in 'The Boat' that night, reminiscing about our days together and the fun we had had, not to mention the shovelling of coal and the heaving of timber! Not forgetting bow-hauling up Saltley either! In the morning I waved them off and stood watching as they headed away round the curve leading into the cutting. A final wave was exchanged with Lil before she disappeared from my view. Seven years were to pass before we would meet again.

The process of change, once begun, often speeds up and goes much further than one would ever have thought possible. That autumn my parents decided to sell the cottage at Stoke Bruerne. I could see the logic behind their decision and, despite all it represented, agreed with it, both at the time and with hindsight. The canal side had changed very considerably in the relatively short time we had known it. Like the rest of the cut its old way of life was over. Sister Mary had retired to London and Olive and Ricky seemed to use their cottage less and less. Mrs James had died, Christine had married and moved to Roade, and Noel no longer tied his immaculate pair of Barlow's up for the night outside the Mill. Old Gibby was gone and his cottage stood empty awaiting an uncertain future. Colonel Ritchie, a retired military policeman, had bought Sister Mary's house and had strongly encouraged the setting-up of the Museum in the Mill. This decision was eventually to turn Stoke into a kind of theme park, but even in 1964 the number of visitors had increased alarmingly. Sitting on the step in peace on a Saturday afternoon was very much a thing of the past and we had even discovered people in our own front room under the mistaken impression we were part of the exhibits! Peace had gone from Stoke but so too had that intangible sense of community, all wrapped up somehow with the old life of the cut. The heart had gone out of the place and it was time to move on. At the end of September I packed away my windlasses, my leather belt, the handbowl and can Alec had given me as a memento, and went off to College. When I came home again that Christmas the cottage had been sold to Colonel Ritchie and a line seemed to have been drawn under my days on the cut.

I worked hard at college, not wishing to return to the boredom of office life, and tried to adapt to life without the cut. In one sense it was easy because it had largely gone. The pairs I worked with had gone, the cottage was gone, even my old friend Meadows was gone, killed by a lorry in Blisworth village. The cut itself, of course, remained and sometimes it tempted me back. I had found a place where, with a spot of careful climbing, it was possible to get on to the towpath in the middle of the Saltley flight, all no more than ten minutes away from my room in college. Once again I had my secret world as I slipped away some afternoons and dropped back into the old familiarity. Wednesday afternoons were free and one warm day in late October I walked down the Saltley flight, round past Salford Bridge, and then up the New Thirteen before bussing back to Saltley, my memories walking every step of the way alongside me. On another occasion it was up the locks, then along and up Camp Hill and past the deserted wharves of Sampson Road and Tyseley before once again seeking the bus. A few 'joeys' were still sporadically moving about, but I saw no pairs at all on these forays and the once busy locks were largely still. A favourite sortie was to bus into the city and join the towpath through the little wooden door at Gas Street before walking down the Farmers Bridge Thirteen, through the Digbeth Arm, and then along to 'my bridge' in the Saltley flight from which I could return to college and a welcome cup of tea. If I was lucky I got to shut a few gates and drop paddles for a 'joey' boat or the occasional cruiser, but as often as not the grimy flights were simply deserted. Nevertheless I always enjoyed these solitary rambles and remained hopeful of one day encountering a pair working through on their way to the 'Bottom Road'. As I later learned there were still a steadily dwindling few travelling this way, but I was always out of luck and the flights remained bereft of bright cabin sides and shining brasses.

I qualified in 1967 and returned to Northampton to begin teaching at Vernon Terrace Primary School. The job was all-embracing, especially in that first hectic year, but I found myself very much enjoying it despite the heavy demands on my time and energy. The cut had mostly faded into the background although one week-end I dusted the bike off and cycled nostalgically through the lanes to intercept the Grand Union at Banbury Lane. Everything looked much the same as I followed the towpath up as far as High House Bridge before returning home along the picturesque lanes through Flore, Little Brington, and Nobottle. I saw a number of hire boats and cruisers, ran my fingers through the ropemarks cut into the iron protectors fitted to many of the bridge holes, but found no sign of any pairs. By now, with so many other pressures in my life over the last years, I had become completely out of touch with the situation and now realise that, with so few pairs left running, I would have been very lucky to have seen anyone on that particular afternoon. With the scarcity of money during my student years I had even allowed my I.W.A. subscription to lapse, indeed the cut seemed to have become very much a thing of the past.

After two happy years at Vernon Terrace I achieved my first promotion and moved schools to Chiltern Junior School, close to where I lived on the west side of the town. In the summer of 1970 a little note was circulated from the Education Office, it concerned the participation of local primary schools in week-long canal cruises aboard a pair of narrowboats operated by Union Canal Carriers who were based at Bottom Lock, Braunston. This was a chance not to be missed! The Head agreed to the venture and later that term I found myself in charge of twelve boys and girls who were to share a week on a pair with another twelve from Parklands School on the eastern side of the town. The Parklands children were accompanied by a fresh faced young teacher called Gill who was in her first year of teaching. Gill was a naturally sunny and open person, a real pleasure to work with, and we very soon established a good rapport in, what was for her, a completely new experience. The bottom of Braunston had changed somewhat since my last visit and I found that Union Canal Carriers were based in the shed adjoining what used to be the oiling point for the British Waterways pairs. Trailing over the bridge from the bus we made our way along the dusty towpath to *Petrel & Moon*, a smart pair run by George and Helen Smith. Helen greeted us in what I was to soon recognise as her characteristically effusive manner and we settled in with boys on the motor and girls on the butty. Double bunk beds were arranged along the holds and an Elsan bucket, an object of considerable interest to the children, was sited in a small cupboard under the cratch. Gill and I got the excited children settled in and unpacked ready for their week of adventure. Standing on the back beam I took in the familiar scene, my eyes straying to the old Willow Wren base opposite where we had tied so often. At long last I had come back.

TOWARDS AN END

Seven years had passed since I had waved goodbye to Lil and much had changed. Union Canal Carriers, an unknown company then, had occasionally traded coal down to Croxley in the late 60s, but now concentrated on being 'people' carriers. We had only been at Braunston about ten minutes when I heard the unmistakeable accent of another old friend as Janusz came over the bridge. A good deal of smiling and back-slapping followed as we greeted each other again. He knew I had gone into teaching and seemed immensely pleased to see me, insisting on taking me along there and then to the little cottage they were renting, adjacent to the bottom lock, to meet Ruth once more. Like true friends always do we picked up where we had left off and the intervening years just fell away as if they had never been. Janusz ran Union Canal Carriers, in collusion with another man called Robin, and he had been instrumental in arranging the Northampton Schools contract in partnership with Jack Riley, the Head of St Paul's School in Northampton. Upon enquiring about Alec's whereabouts I was saddened to learn that he had been very ill and was living near 'The Engine' pub, just round the corner from Sutton Stop. Obtaining his address from Janusz I resolved to write a long letter just as soon as I got back home.

It was just wonderful to be back on the cut and my obvious friendship with Janusz and Ruth, coupled with my previous experience, rapidly broke the ice with Helen and George who were also destined to become good friends. The plan was to make a leisurely five day trip down to Cosgrove and back, this would give the children plenty of time for collecting and identifying grasses and wild plants, doing their logs and canal drawings, as well as visiting the museum at Stoke and the Wolverton Aqueduct. With two long tunnels, three flights of locks, and plenty of time on and off the boats, it proved to be a very valuable and much enjoyed week both educationally and in terms of the children's personal experience of life. At Stoke, Gill, with whom I was getting on very well, was joined for the evening by her young husband, Graham, also in his first year of teaching. We got along together famously from the beginning and three years later he was to be best man at my wedding, the cut was taking a fresh hand in my life and it was good to be back. The week flew by quickly, as all good weeks do, and the children seemed to love every minute of it. We were blessed with fine weather and they revelled in running round and under the aqueduct at Wolverton, following the old tramway up at Stoke, collecting a piece of ballast each from the remains of the S.M.J., and getting a detailed commentary from their teacher in the Museum on how to start a single Bolinder, only the 'bomp, bomp, bomp' was missing! On the return journey I found myself at the tiller of *Petrel* along my 'home' pound from Stoke to Weedon and discovered that, like riding a bicycle or swimming, one never forgets how! The week simply flashed past and had gone before I knew it, but I had a toehold back in a much-changed canal world and I determined to enjoy it while I could.

Having lost my old friends as our lives had diverged I had now, through the mysterious workings of chance, been given the chance to see them again. That summer and autumn I wrote twice to Alec and Lil without reply from him. This didn't surprise me especially or put me off, writing letters was never his forte and besides he had reportedly been very ill. Instead I followed up with a Christmas card containing a further letter and some photos of my class and myself, this time I was rewarded with a card back, profuse apologies for not writing earlier, a photo of Young Lily's children, and a couple of scrawled pages of news. They were clearly very pleased that I had not forgotten them, as if I could, and hoped to see me over at 'The Nelson' in the Spring.

That same autumn I had also made contact with Jack Riley, who ran the boat trips, and we subsequently became good friends. Each Friday night we went over to Braunston together to pay the crews, take Helen's food order from the cash and carry, and then sink a few pints in the 'Nelson' where Hubert and Thirza, also pleased to see me, still benevolently reigned. It had become something of a tradition for the U.C.C. crews to get together in 'The Nelson' at the end of each week and a fairly hard-drinking session would follow, with Hubert still inclined to his practice of allowing the favoured few to remain behind in the bar as his 'guests' for a couple of hours after closing time. A few old boaters who remembered me, particularly Mark and Ted, often stayed and the old times were raked over once more. Jack, who drove an old Ford Popular, had a blissful disregard for such niceties as the new-fangled breathalyser and, despite a considerable intake of beer, was never pulled over. On wet nights his old wipers couldn't cope with the spray and mud thrown up off the road and it was my job to take a Squeezy bottle full of water, wind down the window and leaning round as best I could squirt water across the screen to help clear off the mess. My resultant wet arm was an irrelevance!

These days with the children's trips proved to be very much an Indian Summer for me as far as the cut was concerned. With my interest rekindled I would passionately teach my class an extensive project on canals and canal life and follow this up with a week-long trip on a pair. Enthusiastic lively teaching tends to beget enthusiastic and interested pupils and much of their work was both detailed and imaginative and of the highest quality. It is true to say we enjoyed ourselves. Working happily and hard at school I found my friendships with Jack, with Gill and Graham, with George and Helen, with Janusz and Ruth, all blossoming, it was one of life's good spells. Things got even better one Friday evening in the spring of 1971 when, upon entering the bar of "the Nelson' with Jack, I found myself greeted by a loud and very familiar voice.

"Whay-up then, young John! Get the beer in!"

Seven years vanished in an instant as we embraced and hugged each other, red with pleasure. I even broke all conventions by not only hugging Lil but actually giving her a kiss on the cheek, absolutely unheard of! They looked older and seemed a bit thinner, but otherwise all was quite well and they were going to have one of Janusz's pairs to work that summer! The evening flew by in a sea of remembrances, tales of times past, beer, what I was doing, Lily and Cliff, more beer, Ronnie, the grandchildren, and still more beer. We parted happily, overjoyed to meet again and basking once again in each other's friendship. Truly, they were two of the best and most trusted friends I have ever had.

With the school trips once again back in full swing life established a pattern and Friday evenings over at Braunston became a regular feature of the summer term. About twenty schools now participated in the venture and each week we would drive over and settle our business before repairing to the delights of 'The Nelson'. Crews, now comprising a combination of George and Helen, Andy and Liz, and Alec and Lil, had to be paid, any difficulties resolved, and things set up for the next week. Food, bought in the cash and carry, had to be delivered on board and any minor niggles sorted out before the pleasurable side of the evening could begin. The Friday evening following that in which I had been reunited with Alec and Lil proved to be another turning point, in fact the absolute turning point of my life. Having been to Bottom Lock as usual to see the crews, we ran the old Ford up the field and along the lane prior to turning round and parking on the grass verge just down from 'The Nelson'. On this particular evening we found ourselves having to squeeze in behind a green Austin A30 before climbing out and heading for the bar.

Rounding the corner of the pub we encountered the owner of the Austin, a slim dark-haired girl sitting on the bottom gate and looking slightly forlorn. It turned out that she had completed a trip with Kingsthorpe Grove School the week before and had come over to Braunston in order to renew acquaintance with Helen and George. Having arrived rather early she had been somewhat dismayed to find the pub empty of canal folk and, not liking to go in on her own, had sat down to await their arrival. She brightened up considerably upon seeing Jack, whom she knew by sight, and introduced herself as Sandy. It was love at first sight. Nothing less can be said. I sat in the bar that evening only half-listening to the chat and gossip swirling around me, my eyes focussed on that fine boned face, the dark hair with the centre parting, the pretty smile. I was so absorbed that I even forgot to eat my crisps! They lay, spread out and neglected, on the open wrapper in front of me. People noticed, of course. George, later that evening, decided that I was bewitched! Doomed! He forecast that very night to all who would listen that I would marry Sandy! That he was to be proven absolutely right became something of which he always remained very proud. All this was somewhat in the future of course, but the die was cast. Fate had taken a hand and another path in life had been decided. The cut, which had given me so much, had now brought me the best and most cherished thing of all. Such is the way of destiny.

WINDLASS IN MY BELT

That summer I did another trip with Gill to Cosgrove aboard *Petrel &
Moon* and then Janusz very kindly offered Jack and I the use of *Petrel* for
a trip during the October half-term. This sounded rather good and, with
George away for the week, Helen offered to come along as Cook-in-
Charge, Sandy would come, Gill and Graham, and Pat and Mick. Pat, from
Liverpool, taught in my new school and we had all become very friendly
with each other over the last few months. It was decided that we would go
up to Gas Street and back with fingers crossed for the weather. There were
no problems in that quarter as we left Braunston around Saturday lunchtime and headed off round the Napton pound. It was about nine years since
I had passed this way but very little seemed to have changed. The cut
wound along and the fields and little hills on either side were as beautiful
as ever. We all took turns steering although there was a tacit understanding
with Janusz that Helen and I would share the responsibility for *Petrel* and
ensure no avoidable mishaps. Accordingly I once more found myself at
the tiller on the approach to Shuckburgh turn. Fifteen years had passed
since I had failed to get round on *Canada Goose* and I had not forgotten.
Ease her down, then slowly into the wide bridge hole with the same
massed banks of reeds on the right and that unforgiving concrete coping
dead ahead. I watched the fore-end drift out. Experience counts for a lot
with narrowboats as I had discovered over the years. On *Canada Goose* I
hadn't got it, now I had. At exactly the right moment my hand twirled the
speedwheel and simultaneously thrust the tiller hard over. *Petrel* turned
almost in her own length and we were comfortably round. Phew! It would
have been highly embarrassing to have messed it up!

Eight-handed on a single motor makes for effortless locking and, having
overnighted at the bottom of Itchington, we were soon grappling with the
joys of Hatton on another gloriously sunny day. Shirtsleeve weather at the
end of October, Lady Luck was certainly smiling on us this time! Young
Lily and Phyllis had raced *Redshank* up these locks years before and now
here I was emulating them, but with an empty boat and a much bigger crew.
The locks were empty with all gates shut as was becoming the custom, but
we had plenty of muscle! I made it one hour and three minutes for the
flight, Helen reckoned it was just fractionally under the hour. I won't
quibble, suffice to say it was fast going, certainly a lot quicker than that
ghastly rainy morning long ago when I had found half the pounds empty
and the ascent had gone on for nearly four and a half hours.

We were hoping to reach Tyseley that evening but, just below Knowle
and with Helen at the tiller, there came a sharp 'clunk' from under the
counter and, amid clouds of black smoke, the engine cut out. Just as on
that faraway summer's day on the Oxford Summit the culprit was wire,
another great ball of it wrapped around the blades and rendering further
progress impossible. Remembering the sequence of events only too
clearly, I determined to follow the same course of action as Alec and Lil
had undertaken. With the bottom gates of Knowle only about a hundred

yards distant, it made sense to begin by bow-hauling along and putting her through the bottom lock. *Petrel*, floating in a full lock with a nice solid lockside to stand upon, would be much easier to deal with than attempting an instant solution alongside the rocky broken edge of the towpath. Twisting and tugging with the shaft produced a few spindly bits of wire, but no effective result. Turning the shaft on the handle whilst simultaneously pulling also yielded nothing. History seemed to be repeating itself, the clock ticked on and we were still hopelessly stuck.

However this time there was no call for a volunteer to go into the water to clear the blades. The intervening pounds at Knowle are exceptionally wide, due in part to the presence of the original narrow locks. It would thus be possible to 'wind' *Petrel* and then very carefully 'drop her on the sill'. We swung her round, before pulling her backwards into the next lock which was then filled sufficiently for her stern to float freely above the solid protruding concrete sill, which all boaters are warned never to let their boats catch upon. Then it was a case of dropping the top paddles and, with a thick line running from her dollies around the handrails to secure her against the top gate, raising just a small amount of bottom paddle. This had the effect of slowly lowering the water level until she was resting high and dry on the sill. Only her stern was on the sill and the rest of her was floating free, the paddle being hurriedly wound down to leave the water an inch or two below the sill. Gingerly I climbed down the gate and stepped cautiously on to the slimy wet sill, taking great care not to slip on the treacherous surface. The wire cutters were passed down and, with a clear view of the problem, it was the work of a few minutes to cut the dense ball free, passing it up for disposal in one of the old narrow locks where it could do no further harm. Once again it could have been a lot worse. If we had been somewhere in the middle of the next pound, perhaps in the Solihull cutting for instance, then someone would have had to have gone in. I had a good idea who that someone would have been too!

The very next day Helen did go in! We had tied near Catty Barnes the previous evening and reached Gas Street, after threading through the flights, in early afternoon. A little girl off a boat tied in the basin spotted Helen as we were tying up and ran, full of joy at seeing her again, towards us with loud cries of "Auntie Helen! Auntie Helen!" Helen, ever ebullient, picked her up and swung her round by the arms before somehow or other they overbalanced and fell, one after the other, into the black oily waters. It was funny later, but not at the time. The little girl couldn't swim but Helen, despite the shock of her own immersion, had kept tight hold of her. Holding her protectively she paddled quickly to the side, passing her out to us before clambering back on to the greasy towpath where she stood dripping and offering several unprintable comments! There are cleaner parts of the cut than Gas Street if you must throw yourself in! A cup of tea, a large kettle of hot water, and a complete change soon put them both to rights, although their clothes took some washing! We spent a whole day in Birmingham and then, on the first leg of our journey home, Helen did it again!

We had decided to return to Braunston via the northern Stratford which I had never done, it also seemed to offer a pleasant alternative to locking back round through the city to Camp Hill. In the early 1950s the northern Stratford had been in a very weedy and neglected state, barely navigable in fact. However once work had begun on the major task of restoring the southern end of the canal, its northern counterpart had found itself being thoroughly dredged out. Indeed, in the early 1960s, it had even seen a little commercial traffic in the form of Willow Wren timber bound for Great Bridge, and for us it was a perfectly feasible proposition. The only problem was that, from time to time, a stream would flow into the canal and put a temporary bar of silt across the channel. Just south of the short Kings Norton tunnel I was jogging along gently, whilst people were enjoying coffee and biscuits for 'elevenses', when we encountered one of these bars whose existence we had been warned about at Gas Street. *Petrel* slewed round and halted as I took her out of gear, cautiously working on the premise of investigating the problem first before trying to force through by dint of 'winding it on'. Helen poked about with the shaft from the towpath and then decided to hold *Petrel*'s fore-end out whilst I took a run at it. Afterwards I was never quite clear how she managed it. But, from standing on *Petrel*'s deck shafting her off, she suddenly found herself off the boat and clutching a shaft which was still dug into the grass at the edge of the cut. Very slowly, almost in slow motion it seemed, her weight drew the shaft downwards and she found herself gently lowered stern-first into the still waters. Her comments as she sank slowly in were delivered in stentorian tones and again, without any shadow of a doubt, were completely unprintable! No real harm done, of course, and a cup of coffee followed by yet another change of clothes soon had her smiling once more. No more of these 'bars' were met with and a good run down the nineteen Lapworth locks allowed us all to work up a good appetite for our dinner that evening.

It was Thursday and the fine weather had lasted throughout the week. Each day the warm Autumn sun had shone down upon us and we were remarkably brown for the time of year. It couldn't last indefinitely, of course, and on Friday, our last full day, the weather finally broke. We awoke to grey skies and a fine drizzle seeping down as, making an early start, we swung out on to the Grand Union only to find Hatton completely against us. Many hands make light work however and, with four lock-wheeling and four bringing her through, we were soon down and heading for Cape Two. Sometimes a bad start can change, the drizzle will disappear and blue skies return. Not so today. Just to further complicate matters on an already dank and cheerless day we found half the pounds to be in a very low state at Radford. Some of these pounds are quite long and, with water having to be run down, we found ourselves quite considerably delayed and finished up ascending Itchington in the dark to tie by the pub on the Southam Road bridge. Despite this slight unforeseen hiccup it had been a splendid week. Saturday morning would see us comfortably into Braunston and leave me nicely set up for the winter.

The following year brought more changes and life moved on again. Jack Riley was offered the Headship of the new Lumbertubs Lower School in Northampton, I was appointed Deputy-Head and Sandy moved from Kingsthorpe Grove on to the staff. That year I took the Lumbertubs children on a boat trip, this time on the pair crewed by Alec and Lil. It was to be our swansong together. Down the Junction we went to Leighton and back, a somewhat longer trip than normal but with plenty of interest for the children. Sandy came out to see us in the evening at Stoke and again, later in the week, at Weedon. On both occasions Alec made a point of being very taken with her, obviously considering it well past time that I was married! It was an ordinary week, running smoothly and without problems, but quietly memorable for all that. We had first worked together over fourteen years before and they had taught me so much, both about the cut and about the true values of life. To steer the motor, *Kimberley*, and look back at Lil on the butty was like winding back the years for both of us. They took a great pride in me and told everyone they knew that I was now a deputy-head and heading up in the world. "We taught him how to work," said Alec, "Look how well he's done!" It was certainly true that I had absorbed a goodly number of their values and I readily acknowledged that, not withstanding my parents enormous contribution, I owed them a great deal. They were very fond of Sandy and had immediately accepted her as part of the family, going out of their way to make her feel very much at home. My friends were their friends, that was the way of it with no questions asked. Like me Sandy found them to be a very warm and genuine couple whose trust and friendship, once bestowed, was with you forever. That week, like all the others, seemed to pass very quickly and, although we would still see each other at Braunston, it proved to be our very last trip together. A neat and unexpected little tailpiece after the many shared miles of the Willow Wren years.

That October Janusz lent us *Kimberley* for a week and we set off up the Leicester Cut. There were less of us than previously, this time it was to be Gill and Graham, Sandy, and Liz, a new teacher who worked with us at at Lumbertubs. After the rigours of teaching it proved to be once again an enjoyable and refreshing week, marred only by periods of heavy and persistent autumn rain. The long solitary windings of the twenty-mile summit were followed by the spectacular flight at Foxton and then on as far as the southern edges of Leicester before retracing to Market Harborough for a day off. This time it was to be Liz who fell in, losing her sense of place and absent-mindedly stepping backwards off the counter in the pound below Foxton, at least it was reasonably clean water this time! I was still collecting new pieces of cut and so we turned off into the

Welford Arm on the way back round the summit. Here we found a good deep mooring place at the end of the nicely restored little Arm which I had last remembered seeing in a totally derelict state during one of my long bike rides at the end of the Fifties.

I have a particular memory of the last Friday morning as we left Welford. An early start was needed if we were to reach Braunston in good time and, after a good night in the pub, everyone had decided that being as it was a very long pound the early start could be left to me! Nobody stirred as I started up and nudged into the solitary lock at about half past seven, positively late by boating standards! Locking through I set off in the damp greyness along the narrow waters of the little arm, the cabin doors closed snugly around my legs. As I eased her gently down, watching the wash die away and getting ready to swing hard round on to the main line, it occurred to me that I couldn't have been any happier. It was one of those timeless moments. As we turned I looked back across the swirling waters to the junction of the two waterways, the tiller held firmly in my hand and our brown wash running and gurgling along the grassy banks. A whiff of diesel mingled with the cool morning air and the canvas stretched over the top planks was puddled with dew. Once more I was in my element, the cut still held me in its magical grip and my heart soared. For nearly two hours I steered alone, winding back and forth among the lonely fields adjoining the summit pound and savouring the peace of it all. Eventually Graham appeared with a mug of tea and apologies for sleeping in. I waved them away, I had been thoroughly enjoying myself and was not ashamed to admit it. That Friday night at Braunston had an end of season feel to it as we sank our pints and chatted together for the last time before the winter closedown. Alec and Lil would return to their house, the U.C.C. crews would fill in the time as best they could, we would teach, and the cut, now bereft of its commercial traffic, would largely sleep until the spring brought a new awakening.

Sandy and I were married the following year and went to live in the quiet Northamptonshire village of Nether Heyford, all very handy for the cut! We continued our visits to Braunston on Friday evenings, although now mostly without Jack who had handed over the administration and organisation of the Northampton Schools trips to me. One day during one our walks along the towpath from our new home we espied an immaculate narrowboat called *Alphons* tied at Stowe Hill. In my memory *Alphons* had been the butty to Jack Boswell's motor, the *Greenock*, and so it turned out to be. We became acquainted with the owner, Margaret Cornish, and her son and daughter, Giles and Helen. Margaret had worked on the cut in the war and was later to write of her experiences in *Troubled Waters*. At this time she was a lecturer in teacher training at Nene College in Northampton and, having recently been relocated from the North, had taken the plunge and had *Alphons* converted from a butty to the resplendent motor boat which had caught our eye. With our shared passion for working boats it was almost inevitable that we became good friends, often comparing times past with the much changed nature of the cut today. *Alphons* was a boat to be proud of and I have an especially fond memory of a lovely day we spent together travelling down my 'home' pound to Stoke and back, I always enjoyed the chance of another steer!

The following year was to see our last October trip. Nothing stands still and the trip was indicative of the waning of that brief Indian Summer which had brought so much. This year it was *Lindsay*, an inelegant 'dustbin' motor from the old BW North-Western fleet, and the plan was the very simple one of running down to Leighton and back. Other people's lives were also moving on and Gill and Graham seemed to be the only friends able to come and, as things turned out, even they found themselves having to cry off at the last minute. Thus it was just Sandy and myself who found ourselves steering through Braunston Tunnel before heading south through the familiar countryside. The late Autumn weather was cool and unpredictable and we opted for a leisurely start in the mornings and a stop for lunch, times really were changing! I was saddened to see that the once beautiful 'Finney' pound was in the midst of being ruined by the construction of Milton Keynes, earthworks were everywhere as we moved south and the herons and hares, once so prevalent along here, had become just a memory. At Leighton the fan belt which charged the batteries snapped and, although Alec and Lil were fortunately on hand with their pair, it could not be fixed until our return to Braunston. Alec had a secondary school group from London on board and we spent a convivial evening together in the pub on Leighton Bridge. He claimed to have been recently advised to drink Guinness for his health! Needless to say the empty bottles were soon proudly lining themselves up around our table! It may have been healthier beer, but his intake level remained much the same as it had always been!

With only dim light on board we decided to make an early start the next morning and go to Heyford. This would enable us both to sleep in our own bed and conserve the fading battery whose light we needed for the tunnels. At a quarter to seven I swung the starting handle vigorously whilst Sandy shoved the compression levers over at the critical moment. With a thunderous roar she 'caught' and we were quickly away, swinging round Alec's sleeping pair and running quickly down to Leighton Lock. After forging confidently round the bends of the Jackdaw, with the rising sun promising a fine day ahead, we encountered our first problem with empty pounds at the Three Locks, not what you want so early in the morning! Sandy produced a second cup of tea as I ran energetically about, heaving on gates and furiously winding paddles in order to get just enough water into the pounds to float us through. We were soon off again and running northwards in good style on the pleasantest day of the week. At 'The Navigation' we were flagged down by a girl whose name now escapes me, she was alone on a butty there and the motor, complete with her feller, was at Braunston! It was a very complicated saga but what could you do? Needless to say we agreed to do our bit in reuniting the pair and took her on the cross-straps in time honoured fashion.

Stoke were solidly against us, but our new friend proved to be a willing lock-wheeler and very little time was lost as we ascended the flight I knew so well. Stoke was full of memories, but I found myself beginning to increasingly dislike going through the present crowded scene so far removed from the peace which once prevailed. Today was little different, the top lock being thronged with 'gongoozlers' as we locked through with classic professional ease, probably only appreciated by ourselves! A pair of narrowboats was an unusual sight by now and, rather like on the Thames all those years before, we found ourselves very much the centre of attraction. I glanced at Sister Mary's surgery window, now a cafe. In my mind's eye I pictured the sash going up and the friendly smile of welcome which greeted the passing crews, all a memory now. We didn't tarry. I eased *Lindsay* forward, picked up the cross-straps and we were away, steadily 'winding it on' through the green cutting and into the welcoming darkness of the tunnel. Braunston was reached early on Friday after a very wet and gloomy last day, we were soaked and grateful to Janusz for running us home in his old Land Rover, once again things seemed to be moving towards an end.

For a number of reasons, both personal and professional, Sandy and I had reached the conclusion that the time had come to grasp the nettle and take a different fork on our road through life. For better or worse, this decision would have ramifications beyond anything then present in our carefully calculated thinking at the time. That winter we took the momentous decision to leave our home town, which had nurtured and influenced us both, and to strike out on our own, determined to build a new life elsewhere. With no more ado I set about applying for headships and was rewarded by securing an appointment to a village school, Nunney in East Somerset. I was to start the following September. That July, amidst frenzied planning for the move and with Sandy now pregnant, we went over to Braunston on that last Friday of term to wish everyone well. It was a poignant moment. Bidding farewell to Janusz and Ruth, George and Helen, Andy and Liz, was one thing. Saying goodbye to Alec and Lil was something else entirely. Sandy's pregnancy was the excuse for a few jokes and dire instructions from Alec, mostly concerned with not letting her wind up overstiff paddles! Not in Somerset, I thought, suddenly only too aware of all that we were leaving behind. It was not the easiest evening for any of us, the conversation struggled from time to time and little gaps and silences crept in. Everyone was aware of the significance of these last moments together and, just for an instant, a little doubt nagged at the back of my mind. I pulled myself together quickly, it was far too late to change the decision now. Life has a habit of moving us all on like corks in a flowing stream, it was time to say goodbye.

TOWARDS AN END

As always, we were all very stoical about it. Hands were shaken firmly, last rather shaky smiles were exchanged. No point in prolonging matters. Sandy and I walked slowly along the towpath in the fading evening light and up on to the old hump-backed bridge, it was very quiet with just the gentle trickle of water to be heard escaping through the old gates behind us, the brickwork on the parapet warm to my touch. With a lump in my throat and a prickling behind the eyes I looked down at the cut and my two dearest friends standing closely together in the hatches watching our progress. We waved at each other and smiled encouragingly. It was just as if I would see them again next week-end as we headed south with coal. Just as if nothing had changed, except that everything had. Sandy gripped my hand tightly as we turned resolutely away, not daring to risk a backward glance on the long walk up the field to our new life.

The End

Postscript

The move to Somerset proved to be the defining moment in my old links with the cut. In the Sixties these had withered and almost died, but revival had come during those summer weeks in the early Seventies. For me the old life had ended with *Redshank* as we locked down together for the last time at Napton, but my Indian Summer of boating in the Seventies, against the background of a much changed canal world, was a time of much enjoyment and new friendships. In Somerset we were in another world. My village headship was to give me the most enjoyable and rewarding years of my teaching career, but I missed the cut with only the still derelict Kennet & Avon offering a tenuous link with my once all consuming passion.

By the time of our move to Oxford the continuing momentum of change had almost completely swept away the cut as I had known it. This time there was no chance of going back, the old times had vanished almost as if they had never been. For a time we considered having our own boat, but it was not to be. We were both teaching in very exacting jobs, would we ever have had time to use it to any great effect? In retirement, I decided to set the story down as I remembered it from the time. Many of the participants are dead or, like me, getting ever older and I am in touch with very few of them, however they continue to live on in my memory and I will always be grateful for the warmth of their friendship. Sometimes Sandy and I walk the towpaths and look again at the old places, Maffers, Stoke, Braunston, Hatton, Napton, Claydon, Banbury. Some, such as Maffers or Hatton are surprisingly little changed. Others like Braunston, Banbury, and especially Stoke Bruerne, have seen dramatic developments which are still continuing. Hire fleets predominate, but there are still a goodly number of smart privately owned craft whose crews are almost universally pleasant, particularly when I offer to shut the gate behind them as they lock through.

The once secret world has gone for ever. The cut is secret no longer and is probably carrying as many boats now as it ever did. People lock through and answer their mobile phones as they do so, the wider world has caught up. A very occasional narrowboat may pass by, sometimes with bags of coal for sale, and it is nice to see. But it is not the same. The old close-knit hard working community with its unique way of life has vanished into history.

But come with me along the shady towpath on a quiet evening and if you look carefully you can see them again in your mind's eye. Look! Here they come, gliding along low in the water with the coal piled high in their holds. Surely you can see them too! The soft light on the green cabin sides

POSTSCRIPT

and the little wren perched on a willow twig in the roundels. Brasses proudly gleaming, ropework scrubbed to pristine whiteness, and the redolent smell of a stew simmering gently on the range. I hold up a hand in friendly greeting as they drift past and fade softly away into the gathering twilight.

*****

Glossary

Arm	A branch canal leading off the main line of the waterway.
Arm End	The junction of such a branch with the main line. Especially with regard to Gayton Junction where the Northampton Arm of the Grand Union Canal joins the main line and always referred to by boatmen as 'Arm End'.
Back-end	The section of hold immediately forward of the cabin.
Barge	Or lighter. Any vessel with a beam of 14ft or more.
Bad road	When travelling with all the locks against you.
Berko	Berkhamsted on the Grand Union Canal
Beam	Four removable lengths of thick plank laid at intervals across the hold. When travelling empty the top planks were laid along the beams to form a walkway from the cabin to the mast beam. Beyond this the top plank from the mast to the cratch was normally left in position.
Blades	The propellor. Getting a 'bladeful' refers to a fouled prop and was especially likely in urban bridgeholes, or on 'Cabbage Turn'!
Bottom Road	The term for the route from Birmingham to the Warwickshire coalfield via the Birmingham & Fazeley Canal. 'Top Road' indicated the same journey via the Grand Union Canal and Braunston.
Bow haul	Pulling the butty through a flight of locks by means of a long line attached to the mast and looped over one's shoulder. Alternatively any situation where the boat is pulled along manually. Pronounced as in the bow in one's shoelaces not the front of the boat – to which the line is not attached anyway.
Breasting-up	Bringing the motor boat and the butty boat together and securing them side by side.
Bridge hole	The arch under a bridge. 'Hole' was a well used expression for any space e.g. 'engine hole', door-holes, soap holes, the Kearley & Tonge factory known as the 'jam 'ole'.

GLOSSARY

Butty
: An engineless narrow boat pulled by the motor boat, ie motor and butty, usually described as a pair of boats, or pair.

Chains
: Chains attached to each side of the boat were stretched across under a beam and joined together with a bottle screw which could be tightened to hold the sides of the boat in and prevent spreading under pressure from the cargo. Chains were undone whilst loading and unloading so as not to obstruct the hold. Sometimes known as bracing chains.

Chucking-back
: Going into reverse gear in an attempt to clear the blade of any minor fouling such as weeds or small miscellaneous items of rubbish.

Company Man
: An employee of British Waterways.

Counter
: The rounded stern of the motor boat. This extends above the blades and is designed to offer protection in the event of collision with copings or lock gates.

Cratch
: Triangular tent-like structure of wood and canvas at the front of the boat usually decorated with white strings. Used to store top cloths and spare lines.

Cross straps
: Two short lengths of rope running from the two dollies on the motor's counter around the butty's stern post to the stud on its fore-end and thus drawing the butty up close behind the motor when running empty.

Deep
: A deeper than normal length of pound i.e. Heyford Deep on the Blisworth Pound. A lock with a particularly deep rise and fall ie Denham Deep on the Grand Union or Somerton Deep on the Oxford.

Dolly
: A small iron stump on the motor's counter used for towing or tying up.

Door holes
: The space above the footboard and between the two doors giving access to the cabin.

Draw
: Raise a paddle to fill or empty a lock.

Elum
: The rudder post on a butty boat.

Finney
: Fenny Stratford on the Grand Union Canal. Also the pound between there and Cosgrove.

Flush
: A sudden rush of water often created by raising the paddles.

Fore-end
: The front of a narrow boat and particularly the triangular deck just forward of the cratch.

Ganzies
: A flight of locks on the Rushall Canal.

Gas boats
: Boats used for transporting gas liquor or tar with tanks under a continuous wooden decking. Thomas Clayton of Oldbury being a particularly well known carrier.

Getting 'em ahead	Keeping the boats moving without wasting time. Sometimes used as an instruction to get going eg "get 'em ahead, John!"
Good road	Travelling with all the locks ready for you.
Hatches	The well deck and surrounding area at the stern of a butty.
Hayes Cocoa	The Nestlés factory at Southall.
Hold back	Engage reverse gear.
Inside	The towpath side of the canal. 'Outside' being the side furthest from the towpath. When steering it was sometimes necessary to 'hold in' or 'hold out' in certain situations.
'Joey' boat	Boats used for short distance work around Birmingham and the Black Country. Often cabinless or with just a small day cabin for shelter.
Josher	A boat formerly belonging to the firm of Fellows, Morton & Clayton Ltd. A very large general carrier whose boats were sold to BW in 1949.
Lockwheeler	A crew member going ahead along the towpath to make the locks ready. This job was usually undertaken by bicycle, but the term was also used to describe anyone walking ahead.
Looby	Spring loaded pin on the top of a boat's mast to which the towline is attached.
Loosing 'em by	Allowing another pair of boats to overtake.
Maffers	Marsworth on the Grand Union canal.
Mast	A square wooden post about twelve to fourteen feet from the fore-end to which the tow line is attached when bow-hauling or horse boating.
Mast beam	The beam running across the boat supporting the mast.
Number One	A boatman who owns his own boat.
Paddles	Sluices for admitting water into the locks. Ground paddles are situated at the lockside, gate paddles in the gates.
Pigeon Box	A small detachable skylight box situated above the engine hole.
Pound	A length of water between two locks. Many had the own name eg Blisworth Pound, the length between the bottom of Buckby locks and the top of Stoke.
Ricky	Rickmansworth on the Grand Union Canal.
Rods	The controls of an engine leading from the steerer through into the engine hole.
Road	A particular route eg 'the Oxford road' from Napton southwards or 'the Birmingham road' from Napton Turn to Birmingham.

GLOSSARY

Shaft	A boathook attached to a pole. Short shafts lived on the cabin top whilst long shafts lay in the hold. Shafting describes the action of moving a boat with such a shaft eg 'pushing her off with the long shaft'.
Shroppie	Shropshire Union Canal.
Stour Cut	Staffs & Worcs (or Staffordshire & Worcestershire) Canal.
Single out	Work the boats one behind the other, either on the cross straps if empty or the snubber if loaded.
Slide	The sliding hatch above the door-holes.
Snatcher	A short towing line often used by loaded boats in short pounds.
Snubber	A long 70ft towline used on long pounds. Being further back rendered the butty less susceptible to the motor's wash thus making steering easier.
Speedwheel	The control wheel, in the motor boat's cabin door hole, attached to a rod which operates the engine throttle.
Strap	A rope. Often used to describe that used for checking a butty as she entered the lock or elsewhere eg 'strapping her in'. Hence strapping post on a lockside or gate.
String	Decorative ropework on the boats often scrubbed clean eg 'white strings' around the cratch. Also used to describe thin pieces of line used around the boats eg side cloth strings, tiller string, stern string.
Sutton Stop	Or Suttons. Hawkesbury Junction, near Coventry where the Oxford and Coventry Canals meet. Loading orders were usually obtained here, hence 'back empty to Suttons'.
Swim	How a boat moves through the water. The cargo would often be trimmed to ensure she 'swam' well. A good 'swimmer' was easier to steer.
The Fields	The stretch of the Grand Union Canal between Leighton Buzzard and Marsworth.
Thick	Used to describe a section where the locks are very close together eg the 'thick of Hatton'.
Tipcats	Sausage shaped rope fenders attached to the counter of the motor boat and designed to offer protection particularly in lock chambers.
Turn	A junction eg Braunston Turn or Napton Turn. Also used to describe a very big bend in the canal eg Ansty Turn or Cabbage Turn.
Wigrams	Napton Junction or Calcutt Locks on the Grand Union Canal.

WINDLASS IN MY BELT

Wind	Turn a boat around.
Winding hole	A place on the canal specifically designed to enable a boat to be turned around.
Winding it on	Increasing the speed. Often effected by winding round a speedwheel connected via a rod to the engine-hole.
Winding it off	Slowing down.
Windlass	A portable handle used for operating the lock paddles.

******